BUILDING THE SIAM-BURMA RAILWAY DURING WORLD WAR-II
—A Documentary Study

BUILDING THE SIAM-BURMA RAILWAY DURING WORLD WAR-II

(A DOCUMENTARY STUDY)

T.R. Sareen

KALPAZ

Published by

Kalpaz Publications
C-30, Satyawati Nagar,
Delhi – 110052
Ph.: 011-47034999, 9811692060
www.kalpazpublications.com
E-mail: kalpaz@hotmail.com

Distribution Network
gyanbooks.com
India, USA, Canada, UK, Australia, France

ISBN: 978-93-5722-930-2 (PB)

First Published, 2024

Printed at: Gyan Press, Delhi.

Building the Siam Burma Railway During World War-II
Author: T.R. Sareen

To

Raghav

and

Rohan

Contents

Introduction

No subject created so much controversy during and after the Pacific War as the Japanese treatment of the Allied Prisoners of War (P.O.W.) in flagrant violation of the Geneva Convention. Whether it was due to the racial war carried out by the Japanese or was the outcome of the mistaken value of " Bushido"- the question has never been resolved. The harsh and brutal treatment of the P.O.W. was fully demonstrated, when the Japanese decided to utilise them for the construction of Siam-Burma railway. The worst P.O.W. and forced labour camps during the war were located, as Arnold writes, along a 258 miles strip of rail-road track running through the almost impenetrable jungles of Thailand and Burma.[1] Driven like slaves and with semi-starvation diet, the Allied P.O.W. were left with no stamina to fight tropical diseases. As a result thousands of them from these camps died while working on Siam-Burma railway, which came to be known as " Rail-road of Death".

Hundreds of men who spent the time in these camps have published their memoirs, diaries and accounts, but still our knowledge about the events is not complete on account of non-availability of records under the access rules. Moreover, the systematic destruction of a great bulk of their records by the Japanese towards the end of war has deprived the scholars about the Japanese side of the story. At the same time the Japanese scholars have deliberately ignored the subject in their history books treating it as a footnote to the Pacific War. "Herein lies the difficulties for the historian" point out Water Ford, "to present a true picture of the Japanese atrocities inflicted on P.O.W. when only a Western view-point on the occurrences exits and personal accounts of atrocities are either biased by speedy publication or shattered by selective memory because of the time that have passed."[2] Many of the reminiscences written after the events, described "the bitter years of captivity, but they lack the authentic detail and intensity of feeling that lend such power to contemporary and near contemporary narrations". Surviving journals written during captivity are very scarce. Writing materials virtually impossible to replace as many of the uncompleted journals were found confiscated by the guards.[3]

British and American official histories of the war against Japan have devoted some attention to the treatment of the P.O.W. which actually became a big issue at the International Military Tribunal for the Far East. As a result major documentary sources on the subject are the testimony from war crime trials held at Singapore and Tokyo. Their transcripts at the Public Record Office, London run to thousands of pages.

It was while consulting records for my study on the *Japanese Prisoners of War in India* that I came across some reports on the Japanese treatment of the Allied P.O.W. especially those relating to their employment on the Siam-Burma railway. These reports along with the memoirs of few Allied officers who were connected with the railway were also found in the military archives. These were written as a part of their official duty after the war. As such these "are quite different from the personal memoirs" which " vary enormously in quality, balance and perspective, some are out-pourings of bitterness and hate at the appalling treatment meted out to the prisoners by the Japanese captors".[4]

The study is neither intended as a justification of the Japanese treatment of their captors, nor there is any motive to exploit those shocking conditions which have been made public by many survivors of the " Death Railway". It is mainly devoted to the reproductions of the reports from Indan Archives which have remained beyond the reach of scholars. These original documents give us an insight into the highly controversial story of Siam-Burma railway, which should be presented within the framework of the wider perspective of Japanese treatment of the Allied P.O.W.

II

Western scholars have tried to project the Japanese treatment of the P.O.W. as a part of the racial war. In their view, the Japanese did it to " humiliate the Americans, British, Dutch and Australian who for so long had looked down upon the Japanese, as inferior beings"[5]. While the element of racial bitterness cannot be denied, but it is not easy to perceive that the Japanese had pre-determined the nature of treatment, when they started the Pacific war. The sources do indicate that the Japanese expected to face a situation of looking after of P.O.W. in the areas which they were likely to occupy in South-East Asia. But they were not aware of its size. For example, after the fall of Singapore on 15 February 1942, the Japanese were not even remotely aware that they would be having more than 85,000 prisoners in their custody. It is doubtful whether they had earmarked the economic resources or even adequate space for looking after such a huge mass of people.

At the same time, the Allied Governments became aware that the Japanese had scant respect for the Geneva Convention which had laid down certain minimum conditions for the treatment of the P.O.W. by their captors. Since Japan had not signed the convention, it was known that she was not likely to give the prisoners even the minimum treatment stipulated in the convention. On the other hand Japanese scholars have tried to show that Japan had been consistently adhering to the guidelines laid down by the International Law and, as Prof. Hata says "Japan gained a good reputation internationally by faithfully carrying out her obligations under the Geneva Convention of 1864 and the Brussels declaration of 1874. She followed the instruction during the Russio-Japanese War (1904-5) and during the

First World War. But surprisingly she refused to follow the Geneva Convention signed in 1929. Among the reasons given for this was the following, "although to be taken prisoner is contrary to the ideology of Japanese serviceman, those of foreign nations may think differently. Accordingly, although convention in form appears to impose reciprocal obligations, in actual fact, it would mean duties only on us"[6]. Under this mistaken notion, when immediately following Japan's entry into the War, the United States and British Government raised the question of the applicability of 1929 Geneva Convention, Foreign Minister Togo replied that Japan, although not bound by the Convention would apply its provisions *mutatis mutandis*[7]. Allied powers concluded on the basis of this specific undertaking that Japan was morally bound to comply with the provisions of the convention "in all possible circumstances and where liberal compliance was not possible, she was under an obligation to apply the nearest practically equivalent".[8] Contrary to the assurance given by the Japanese, the rules laid in the Geneva convention were hardly followed. Japanese introduced their own code of conduct for the P.O.W. The Japanese advance in South- East Asia in 1941-42 made their captive many thousands of Allied soldiers and placed in internment large number of civilians residing in those areas. The problem was quite formidable but the Japanese gained control over South-East Asian countries very quickly and as it was obtained, prisoners of war were moved to countries other than those in which they had been captured. Since the Japanese had never anticipated such an overflow of the Allied P.O.W. no adequate steps or even plans had been drawn up to meet the eventuality. It was only on 31 March, 1942 that the Japanese Army established an Army P.O.W. Management Bureau, which laid down certain guidelines, issued on 21 April 1942, under the title, *Prisoners of War Detailed Treatment Regulation*. Many other guidelines were issued from time to time for the control of Allied P.O.W.

According to Japanese sources, about 300,000 were placed under the control of Southern General Army Command. They were distributed at different places in Siam, Singapore, Philippines etc. In all, the Japanese established nearly 227 P.O.W. camps all over South East Asia during the war. The distribution of P.O.W. under the Southern General Army Command was as follows: 120,000 P.O.W. in Thailand and Malaya camps respectively, 115,000 Philippines camp, 3,500 Java camp and 500 in Borneo camp. There were P.O.W. camps in Taiwan, Korea and other places like Shanghai and Hongkong[9]. It was from here that around 60,000 P.O.W. were recruited to work on Siam-Burma railway. This project created an image of the Japanese which has persisted to this day as to be the most barbaric nation in the world. The horrid conditions and thousands of deaths which occurred during the construction of the railway stirred the conscience of the whole world. How far the deaths were due to insufficient medical facilities or lack of food or harsh treatment by the Japanese, are reflected in the reports given here. Harsh treatment apart what increased the humiliation of the Allied soldiers was the kind behaviour the Japanese adopted towards the Asian prisoners at the same time. On 14 March, 1942 Supreme Headquarters instructed the Chief of Staff of the Southern Army command that Indian P.O.W. should be freed and put under the command of the Indian Independence League.[10] Similarly, the Indonesian national P.O.W. were also freed. During 1942, nearly 153,000 Indians, Indonesians, Philippines, Malayan and Burmese P.O.W. were liberated.[11] For the guidance of Allied prisoners the Japanese circulated an account of their old "Bushido". This had been "an alleged code of honour and chivalry that was traditional in the Japanese nation under which " the captor is gracious and generous to his captors."[12] But possibly this traditional code was followed by a very small percentage of Japanese commanding officers. It was a mere paper circulation and not meant for follow up.

On the other hand, the revised concept of "Bushido" which had emerged under the militarist regime was followed strictly. Under the new code P.O.W. was a disgraceful person, who was to be treated harshly and exploited for the benefit of the war. As Lord Russel has pointed out, "uncivilised ill-treatment of the P.O.W. by the Japanese was the natural outcome of the revised code of Bushido, which was inculcated into the Japanese soldier as part of his basic training". For a Japanese soldier "death was more honourable than surrender". Naturally under this mistaken belief they developed, "a feeling of utter contempt for those who had surrendered to the Japanese forces. In their view after having become P.O.W. they had forfeited all right to any consideration".[13] However, in the initial stages, the Japanese supervision in Singapore and Burma over the P.O.W. was not very strict. Many of them did escape to India since majority of them were from the Indian Army. From these persons and other sources the British came to know as to how the Japanese were treating the P.O.W. and civilians in occupied territories of South-East Asia. While the Chinese were mercilessly killed by the Japanese, their attitude towards the Indian P.O.W. was not so brutal, who were encouraged to fight against the British for the freedom of their country. For example, when the Indian P.O.W. were asked whether they wanted the British in India. "An affirmative answer produced slaps- a negative might win a cigarette."[14] Slapping was quite common and even religious sentiments had been hurt of the Indian soldiers. On the basis of the information received, the British analysed that the higher the rank of the prisoner, the harsher would be his treatment. Vague answers during interrogation only resulted in beating. The local Japanese commander down to a 2 Lt. had complete power of life and death. No question were asked by the higher authorities. The Japanese regarded the P.O.W. as a complete outcast. There was no fixed rules for the treatment of the P.O.W. much depended on the attitude of the person incharge of the prisoners. There were occasion when the P.O.W. were executed even though they gave straight-forward answers, and it was impossible to guarantee that any given attitude would protect a prisoner from ill-usage or even death.[15]

The Government of India considered the information thus received as a good propaganda material. They were already contemplating a programme of anti-Japanese propaganda especially after the formation of the Indian Independence League and Indian National Army which was serving in their opinion as "Japanese Indian Fifth Column". The idea was to project the Japanese as barbaric and uncivilised, so that Indians who were having pro-Japanese leanings could be alienated. It was also anticipated that further desertion in the Indian Army could be stopped by revealing to them the horrible atrocities committed by the Japanese military on the captured P.O.W. especially Indians after their surrender.

This became all the more necessary in view of the Japanese "Intelligence Offensive" mounted towards the British in India, with the help of the Indian nationalists. The Japanese offensive was both strategical and tactical. Strategical drive aimed "at undermining of India's war efforts by discouraging recruitment and encouraging desertions. While tactical side was directed towards Indian troops in forward areas with a view to damage their morale.[16] To defeat Japanese designs, the Government of India proposed to expose the Japanese atrocities and their ill-treatment of Allied P.O.W. For this purpose they proposed to utilise the services of the escaped P.O.W., who had been treated badly and had seen other brutally dealt with. Alongwith the civilian refugees, the British thought that it would "make an excellent platform". This was to be combined with the force of Chinese evidence, which would depict the cruel and harsh treatment meted out to the Chinese in Hong Kong and China. But the main aim of the propaganda was to foster distrust between Indian nationalists and the Japanese who were collaborating with them as allies against the British in India.

More than the other Allied Powers, the British had great involvement in the Japanese treatment of the prisoners of war, since bulk of them belonged to the Indian Army. The general staff branch carried out detailed studies not only about the decline of the morale of the Indian Army, who did not put any resistance before the Japanese in Malaya, but also suggested the methods for further safeguarding their loyalty in the face of Japanese impending advance towards India.[17]

We need not go into the various dimensions of the propaganda which the British mounted from India against the Japanese. Here it will suffice to say that the main purpose was to malign the Japanese in the eyes of the Indians, and to make them understand that "unless the Indian beat his declared enemy the Japanese, he too may expect to undergo the same physical violence, and economic expoilation as has been the lot of those others who have failed effectively to oppose the Japanese"[18]

Before starting the propaganda, the General Staff carried out a detailed analysis about the factors which were responsible for the harsh treatment of the P.O.W. by the Japanese. It analysed that the position and treatment of the P.O.W. in Japanese hands differed materially from those in German hands. According to their study there were various factors, which contributed towards this state of affairs. British opinion, though not very sympathetic, still reflects the true picture. In a secret report, they listed the Japanese limitations and her helplessness in this respect. Firstly, it was due to the wide differences in Japanese outlook and general conditions of living. But more than attitude, the great and far-spread area over which camps were scattered in which P.O.W. were detained made it rather difficult to have uniform policy of management. Much depended on the men on the spot. At the same time, the climatic conditions to which the prisoners were subjected did effect their mental and physical behaviour. These varied " from the tropical heat of the equator to the seasonal cold of Korea and Manchuria".[19]

What contributed more to the sufferings of the P.O.W., the study pointed out was the lack of proper administration which was difficult to maintain due to thousands of miles between Japan and the outlying areas of detention such as Burma, Siam and Netherlands East Indies, combined with the inadequate means of communication or of carriage for supplies such as existed in Europe between the seat of the Central Government and the location of the camps. As such the treatment of the P.O.W. while in Japan was slightly better than what it was in the camps of South-East Asia. During the war-time the medical supplies were definitely affected alongwith the shortage of foodstuffs which was not entirely of Japanese making. What further prevented the Allied powers to have any meaningful dialogue with the Japanese the study pointed out, was that there was no country in the Far East from which the International Committee of the Red Cross could function as they were able to do so in Europe. More than the above factors the Japanese adhered to their own valued notions about the position of the P.O.W. Much depended on individual Japanese officers in charge of the P.O.W. Some Japanese commandant of the camps did behave in a disgraceful manner towards the P.O.W. in violation of even the official orders, which forbade them as not to behave "contrary to humanity with the prisoners".[20]

Mild protests were followed by the Allied broadcast giving details of "Japanese atrocities and warning Japan of the retribution to come". Subsequently, letters of protests were sent through the Swiss Embassy. The protests were taken lightly and replied to by the Japanese Foreign Minister Shigemitsu, who, of course was not convinced by these protests and dismissed them by saying that "prisoners were equally treated and all those who were sick received medical attention"[21].

Initially, London was hesitant to permit the Indian Government to indulge in propaganda against the Japanese treatment of the P.O.W. They were afraid that it might jeopardise the fate of large number of prisoners in Japanese custody. Indian Government, however, reacted sharply when they were asked to publish a message by Howard Vyse, from London. The message stated in contradiction to American viewpoint that there was not "a single case of atrocities in the P.O.W. camps in Japan and giving relatively satisfactory account of the conditions". Commander-in-chief of the Indian Army noted with dismay, "I do not understand this policy of white-washing Japan and concealing truth regarding barbarism of Japanese". In his view the above statement had given the impression which was "far from truth and was misleading" as only a very small proportion of Allied prisoners were held in Japan itself[22]. Both the Viceroy and C-in-C tried to convince the Chief of the General Staff, London about initiating a vigorous propaganda against the Japanese. They argued that there was hardly any ground to suspect that, "such campaign would prejudice" negotiation for further exchange of civilians and for despatch of food and medical supplies to P.O.W. On the other hand they pointed out that there were good grounds for belief "that exposure of Japanese shortcomings" was " the best and quickest way to effect improvement owing to the Japanese sensitiveness to world opinion".[23]

The Government of India had valid reasons, " for informing allied public true facts as soon as possible" in view of the reports received about the employment of the P.O.W. for the construction of the Siam-Burma railway. In addition they wanted to warn the people about the Japanese intentions towards India. Alongwith the sustained anti-Japanese propaganda the Government of India pressed the Chief of the General Staff, London to strengthen their Air-Force which was needed for attacking, "Japanese line of communication wherever possible" but especially the Siam-Burma railway which was likely to reduce the line of communication between Siam and Burma for supply and reinforcement.[24]

III

It is not intended to give a detailed account of Siam-Burma railway, which has been extensively covered by those who actually took part in it. Here it is proposed to give the minimum facts and to hint at the certain discrepancies in the published accounts. It is generally stated by many that the Allied powers came to know about the true facts regarding the Japanese treatment of the P.O.W. who were employed for the construction of the Siam- Burma railway, when a ship named *Rokayo Maru* was sunk by torpedo in South-China sea in September, 1944 with 1300 Allied P.O.W. on board. Only a hundred of the Australian and British prisoners were picked up and when eventually, they reached home, they told the whole story[25]. It is only a partial truth. The British intelligence agencies in India were aware that the Siam-Burma railway was being constructed with the help of the Allied P.O.W. From the very beginning, besides obtaining information about its progress by aerial photographs, they were being supplied details through different secret sources. Weekly Intelligence reported in November 1942 stated that the Siam Burma railway, a "project to join Thailand with Burma" had been welcomed by the Japanese and Thai officials' and " this railway line will be constructed in accordance with the treaties existing between Thailand and Japan. The line will be 460 km long and will start from South Thailand. From South Thailand, the line will run along the Mokong River and will cut across the Thai-Burmese border at a point 160 km south of Moulmien"[26]. The report clarified that it now appears that the proposed link up between the railways of Siam and Burma would follow the alignment Banpong-

Kanchauburi—Three Pagodas Pass and not the preliminary suggested route-Prachuab-Kirikan-Mergui or Raheng-Mesord-Kaw-Kareika-Moulmien. Subsequent information received referred to the difficulties involved in the construction of the railway. The entire route of the railway, the report pointed out," ran largely through hilly and completely underdeveloped country with extremely heavy monsoon rainfall". The report concluded that the conditions "suitable for rapid railway construction were almost entirely lacking".[27] After the construction began details about the working conditions were gained from the letter of a P.O.W. addressed to the International Committee of the Red Cross which stated that the P.O.W. were living in a jungle had been, "reduced to almost starvation and without hygiene of any sort". "Food" according to the letter was not only insufficient for the European, but was causing "vitamin deficiency" which had resulted in the disease such as "beriberi". Due to the lack of meat, the P.O.W." were greatly delibatated and suffering from dysentery and malaria".

It also referred to the long hours of work daily " in all weathers" and without sufficient clothing particularly shoes and trousers. In the last part of his letter, the P.O.W. referred to the "deaths which continuously were on the rise in the jungle and mentioned that 3,000 men have died to date. An epidemic of Cholera has broken out and medicines are lacking".[28]

The above letter revealed the wretched conditions of the P.O.W. working on the railway, but it is not clear whether any steps were taken by the I.C.R.C. to provide relief to the P.O.W. In reality the I.C.R.C. was helpless to do anything as the Japanese were reluctant to receive any substantial help from I.C.R.C. for mitigating the sufferings of the P.O.W. However, it is on a record that the P.O.W. did get some monetary help secretly from I.C.R.C. from time to time[29].

Further reports warned that more than 40,000 allied P.O.W. were working in the most appalling conditions in the valley of Quoa Noi River. They had no drugs and only one-third ration. Their conditions were worst during the monsoon and if no steps were taken, it was expected that at least 20 per cent of the P.O.W. would die due to lack of "drugs, food and exposure".[30]

Different motives have been assigned as to why the Japanese undertook the construction of Siam-Burma railway immediately after the fall of Singapore. Some scholars say that this project was closely linked with Japanese "decision to mount the offensive into India". Though it is doubtful that the Japanese were keen to start an offensive towards India in the beginning of 1942 yet after they had captured Burma, it was definitely expected that the railway line would, "facilitate the transfer of men and supplies to support Japan's large army in Northern Burma which faced the British from India and the Chinese and Americans from Yunnan". At the same time, it had been realised by the Japanese High Command that, "the supplies and re-inforcement required for Burma, front were to be supplemented by a land route since the "Allied navy and Air-Force were becoming a threat to the marine route following the battle of Midway on June, 1942 when the Japanese fleet had suffered a considerable losses"[31]

The British had realised the strategic importance of railway but at the same time were aware that there was no threat to their position in India in 1942, as the intelligence report pointed out that "while operations may not be started immediately yet the Japanese know that India is being used as the base on which a major offensive against him is being mounted. He must therefore, use everything he has to weaken that base". For the Japanese, the presence of the British in India was a constant threat to their contemplated co-prosperity sphere, while for the British, any Japanese advance towards India meant the liquidation of their empire. But by late spring 1942, the Japanese Imperial Army occupied the whole of Burma and was in process of consolidating its positions there. To maintain this Army and prepare it for the inevitable counter-attack to come, meant moving in of supplies and reinforcements on a large scale. Moreover, the initiation of any positive action, e.g., invasion of India would double these demands.[32]

Arnold, however, refers to the Japanese need to the exploitation of tungston ore deposits along the route (Tungston is used in the manufacture of munition). '"There may have been another, ultra secret motive" writes Arnold, "for rail road Burma was thought to be a site of Uranium deposits necessary for Japan's atomic bomb projects."[33]

There was nothing new in the proposal for Siam-Burma railway which had been debated earlier also in Burma and Siam. But was given up on account of its being considered as uneconomical and also difficult to manage due to dense forests.[34] From the Japanese side the Fifth and Ninth Railway Regiments, comprising of 12,000 Japanese troops were assigned to undertake the project together with 3200 Japanese and Korean civilian guards. For the manual labour it was decided to employ Allied P.O.W. and labourers to be recruited from Burma, Malaya and other places. Due to initial opposition by the Siamese Government and other reasons, the work was delayed and started only in November, 1942 which was originally scheduled to be begin from June 1942.[35] The entire work was to be completed in eighteen month despite the doubts expressed by the men on the spot. Although the engineers eventually convinced their superiors of the utter impossibility of this, they were still ordered to press ahead with utmost speed.

Despite initial opposition from Thailand, an agreement was signed on 16 September, 1942 between Premier Phibun Songkhram and Japanese Military attache General Moriya Seiji, which pledged the provision of accommodation for the construction units, land for the right of way, rail road ties (sleepers) wooden poles, bumper, cement and sand. Thailand as per the agreement was also to provide engineers and labourers, and assist the Japanese Army in obtaining trucks, boats and work elephant. The Japanese army, however, would direct the construction and operate the completed line. In addition large sum of money was given as loan by the Thai Government.[36]

From the Burmese side, the Japanese got full support in recruiting the labour. Estimates of the number of Burmese who laboured on the railway vary. Ba Maw claimed 65,000, while a Burmese official told a Dutch officer after the war that 90,000 were involved. The labourers were recruited from different countries by the agents on voluntary basis and were not conscripted. However, the facilities promised at the time of recruitment were never adequately provided by the Japanese. The estimate of labour employed vary, but the official figures are, that about 1,18,000 labourers were employed before the end of 1942, while another 1,40,000 coolies from Burma and Malaya were employed till the completion of the railway.[37] Some believe as many as 100,000 lost their lives.

In addition to labour, the Japanese High Command permitted the Southern Command to employ Allied P.O.W. to work on the railway. As to why only around 61,000 allied P.O.W. were employed when the Japanese had tens of thousands of P.O.W. in their custody in South East Asia it is difficult to understand. However, the study of the report of "F" Force gives a partial answer. Perhaps the Japanese were aware that the - employment of P.O.W. for military purposes was against the rules of Geneva Convention. But their interpretation of those who surrendered at Singapore was quite different. According to Geneva Convention, "belligerents may employ as workmen prisoners of the war who are physically fit other than officers and persons of equal status, according to their rank and ability"[38]. But the Japanese did not follow the Geneva Convention when they employed sick and physically unfit men on the construction of the military project.

The Japanese explanation given to "F" Force was that their status as P.O.W. was quite different from those who had been captured, and their "unconditional surrender at Singapore placed them outside the terms of Hague and Geneva Convention". Harris who was commander of the " F" Force forcefully argued against this interpretation, but without any success. His argument was that " the position of any prisoner who is captured on the field of battle is closely that of the unconditional surrender". He further pointed out that the surrender at Singapore was conducted on the written request of General Yamashitia " in order to avoid further useless loss of life on both sides and especially the lives of civilians in the city. In view of this he pleaded that it was not proper to place the garrison of Singapore outside the terms of the convention"[39].

The Japanese were adamant to follow their own rules and perhaps recruited mainly the Allied prisoners from Changi prison specifically so as to avoid any legal or moral complications in the future.

The figures and total number of prisoners employed on the railway and those who died differ considerably, but the details given by Brett in his official report were calculated on the basis of figures given by War Grave Commission. These are as follows:-

Nationality	*Total employed*	*Died*
British	30,000	6,540
Australian	13,000	2,710
Dutch	18,000	2,830
U.S.	700	131
Total	62700[40]	12,624[41]

Originally the deadline for the completion of the entire rail line had been set for December, 1943, but the pressure on the Burma front by the Allied caused the Japanese high command to advance this to August, 1943. When it appeared that deadline could not be met, more civilian labourers and Allied P.O.W. were sent from Singapore. The story of these groups sent from Singapore is fully documented in the History of "F" Force and "H" Force. They were in addition to those already sent earlier, and were to speed up the construction of the railway. It was the deployment of these two forces contrary to the promises made and ordeal suffered by them which gave the railway its notoriety as the " railway of death". The two groups comprising of nearly 10,000 men were also different from all other parties sent north in that they remained under Singaporean administration throughout their time in Thailand and were returned to Changi Prison as soon as the railway project was completed.[42] This dual administration created many problems for the men and went against their interest as has been pointed by Harris in his report. From the start, the prisoners were kept in the dark about the nature of work and the ordeal which they were to face during the journey to the site of the Siam-Burma railway.

After reaching Banpong, the members of the force were asked to proceed to the different camps, along the railway line on foot. The heavy stores which they had brought with them alongwith the medical stores, were either abandoned or sold at cheaper rate to the unscrupulous traders. Banpong was the base camp for the railway working parties with one hospital for the P.O.W. The net result of the misinformation and poor organisation of the move was that when "F" force marched north towards the Burmese frontier it did so without any idea of what they were supposed to do. The report gives full details about the promises which were made by the Japanese to the P.O.W., when they were drafted from Changi. It is not clear as to why all these promises were never kept or whether these were given without the sanction of the higher authorities. Since nearly 30 per cent of the force consisted of unfit men, the Force commander Major Wild had several interviews with captains Miyosaki and Tanoka of the Imperial Japanese Army at Changi before their departure.[43] At the interviews, the actual figure of fit and unfit men were shown to them. It was further explained that even the so-called fit men in Changi had nearly all been in hospital as P.O.W. for one reason or another. In fact, they were not fit for heavy work or for marching long distances. In the light of the above discussions, the Australian re-examined all their men and re-classified as fit previously marked as unfit. This was done on assurance from the Japanese that, "the force would have good chance of re-habilitation with good food". The British troops were also re-examined before selection, but the inspection did not amount to more than establishing fitness to travel.

Harris did not believe that the Japanese in-charge at Singapore had any knowledge about the purpose of the party being sent to Thailand. "This" Harris says, "must have been to their knowledge untrue and it is on these therefore, that full responsibility for what followed must lie". The party reached Banpong under extreme hard conditions and were very politely told to march on foot towards Burma. From the very beginning something or the other went wrong. Due to shortage of lorries, Japanese asked them to move on foot and travel by night to avoid the heat during the day time. On the other hand, the Japanese engineers were also not aware of the situation. The orders from the Imperial Headquarters as recorded by one Japanese engineer were to "go into the jungle and build a railroad". He describes that "the jungle was incredible. It was deep, dark and dense, with green trees. There were no roads. There were no reliable maps, only a primitive chart made by the British Army long before"[44]. The Japanese engineers depended on the old survey reports as there was no time to undertake the new survey.

The initial orders for the move of the force in thirteen trains was altered to send Australians in the first six trains and rest of the British in other trains. The train which was to carry all heavy luggage and medical gear instead of the first became the 7th in the process, which the report says had far reaching consequence.

"If the medical and other essential gear had arrived with H.Q in Banpong on the first train there would have been nothing to prevalent its being moved up into the forward area before arrival of the troops and before the rains broke, rendering the road impossible to M.T."

The change of schedule also made it impossible for the Australian contingent to have their second cholera inoculation before leaving. The Imperial Japanese Army had also given instruction to all those leaving to have inoculation against typhoid, plague, dysentry and cholera.

The above neglect had disastrous consequences for the British force, when they were face to face with cholera while working on the Railway line, which made its appearance in the middle of 1943. It is recorded that even before the march started many of the P.O.W. were beaten by the Korean guards especially one called Toyama, who thrashed prisoner for no cause with the steel shaft of a golf club "inflicting more or less serious injuries on a number of officers and men." They were then asked to march, the distance was not disclosed. They started off with very heavy load bulging packs and haversacks and rolls of bedding. On the other hand, the Japanese guards carried a rifle and a sling haver-sack for food. The march went on and on. They marched at night and slept in the day-time. After each day march they had to discard some items of what they started with. It became difficult for the sick to walk and many died during the march. In order to avoid heat, the marches took place at night, sleep for the majority was out of the question as men were compelled to restart their marches in an exhausted and dehydrated conditions. This treatment contributed substantially to the subsequent disease epidemics which decimated personnel of the Force. After a strong protest by the Allied Officers, Japanese gave a few concessions. These included the leaving of seriously sick persons in a Japanese hospital at Banpong and a few more in an extemporised hospital in the camp, while rest were to march. Medical stores were to follow on priority basis. Officers were asked to go by Motor transport to Tarso, which was to serve as the base camp of the final construction area.

While on the march, due to the refusal of the authorities to change Malay currency into the Thai, the P.O.W. brought extra food, water etc by means of selling Thais or the Imperial Japanese Army (I.J.A.) guards their personal belongings. Naturally in the climatic conditions, they had to work naked exposed to sun and rain. The march lasted about two and a half weeks over a distance of 300 kms, covered in the 15 stages of about 20 km each. Perhaps under normal circumstances marching 20 km daily would not have been tiresome for a normal soldier, but conditions became worse with the outbreak of the monsoon. The road surface became slippery and treacherous and long stretches were flooded and eventually washed away. The march became a nightmare for those, who were not physically fit. The condition at the staging camps were even intolerable due to constant rain. Accommodation consisted of coal house and open trench latrines and flies abounded with no shelter. Food which consisted of rice and vegetable stew; was supplied in insufficient quantities. Anticipating worst conditions, Harris had warned Lieut Fakuda that "a tragedy was in the making". But in the middle of 1943, the Japanese were too much intoxicated with their dream of achieving the co-prosperity sphere, that the miserable conditions of the P.O.W. had no effect on their thinking. Very soon, majority of the men became ill due to dysentery or beriberi and malaria. Even in such conditions, they were forced to march.

At Tarso, which was thought to be the base camp and headquarters of Thailand P.O.W. administration, Harris could realise that there was a sort of difference between the I.J.A. Railway Engineers and Thailand P.O.W. administration. This was, "presumably owing to the jealously at Malay's retention of control over "F" Force". It was due to this the P.O.W. staging camps on the march were left incomplete, by the authorities. The primitive huts in which they lived were full of water during the monsoon and at times with sewage. After reaching Tarso, the P.O.W. had a serious confrontation with the I.J.A. Major Wild took 50 sickmen for inspection by the I.J.A. medical officer, who told the corporal that 36 of them were quite unfit to march that night. Despite the certificate by the Japanese Medical Officer, the Corporal ordered 36 men to take the march. When Major Wild again protested, he was beaten up with bamboos, but at last it resulted in only 17 for the march.[45]

But worst happened when the force reached Knokita, where cholera had broken out. As a matter of fact, when the force reached its destination in May , it was heavily infected with malaria, dysentery, diarrhoea etc. Col Banno, then distributed the Force at different camps situated at Shimo-Sonkru, Sonkari Kami Sonkrai, Chokata, and Nieke to work on the railway. As the report says, "without warning cholera epidemic swept down amongst us as cessation of movement were spurned and in point of fact, owing to the depletion of labour force by death, movement became increasingly frequent and longer in character. The result was inevitable. The disease spread as not withstanding the noble efforts of our own medical personnel, every camp throughout the Force was quickly effected. The death rate was very heavy."[46]

Even before they started work on the railway, "F" Force had lost nearly 595 persons. And immediately after the march ended, cholera broke out, which proved to be a great killer, causing half of total deaths. However, with the deployment of already sickmen from September to December 1943, the death rate increased to a considerable extent. During this period nearly 841 died. Barring the last period from January to April 1944, death-rate fell rapidly. The death rate per month was as follows:-

1943							
May.	*June.*	*July.*	*August.*	*Sept.*	*Oct.*	*Nov.*	*Dec.*
314	*748*	*451*	*1048*	*1082*	*928*	*1006*	*778*
1944							
Jan.			*Feb.*		*March.*		*Apr.*
226			79		37		373

Henceforth, it was a constant struggle between the I.J.A. to recruit as many persons as possible to carry on the job of construction and it was the task of the Allied forces to have all round reduction, "in working number, reasonable hours and rest days". It goes to the credit of the Allied forces that many of the officers were deployed - of course against the Geneva Convention- under what is known as "officers working to save their men". But inspite of this, the condition deteriorated rapidly and with "starvation diet and with cholera, dysentery, diarrhoea, malaria, beri-beri, tropical ulcers , it was not long (by end of June), before the total number of men working outside the camps for the whole force was 700 men out of 7000 strong".[47]

It is not possible to generalise as to why the Japanese treated the P.O.W. so badly. Harris got the impression that the attitude of the I.J.A. depended on orders from Tokyo (with an alleged message from the Emperor, that the railway was to be finished at all cost). Perhaps the attitude of the Japanese was also determined to a great extent on account of their deep rooted notion that the " prisoners had no right whatsoever and that the prisoners from the unconditional surrender of Singapore in particular were I.J.A. chattels and were outside the preview of any international agreement.[47] Things took a different turn, when the time for the completion was reduced as per orders from Tokyo. During this " Speedo", period - as it is known more popularly," the men were driven like slaves, but food was reduced and the system was begun by which the sick were forced to work"[48]

It did not matter to the guards or to the engineers who laid down the daily task how hard or difficult the ground or what natural barriers obstructed the work. The final task had to be completed whether it meant seven hours of toil or ten or twelve. Day by day, stretched over four hundred kilometres of jungle; the men from two score camps picked and dug, chunkled and carried long hours and the fierce sun slowly drained away their resistance, never bolstered by a single square meal"[49]. The inhuman condition and the brutal behaviour earned the Japanese the name of what one prisoner described as an inhuman devil with a human face". However, there were others who did try to improve the conditions[50]. All said and done, the reports bring out the fact that death rate was more from disease and malnutrition than by hard work on the railway. The death rate amongst the British was more than the Australians. Despite the pressure mounted by the Allied P.O.W. and constant appeals to General Arimura in Singapore, to the International Red Cross at Tokyo and to the Japanese Governments, the conditions on Siam-Burma railway did not change, till the railway was completed. There were number of difficulties, which were beyond the power of the Japanese to minimise. Even Harris has admitted that in May,1943 railway construction was several months behind the schedule and the orders from Tokyo for its speedy finish entailed working throughout the monsoon, mid-May to mid-September, which led to the death of thousands of P.O.W. by disease and malnutrition. As a matter of fact maximum death occurred during this period. It is very difficult to put the entire responsibility on the Japanese alone, the natural physical conditions were also against the Allied P.O.W. Japanese had neither the means nor perhaps the will to evacuate the sick at a safer place. The harsh treatment by those who were asked to finish the work quickly led to the death of many P.O.W. No amount of pleading, protests or even flattery had effect on the Japanese attitude. Harris even tried to flatter the captors by describing them as belonging to, "a great and powerful nation" whose doctors and scientists were the best in the world "and who were proud of showing chivalry to the vanquished. "It is very difficult to understand", he wrote that "why such treatment is meted to the prisoners" by such noble people.

Food was always in short supply. Tentage at many places was almost non-existent, which necessitated large number of prisoners sleeping outside. The commander of "H" Force recorded that," in no single instance was sufficient cover available to house personnel attached to the area. In every case all consideration were subordinated to the demand for labour and still more labour for carrying out the railway construction undertaking". But in spite of terrible hardship the bonds of discipline and morale of the Allied P.O.W. never broke. The bond was stronger amongst Australian as such they suffered only 28 per cent deaths, the British suffered nearly 60 per cent. Moreover, the average physical standard of Australian Force was higher than those of British. At the same time, the Australian were accustomed to jungle conditions and had occupied the camps before the monsoon broke out. By the time, the members of "F" Force left for Singapore, after completion of the railway it had lost 3087 person, while the "H" Force had lost 702 persons. The deaths were due to various diseases which the prisoners inherited while on the march from Banpong to the camp sites. Torture and brutal treatment by the Korean guards added to the sufferings of the prisoners. All the authorities agree, that the Japanese relied heavily upon their Korean menials, for carrying out their orders. The regular Japanese troops writes, Bergamini, "in the area mostly averted their eyes or made sporadic efforts to ease the prisoner's lot. "Instead of demanding better equipment and food for their slaves, the Japanese engineers insisted on turning them out in numbers sufficient to meet work quotas. The doctors were still more knowingly inhuman in that they regularly certified sick men fit for work"[51]. Even where the Japanese doctors certified some persons not fit for work they were ignored by Japanese guards and doctors orders were never carried out.

There is a difference of opinion as to whether the treatment of the prisoners became better after the completion of the railway. The official estimate was that it improved to a considerable extent, while those who participated in the construction work, considered that it was only for a short duration. "With the railway completed" Evers writes "the Allies became aware of its strategic importance, stepped up their air attacks, which, so far, had been sporadic. The smaller viaducts, and bridges, now becoming subject to frequent bombing raids were regularly destroyed and repaired again and again, by those prisoners held back for the purpose".[52] The records of reconnaissance and aerial photographs show that the South East Asia Command was fully aware of the progress being made in the construction of the railway. Between January, 1943, when the first photographs were taken, till March, 1944, nearly 750 sorties were undertaken, which resulted in over a quarter of million photographs of the Siam-Burma railway. The above photographs provided detailed information to the Allied powers about the progress achieved by the Japanese meter by meter in the railway construction. The photographs also helped them to launch their programme of what was officially known as the, "Battle of Bridges". With concrete information at their disposal, many important main-line bridges were destroyed by Allied bombing. They were rebuilt as the report says by the "Japanese only to be destroyed again". At the same time, the successful attacks by Bean-fighters were carried out against locomotives and rolling stocks.[53]

Under Japanese discipline or what is called as Japanese brutal behaviour, P.O.W. definitely achieved tremendous progress in the construction of the railway even with inadequate resources and implements. South-East Asia Command estimated that in nine months time "approximately 200 miles of railway had been constructed" which it regarded as " a prodigious feat bearing in mind the nature of the country through which the railway passed. The report further praised the achievement and recorded that, " practically throughout its length clearing had to be made through dense forests, many large embankments and cuttings had to be made in order to negotiate the hilly country, and hundred of bridges and culverts had to be constructed to carry the line over the many rivers and water courses".

The construction of this railway in its opinion represented "a major feat of engineering, made possible only by the employment of large number of prisoners of war and the urgent necessity to the Japanese of establishing through communication between, Burma and Siam"[54]. Naturally for the Japanese, the railway was quite important as it shortened lines of communication by many hundred miles as formerly suppliers had to be shipped to Rangoon via Singapore". However, for the British, it posed a strategic threat. As such, every Japanese target meant for making the advance towards India a success was to be weakened.[54]

For the defence of India, the British did not bother to calculate the damage bombing was having on the P.O.W. It is difficult to estimate as to how many died in the bombing raids, but one can say that hundreds emanciated and oppressed whitemen died while reconstructing the bridges destroyed by the Allied powers. The British carried out a systematic and regular bombing of the railway line and they succeeded to a great extent in making the railway quit ineffective during 1944-45. A secret report confirms that "railways and roads were largely useless and important bridges were destroyed. Transport both by road, rail and water was literally brought to a standstill during day-time". While their propaganda against the inhuman treatment succeeded in bringing about a change in the attitude of the Japanese towards the P.O.W. especially after the railway was completed.

The Japanese order issued in the beginning of 1944, stated that hitherto the P.O.W. control had attached " importance to the use of P.O.W. as labour and although there have been not a few good results in the way of direct contribution to the war efforts etc conditions have been such that we have been unable to avoid material stringency". " It cannot be said", the order admitted that, "conditions of health have not been good and it is essential that attention should be given to improve the health of the P.O.W. alongwith increased food and clothing as per the fixed regulation[55]. The order admitted that while the sick and weak were compelled to work on the completion of the railway" it was now laid down that, "compelling persons to work who are sick or need a rest, or giving excessive work to those who are weak in order to keep up the formal work ratio of P.O.W. labours was, is to be avoided". Instead, the P.O.W. were to be treated cordially. The Japanese commanders in charge of P.O.W. were instructed to strive to " eradicate the mistaken hostile feeling amongst those, who had been forced to work on the railway". Full investigation was to be carried out about their health and steps were to be taken to reduce deaths in future.[56] Further evidence of the impact of anti-Japanese propaganda, was reported by the Indian army 3rd division when an order dated 27 February, 1944 by the Japanese commander came into their hand. This referred to the large scale and consistent propaganda campaign of the Allied powers "accusing the Japanese army of butchering prisoners and committing other atrocities". This the order said was being done with the object of arousing animosity against the Japanese of the Indian Army and the local authorities. To defuse the aim of Allied propaganda, the Japanese divisional commander suggested that, "all units must treat prisoners properly and avoid all atrocities" on allied prisoners. Perceptible change was found in subsequent Japanese orders regarding the P.O.W. These orders stated clearly that the, "wounded and sick prisoners, will be treated humanely and will be tended and cared for as for as the situation permits". For this purpose a proportion of the army's medical facilities and medical supplies will be provided and those who were killed due to wounds would be buried or cremated with due reverence".[57]

Whether the railway was ever fully used for the purpose for which it was constructed would remain a matter of conjecture. South-East Asia Command found that there were many obstacles for the proper utilisation of the railway. It referred to two important problems. One was, "the break in the line imposed by the ferry between Moulmein and Martaban" and the other was that "two of the 150 spans of the bridge carrying the railway across the Sittang River had been destroyed during the evacuation of Burma by the British and it was not easy to repair them. In addition at Moulmein the sidings and Jetty facilities were insufficient for handling the increased traffic expected. With the opening of the new railway, accordingly a new goods Jetty had to be built, whilst a similar Jetty and new sidings were built at Martban"[58]. Since the utility of the railway depended on the repair of Sittang Bridge, the Japanese took its repair earnestly and got it repaired by Feb, 1944 but it was destroyed again by Allied bombing. According to British Intelligence by April 1944, four trains were running each day usually of 20 trucks. Signalling was by red and blue flags during day and lamps by night. The speed was 40 miles per hour [59].

Under the circumstances the Japanese aim of utilising the railway fully in their scheme of advancing towards India was never fully realised. The British made it impossible for the Japanese army on the Imphal battle-front to adequately receive the reinforcement from Burma. The Allied Powers were aware that the line was extremely vulnerable to Air-attack owing to the nature of the country and the number of bridges. There were about 688 bridges on the entire track of the railway which were constantly under air-attack especially those which were on Burmese side.

IV

A contemporary report has recorded that despite the hardship the P.O.W. did not express resentment against any authority during their captivity, but they definitely displayed intense contempt for their captors, " though slightly less intense hatred". They regarded the Japanese as "not natural" or even "not civilised". The Japanese in-charge of P.O.W. were aware of these feelings and sometimes did take revenge on those who jeered at them. Harsh and brutal behaviour alongwith the violation of Geneva convention, however increased the contempt for the Japanese. Naturally after their release and recovery, there was no temptation to fraternise or even to show any sympathy towards the Japanese in their hours of complete defeat[60] by the Allied prisoners. But in the post-war period, more ex-P.O.Ws, however, remained embittered.

It is difficult to say as to whether there was any deliberate intention on the part of the Japanese to treat the prisoners harshly. The great deal of hardship which the prisoners had to undergo was attributed by the commandant of the "H" Force " to Japanese incompetence and inefficiency as well as to a complete apathy on the part of the officers of, IJA". These officers seemed at all times incapable or undesirous of regulating the conduct of their subordinates, with the result that illiterate NCO and soldiers entrusted with the responsibilities of supervision and administering P.O.W. were enabled to give full play to high degree of vindictiveness and sadism which seems to be an inherent part of the Japanese temperament"[61]. It has been testified by many P.O.W. that the behaviour of the Japanese was less brutal and inhuman as compared to the Korean guards. The reason being their abnoxious treatment by the Japanese. As Payne says the Koreans were even more villianous than their Japanese masters. Koreans were in charge of British and commonwealth officers and Japanese soldiers were incharge of Koreans.[62] The Korean guards were despised by the Japanese and hated by the P.O.W. Added to the insults received from the Koreans, the P.O.W. received a further emotional shock, when they were kept at par with Tamil coolies. As the report has pointed out," no regard was paid to the location of the camps beyond their convenience to the working site concerned, with the result that the camp were frequently situated cheek by jowl with native coolie camps in all of which sanitary arrangements were entirely absent throughout most of which deadly diseases were already stalking".[63] Japanese also made the P.O.W. to work side by side with the coolie of every colour and caste" and submit to standardised form of supervision and summary punishment with these people. However, there were many European P.O.W. who definitely felt sorry at the plight of the Asian workers, but they were unable to control the social prejudices of their comrades. The dignity of the P.O.W was further lowered when they saw their officers being forced to work as coolies, which was done as "H" Force, commander recorded, "to degrade in every considerable way the officers of various Allied Forces who had been unfortunate enough to fall into their hands."[64] Much against the international rules, the Japanese did not spare the Allied officers who were used in the task of construction of the railway. Though they were to serve as supervisors, but many of them served as labourers in order to what was called to save their comrades from virtual death. When the demand for more and more labour was received many allied officers went for constructions work, so that utterly sick comrades could be spared for rest. In this manner many prisoners were saved from death. Beatings were common, while hours of work were long. It was a daily sight to see officers practically nude, engaged in labour tasks of the lowest and most arduous of types.

Japanese scholars have tried to defend that in the tropical conditions, there was a general scarcity malnutrition and disease and epidemic among P.O.W. and the Japanese[65] sufferred and lived in the same places. But the statistical details do not support this. The deaths amongst the P.O.W. not accustomed to living in tropical climate were much more than amongst the Japanese. By denying food to the sick or non-working people, the Japanese guards " were heard to say that they hoped the sick would die and then save Japanese rice" for their use[66]. The medical supplies alongwith the shortage of food were no doubt affected by the war and the Japanese tried to provide what was readily available and in many cases, the delay occurred through sheer carelessness rather than deliberate attempt. But it should not be presumed as Kinving writes that "all cases of sickness were the result of Japanese neglect and their failure to provide the necessary drugs", the climatic conditions were against the prisoners. At the same-time one has to consider the Allied policy of making the completion of the railway as difficult as possible. Besides the sabotage by P.O.W. " the Allied action cut the sea supply lines, damaged the lines itself by constant bombing". As a mark of retaliation every P.O.W. whether sick or unfit was forced to reconstruct the lines and bridges repeatedly destroyed by the Allied bombing[67]. Japanese engineers have further recorded that the enemy air raids damaged the line's carrying capacity immediately after its openings. Abe writes that from "Jan to December, 1944 when the Japanese were on Myitkyina line, which stretched north from Manalong towards Indian and Chinese borders, the British approaching it from the East, attacked it practically every day. In day-light, the British planes bombed and we repaired the lines all night.[68] In addition the Siam-Burma railway, the British concentrated their bombing within Burma itself and on "the major communication centres such as Rangoon, Mandlay, Pegu and Bangkok together with major bridges within range"[69].

After the war was over, the Supreme Allied commander South-East Asia, Lord Mountbatten was in favour of retaining the Siam-Burma railway. His arguments were that the railway had been built at an enormous cost of Allied life and if steps were not taken, to maintain it, it would become useless. He further argued that there were good reasons for the retention of the railway especially as no airline would replace it. More than the facility, it would provide between the two countries, it would also make it easier for troop movement and maintenance of Allied Forces. The British were still not reconciled to the fact they were to withdraw from South-East Asia. However, the decision was kept for a meeting in London. Quite contrary to Mountbatten's view the Inter-command meeting held on 7th November, 1945 decided that India had no special interest in the railway reconstruction and it had no strategic importance for her as such it " should be handed over to Siam"[70]. Like

India, Burma was also not interested in the maintenance or reconstruction of the railway line. The decision of both the countries was based on the realistic thinking. The railway line, they were aware had been damaged by the Allied bombing to such an extent, that it would cost them nearly 8 to 10 crores of rupees, to reconstruct and make it worthy for traffic for maintaining the daily capacity of 1200 tons. The railway line on the Siamese side was handed over to the Siam Government, who paid nearly 50 million Baht to South-East Asia Command. The money was utilised for the P.O.W. who had worked on it.[71] Closely linked with the decision to the disposal of the railway, was the question of the recovery of the P.O.W. in Japanese hands. Surprisingly, the report of the South East Asia Command has given a slightly different picture of the P.O.W. under Japanese captivity as compared to what was depicted during the war time. According to its findings the position of the Allied P.O.W. in the Japanese Prison camps was not so bad as had been projected during the war-time. Prior to their liberation the reports received from various sources suggested that the health of the prisoners and internees was very poor. But all the medical officers "who visited these camps at the time of recovery found that the health of the prisoners was far better than was expected"[72]. They ascribed the good health due to improved nutrition provided by the Japanese during the weeks prior to victory. The report endorsed the hardships and sufferings, which the P.O.W. had undergone during their captivity and agreed that some of the P.O.W. were under-nourished, and weak and sullen, but none was on death-bed. "It was gratifying to realise that while all required much medical treatment", the report noted only about 50 per cent required hospitalisation for only 3 to 7 days and not more than 10 per cent who had been in the worst camps required prolonged treatment for ten days or more".[73]

Out of 34,985, P.O.W. who were recovered from Singapore, 76 per cent were fit for immediate evacuation to U.K. on convalescent diet by Troop Ship or Ambulance Transport, 21 per cent were fit for immediate hospital ship evacuation. Only 3 per cent required hospital treatment prior to evacuation. There were only marginal cases, who were dangerously ill. Their percentage was only 1.4 per cent. On the whole, the report concluded that less than 25 per cent of the liberated British personnel were ill and that the majority of those required relatively little hospital treatment.

The details given by South-East Asia Command do show to some extent, that the Allied propaganda about Japanese treatment of P.O.W. during the war did contain some element of exaggeration. But at the same time there is no justification also to defend the Japanese for the harsh treatment and violation of the rules. One can say that these were not deliberately carried out and may be regarded as what Adochi termed as " unprepared regrettable events"[74]. More than the health, the Committee was surprised to note the excellent mental condition of the P.O.W.

How amid disease, slave labour and the perpetual monsoon rain and harsh treatment, the P.O.W. kept their sanity intact. It could be that the P.O.W. had no alternative but to laugh at the odd behaviour of their captors. Of course not all

Japanese were brutes. There were sympathetic and comical characters. Moreover, the help received from Thais, and other unknown persons kept them slightly cheerful. The South-East Asia Command was rather surprised at this phenomenon. They recorded that the psychological shock which P.O.W. received in Germany was missing in the Far East.[75] The report goes on to say that the " studies of the P.O.W. released from German or at their hand in 1944-45 showed that many were suffering from psychological disorders. Apart from cases of illness, so many were mildly abnormal ". Expecting that the conditions of P.O.W. in Japanese hands would be in the same or worst state instructions had been issued as to the best way to treat them. It was, therefore, a great surprise for them to state that their mental health was unbelievably good and relatively even better their physique".

Surprisingly, the P.O.W. had no grudge against working rather they found work as their salvation, work of practically any nature even at the harder and dullest manual work but perhaps the misbehaviour of the Japanese made it difficult for them to have an honourable and peaceful existence. Shortage of food and medicine continued with unhealthy living conditions in the dense forests of Siam-made them very bitter, but still many survived. For their misbehaviour and ill-treatment of the Allied P.O.W., the Japanese paid a much higher price as the Allied had announced that they were not going to forgive Japan for her misdeeds. Inspite of hardship of prison life, the P.O.W. did show what the Report says, "incredible ingenuity in improvising all sorts of equipment, wireless sets, surgical instruments and breweries, from whatever came to hand. The effort and success in concealing them from the Japanese increased their own self-respect".[76]

Although the Japanese atrocities against the P.O.W. cannot be condoned or justified, but for proper understanding, it will be necessary to keep the diverse factors in mind, which generated such behaviour from their captors. Japanese supervisors followed blindly the orders - whether right or wrong—from their superiors and there was no questioning. The documents included however, do not support the general charge against the Japanese that their treatment of the prisoners was a wilful and malicious act done with purposeful cruelty. While it is difficult to overlook the suffering and death of hundreds of P.O.W., the Japanese incharge of the P.O.W. were definitely guilty of " mall-administration, inefficiency and callousness".[77] The cruelty inflicted on the P.O.W. in some cases was the outcome of personal behaviour of the Korean guards, who did it out of spite rather than as per instructions from the Japanese masters.

V

As mentioned earlier, this is a documentary study and some reports on this controversial topics have been retrieved from the Indian Archives and are presented here for the benefit of the scholars. These include three reports prepared by the British officers. The report by Lieut. C.Brett, who belonged to Canadian Intelligence was prepared on the basis of extensive interrogations, translations and documentary research and personal observations of the Siam-Burma railway. The research was carried out over a period of seven months in Siam, Burma and Malaya. Brett's report is divided into five parts. Besides giving the background as to how the railway came to be built, it deals with the construction, problems, its operational side, employment of coolies and Allied P.O.W., their trials and turbulations. Much more than the factual account, what enhances the value of the report is the large number of appendices, correspondence and notes, which are not easily traceable now. Besides reproducing a sizeable portion of Lieut. Harris's report on "F" force, Brett has also included the report of the commander, "H" force, statistical details of the Allied P.O.W., and coolies, note on the 5th and 9th Japanese railway regiments, translation of Japanese documents, medical report by a Japanese doctor, conditions in coolie camps etc.

Besides having access to records of the Allied powers, much of the materials in the preparation of the report was obtained by Brett from interrogation of Japanese connected with those units.

This report is quite well known, but I would like to draw attention of the scholars to the fact that the report of Lieut. Col. S. W. Harris who was commander of F Force at Appendix 'I' in the above bulletin is not complete Brett excluded nearly 30 paragraphs from the original report, which is available in the History of 'F' force . This is described below along with the supplementary report on 'H' force.

With a view to have a proper perspective about the events, Brett's report should be read with the compilation entitled History of the 'F' Force. This is perhaps the most detailed account of the trials and tribulations suffered by the Allied P.O.W. while working on the railway. It deals with the deplorable conditions under which more than three thousands British and Australian prisoners died between April 1943 and April 1944. A party of 7000 men half British and half Australian were taken under the care of Lt. Col. Banno of Imperial Japanese Army [I. J. A.] from Changi POW Camp, Singapore to work on the railway in the vicinity of three Pagoda Pass. All of them were under the overall command of Lieut. Col, Harris. The force left Singapore in April, 1943.The first six trains carried the Australians, the next seven, the British and the main Japanese party. The conditions during the thousand mile journey were extremely bad and the prisoners were not given adequate food or water. The camps where they were kept were a squalid mess with poor sanitation facilities. After a stay of few days in the make-shift camps, the personnel of F Force were ordered to march for roughly 300 kilometers travelling by night and resting by day for about 17 days. This march in the rain led to the decline of health of those prisoners who were not fit to travel. As a result of this many died on the way even before they reached the destination. Nearly 595 POW had died even before they were put to work on the railway.

The History of 'F' Force is divided into two parts. Part one of the report contains, the Japanese orders for the departure of Allied POW from Changi and deals with the most crucial question as why the prisoners were selected from Changi prison for the work on the railway when thousands of Allied POWs were available to the Japanese at other places. It appears from the study of this report that the Japanese did not treat them as prisoners of war under the Geneva Convention. The Japanese had signed the Hague Convention of 1907 on the law and customs of war ,but had refused to sign the more detailed 1929 Geneva Convention on the treatment of the prisoners of war. They had ,however, agreed to apply the Convention during the duration of the war when a representation was made to the Japanese. As per the Convention 'belligerent may employ as workmen prisoners of war who were physically fit other than officers and persons of equal status according to their rank and ability,' and the employment of the prisoners of war for military purposes was also against the Convention. As such they were treated as sunendered soldiers and not those captured during the course of the war by the Japanese. This was a lame excuse, the very idea of treating men who had surrendered as worthy of consideration was alien to their thinking. As such the pleadings of the prisoners in this respect had no effect on Japanese attitude.

From the study of the above report, it comes out that the British commander drew the attention of the I.J.A. to the spirit of the Geneva and Hague Conventions and explained that the unconditional surrender of the POW at Singapore did not place them outside the terms of Hague Convention as claimed by the I.J.A.. It was further clarified that the position of 'any prisoner who is captured on the field of battle is clearly that of unconditional surrender, but no one would suggest that he was not covered by the Convention'. Their plea was that the surrender took place at the written request of General Yamashita 'in order to avoid further useless loss of life on both sides'. But in spite of these pleadings the I.J.A. followed their own policy towards the POW and recruited the personnel for the F and H Force from Changi only, when the deadline for the completion of the railway was advanced from December to August, 1943.

The report reproduces the correspondence between Commander of the F force and General Banno regarding the conditions of health of the prisoners and how these could be improved with the adequate supply of medicine and food. But there was no positive response. As a result of this callous attitude of the Japanese by the time the railway was completed, out of 7000 POW nearly 2500 were dead, 2000 were ill in the hospital and only 1500 were fit for light duty and not more than 1000 fit for work.

As mentioned above about thirty paragraphs which Brett omitted from his report throw considerable light on the Japanese side of the story.For instance these paragraphs from 8 to 12 describe the meetings which took place between Major Wild, who was Force interpreter and Miyasaki and Tanaka, officers in charge of Changi in which the question regarding the fit and unfit POW were discussed before their departure. The selection of the POW was revised, but it appears that the instructions were not implemented seriously even with regard to the question of inoculation before the departure of the POW. In other paragraphs the position of the officers is given by Harris as to how they were asked to do labor duties in spite of their protests. In other paragraphs, the reasons for the harsh attitude of the IJA, are discussed which were dependent 'on orders from Tokio [with an alleged message from the emperor] that the railway was to be finished at all costs'. Their attitude was also determined by the reports which the IJA was getting about the inhuman treatment of the Japanese POWs by the Americans. [para75] In subsequent paragraphs Harris has also given the local Japanese difficulties for the construction of the railway along with the failure of the IJA administration to cope up with the situation. The last three paragraphs [101 -103] refer to the morale of the POWs which was stretched to the breaking point by the Japanese but they were unable to break it. 'If they had probably not one man would have returned alive.' It appears from this report that the POW were kept in the dark about nature of work and the ordeal which they were to face during the journey and subsequently on the construction of the railway.

The report by Harris is followed by an interesting account submitted by Major Cyril Wild and Col. Dillon 'On conditions of POW IN Thailand May to December, 1943' to the IJA. But they neither answered it nor challenged it, though the British Commander was asked to destroy all copies of this report. This report gives factual details about the health conditions in different camps and the suggestions for their improvement and tried to avoid the impression that it was protest of the prisoners.

Part II of the report deals with the supply of food, health of the prisoners and the medical facilities made available to the Allied doctors by the Japanese authorities. There is comprehensive report by J. Huston S M O along with the extracts from the reports of Major B.A.Hank and extracts from the medical report of Assistant Surgeon Woelf, M. D. These reports give a day to day account of deaths which occurred due to diseases like cholera, malaria, dysentery, beri-beri, tropical typhus, jaundice, etc. There is a interesting report on sickness and death rate prepared by T. Wilson due to malnutrition. The number of deaths increased in July and August and continued till the end of the year and decreased from January 1944. Besides these details this part of the report contains the copies of correspondence which passed between J. Huston and the Japanese army from November 1943 for improving the health of the prisoners. Most interesting is the report on the Tanbaya hospital by Bruce Hunt. These medical reports are very useful to understand as to how the POW died while constructing the railway. From these reports it is known that the treatment of the troops and in particular the sick by the 'IJA guards varied from camp to camp. At some camps the M.O. of the party was allowed to leave behind without interference such men as he considered unfit to march,. On other occasions the M. O. was subject to interference and at several places men with malaria or dysentery were compelled to do a whole night march to the great detriment to their health.' What enhances the value of this comprehensive history is the copies of correspondence which passed between the British officers and the I.J.A. At times the British officers tried even flattery in their letters to get concessions from the Japanese for the sick prisoners. For instance Bruce Hunt wrote in one of the letters that 'if we had been taken prisoners by a barbarous race unaccustomed to the ways of civilized nations, with complete lack of medical precautions.....it would be readily understandable.' But he regarded their captors as belonging to 'a great and powerful nation whose doctors, and scientists are amongst the best in the world. 'Naturally it was difficult for him to understand as to how such treatment was meted out to the prisoners by people who were 'proud of showing chivalry to the vanquished.' But it had no effect on the Japanese guards, who were to follow the orders from above and to see that the railway was completed in time. This comprehensive history clearly establishes the fact that the death rate was more due to harsh physical conditions, tropical diseases and malnutrition than by the hard work on the railway.

Scholars are familiar with the report on 'H' Force as given by Brett in the bulletin mentioned above. This report was prepared by Col. H. R. Humphries, British commander of H force. The force consisted of 3270 mixed Australian Imperial Force [AIF] British, Dutch and American POW personnel who were sent to Siam under orders of the I.J.A. In the Indian Archives I could not trace the copy of the above report, but found a supplementary report on H Force by another British officer Major J.F. Grossby. As compared to the above documents, this is a very important and critical report. It highlights the specific instances of the harsh treatment accorded to POW by the Japanese which were not included in the other reports and tries to find out as to who was responsible for the death of so many prisoners. It attributed the hardships and sufferings of the prisoners to 'the Japanese incompetence and inefficiency as well as to the complete apathy on the part of the officials of the I.J.A.' These officers of the I JA were not only incompetent, but they were at the same time in capable of 'regulating the conduct of the subordinates' with the result that the illiterate Japanese N.C.O.s and soldiers entrusted with the responsibilities of supervising and administering POW were enabled to give full play to high degree of vindictiveness which seems to be an inherent part of Japanese temperament.'

The most revealing part of the report deals with the way the officers of the Allied powers were treated by the I.J.A and how they were forced to work on the railway. The officers were shocked when they were ordered to do the manual work as they were not accustomed to it and they were not supposed to do the work under the Geneva Convention. The report shows that the Japanese supervisors were determined 'to degrade in every conceivable way the officers of the various Allied forces who had been unfortunate enough to fall into their hands'. According to this report the employment of the Allied officers on the labour duties on the railway was not only against the Geneva Convention, but also against the assurances given by General Arimura that the 'officers would be employed on administrative and supervisory duties.' and 'despite the protests of the officers, they were made to work as coolies with native coolies. Every conceivable insult was thrust upon them. Beating was common. Food was scanty and poor, and in addition to working at the railway undertaking, officers of all ranks were compelled to act as porters carrying equipment and rations often over a distance of six kilometers. During the cholera epidemic an officer party was compelled to carry and bury dead and dying Asiatics in a site adjacent to the British camp.'

This report also throws light on the appalling conditions prevailing in different camps and how the sick prisoners were saved by the British medical doctors, otherwise the feelings of the Japanese guards was that the sick should die and then save Japanese rice for them. It is believed by many scholars that nearly 1702 POW died out of 3270 who formed H force and were sent to work on the railway.[78] This report however clarifies that only 880 POW died while working on the railway.

In addition to official reports, the account by three officers of the British Indian Army, who were connected with the railway are included in this study. These accounts are important in sense, that a large collection of these reports of this category are still not available for research. "Given the number of British officers "writes Flower,"in Japanese captivity, the refusal to allow access to the documents, coupled with the reluctance of the officers to publish their own accounts has prevented the full story being made available"[79]. In view of this, the accounts of the officers who spent several month in Changi and then went to Thailand and other places, is very important for forming a correct perspective about the Japanese. The first report is by Captain J.Gibson, who was in the Royal Artillery 5 Indian Division and was recovered by the United States forces from the Philippines in January, 1945. Gibson, gives a detailed account of the surrender of British forces at Singapore, the life at Changi Prison where rations were not bad in the beginning and even the supervision was not strict. But gradually insufficient and diet started having effect on the general health of the P.O.W. The cases of malaria and dysentry began to increase. At Changi, Gibson found the behaviour of the Japanese as "quite reasonable". About the middle of June, he went north for working on the railway, with a party of nearly 1800. They were put in cattle trucks for an unknown destination. He describes, "we spent 4 days and nights in the train in the most uncomfortable conditions, being fed at irregular intervals and finally reached at destination in an extremely dirty and tired condition. The destination was Banpong in Thailand" Gibson was incharge of making the prison camps which had been left incomplete by the native coolies. Gibson had a fairly good opinion of the Japanese engineers he writes, "work on the railway was now started in earnest and only on rare occasions did the men have to work excessively long hour". During this period, he found the Japanese engineers fairly reasonable. The food at Wantakien camp had been, according to Gibston "the best we had ever had from Japanese and we were sorry to leave the camp".

Gibson's comments on the Korean guards are very interesting. Their behaviour towards the Allied, P.O.W., writes Gibson, was quite horrible and even " friendish" and "inhuman". He describes their arrival. "They arrived from Korea about the middle of July and as they marched into camp they presented a most ragged and dirty appearance. Their uniforms were worn out and most of their boots were in extremely bad conditions". Of course, they were given new uniform and all of them were armed. The P.O.W. as per the account of Gibson found them " to be extremely unpleasant in every respect". Gibson's assessment of the Korean guards is supported by many others. But when they were interrogated after the war, the Koreans blamed the Japanese. They even quoted the orders of the Lt.Col Nagatomo who told them that "P.O.W. are our enemies to the end, treat them drastically within the limits of humanity". Some of them even were told to think of P.O.W. as "though they were cattle or horses". Korean guards also testified that some of the P.O.W. were shot who tried to escape and even revealed that letters of P.O.W. which "had crossed many thousands of miles overland and sea were not delivered to the rightful recipient, but were burnt"[80] From Gibson's account, it appears that the Japanese treated them with utmost contempt. Naturally this provoked the Koreans to vent "their spleen", on the Allied P.O.W. On the other hand, the Japanese behaviour towards the officers amongst the P.O.W. was the result of the news which they had received that "Japanese nationals had been ill-treated by the Allied in concentration camp in America" because of this, the Japanese told the P.O.W. especially the officers that they had to work on the railway.

Perhaps, the best part of his account pertains to the "speedo" period and how the conditions became worse day by day" and how men were dying in large number daily and all appeals to the Japanese were without avail".

The second report is by Capt. J.W. Chapman who served with the 1st Gorkha Regiment. He was also a P.O.W. from Feb. 1942 till the war ended.

Chapman has given a detailed description of the Chungkai camp a jungle camp in Thailand, which served as a base camp. This camp had many P.O.W. who had worked on the Siam-Burma railway and how things began to change after the completion of the railway.

In his view Changhi camp was more elaborately planned "where the food supplies were in plentiful. But it also presented some shocking cases of erstwhile robust men, "now reduced to living skeletons." Though the ration was still insufficient, but it was much better than it was during the construction of the railway. The basic ration, according to Chapman "as issued by the Japanese seldom consisted of more than three meals a day with just sufficient scraps of meat and vegetables to go with two of these meals. Tea without milk or sugar was also provided. Chapman also refers to the secret radio sets in the camps, which provided the news. Red Cross parcels were also received, but distribution was eleven persons to get one parcel which usually contained tinned milk, chocolate, coffee, soap powder, cigarettes etc.

The most interesting, but brief account is by Major F.S.G. Nelson, Royal Artillery, who moved from one camp to another during the period of his captivity from Feb. 1942, adds to our knowledge about the events. He served in Change Prison and was involved in the construction of Siam-Burma railway for about ten months.

He agrees that supply of medicine in the tropical jungle was always short. Nelson description of the Japanese treatment of P.O.W. and how they used to maintain discipline by face-slapping or "standing outside guard rooms for period upto four days without food or drink is very interesting. The whole camp would be punished for the misdoings of one man which was strictly against International law. His description of work during the "Speedo" period is quite revealing, he writes that "sickman were carried out on stretchers and were made to work, malaria was not recognised as a disease. Many sufferings from had to have amputation and often died."

"Every available man and officer was made to work on the railway with the bare minimum allowed for camp duties. At the time, accommodation was in leaking tent and on the wet ground. Nelson also confirms the change of behaviour after the completion of the railway. He writes that "Politeness in them was in evidence and there was great courtesy between the officers and the commanders in the personal dealings". The frank appraisal, by these officers of the Japanese alongwith the contribution they made to save the lives of their subordinates by offering their services will definitely add to our kowledge about men and events connected with the railway. There are likely to be many more reports available in England and India, but I hope the documents included here will definitely broaden our knowledge about the Japanese treatment of the Allied P.O.W. and especially their employment on Siam-Burma railway and how they died in Japanese captivity.

New Delhi **T.R Sareen**

25 Mar 2003

References

1. Arnold, C.Brockman, *The other Nuremberg: The Untold Story of Tokyo War Crimes*, New York 1987, p. 253.
2. Van Waterford, *Prisoners of the Japanese in World War II*, New York 1994, p. 2
3. Sibylla Jane flower, "Captors and captives on the Burma Thailand railway" in Bob Moore and Kent Federowich (ed), *Prisoners of war and their captors in World War II*, Washington 1994, p. 229.
4. Clifford Kinvig. *River Kwai railway - The Story of Burma Siam railway*, London 1992, P XIIIV
5. *Ibid.*, p.31.
6. Ikuhiko Hata, "From consideration to contempt: The changing Nature of Japanese Military and Popular Perception of prisoners of War through the Ages" in Bob Moore and Ken Federowich, *op. cit.*, p. 254.

7. *Ibid.*, p. 264.
8. Lord Russel of Liverpool, *The Knights of Bhushido,* London 1958, p. 58.
9. The details of the Japanese policy towards the P.O.W. are summarised from Sumio Adochi. *A Brief History of Japanese Practices on Treatment of Allied War victims During the Second World War,* Tokyo 1982. Many orders not included by Adochi definitely proclaimed the superiority of the Japanese people, who will treat P.O.W., by " their own regulations". See these orders in *The History of Non-Military Activities of the occupation of Japan,* Vol.5 U.S.A. 1951. pp. 1-20.
10. F.No. 601/7378/H.S. Ministry of Defence. This file contains the *Weekly Intelligence Summary* prepared by the General Staff headquarters, Government of India and are very important for the study of the events connected with the Pacific War.
11. Adochi, *op.cit.*
12. John Coast *Railroad of Death.* London 1946. p. 43.
13. Lord Russel, *op.cit,* p. 55.
14. F.No. 601/7378/H.S.
15. *Ibid.*
16. The details about the Japanese Intelligence offensive against India are fully covered in the Weekly Intelligence summary referred above. For the counter—measures undertaken by the British Government in India see *Note on Japanese Subversive Activities Against the Indian Army* F.No.601/10569/H.S.
17. *Ibid.*
18. General Staff Quarters Publication "Against Japan", New Delhi 1944.
19. F.No.F 17/H.S.
20. Adochi, *op.cit.*
21. Though the exact figures were never published, but the records show that about 85,000 Indians, Australians and British soldiers became Prisoners of War in addition to large number of British and Allied civilians. For details See F.No.601/7816/H.S.
22. The correspondence between the Government of India and War office London on the question of propaganda against the Japanese about their treatment of the Allied P.O.W. is available in F.No.601/10534/H.S., but it is not complete and covers only one year. The subsequent correspondence may be available amongst the records of the War office at Public Record office, London.
23. *Ibid.*
24. F.No. 601/7378/H.S.
25. Lord Russel, *op.cit.* Even Brett in his official report has referred to this incident, which prompted the Allied powers to protest against the Japanese treatment of the P.O.W. through the Swiss Government. Some say that there were 1500 Australian and British prisoners on board the ship *Rukuyo Maru,* when it was torpadeoid by American submarines out of this only 151 survived. They revealed the horrible treatment meted out to the prisoners by the Japanese. However, by the time the protest was lodged, there was a perceptible change in the Japanese policy towards the P.O.W. It is not known as to how many allied P.O.W. died during their captivity either by Allied bombing or by the submarines. See Richard Garett, *P.O.W.* Great Britain 1982, p. 186.
26. F.No. 601/7378/H.S.
27. *Ibid.*
28. *Ibid.*
29. The Japanese did not allow the International Red Cross delegates to visit P.O.W., camps in Singapore inspite of repeated request, and especially the camps on Siam-

Burma railway. However, they did not object to the despatch of medicines etc. For the Allied P.O.W. it is recorded that the first consignment of 6000 tons of medicines and other goods were sent from India. Out of this 3000 tons were unloaded at Singapore, 1000 tons at Hong Kong, the balance being distributed among allied P.O.W. elsewhere in the Far East. The first consignment was sent in August 1942. Subsequent consignments irregularly were sent through the medium of the Protuguese, from the Marmagoa Port. Regular supplies became possible after the conference held in Washington in November, 1943. The supplies were allowed to be sent by the Japanese through Vladisvostok which was quite a long route.

30. F.No. F17/H.S.
31. Corenelis B. Evers, *Death railway Bangkok* 1993. p. 5. see also Earnest Gordon, *Through the Valley of the Kwai* U.S.A. 1962.
32. South-East Asia, *Translation and Intelligence Bulletin* No. 246.
33. Arnold C.Brockman, *op.cit.* p.254.
34. For the earlier efforts to construct the Siam Burma railway. See the *official report* by C.C.Brett, and also C. Bruce Renolds. *The Thailand-Burma railway,* a paper presented at the symposium on the Japanese Occupation of South-East Asia, National University of Singapore. December 14-16, 1995.
35. South-East Asia, *Translation and Intelligence Bulletin* No. 246.
36. The details of the agreement are contained in Viboon Leesuwan, et el. *Kanchanaburi Sprit of the Death railway and River Kwai Bridge,* Thailand, 1987, pp. 20-22.
37. Ba Maw, *Breakthrough in Burma,* New Haven, Yale 1968, p.290.
38. F.No. 21/4/1939. Home Department (Political) *National Archives of India.*
39. History of "F" Force
40. Different figures have been given with regard to the employment of P.O.W. for the construction of the railway. Arnold places them around 51,000, Japanese official account says 55,000. Lord Russel thinks only 46,000 were put on the job. Brett was quite near the total figure when he wrote his account and placed it at 61,000. Recent researches have calculated the number as 64,000, of these more than half were British. See Jane flower. *op.cit.* p. 240.
41. Similarly there is a difference of opinion as to how many Allied P.O.W. actually died on the railway. Hardie gives the figure as 16,000, while Chapalkar estimate was around 20,000. Japanese official report places the number at 10,000. Brett's figure of 12,364 has been accepted by many.
42. Kinvig, *op.cit.* p. 20. See also History of "F" Force.
43. This portion is summarised from the history of "F" and "H" Force.
44. Hiroshi Abe a Japanese railway engineer who escaped execution by sheer luck, has given the account on *Building the Siam-Burma railway* published in H.T.Cook and T.F Cook, *Japan at War, An Oral History,* New York 1992, p. 100. It is an interesting account which shows as to how Japanese engineers were ignorant about physical condition in the jungles of Siam-Burma where they were asked to construct the railway.
45. *History of "F" Force.*
46. See Report on conditions and incidents during expedition of 3270 mixed prisoners of War designated as "H" Force. This was prepared as an appendix to the earlier report by Lieut-Colonel H.R.Hamphries, which has been produced by C.C. Brett. This official report is very precise and full of details not included in other reports. In future referred to as History of "H" force.

47. History of "F" Force.
48. Too much of publicity was given to the trials of those Japanese officers, who were connected with the Siam-Burma railway. The idea was to expose the Japanese atrocities and denigrade them in the eyes of the South-East Asian people, who had collaborated with them see *The Strait Times,* March-May, 1946.
49. Rohan H.Rivett, *Behind Bambo, An inside Story of Japanese prison camps,* London, 1946, p.153. Rivett served as a War correspondent before he became P.O.W. and worked on Siam-Burma railway.
50. F.No. F 70/H.S.
51. Bergamini H. *The Pacific War,* New York, 1996, p.70.
52. Evers, *op.cit.*, p.8.
53. See *Review of railway Activity in Burma - Analysis of Siam-Burma railway* in South East Asia Air Command Weekly Intelligence summary. F.No.601/9336/H.S.
54. *Ibid.*
55. South-East Asia Translation and Intelligence Bulletin No. 229.
56. F.No.601/7583/H.S.
57. F.No.601/7378/1 IS. See also S.E.A.T.IC.Bulletin No.229. See also Robert S.La Forte and Ronald E.Marcello, *Building the Death railway,* Wilmington 1993, pp. 215-216.
58. F.No. 601/9336/H.S.
59. F.No. 601/7378/H.S.
60. See South-East Asia Command Report *on the Recovery of Allied P.O.W. and Internees.*
61. History of "H" force.
62. Harold Payne was taken prisoner at Singapore when serving as second Lieutenant with 137th Army Field Regiment of the Royal Artillery. His account is quoted by Richard Garrnett, *P.O.W.*, Great Britain 1981, pp.188-190.
63. History of "H" Force.
64. *Ibid.*
65. Adochi, *op.cit.*
66. History of "H" Force.
67. Cliffod Kinvig, *op.cit*, pp. 207-208.
68. H.T. Cook, *op.cit.* p. 103.
69. Rohan Rivett, *op.cit.*, p.175.
70. F.No. F.592/H.S.
71. Evers, *op.cit.*, p.10.
72. South East Asia command, *Report on the Recovery of P.O.W. and Civil Internees* F.No. F. 70.
73. *Ibid.*
74. *Ibid.*
75. *Ibid.*
76. *Ibid.* - See also Robert Hardie, the Burma-Siam railway, U.K. 1984.
77. History of "H" force
78. Evers. *op.cit.*, p. 60
79. Jane Flower, *op.cit.*, p. 223
80. For details about Korean guards and their defence of their behaviour in the interrogation report in South-East Asia Translation and Intelligence Bulletin No. 225.

I

Report on Siam-Burma Railway By Lieut C.C. Brett[1]

Introduction

This Bulletin is the work of Lt. C.C. Brett, Canadian Intelligence Corps., and is the result of interrogations, translations and documentary research, and personal observations of the Burma - Siam Railway, carried out by him over a period of seven months in Siam, Burma and Malaya.

It is hoped that this history compiled from all the available sources, will provide the framework of any further research on the subject, and will serve to set the history of this railway against a general background of the War in the Far East.

Summary

In 1942, the Japanese Southern Army in order to alleviate a critical shipping situation as well as to meet increasing demand from the Burma theater decided to build a railway some 260 mils in length from the vicinity of Bangkok, Siam to the Tanessarin coast of Burma. Working against difficulties of terrain and climate they nevertheless completed it in record time and less than a year after construction started. Trains were running on regular schedule moving supplies to Burma.

But the cost was not small. To carry out this tremendous task the Japanese employed upward of some 300,000 Prisoners of War and civilian coolies. As construction advanced into the hinterland from both ends, the problems of administration of this great army of labourers increased. Ultimately these developed to an almost complete breakdown in transport, supply and medical arrangements resulting in much hardship? The losses were heavy. Mortality has been estimated to be between eighty and one hundred thousands.

The Railway shortened the Line of Communication of the Burma Area Army by many hundreds of miles and enabled much vital shipping to be diverted to New Guinea and other areas in the South Pacific.

There is evidence to show that the operation of the Railway to full capacity was never realised and this in large part be due to Allied Air Forces, which by their continual assaults on bridges and other vulnerable points reduced the effectiveness to something less than fifty percent.

1. F. No. 601/7741/Historical Section, Ministry of Defence, New Delhi.

How the Railway Came to be Built

1. Strategical Situation

(A) *Burma:* By Late Spring 1942 the Japanese Imperial Army had occupied almost the whole of Burma and was in process of consolidating its positions there. To maintain this Army, and prepare it for the inevitable counter-attack to come, meant the moving in of supplies and reinforcements on a large scale, Moreover the initiation of any positive action e.g., invasion of India would double these demands.

(B) *Shipping:* This, in turn, would place a heavy burden on sea transport, which was already feeling the strain in the South Pacific. The long sea-haul of Rangoon by way of Singapore would require the withdrawal of shipping from vital areas. Moreover, such an extended line of communication was highly vulnerable, placing the Burma Army in constant danger of being out off from its main source of supply.

2. Land Route

(A) *Advantages:* The answer to the problem was the opening of a land route between Siam and Burma, the advantages of which would be:

(a) to ease the shipping problem

(b) to protect L of C

(c) speed of movement.

(B) *Decision to Build a Rail-Road:* Conceivably a motor-road could be built and operated at less cost than a railroad. But, at the time. there was a general shortage of motor transport both in the home, and and in the occupied countries. As opposed to this, quantities of roling-stole and railway equipment were readily available.

Thus, according to the Japanese, the decision to build a railway through some four hundred, kilometres of mountain and jungle was made. It was understood at the outset that the difficulties involved in such an undertaking would be enormous: yet, according to the foregoing appreciation, they considered that the success, perhaps even the survival, of the Japanese Army in BURMA depended on the speedy completion of this project.

3. Authority

Imperial General Headquarters, TOKYO, in the month of June, 1942 ordered the Southern Army to commence porprations for construction of a railway from SIAM to BURMA. Instructions for this task were passed on to the Southern Army's Railway inspection office and a Commander of Railway Construction was appointed. These links constituted the chain of higher command.

4. Responsibility

Allotment of responsibility was as follows;

(A) Imperial General Headquarters (Gen SUGIYAMA, Chief of General Staff; Gen TOJO, War Minister)

- (a) Negotiations with Ministry of War concerning estimates and materials.
- (b) Diplomatic Negotiations through Ministry of War (e.g., with SIAMESE Govt. etc.),
- (c) Order concerning railway construction (directives of Imperial G.H.Q.)
- (d) Supply of Materials necessary for construction.
- (e) Directions for construction to comply with operational needs.
- (f) Decision to employ Prisoners of War

(B) Southern Army (Gen. Count TERAUCHI, C-in-C)

- (a) Estimating military strength and labour needed to build the railway and the recruiting, supply and maintenance of these forces.
- (b) Planning of construction
- (c) Coordinating the efforts of Japanese Railway units and the attached POW and Labour forces.
- (d) Maintenance of traffic routes and waterways necessary for construction.

(C) Railway Inspection Office (Maj. Gen. SHIMODA, Commander of Construction. Later replaced by Maj. Gen. TAKASAKI).

- (a) Inspection, Survey and construction of route according to railway construction plan.
- (b) Employment and coordination of work of Japanese and attached labour units.
- (c) Billoting.

(D) Under the Railway Inspection Office, responsibility was apportioned out as follows;

- (a) Railway Regiments
  - (i) Construction of the railway in their respective areas.
  - (ii) Administration of Civilian Labour,
  - (iii) Supervision of POW and Civilian Labour.

(E) For diagram of Construction Organisation and Chain of Command See Appendix "A" attached here to:

(b) Internment Camp

(i) To provide railway construction units with the POW

(ii) Supervision of POW Labour Camps.

II
Construction of the Railway

1. Factors Entering into Construction

A. Time

Since the need for the railway was tactical, time was the chief factor. It was originally intended that the railway should be completed by the end of December 1943. Taking into consideration materials and labour available and the time required to assemble them, fourteen months was calculated as being the minimum time in which the railway could be built.

Subsequent changes in the military situation did, as will be seen later, bring about a further reduction in the time allotment.

B. Land

(a) Previous Survey: Although it is not acknowledged by the Japanese, there is evidence to show that their survey followed the route of a survey made many years previously. According to former Prisoners of War, old survey posts with old marking on them were frequently seen during the construction. Also along the route followed was an old earth-return circuit, parts of which the Japanese were actually able to put into the use. Ex-prisoners of War state that the railway closely followed this old surveyed route with few deviations.

(b) Route and Terrain: The route was to connect the SIAM and BURMA railway systems (the SIAM junction at NONPLADUK and the BURMA junction at THANBYUZAYAT). Starting at NONPLADUK the railway was to follow the MAEKMLAUNG River to TAMAKAN where the river splits into two tributaries; the railway was to follow the northwest tributary, the KHWAF No. 1, continuing across the frontier to THREE PAGODAS PASS.

In BURMA it would descend along the courses of the ZAMI and AIRAN Rivers for a distance, then proceed on, following various small streams, to THANBYUZAYAT.

The route was to traverse literally the formidable BILAUKTBUNG Range of mountains, whichforms the natural boundary between the two countries, as well as the Taungamyo Range in Burma. Seventy per-cent of the route was to pass through thick, malaria infected jungle. The terrain was precipitous; in Many places, solid rock wall was to be hewn through and hundreds of streams and dry gaps had to be bridged.

(c) Right of Way: A circumstance which undoubtedly played some part in delaying the start of construction was local opposition from the Siamese. From the outset landowners protested at having to give up their property to the Japanese. According to Japanese Railway Officers, a series of conferences were held in Bangkok with the Siamese Government. Major General Shimoda is said to have been the Japanese representative. After many conferences, an agreement was finally concluded. It is said to have contained, among others, the following conditions; that Siam would provide the land for the right-of-way, and bear the cost of construction of a road parallel to the railway, and also to supply a portion of the labour and materials.

C. Labour

Labour came directly under the 2nd Railway Inspection Office, frequently referred to as the 2nd Railway Administering office. This was located at Kanburi. Labour came under three classifications:-

(a) Japanese Army Units;

(b) P.O.W Labour;

(c) Civilian (sometimes referred to as "Coolie") Labour.

(a) Japanese Army Units engaged in construction were known as the Southern Railway Corps, chief among were the following: 5 Railway Regiment, with H.Q at Thanbytuzayat, 9 Railway Regiment with H.Q at Kanburi, and the main strength of the 1st Supply Depot located at Nonpladuk with the remainder of the strength at Rangoon. To the railway regiments were attached various smaller engineering and building units. Total number of Japanese involved in construction of the railway was about 12,000.

(b) Prisoners of War and Coolie labour are discussed in a later Section.

D. Materials

Materials and equipment for construction came largely from Malaya, Siam and Burma. That which could not be obtained locally was brought from Japan i.e, a part of the bridging material, steel rails and rolling stock. Lack of heavy construction equipment and excavating machinery had to be made for by manual labour. Throughout the period of construction an acute shortage of motor vehicles for road transport prevailed.

Generally equipment is believed to have come from the following sources:

Locomotives brought from Japan	:	45
Locomotives brought from Malaya	:	30
Locomotives brought from Burma	:	25
Locomotives brought from Siam	:	4
Locomotives brought from Java	:	9
Total		**113**

Stock Wagons brought from Japan	: 400
Stock Wagons brought from Malaya	: 1000
Stock Wagons brought from Burma	: 400
Total	**: 1800**

Steel Rails: According to the Japanese, 50 percent of these came from Japan, and the balance from Burma, Java and Malaya.

Workshop Equipment: The greater part was obtained from Malayan tin mines- the remainder at Kula Lumpur, Java and Sumatra while a very small portion was brought from Japan.

Railway Regiments

9 Railway Regiment was placed in charge of construction of the section lying between Nonpladuk and Konkuta, generally referred to as " the Siam side"; 5 Railway Regiment was placed charge of construction of the line from Konkuta to Thanbyuzyat- the Burma side.

From information supplied K.A WARMENHOVEN ALLIED Railway officer, Kambui, Siam. See Appendix "D" for History and Organisation of 5 and 9 Rly. Regts.

3. Labour

A. Prisoners of War

(a) For the purposed of construction the railway was divided into sections, a body of PWs being allocated to each section. This body was known as a "Branch" of a " Group" and came under a Japanese Commander who was responsible for all matters of accommodation, supply, administration and camp control. Each group was normally divided into several labour camps and were located at various points along the line. The whole came under an organisation known as the " Thailand Internment Camp" or alternatively the "Thailand P.O.W administration". For example No.5 Group comprised American, British, Australian and Ditch Prisoners of War who worked from THANB YUZYAT to a point about 100 Kilometers south of the line. The base camp was at THANB YUZYAT until 21 April 1943 after which it appears to have been at 80 KM and subsequently at 83 Kms. Other camps were set along the line as follows:-

18 Km work Camp from 23 Jan 43 to 19 Mar 43

83 Km work Camp from 19 Mar 43 to 6 Apr 43

80 Km work Camp from 6 Apr 43 to 29 May 43

100 Km work Camp from 26 May 43 to 27 Dec 43

83 Km work Camp from July-August

30 Km work Camp from casualty during station in April 1943

80 Km Hospital from 16 June 1943 to 28 August 1943.

Altogether 10 P.O.W Groups were established. In May 1943 two additional Groups known as "F" Force and "H" Force" were brought from Singapore to work on the line. These two groups, however, unlike the others, were controlled throughout by the Malaya P.O.W Administration.

Each Group was organised as a self-contained unit. White supervised by Japanese themselves. The function of these labour camps was to supply daily working parties as required by the Japanese construction units, at which time PWs came under supervision of the units concerned.

(c) Number of PW's Employed

In all some 61,000 PWs were employed on construction, this figure may be broken down as follows:

Area sent from	*Total*	*British*	*Australlian*	*U.S.A.*	*Netherlands*
Malaya to Siam	30,305	28,931	8,507	494	12,378
FIC to Siam	700	700	–	–	–
Malaya to Burma	7,201	–	4,497	191	2,512
Sumtra to Burma and Java	3,600	500	–	–	3,100
Total	**61,806**	**30,141**	**12,994**	**686**	**17,985**

Following construction, some 17,110 PWs were sent back, 6,340, being returned to Singapore and 10,770 being sent to FIC and Japan. The balance remained on the railway employed on maintenance until the time of the surrender.

B. Civilian Labour

(a) From Malaya

Labour from Malaya for work on the railway was, for the most part, recruited on a voluntary basis through the labour agencies existing at that time. The conditions offered were said to have been:-

(i) When construction was completed they would be returned to their homes. This, they were told would be in from 3 to 6 months time.

(ii) Pay would be 1 dollar as a plus a family allowance of 50 cents.

(iii) Food and accommodation to be supplied by the Japanese.

Between March 43 and March 44 approximately 75,000 coolies were recruited from Malaya, chiefly Malaya and Tamils. In addition about 7,500 Japanese and 5,000 Chinese from Siam were brought to the railway railway in the early part of 44.

Coolie Work Camps came directly under the supervision of units of the railway Regiments who were responsible for accommodation as well as for much of their internal administration.

(b) From Burma

Labour was originally recruited into the "Sweat Army" on a voluntary basis. About 87,000 were recruited in this way. Recruiting of labour for railway was later taken over by the Labour Service Corps into which there were fourteen recruitments. The Labour Service Corps appears to have been designed exclusively to provide labour for the Railway. For each recruitment the Ba Maw Government laid down a quota for the whole of Burma and this was split up into a quota for each district.

The conditions of service were similar to those offered to the Malaya except that pay was 1 Rupee 4as. perday and they were premised repatriation at the end of three months.

That the labour was conscripted and not voluntary is apparant. Of the 166,000 coolies recruited by the labour Service Corps, 74000 deserted on route to the line while a further 13,200 of this figure deserted soon after arriving on the line.

(c) Labour Requirements.

Before the start of construction, while the project was still in the planning stage, requirements for labour, in addition to railway troops was estimated to be in the neighbourhood of 1,00,000. An analysis of the labour statistics would indicate that roughly, 1,18,000 labourers (PWs and Coolies) were brought into the construction area before the end of 1942. From early in 1943 to the end of construction the labour strength was increased by another 1,70,000 (30,000 additional PWs, 70,000 coolies from Burma and 70,000 from Malaya).

Reasons for this increase were : the change in strategical situation and labour wastage.

It was found that the heavy casualties resulting from sickness and mortality among labourers caused a reduction in labour potential. This, in turn, seriously retarded construction.

1 Appendix "B" Table 9

2 Appendix "B" 10

The ratio of labourers employed on construction to the total strength in labour camps was said to be, at best, 50 per-cent, those not employed on construction being either on camp duties or in hospital. Through the spring and summer of 43 this condition is said to have deteriorated causing a further decrease in the ratio, so that at the point of highest production and labour capacity (approx 2,00,000), frequently the number of labourers available daily for construction could not have been more than 50,000.

Another factor which caused a reduction of the labour potential was large scale desertions on the part of the Coolies. According to reports available approximately 45,000 deserted but the actual number may have been considerably greater.

(d) Brief History of Construction

Preparations for construction began in June 42, and were not completed until November. During this time survey parties were sent out, materials collected and bases established and personnel assembled. Towards the end of the Mansoon, labourers began to push through the jungle in parties to set up working points along the route.

Actual construction began in November. It is significant that the survey of the road, at this time, was still in progress, which meant that the Japanese were unable to estimate with any accuracy what the requirements in labour and materials would be. Construction started simultaneously at NONPLADUK, SIAM, the southern terminus, and at THANBYUZAYAY, BURMA, the northern terminus.

In Feb 43, plans were made by Southern Army to shorten the construction period by four months, that is to complete the railroad by 31 Aug 43. The reasons for this action were:

(a) increase in shipping losses.

(b) the situation in NEW GUINEA had become critical and all available shipping was required to move reinforcements into that theater.

(c) A strong Allied counter-attack was expected in BURMA after the end of the rainy season.

(d) since the rivers in SIAM, the main source of transport for construction, were navigable construction while the monsoon lasted.

Accordingly additional labourers were brought in from MALAYA and a strong recruiting campaign was undertaken both in the south and in BURMA to produce a flow of fresh labour. These labour reinforcements were needed not only to cope vith the accelerated programme but to replace casualties which were steadily increasing in number.

As the summer advanced it became clear that the railroad would not be completed by the end of August. The reasons were:

(a) **Transportation**—Demands for road transport increased daily. As construction gradually pushed further and further into the mountains and jungle away from the bases, the problem of bringing up materials and supplies became critical. The road, which was constructed parallel to the track, was rendered impossible in many places by the monsoon rairs. For some time after the monsoon started the rivers did not rise suf.iciently for river transport; consequently for a time there was a complete tie-up of transportation.

(b) **Labour**—Notwithstanding the inflow of replacements and reinforcements the labour potential had been drastically lowered by the high incidence of disease among PWs and coolies alike.

Accordingly, despite the tractical requirements, the date of completion had to be postponed until 31 October.

The final phase in the construction is described in the Official Japanese Report as follows :

"Major General Ishida was newly appointed director of construction for perfect realisation of the scheme. He aimed at completion of the work by the end of October, renewed the organisation of the staff and endeavoured to stimulate morale. He cherished the slogan "Prisoners of War and Labourers are the fathers of constructions', and corrected the erroneious idea 'Mastership' prevailing among officers and men.."

The rainy season which culminated in August gradually reduced the amount of rainfall and working parties did their best for the completion of the work, surmounting ever-increasing difficulties in the innermost regions;

Thus, on 17 Oct. 43, the two railways started from east and west 415 kilometres in length, were joined together at Konkuta and formal ceremonies for the opening took place on the 25th of the same months".

Notes from the diary of a former Prisoner of War on the Railway describing various incidents which occurred during the construction appear in appendix "C" attached hereto.

(e) General Description of Railway

A. The Burma-Siam line connects the Siamese Southern line at Nonpladuk with the Moulmein-Ye line in Burma and so provides a direct route to Moulmein from Bangkok, connecting at Nonpladuk with the line down the Malay Peninsula to Singapore and at Bangkok with the other lines of the Siamese system (including the Eastern line, which is continued by a line in Indo-China to Phnom Penh). At Moulmein there is connection by ferry across the Salween to Martaban and so to the rest of the Burma system. The line thus shortened the Japanese lines of communications by many hundreds of miles, since formerly all supplies for Burma had to be shipped for Rangoon by way of Singapore.

The line is about 270 miles (415 kms) long; it was built by the Japanese between November 1942 and November 1943, by which latter date, the track was completed and traffic operating. In this period clearing had to be made for almost the whole distance through dense forest, many large cuttings and embankments constructed to negotiate hilly country, and about 700 bridges (as well as a number of culverts) built over rivers and chaungs.

From Thanbyuzayat the line runs south-eastward for 70 miles (114 km) up to the Burma-Siam frontier at the "Three Pagodas Pass" (about 900 feet above sea-level) ; in its course through Burma it follows in turn the valleys several different streams and crosses several low divides between these valleys. From the frontier for the whole way to its junction with the old Siamese line at Nonpladuk it descends along the east (Left) bank of the Khwae Noi and then along the Hae Khlong. The country is, for the most part, completely undeveloped : there is a very heavy monsoon rainfall on the Burma side, though not so heavy on the Siam side.

B. Route Length and Gauges

Length : 262 miles (415 km), all single track

Track Gauge : 1 Metre

Leading Gauge : Corresponds with Burmese and Siamese

railways which this line connects.

6. Payment and Works

(a) **Type and weight of Rail:** Rails are mostly old rails (flat bottomed) from lines in Burma and Malaya dismantled by the Japanese. The Malayan rails (used for the southern pact of the line) are probably mostly 60 lb/yd. (29.8 kg/m.) in 30 foot lengths; the Burma rails are mostly 60 or 75 lb./yd. (29.8 or 37.2 kg/m), in lengths of 30 to 39 feet. (Some reports also speak of rails of 65 lb./yd. m of rails in 7-metre (23 feet) lengths, and of rails of German and Japanese manufacture).

(b) **Type of rail-fastening:** Rails are spiked direct to sleepers, with four spikes to each sleeper.

(c) **Sleepers:** Hardwood, 10 by 6 inches in section. The number to a mile is reported to be 2,200-2,300 (2,200 to a mile would be equivalent to 13 to a 30-foot rail length).

(d) **Ballast:** Broken stone from local quarries and river-bed gravel. It is generally laid to a width of 5 feet, and where construction is best, to a depth of 10 to 12. I.S.I.S. Report on Kra-Isthmus Railways.

(e) **Standard of Maintenance:** The early construction at either end of the railway was done resonably well : cuttings were wide and the road-bed was sound. As construction progressed this standard noticably deteriorated other faults, in consequence, developed: e.g. sleepers sank flush into the formation, collapses occurred, and there were landslides in cuttings. Bridges which at their best, were only meant to be temporary, are in a very bad state, particularly on the Burma side. This is said to be one of the reasons why the Burma side of the line was closed down in June of this year.

(f) **Gradients:** According to officers of 5 Railway Regt, the highest point on the line is 903 feet above sea-level. This point is located at 300. 72 km at Three Pagodas Pass. The steepost gradient is also said to be at this point being 29/1000. The steepost gradients are in the section comprising ascent to this pass and are located at the following points: 306.00 km 27.5/1000, 317.70 km - 27/1000, 318.00 km - 29/1000. It was customary in these areas to use two locomotives, one pushing and one pulling.

(g) **Maximum axle-load:** Presumably about ten tens: this is indicated by the weight of the Japanese C 56 locomotives which were running on the line. A rail of 60-75/lb/yd would bear a maximum axle load. Many of the bridges are of filmmy construction and were crossed at 'dead slow' speeds.

(h) **Bridges:** There are 688 bridges on this line. Most bridges are of standard design, and 680 of the existing number of bridges have been constructed out of locally cut timber. The Japanese engineers responsible for the design gave full consideration to such matters as strength of material, lead carrying capacity, etc. adapting the American Merriman-Wiggin standard practice for timber structure.

The construction policy, however, seemed to sacrifice the factor of safety in favour of speed, exemplified by their almost entire use of soft wood throughout when hardwood was readily available. In this connection, it must not be forgotten that the Japanese knew they had unlimited labour at their disposal and were in a position to effect rapid renewals when necessary.

Due to Allied bombings many bridges have had to be rebuilt as often as six times. As may be imagined, the rebuilding of each successive section was more hastily carried out and received less careful consideration.

(i) **Stations:** The line was not intended for civilian traffic (although there has been some civilian traffic since the surrender). The stations are not, generally speaking, stations in the usual sense of the word. Points on the line where there are passing loops or sidings have been treated as stations, and have been given arbitrary names taken from the nearest village or physical feature on the map; at many of these there are few, if any, facilities other than the passing loops or sidings, though at others there are various facilities for goods, locomotives etc.

(j) **Telegraphic communication:** There is a telegraph line alongside the track with four pairs of wires (one wire said to be 200-lb copper, the rest 200.1b galvanized iron); the poles were cut locally and untreated.

(k) **Passing Loops:** The average distance between passing loops is about four miles. Most passing loops are between 350 and 450 metres long and some are shorter.

(l) **Spur Tracks :** At intervals of about ten miles spur tracks branch off into the jungle, mostly on the east side of the railroad. These spurs average about 500 metres in length; they appear to have been an expedient adopted for day time protection from air-attack (from early 1944 onwards) when all movement took place at night.

From report by Major J.F. CLEGG, O.C. 318 Ind. Rly. Bridging Coy

(m) **Workshops:** There is a most excellent railway workshop at Kanburi reputed to be the best equipped in South-East Asia. The total capacity of this workshop exceeds the needs of the line provided it can be adequately staffed, its requirements being 1,100 men, apart from labour. The workshop can handle 500 cars a year. It can also handle 12 engines simultaneously. It is a completely independent unit and includes, among other things, 3 forges, 3 engine shops, 1 foundry, 3 power stations, 1 saw mill, 1 water conduit and an installation for refinning crude oil.

III

1. Changes in Organisation

In Nov. 43, after construction had been completed, 5 Railway Regt. was moved to North Burma to take over operation of the Myitkyina - YE-U Railway. At the same time, 9 Railway Regt. moved north and took over operations of the section Moulmein Thanbyusayat - Neekey. The line between Nonpladuk and Neekey was placed under charge of 4 special Railway Unit which had been brought up from Malaya in September.

2. Traffic

A. **Capacity:** The physical capacity of the line in working order is said to have been eight trains per day each way throughout. Former prisoners of war state that they have observed, on occasion, as many an eight and sometimes ten trains moving in each direction in one day. Staff officers of the Burma Area Army have estimated that 400 tons of supplies were received daily on the average. Train leads are estimated to be 200 tons (20 wagons x 10 tons per wagon) which would suggest an average of two trains per day. 9 Railway Regt. places this average slightly higher. They state that in the latter part of 1944 an average of 4-5 trains was maintained daily. (See Appendix "C" 1).

B. **Supplies:** Generally, the load of each train was made up of from 2 to 5 carloads of ammunition (always in the centre of the train), Ordinance Stores, Supplied etc. (in the forward part) and Petrol stores (in the rear). 9 Railway Regt gives the distribution for the total period as follows:

Ordnance Stores	28,050 tons
Ammunition	68,900 tons
Clothing	6,800 tons
Provisions	60,000 tons
Petrol	53,020 tons
Oils, Lubricants	2,780 tons
Miscellaneous	10,000 tons

This represents movements for total period of operations, i.e.; Dec. 43 to Aug. 45. (For details of movements see Appendix "G"2).

In addition their records show movements of the following commodities to Burma.

Between May 44 to March 45	960 tons of lead and tin
Between September to March 45	900 tons of Ore (Kind not specified)
Between November 44 to May 45	300 Wagons loads of oil pipes
Between December 1944 to April 45	40 Wagon loads oils refining machinery.

C. **Reinforcements:** Personal movements into the Burma theatre included seven or eight complete divisions as well as numerous Corps and Army troops (Appendix "G" 3) Prior to the surrender, complete divisions and elements of many others were moved into Siam. Approximately 10,000 casualties were evacuated to Siam while the railway was in operation.

3. Allied Air Attack

A. Vulnerable points

The line was vulnerable chiefly in respect of the many bridges. There were nearly 700 of these. 63 bridges were more than 50 metres (164 feet) in length. Other vulnerable point included the engine sheds and shunting yards and the junctions at Thanyuzayat and Nonpladuk.

B. Bombing and Strafing

According to reports by the Japanese, Allied long distance bombers began to appear regularly early in 1944. During the spring months attacks were particularly heavy but decreased in intensity during the summer. During this period the Japanese built shelters for locomotives at stations and watering points and built numerous spur lines into the jungle. From this time on, traffic as a rule came to a complete standstill during daylight and moved only during night time. Reports indicate that these spur lines were well camouflaged and gave complete protection to trains harbouring there in the day time.

From Dec 44, onward it appears that air attacks increased in number and intensity, the main target the numerous bridges along the route.

C. Effects of Continual Air Attacks

(a) Strafing of Locomotives and Rolling Stock

(i) When a strafing attack was anticipated, in about 50 per cent of the cases the train would be stopped, with all crew members seeking cover.

(ii) Strafing was often very effective, and caused great difficulty, helding up shipments and breaking up schedules. After each strafing attack, schedules had to be changed.

(iii) Locomotives put out of commission usually took a month or longer to repair. Time walot in effecting repairs because of shortage of spare parts and materials.

(b) *Attacks on Railroad yards and workshops*

(i) **Raids on the yards caused great disorganisation:** after a raid the average time required to restore through running traffic was about three days. Normal traffic would usually be restored in about one week after a raid on the yards.

(c) *Attacks on Tracks and Bridges*

(i) Breaks in the track could usually be repaired in from one to two days. Even this had a serious effect in hampering traffic movements.

(ii) Bridge repair depended entirely on conditions of damage, type of construction and topographical factors. A 40 foot bridge would usually take about one week to repair and a 25 foot bridge required about four days.

In many cases, a damaged bridge was not repaird but a bypass substituted in its place. When repairs could be made they were usually carried out in a hurry, and the bridge would, on the average, only carry about half its former capacity.

The expedient was adopted of using a ferry during the period of repair. Small beats would be leaded with carge and unloaded into a train at the other side of the stream. Another expedient was to use coolies to carry the carge across a temporary foot-bridge. Wherever a bridge was blown a battle-neck occurred and as many as ten trains have been tied up at one point.

D. Speed of Reconstruction

Japanese engineers state that the time required to rebuild even the largest bridges was not more than ten to twenty days. They attribute this speedy repair to two factors. First was that large quantities of timbers out into the proper lengths were concentrated near each bridge; Secondly, that they had an unlimited supply of labour. A labour officer from 4 Special Railway unit, when interrogated on this point, stated in part as follows:

"In 1944 I was in charge of maintenance of the section of the line between Neekney and Plankashi, a distance of about 100 kilometers. Labourers were dispersed in about sixty camps in this section, about ten thousand in all. The chief task was the repairing and rebuilding of timber bridges of which we had more than 200 to look after.

Rebuilding of a bombed bridge started without delay and continued night and day until the job was completed. The average moderate sized, bridge took about a week to rebuild. While the construction was in progress, a gang of coolies was employed in unloading, trains on the one side of the gap and reloading trains of the other. Generally it took about four hours to unload one train.

The Neekey bridge was destroyed three times. It was the longest in my section and measured some 200 metres in length. By working three shifts daily with about 500 men in each shift we were able to rebuild the bridge in about two weeks. We have had as many as twenty bridges hit in one day.

3. Plan to evacuate the Japanese Army in Burma

Following reverses of the Japanese army on the Burma Front, in the summer and autumn of 1944 it became necessary to send back into Siam four or five Army divisions which needed reorganising. But it would appear that even at that time plans were also being considered for the eventual withdrawal of the whole Burma Area Army, should that become necessary.

In Dec 44 work was started on construction of an automobile road east from Wampe. This road was to cross the frontier at Bondei Bon, and from there, following along the Tenasserim River, would connect with the Tavey road at Nyitta, in Burma. This road was ready for use in April 45.

Later that spring a system of defence was organised at the railway terminus, Nonpladuk and round workshops situated at Kanburi, in anticipation of an Allied airborne assault.

At about the same time it was decided to fortify a height near the Burma-Siam border at three Pagodas Pass (presumably to be used in the event of a rearguard action). The down ward slope to the east offered a clear field of fire while access was made difficult both by the river and by the rugged nature of the terrain. In June the construction of a system of pillboxes was started on this height. These were connected by an elaborate system of tunnels and underground storehouses. Pagoda Pass was obviously the place chosen for a last ditch stand. Work on this project was carried on night and day under pressure and it was completed by the first of August. Following this anti-tank ditches and obstacles were set up along the track. By the time of the surrender these had been built as far east as Apalon.

IV
Prisoners of War and Coolies

1. Conditions–P.O.W. Camps

A. Camps

It is difficult, unfortunately, to obtain records or documents which can be said to give a comprehensive picture of the living conditions of Prisoners of War on the Burma-Siam Railway. To gain any kind of general impression necessitate reliance on hear-say or the testimony of individual witnesses, which vary in many respects. Sources, however, are in agreement on many points and certain conditions appeared to prevail throughout the railway and were the common experience of all.

PW Camps varied in strength from 500 to 2000. Each camp was controlled by a Japanese Camp Commandant but the internal administration was done by the PWs themselves. Housing, in almost all cases, consisted of huts built out of locally cut bamboo. Sanitation, from all accounts, was primitive; i.e. latrines were merely open trenches cut in the ground. Shortage of water for washing was a general complaint.

B. Rations

The quantity of rations varied widely, depending on the locality; i.e. the farther away from the railhead, the smaller the rations became. All sources seem to be agreed on one point; that the rations received seldom, if ever, even approached the quantities as laid down on the Japanese ration scale. All PWs seem to have suffered in varying degrees from malnutrition and this is believed to have contributed in no small measure to the high incidence of disease.

C. Work

Heavy work and long hours seems to have been the rule everywhere along the line. It was said to have been a common practise for Japanese construction units, in their anxiety to maintain schedules, to demand that the sick, as well as the fit, work. Days of rest were rare.

2. Conditions–Coolie Camps

Coolie Camps were under administration of Railway Regiments. General camp conditions appear to have been similar to those of the PW camps. But judged by the same standards the Collies were no doubt considerably worse off because : i) they lacked the advantages of army organisation and discipline, ii) much of their sickness was caused through ignorance of hygiene, and iii) they were almost completely dependent, for medical care on the medical staff of the Railway regiments.

Condition in Burmese

Coolie Camps are described in a report by U Aung Mik Relief Burma Government Labour Administration. Appendix 'I' 3 of this report.

3. Health

From the time construction started health of the P.Ws and Coolie alike began to deteriorate rapidly. Conditions were very hard and diseases and sickness became prevalent. In particular the men suffered terribly tropical ulcers which ate away large areas of flesh and, in many cases necessiated amputation of the affected leg. Beri-Beri, dysentry and malaira were also common diseases.

A situation came to prevail in almost all camps where the preportion of men in hospital to men working was more than one half. The Japanese have acknowledged that 50 per cent in hospital was uncommon. Often the ratio was higher. Certain records still exist showing daily number of sick and number at work. Here are a few examples:

Camp	*Date*	*Total*	*Number sick*	*Number demanded for I.J.A. work*
Shimo-Sonkrai	19 July	1850	1350	343
Kami-Sonkar	16 Aug	1670	1075	450
Takenun	15 Jul	564	464	160
Songkroi	25 Jul	1300	1050	280

Medical Report: A very frank account of the medical situation from the Japanese points of view, written by the Chief medical Officer of 9 Railway Regiment, is given in Appendix J of the report.

"F" & "H" Forces

Of the various groups of PWs who worked in the construction of the railway, the records of two only are in existence. These are contained in the official Report on "F" and "H" Forces. These two Forces, comprised of British, Australian. Dutch and American P.Ws left Singapore in the Spring of 1943 and returned early in 1944.

The story of "F" Force as related by its commanding Officer is reproduced in part in Appendix "I" 2 of this report.

"F" & "H" Forces, unlike the other Groups of the PWs remained throughout under the Malayan PW Administration. Casualties occurring in these two forces seem to have been much greater than those suffered by other Groups. A summary of their losses is shown below :-

Force	*No. Sent to Siam*	*No. of death*
"F'	6,997	3.087
"H"	3,270	1,702
Total	**10,628**	**4,7891**

1. From Records of "F" Force. This figure represents death in the force upto 27 April 1944, the date in which evacuation from Siam was completed. As some of the deaths occurred after the force had actually left the railway, this will account for the discrepancy in the figures supplied by No 1 Searchers Organisation (Appendix "B" 7, which accounts for the deaths actually on the railway.

5. Morale

The British Commander of "H" Force in a report on living conditions states that discipline and morale in the Force "remained at a high standard throughout". He describes attempts to encourage and maintain morale during most trying conditions. In particular he pays tribute to the men of his Force who" when the hour was blackest ...."braced their shoulders"- "tightened their belts" and went forward to their labours with that renewed resolution which has never been the characteristics of the British Soldier in adversity.

6. Desertions

(A) **Coolies:** During the period of construction and subsequent operation many coolies deserted from both slides of the line. The Japanese estimate the number of desertions on the Siam side of the line, that is among Coolies recruited from Malaya, Siam etc., to be 28, 594. The figure on the Burman side, according to U Aung Min, was considerably greater, though no even approximate figure could be given. The reason for so many desertions was the fact that because of their race, Coolies could absorb themselves among the local population in Burma and Siam and thus escape detection.

(B) **PWs:** This was not the case amongst PWs. Though many attempts to escape were made, few, if any, ever reached friendly territory : Appendix "E" is the translation of a Japan Court Martial and summary of evidence relating to an attempted escape in which the participants remained at large for several months.

7. Mortality

Below is a summary, based on the latest information available. Of mortality among PWs and Coolies on the Burma-Siam Railway. For purpose of comparison, figures for total employment in each category are shown; the table covers the period Jul 42- Aug. 45.

Classification	*Total employed*	*Total details*
Allied P.O.W.	61,806	12,399
Labourers from Malaya, Siam, Java and F.I.C.	91,112	32,996
Labourers from Burma	1,78,836	40,000

1. Approximately only. Some authorities estimate the number to be as high as 60,000.

8. Evacuation from Railway

Roughly, the strength of PWs and Coolies on the line at the time of the surrender may be estimated to be:

PWs	32,000
Coolies from Malaya, Java etc.	25,000
Coolies - Burma	40,000
Total	**97,000**

According to RAPWI records, 30,789 PWs were repatriated before 30 Nov. 45, but a number of Dutch PWs remained on the railway after that time.

In October and November 1945, 24,111 Tamils, Chinese, Malayis and Japanese had been registered and awaited repatriation. But it is not known how many had proceeded to their homes before registration took place.

The situation with regard to the Burma Coolies was different. A count made in October showed some 6,000 mostly sick, at various points along the line in Burma. But it appears that all these who were able to do so had proceeded independently to their homes, and no records seems to have been kept of these people.

9. Burial of the Dead

Coolie dead appear to have been buried indiscriminately and in the majority of cases, no very close check on names and locations seems to have been kept.

Records of burial were kept in all PW Camps and, on the basis of these, Allied War Graves Registration have been able to located the graves of all but a very few of those reported dead.

The work of locating, exhuming and reburying bodies in proper cemeteries has all but been completed. Main cemetries are located at Thanbyusayat, Burma and Kanburi, Siam.

The number of graves thus relocated are shown below, classified as to nationality:

British	- 6,318
Australian	- 2,646
Dutch	- 2,490
Unknown	- 589
	12,045

Bodies of American dead (believed to be 337) were repatriated early in 1946.

1. Figures supplied by War Graves Registration
2. Appendix B (9)

10. Japanese Memorial to the Dead

A Monument bearing the above inscription stands by the side of the railway at Tamarkan, Siam. Standing on an elaborate base, this stone and concrete structure, measuring some thirty feet in height, was built by PW and Coolie labour in the months following the completion of the railway, Translated into English it has the following meaning:

> "Comfort to Departed Souls
>
> This monument is erected to comfort the souls of those prisoners of war and Labourers from the countries of the South who died as a result of diseases contracted during the building of the Railway connecting Burma and Thailand

11. Maltreatment

(a) **Protest by British Government:** The first concrete evidence of maltreatment of PWs on the Burma-Siam Railway came to light in the Autumn of 1944, from survivers of the torpedded Japanese transport ship, "Ryakuyo Maru". This ship was bound for Japan carrying Prisoners of War who had been taken off the railway. Picked up by American submarines, the surviving British and Australian PWs, numbering some 150, brought to the world tales of terrible living conditions and outrageous treatment by the Japanese along the Burma-Siam Railway.

The British Government, when the facts became known immediately lodged a strong protest through the agency of the Swiss Government. Shortly afterward information was received from the protecting power that the Japanese Government would permit representatives of the International Red Cross or of the Protecting Powers to visit Prisoner of War Camps in the Areas occupied by Japan.

(b) **War-Crimes Investigation:** Subsequent investigation, following the surrender gave proof that, in connection with the building of the Burma-Siam Railway, the Japanese had been guilty of:

(i) breaches of international conventions regarding Prisoners of War,

(ii) maltreatment of Prisoners of War.

In order to being the criminals to justice, British Domuicous and Allied invetigating teams have been gathering evidence and building up cases for several months past. To date (Aug. 31, 1949) 11 cases have been tried in the Singapore War Crimes Courts, dealing with the Railway, involving some 30 Japanese charged with ill treatments of PWs and coolies. 16 of these tried have been sentenced to death.

A specimen charge-sheet is shown in Appendix-L. It is the case of Major Mizutani Totare, who is described as being the worst individual criminal connected with the railway. He was found guilty of all three charges and sentenced to death.

Appendix A

Burma-Siam Railway Construction Organisation

	Malaya P.O.W	*Tokyo*
1.	Administration	Southern Region Army
2.	"F" Force "H" Force	22nd Marshall Court Terauchi
3.	Banno Hachisuka	(Kanbusi)
		Major-General Shimoda Senriki (dead)
		Major-General Takasaki Sukemosa (dead)
		Major Takasaki Hide Kumn (July 43 to August 45)
4.	From Thanbyuzat	From Konkuta to 1st Rly 4th Special Rly Burma-Siam P.O.W. Admin
5.	To Konkuta	Nongapalduku Material Deptt. Corps Aug. 42-Jun. 43 Maj. Gen Sad July 43-Aug. 44 Col. Nakamura Aug. 44-Aug. 45 Col Sugasawa.
6.	5th Railway Regiment	9th Railway Regiment (Not responsible for P.O.W)
		1 Bn, 2 Bn, 3Bn, 4 Bn
	1 Bn, 2Bn, 3Bn, 4Bn	Administration and Maintenance Coolie Camps

In order to bring the criminals to justice, British Dominion and Allied investigating teams have been gathering evidence and building up cases for several months past. To date (Aug 31, 46) 11 cases have been tried in the Singapore War Crimes Courts, dealing with the Railway, involving some 30 Japanese charged with ill treatment of PWs and Coolies. 16 of these tried have been sentenced to death.

A specimen Charge-Sheet is shown in Appendix "L". It is the case of Major Mizutani Totare, who is described as being the worst individual criminal connected with the railway. He was found guilty on all three charges and sentenced to death.

Appendix B

Statistics Concerning Employment of Labour During Construction and Operation of the Burma-Siam Railway

Tables contained in this Appendix

1. PS. O.W. Sent to Siam from'Malaya
2. PS. O.W. Sent to Siam from Other Areas
3. PS. O.W. Sent to Siam from Burma, Malaya
4. PS. O.W. Sent to Siam from Other Areas
5. PS. Returned to Singapore before Surrender
6. PS. Transferred F.I.C. and Japan before Surrender
7. PS. Deaths on Railway
8. PS. Repatriated Following Surrender
9. Civilian Labour brought from Malaya, Java, Siam & F.I.C.
10. PS. O.W. Sent to Siam from Burma

1. Table showing Numbers of Ps. O.W. Sent from Malaya to giving Nationalities and Time to Move

Date	Total	British	Australian	USA	Netherlands
1942					
18-26 Jun	3,000	3,000	-	-	-
9-15 Oct	3,250	3,250	-	-	-
14 Oct	390	390	-	-	-
14 Oct	401	401	-	-	-
17-22 Oct	2,600	2,600	-	-	-
23 Oct	650	650	-	-	-
24 Oct	650	650	-	-	-
25 Oct-6 Nov	8,450	8,450	-	-	-
7-9 Nov	1,260	1,260	-	-	-
Total 42	**20,651**	**20,651**			
1943					
7 Jan	1,002	4	383	456	156
14-30 Jan	10,000	-	1,250	-	8,750
14 Mar	7	3	-	-	4
14-23 Mar	5,000	2,780	2,220	-	-
13-17 Apr	3,000	3	155	11	2,831
18-30 Apr	7,000	3,334	3,686	-	-
5-17 May	3,270	1,949	705	26	590
25 Jun	230	183	55	1	11
24 Aug	115	42	73	-	-
Total	**29,624**	**8,278**	**8,507**	**494**	**12,345**

1. From information, supplied by No 1 Searcher Org Clearing House, HQ/ALFSEA
2. PWs from F.I.C. to SIAM

   On 4 April 42, 1,125 British PWs were sent to SAIGON, F.I.C. In April 1943, 700 of these were taken to SIAM for work on the Railway.
3. Table showing Numbers of PWs sent from MALAYA to BURMA by Nationalities and giving time of move.

Date 1942	*Total*	*British*	*Australian*	*U.S.A.*	*Netherlands*
14 May	3,000	-	3,000	-	-
16 Oct	1,800	-	1,497	192	111
20 Dec	1,000	-	-	-	1,000
27 Dec	401	-	-	-	401
Total	6,201	-	4,497	192	1,512
1943					
10 Jan	1,000	-	-	-	1,000
Total from Malaya	**7,201**		**4,497**	**192**	**2,512**

4. Table Showing Numbers of PWs sent to BURMA from SUMATRA and JAVA by Nationalities and giving time of Move 1.

Date 1942 From SUMATRA	*Total*	*British*	*Australian*	*U.S.A.*	*Netherlands*
15 May	2,000	500	-	-	1,500
From JAVA					
20 Oct	1,600	-	-	-	1,600
Total to Railway in Burma	**3,600**	**500**	-	-	**3,100**

5. Table showing No of PWs who were returned to SINGAPORE before the Surrender ("F" and "H" Forces)

Date 1944	*Force*	*Total*	*British*	*Australian*	*U.S.A.*	*Netherlands*
Apr	"F"	3,941	1,305	2,636	-	-
Apr	"H"	2,399	1,298	529	23	549
Total Returned		**6,340**	**2,603**	**3,165**	**23**	**549**

1. From information supplied by No 1 Searcher Org. Clearing House, HQ ALFSEA. 8. Table showing numbers of PWs Repatriated from Railway from time of Surrender until 30 Nov. 45 by Nationalities & Races

Nationality	Number
British	13,328
Australian	4,584
Indian	754
New Zealand	18
U.S.A.	294
Netherlands	11,672
Europeans	7
Asiatics	132
Total PWs Evacuated	**30,789**

9. Table Showing Numbers of Labourers (Civilian) Recruited from Malaya, Java, Siam and F.I.C. Number of Deaths Occurring in each Group and Period

Group	*Number Recruited*	*Number of Deaths*	*Period of Supply*
1st Malayan Labour Party	70,000	28,928	Apr 43-Sep 43
2nd Malayan Party	2,300	383	Nov 44-May 45
Specially Employed Labourers	727	12	Dec 43-May 45
Labourers' Families '	2,100	186	
Malayan Railway Employees	1,057	77	Aug 43-Jul 44
Malayan Electric Bureau Employees	166	16	Mar 44
Malayan General Employees	839	31	Jan 44-Aug 45
Ambulance Corps Employees	660	10	Dec 43-Dec 44
Temporary Ambulance Corps Employees	53	3	Sept 43
Overseers	214	10	Sept 43
Malayan Post Office Employees	88	1	Oct 43-Aug 45
Javanese Labourers	6,173	2,806	Jan 44-Mar 44
Javanese Employees	1,335	88	Dec 43-Dec 44
Chinese Association in Siam	5,200	500	Dec 43-Feb 45
Indo China Labourers	200	25	Apr 43
Total	**91,112**	**32,996**	

Note: From the Records containing the above data 7,906 are shown as having returned to their country of domicile before the surrender, 28,594 as having deserted from the Railway and 21,616 as having been on the Railway as at the end of Sept. 45 awaiting repatriation.

1. From files compiled by RAPWI

2. From records of the Labour Dept HQ (Japanese) 4th Railway Corps

6. Table showing Numbers of PW Transferred from SIAM to F.I.C. and JAPAN on Completion of the Railway by Nationalities and giving Times of Moves.

To Japan	*Total*	*British*	*Australian*	*U.S.A.*	*Netherlands*
4 Jun 44	2,200	1,000	200	-	1,000
4 Jul 44	1,663	300	913	-	450
4 July 44	1,800	750		-	1,050
4 Sep 44	2,266	1,550	716	-	-
23 Dec 44	525	-	407	32	86
Total to JAPAN	8,454	3,600	2,236	32	2,586
To Saigon					
29 Dec 44	286	286	-	-	-
2 Feb 45	2,030	1,592	200	-	238
Total to Saigon	2,316	2,878	200	-	238
Total to SIAGON & JAPAN	**10,770**	**5,478**	**2,436**	**32**	**2,824**

7. Table showing No of PW Deaths on the Railway from August 1942 to July 1945 by Months.

Month	*1942*	*1943*	*1944*	*1945*
Jan		120	679	98
Feb		160	416	37
Mar		190	145	54
Apr		207	57	54
May		279	64	34
Jun		662	60	119
Jul		722	40	118
Aug	2	955	37	
Sep	6	1,054	120	
Oct	13	826	13	
Nov	67	538	27	
Dec	81	345	70	
Totals	**169**	**6,058**	**1,728**	**514**
Total 8,469				

	Total	*British*	*Australian*	*USA*	*Netherlands*
	8,469	4,224	?	?	?
"F" & "H" 3 Forces	3,930	2,680	1,206	3	41
Total Deaths	**12,399**	**6,904**	**?**	**?**	**?**

1 No.1 Searcher Org. from Japanese records.

2 Japanese Records-SIAM PW Administration.

3 "F" and "H" Forces shown separately as they came under the Malay PW Administration. The figure are from the official Histories of "F" and "H" Forces.

4 From British Records as compiled by No 1 Searcher Org Clearing House.

CONFIDENTIAL

ETIN No. 246

Table showing Numbers of Civilian Labourers Recruited for Work on the BURMA &.-SIAM Railway through the Agencies of the Burma The "Labour Service Corps", and in the case of the latter, particulars as to the Numbers Recruited and the actual numbers

a) "BURMA Sweat Army"-Coolies recruited and placed on the' line from July 1942 and January 1943

b) Labour Service Corps - Coolies recruited and placed on the' line from March 1943

Recruitment	*Quota*	*No. Sent from Districts*	*Escaped En Route*	*Arrived Moulmein*	*Escaped Moullmein*	*Repatriated Unfit*	*Sent to Thanbyuz*
Ist	30,000	26,000	4,045				21,964
2nd	21,000						11,174
3rd	20,000						9,279
4th	15,000						7, 747
5th	15,000	9,174	3,135	6,039	1,035	256	4,747
6th	10,000	7,317	2,985	4,332	291	103	3,938
7th	10,000	20,475	6,546	13,929	1,676	319	11,933
8th	10,000	6,112	3,661	2,457	402	52	1,995
9th	10,000	8,184	4,732	3,452	1,697	14	1,740
10th	10,000	8,624	3,552	5,092	801	66	4,222
11th	10,000	10,743	5,067	5,676	495	174	5,007
12th	5,200	4,291	1,658	2,653	685	102	1,846
13th	5,100	4,519	1,224	3,145	438	35	2,722
14th	5,000	4,907	1,240	2,667	101	46	3,522
Total	**177,300**						**91,836**

1. These Figures were supplied by U AUNG MIN, formerly Deputy Director of Labour in the Japanese sponsored BURMA Provist.
2. No details available.
3. Approximate only

Appendix C

Notes on Construction

The following notes, supported by affidavit, are taken from the diary of 2323445 Sgt H. Jones, Royal Signals, who worked as a PW on the construction of the railway. The extracts which are reproduced herein were selected at random from the diary and describe various incidents which occurred during the construction of the railway.

"On the 8 November two working battalions (1000 men approximately) under Lt Col Knight, 4th Norfolk Regiment, marched into the jungle. Our guards were Korean private soldiers under command of a Japanese Lance Corporal....The idea of the Japanese was to march the prisoners of war into the jungle and from camps right along the entire route on which the railway was to be built, these camps to be formed approximately 12 kilometres apart.

The Japanese seemed to be following an old trail, marking which was old earth-return telephone wire. This we learned, was built by a firm that had attempted to build a railway some years before and had given up owing to the seeming impossibility of the project.

Japanese engineers arrived at Toncha and built their camp on the bank of the river. They had nothing to do with us except supervise the construction of the road and railway.

December—The road was completed in our section and clearing for the railway begun. The Japanese wanted a lane 50 metres wide cub through the jungle.

The Christmas canteen supplies did not arrive and the only extra on our diet was fried rice-ball made out of Japanese tinned meat.

January 1943—The first lorries started to pass along the road during this month but rations did not improve.

At this time external ulcers started to appear and, owning to the lack of medical equipment, the men were using leaves as dressing. The ulcers could not be cured and, owing to the mens weakened conditions they rapidly became worse. The medical officers asked that the worst cases be moved to Tarsao where we had been allowed to build a large base hospital. After many repeated requests, the Japanese Commandant allowed a few to be sent down by barge.

Pay was increased to the following ; Private 25 cents per day, Corporal and Sergeant 30 cents per day, WO 35 cents per day, each man contributing 10 per cent of his pay food for the hospital.

In the last week of this month all work on the railway ceased owing to the Japanese surveyers having made miscalculations which would cause the ends of the railway working towards each other to miss by about 1 kilometers.

February 1943—Another attempt to get news was made and the signal party carried all the spare parts that could be found and took them to Tarsao where four 2-valve sets were constructed by the B.M.B.C. electricians inside large Dutch water battles. These sets from now on kept our group going with news which was carried by our signal section from camp to camp.

The railway embankment was started before the jungle clearing was completed. When unobserved, Prisoners of war would put huge tree legs under the earth. By now these must be eaten away by the ants.

The Japanese Commandant returned from Bangkok and come up the road on a vegetable truck. Prisoners of war working along the embankment saw the vegetables and cheered right along the line. The Japanese Commandant thought that the cheering was for him and stood up in the lorry saluting the men all the way down the last kilometre of the road. On his return to camp he sent for Capt Skinner (our adjutant) and told him that he was quite pleased at this display of happiness at his return.

May 1943—Food just the same. Work carried on as usual. This month I caught sight of a Japanese map of the railway and marked on it was an old route that a Japanese Sergeant said had been surveyed by some company years before. Our route followed this old one except in one or two places.

June 1943—The monsoon broke and the camps were in a bad state of repair. Prisoners of War worked in the heavy rain and on return to quarters found them also wet.

The railway metals were now approaching Tengha. Work was speeded up and some men were doing it a 14 hour day. Tasks were set and no matter whether the terrain was rock or earth men had to complete their task before being allowed to return to their huts. (Men had to build up or dig out one and one half cubic metres of earth or rock each day).

At one of the sub-camps, Toncha South, elephants were brought up to assist in the dragging of logs from the forest, but owning to their slowness, the Japanese soon sent them away. The Japanese said that ten prisoners of war must do the work for one elephant.

Small generating sets were brought up to provide light on the job to enable men to work all night. I was put in charge of the cablelines running to the working points and if anything went wrong I delayed the repairs as long as possible so that the men could have a rest.

All wood used in construction of the bridges was taken from the jungle and the Japanese themselves, estimated that it would last two years.

A Japanese civilian bridge-building unit arrived. The men were very small but they worked harder than any of the other Japanese. Their insignia was a set of small stars in the form of a crescent, worn on the left brears. ("Gunzoku" or attached civilian personnel).

Towards the end of the month Cholera broke out in one of the small camps and very soon spread to Toncha South. Men died at a terrific rate; round the camp we had 2,700 Tamils and Chinese labourers; these died like wild fire. Many ran away to the north and south carrying with them the deadly disease. The Japanese were terribly frightened and built a small stockade around their own quarters and would allow nobody in unless he was first covered with disinfectant. They sent down to Tarsao for a British Medical Official who arrived and completely took over the whole area. He was Lt. Col. Harvey. All the Japanese gave him was line and disinfectant.

For treatment we made our own saline water, two gallons of which infected people had to drink. During this period work stopped for one week and then it was resumed at a tremendous pace.

July 1943—The Party of prisoners of war on rail laying put down three kilometres per day and had passed through our camp by this time. At first the railway was a very poor job, indeed, but the Japanese started parties of prisoners of war on maintenance and improvements.

October 1943—The railway was finished towards the end of this month. The Japanese made the British rail laying party race the last kilometer against a Japanese party on the same work. After two hours the English party was well in the lead so the Japanese stopped them on some excuse, thus allowing the Japanese to win the race.

Appendix D

Outline of Organisation and History of 5 and 9 Railway Regiment

1.Organisation of Railway Regiment

(a) H.Q.

No.1 Bn		No.2 Bn		No.3 Bn		No.4 Bn		Material Depot
1 Coy	2 Coy	3 Coy	4 Coy	5 Coy	6 Coy	7 Coy	8 Coy	
1 PL		2 PL		3 PL		4 PL		

(b) Approximate Strength of Regiment

Officers	75
N.C.Os	300
Men	2, 150
Attd	30 (civilian)
Total	2,55

(c) The Function of Railway Regiments: The construction, repair and operation of railways for military use.

(d) Personnel: At the time a regiment is raised personnel fall into two categories, i.e. skilled tradesmen and general service. Into the first class come the highly specialised such as locomotive engineers, telegraphists etc. who already hold a civilian qualification at the time they are recruited.

Into the second class come the semi and unskilled types (which constitute the majority) : these receive a general all- round training in railway construction, operation and maintenance.

2. Brief History of 5 Railway Regiment

Early in 1938 Regiment was raised in Japan and at the conclusion of a brief period of training was moved to North China. For the next three years, during the period of the "China Incident" this regiment successively operated railway lines in the vicinities of Tiensen, Kaifeng Hankow and Kowloon. During this time it also constructed and operated a light railway between Chinsein and Nanning.

In October 1941, shortly before the start of the Malayan operation, 5 Regiment was moved to Saigon, F.I.C. The Regiment here made preparations for the landing and moving of troops and supplies, concentrating rolling stock and building jetties in the harbour of Cap St Jacques.

In the early part of December 1941 the Regiment was moved to Bangkok, Siam and from there began its movement down the KRA Peninsula. As the campaign in Malaya progressed 5 Regiment took ever operations of the Taiping-Singapore line.

After the conquest of Burma in the spring of 1942, 5 Regiment was sent to that area to take over operation of the Rangoon - Mandalay line. The Regiment remained here until the fall of 42 when it was moved to Thanbyzayat to take part in the construction of the projected Burma-Siam Railway.

3. Brief History of 9—Railway Regiment

9 Railway Regiment was formed in Japan in 1940. In October, 1941 the Regiment proceeded to Haiphong, F.I.C. After the start of the Malaya operation 9 Regiment moved down the Peninsula and eventually operated the East Malaya Railway.

In April 1942, the Regiment moved to North Burma where it was engaged in repair and operation of line north of Mandalay.

In August 1942, 9 Regiment was moved to Siam, setting up HQ at Bampong, close to the southern terminus of the Burma-Siam Route.

After completion of the railway 9 Regiment moved its HQ to Thanbyuzayat and took ever operation and maintenance of the whole line.

In July 1946, 9 Regiment was moved to North Burma and, at the time of writing, it is applying its energies and its resources of skill and experience to the task of rebuilding and repairing the war-wasted railway lines of North Burma.

Appendix E

Translations of Japanese Documents

1 Translation of Cyclostyled pamphlet entitled "Notification for Agreement concerning treatment of PWs detached for Labour" published by Siam PW Camp, 1 Sep 44.

1. Control of PWs

(a) It will be a principle that handling over and return of PWs will be performed near the section or detached station gate, and that handing over and return will be closely supervised.

(b) After PWs have been handed over, it will be the responsibility of the employing unit to guard and control them. It will therefore be responsible for preventing escapes, accidental deaths, crimes and obstructions in the way of PW control after handing over.

(c) Opinions on PW administration will be given to detached unit commanders, and liaison personnel will be sent from detached sections for liaision between employing units and detached sections.

2. Reporting; of PW Services

In accordance with Act 8 of Military Regulations, it is desired that commanders of units employing PWs, should submit reports by the end of the month as per proforma appended (TN : proforma is a table for the entry of unit, Nos. of PWs employed, sick, number of dead, number of escapes etc.)

3. PW Rations

a. Working PW

b. Detached stations are responsible for rations.

b. Detached PW

(i) Pay and Wages are supplied by PW Camps

(ii) Clothing and necessaries are supplied by Camps.

(iii) Food will be supplied by employing units (table 1)

4. Medical Treatment

Agreement will be made with detached stations for medical treatment of PW while they are working and detached.

5. Mail

Mail and books for PWs will all go through the PW Camp Commandant and will be censored.

Table 1 Scale of PW Rations

Main foods	550 gms (cleaned rise, rice flour, etc.)
Subsidiary foods	50 gms
Meat	50 gms
Vegetables	400 gms
Sugar	20 gms
Salt	20 gms
Fats	25 gms
Tea	5 gms
Seasoning	20 gms
Firewood	1000 gms

Notes - Proportionate composition of main foods will be suitably fixed by the PW Camp Commandant.

The rations of those doing heavy labour will be increased by 220 gms of main foods, 50 gms of meat, and 20 gms of vegetables.

2. Document Relating to Attempt Escape—2F PW

Translation of Japanese Court Martial Case and Summary of Evidence selected from a file of Court Martial Records belonging to the Legal Department of 18 Area Army.

Case

Accused	Iran O'Brain Poston Bradley	British Army Sgt
	Peter Richard Jackson	British Army Sgt
	Bernard Bradley	British Army C/Pal
	Fredrick John 'UARDO'	British Army Rank
	Jack Ivor Evans	British Army Cpl
	Willam Henry Dawkins	British Army E L/Cal

Units: 2 Detached Stations, 4 Station, Malay PW Camp.

Offence: Acts contrary to PW Camp Penal Laws.

Sentence: Penal Servitude for Life.

Date of Sentence: 18 Nov 43.

The accussed were captured in Singapore and were sent to 2 Detached Station for work on the Burma-Siam Railway. There was an outbreak of Cholera in early June 43 and the accused felt unhappy and longed to return home.

Among the PWs was a man called Medley who had been in Siam before and knew the language and topography. On 5 June, the accussed got together and planned to escape to China or India and so return home. The accused men and another PW called Singleton sold various articles through Medley to Siamese who were working on the railway, and also got some food from the PW in charge of the cook house. Bradley got a lodestone from another PW and four maps were made.

Preparations for the escape were then complete, and on 6 June the accused and Singleton escaped under Medley's guidance (a total of 8 men).

In the middle of July the party had reached a cave in the jungle near 'Chiyenaboe', 12 km East of "Nonaipon' (Siam) but it was the rainy season and free movement was impossible.

During their concealment, Singleton died on 13 September. On 2 October Evans, Dawkins and Medley went out to buy food and the other four were captured by the Kempeital. Medley continued to do his utmost to escape but on the 7th October Evans and Dawkins gave themselves up to Japanese Officials of the Mitsubishi Mining Co. at 'DAIBU' and they were handed over to the Moulmein Kempei on 14 October.

Signed:

Lt Col Shitamura Chikara, President of the Court

Lt Ishihashi Tsuki, Court Member

Lt Koyama, Mayata, Court Member

Appendix G

Statistics Relating to Volume of Traffic Over the Burma-Siam Railway During its Period of Operation-December 43 to August 45

Tables Contained in this Appendix

Table 1. Showing Average Number of Trains Run Daily

2. Showing Volume of Supplies Moved into BURMA.
3. Showing Reinforecements moved into BURMA
4. Showing Troops Evacuated to SIAM

1. Table Showing Average Trains Daily SIAM-BURMA for Two Month Periods from Dec 43 to Aug 45

	Period	*Trains Run Daily*
1943	Dec-Jan	1-2
1944	Feb-Apr	2
	May-Jun	2-3
	Jul-Aug	3-4
	Sept-Oct	4
	Nov-Dec	5
1945	Jan-Feb	2
	Mar-May	2-3
	Jun-Jul	2

2. Table showing Volume of Supplies Moved into Burma by months giving Distribution by Commodities.

Year Month	*Trains Per Month.*	*Per Train Wagons*	*Tonnage Ordinance*	*Transported Ammunition*	*P.O.L.*	*Miscel*
'43 Nov	45	20	2,800	3,000		1,800
Doc	50	20	2,500	4,200		2,800
'44- Jan	60	20	2,400	4,500		4,500
Feb	65	20	2,000	4,500	1,500	4,350
Mar	65	20	2,150	4,500	1,200	4,500
Apr	70	20	1,150	3,500	1,500	4,000
May	75	20	1,250	4,000	3,000	3,000
Jun	80	20	1,000	4,000	5,700	2,000
Jul	85	20	2,500	4,500	5,700	2,950
Aug	90	20	2,000	4,500	5,700	4,900
Sep	95	20	550	5,500	6,000	6,000
Oct	100	20	1,000	5,500	6,000	7,000
Nov	110	20	2,400	5,000	6,000	7,000
Dec	115	20	2,850	5,000	7,000	7,000
'45 Jan	60	20	400	3,500	3,500	4,000
Feb	65	20	500	1,200	1,000	2,500
Mar	70	20	500	1,000	1,000	2,800
Apr	70	20	400	500	500	2,500

1. The tables in this Appendix were prepared by 9 Railway Regt. As many of the records were unavailable these figures must be considered as approximate only.

Appendix H

Statistics Relating to Major Bridges Destroyed and Rolling Stock Destroyed or Damaged by Allied Strafing and Bombing between Thanbyuzayat and Neekey during 1944-1945

1. Table showing Major Bridges Destroyed Locations and Number of Times Destroyed

Name of Bridge	*Location*	*No. Times Destroyed*
KALEWTHUT R. (No.75)	KWANLHA KALAWTHUT	10
KWANLHA R. (No. 77)	KWANLHA KALAWTHUT	10
THETKAW	THETKAW – RABAO	7
MYETTAW R.	BAKE-TON-ANANKWIN	1
KHONKHAN R.	THANBAYA-TAUNG-ZUN	1
WINYAW R.	TAUNG-ZUN-LONSI	7
MEZALI R.	MEZALI-APALON	7
APALON R.	MEZALI-APALON	2
ZAMI R.	APALON-CANDOW	6
SONGKRAI R.	CHANGARAYA-SONGKRAI	5

2. Table showing Number of Locomotive Damaged by Bombing and/or Strafing, Number repaired and Number rendered Unserviceable.

Model	*No. Damaged*	*No. Repaired*	*Rendered U/S*
C 56	2	2	
P	5	2	3
Q	1	1	
J.S.	1		1
F.S.	5		5
K.S.	2		2
	16	5	11

3. Table Showing Number of Wagons Damaged, Number repaired and Number Unserviceable.

Classification	*Wagons Damaged* Burma	*Malaya*	*Siam*	*Repaired*	*Made U/s*
Passenger Bogies	10			1	9
Covered Wagons	70	40	5	50	65
Open Wagons	40	10	2	17	35
Flat Wagons	15			10	5
	135	**50**	**7**	**78**	**114**

1. No. records are available showing damage to bridges or equipment on the SIAM side of the line.
2. Refers to wagons originally taken from these countries.

Year Month	*Trains Per Month*	*Per Train Wagons*	*Tonnage Ordnance*	*Transported Ammunition*	*P.O.L*	*Miscel*
'45 May	75	20	200			1,000
Jun	60	20				1,000
Jul	60	20				500
Aug	40	20				200

3. Table Showing Units brought into BURMA via Railway with Approximate Times of Moves

Period	*Unit*
Dec 43	RETSU Butai (31 Div)
Feb-Apr 44	OKAMI Butai (49 Div)
Mar-Apr 44	168 Inf Regt (49 Div)
May-Jun 44	YASU Div (53 Div)

4. Table showing Units brought from BURMA to SIAM via Railway showing Approximate to times of moves.

Period	*Unit*
Feb-Mar 45	ISAMU Div (2 Div)-Less AOBA Brigade
Feb-Jun 45	TAKA Div (5 Air Div) Complete Strength.
May 45	HAYASHI HQ (HQ 15 Army)
Apr-May 45	MATSURI (15 Div) Mixed [illegible]
May-Jun 45	AOBA [illegible] Div)
May-Jul 45	CHU Bde (from 55 Div)
Mar-Jul 45	1 Railway Material Supply Depot
Apr-May 45	7 Railway Regt
May-Jun 45	5 Special Railway Corps
May-Aug 45	Naval Troops

Appendix I

Extracts from Official Report of "F" and "H" Force and from Report by U Anng Min

1. Extracts from report of Lt Col W.R. Humphries, R.A., British Commander of "H" Force, and Expedition of 3,270 mixed A.F.F., British, Dutch and American Prisoner of War, Personnel dispatched to Siam under I.J.A. Orders and Administration during the period 5th May 1943 - 23 Dec 43..

   (i) **Command:** The small staff appointed to carry out the executive work of Command and Administration worked with energy and seal throughout. All ranks of the Force Headquarters were actuated by a genuine desire to further the interests of the PW Force and laboured incessantly to this end.

   (ii) **Discipline-Morale:** Discipline and morale remained at a high standard throughout, and the retention by individuals of self respect even during the most trying periods was encouraged by every possible means, e.g., shaving was insisted upon as a Standing Order, and the Camp Committee Co-operated with amazing success in this and other similar direction, seizing every opportunity of insistence on this and complete ablutionary measures even under the most primitive and difficult conditions.

   Payment of compliments was maintained at a high standard within the Camps, at the work sites and at chance meetings up and down the jungle paths.

   Throughout the whole period it was apparent that the men still looked with confidence to their officers for leadership, help and guidance. Even at the height of the cholera epidemic when deaths from this and other causes were very high; the more fortunate of the force threw themselves into the work of succouring the sick and dying. It seemed almost as though they did this as a thanks giving for the fact that they themselves remained active, although in numerous instances they were themselves partially sick. Many deeds of courage were to be observed, and self-sacrifice of a high order was the constant care of all ranks. Such few lapses as occurred were negligible and unimportant, serving only to emphasise the high standard which was extant in the force, and which was well worthy of the best traditions of the services.

(iii) **Work:** The labour tasks were heavy in whatever branch of the activities personnel were engaged. Long hours, great fatigue and rigid self-control being inseparable from the circumstances under which they worked.

Complaints were inevitably numerous and understandable, but in no instance did any lowering of morale make itself markedly manifest. When the hour was blackest, then was the time that all ranks "braced their shoulders" - "Tightened their belts" and went forward to their labours with that renewed resolution which has ever been the characteristic of the British Soldier in adversity.

(iv) **Food :** The difficulties and dangers which had to be faced in the distribution of food and clothing could not but result in a low standard, and this was the invarible case throughout. The question at the height, of the shortage was purely one of distribution; and I am convinced that the I.J.A. Administration was as much concerned with the situation as we, ourselves, were, and that they really did all they could in efforts to overcome these difficulties. But, of course, this was of little consolation to the men who were working so hard on practically empty stomachs, and malnutrition became the order of the day up and down the line of Camps. A peculiar and frightening symptom was manifest at one period, viz ; an intense and fixed, but vacant kind of stare being present in the yees of every man; and if despair could sometimes be detected in the countenance of some, I am certain, in my mind, that in most cases this was purely physical, and a direct result of the low standard of diet.

(v) **Pay:** Pay was received regularly within a day or so of its due date, and distribution to the Camps was immediate. On no occasion was money held at Headquarters for longer than 24 hours before absolute completion of distribution.

On such occasions as the money was collected from TARSOK, payment of the lower Camps was carried out on the return journey and on arrival at Headquarters, messengers from the Camps above would be awaiting its arrival.

C.M.F. was deducted at source and handed over with the Pay together with a complete statement of account. Every party moving between Camps carried with it the unexpired portion of the C.M.F. for the current period.

Some difficulty was experienced in getting Pay to some of the more outlying detached personnel but even this was finally cleared to the satisfaction of all concerned.

Changing of money from Malay to Thai currency, and conversely for the return journey presented little difficulties, but these, too were eventually overcome, thereby enabling all ranks to enjoy the free use of prevailing currency, sometimes, it is true, after slight delay and inconvenience.

(vi) **Sickness :** It is surprising that, in as much as at its formation 40 per cent of the Force consisted of personnel who were certified as fit for Light Duty only, and in view of the fact that no regard could be paid to this in the allocation of work the sickness and death rates in the Force were not considerably higher than they were.

The strenuous march up country seemed to be the factor which, from the inception of the expedition, undermined the physical stamina of all to such an extent that it left its mark on everybody during the whole of the remainder of the period. In theory the march was well planned, and should not have been too strenuous or resulted in undue hardship, but in practise the reverse was the case. The following unconsidered factors contributed to the hardship of the undertaking:

(a) Human nature caused everybody to carry on excessive load. (Nobody wished to sustain further loss of the few regaining cherished possessions).

(b) All ranks were unfit when judged by marching standard. Eighteen months of inactivity had made them physically soft the feet being particularly susceptible to the strain imposed upon them; and it is no aggravation to say that, even including those who were really physically strong, no single individual arrived at the journey's end without some damage to the feet.

(c) The rest period were not really restful, being disturbed by fatigues, meals, washing, medical formalities and water difficulties, as well as general lack of shelter in which to rest during the heat of the day.

The general absence of opportunity for normal precautions such as Mosquito Nets (anti-Malarial), proper sanitation and sterilisation (anti-Dysentery), were further important factors, and the Cholera epidemic which came, as this disease invariably does, like a bolt from the blue completed the disastrous cycle of misfortune.

The conduct of the whole of the medical personnel was of the highest order throughout and, whilst they could not have done more than they did to prevent deaths where they occurred, there is no doubt, as a result of their efforts, many cheated the Reaper and were enabled to return.

(vii) **Burials:** Every camp within the administration maintained a Burial Ground in its vicinity. In view of the high incidence of deaths, and the acute shortage of labour for grave-digging, it was unfortunately impossible, on occasions, to carry out single burials in one grave, but, in every instance, whether buried collectively or singly, the last rites of the deceased religion were performed. Where tha services of a Chaplain were not available, these, rites were carried out by an officer or the denomination concerned - (most frequently the Camp Commander).

(viii) **Commendations:** An expedition of this kind could not possibly be undertaken and completed without the individual acts and general conduct of certain people being outstanding. The case of this force was no exception, and notwithstanding the universally high standard of conduct and performance of duty, there were many who, by their constant devotion to duty, perseverance, and oft times personal courage, raised themselves so much above their fellows in these respects as to render special commendation for their services obligatory upon me as a duty.

In this connection, I submit with a sense of pride and privilege a list of such people, together with a brief resume of their individual meritorious activities with recommendations for awards for the Commander's consideration and submission, where approved, to higher authority.

Appendix I

Extracts from History of "F" Force - by Lt. Col. S.W. Harris O.B.E., R.A. (commanding 13 Div PW Area, Changi)

Introduction

1. In Apr 43 a party of 7,000 PW was sent from Changi, Singapore, to Thailand. By the end of August, 25 per cent were dead and 30 per cent of the remainder were sick. By December 40 per cent of the whole force were dead and the move of the unfit remainder back to Singapore began; It was completed in April. The total dead was then approximately 3,100 or 45 per cent in one year.

Orders

5. The orders received from the I.J.A. (Imperial Japanese Army) stated that:
   (a) The reason for the move was that the food situation in Singapore was difficult and would be far better in the new place,
   (b) This was NOT a working party.
   (c) As there were not 7,000 fit combatants in Changi, 30 per cent of the party were to be men unfit to march or work. The unfit men would have a better chance of recovery with good food and a pleasant hilly place with good facilities for recreation.
   (d) There would be no marching except for a short distance from the train to a nearby camp and transport would be provided for baggage and men unfit to march.
   (e) Bands were to be taken.
   (f) Gramophones, blankets, clothing and mosquito nets would be issued at the new camps.
   (g) All tools and cooking gear and an engine and gear for electric light were to be taken.
   (h) A good canteen would be available in each camp after three weeks. Canteen supplies for the first three weeks were to be bought with prisoners' money before leaving Singapore.

(i) The party would include a medical party of about 350 with equipment for a central hospital of 400 patients and medical supplies for three months.

(j) The force was to include a HQ.

(k) No Red Cross representative was to accompany the Force nor could any Red Cross money be obtained to take with the force. Facilities would, however, be given to communicate with Singapore for this purpose if the need arose.

Preparation

6. Lieut Col. S.W. Harris, OBE, RA (Commander, 18 Div PW Area in Changi) was accordingly appointed by British HQ. Changi, with concurrence of Comd. A.I.F. to command the force, using 18 Div Area HQ as his staff. The A.I.F. contingent was to consist oi' 27 Inf Bed, A.I.F. plus detachments to bring the strength up to the required total, Lt Col C.H. Kappe, AIF, Commanding.

7. The AIR contingent was to total 3,600 and the British 3,400.

Train Journey

13. The force travelled to Bampong in 13 freight trains, leaving Singapore on successive nights in parties of 500-600. The accommodation was one steel bas-car for approx 27 men. The journey lasted 4-5 days. Cooked rations of rice and vegetable stew, provided at various stations, were generally inadequate; drinking water was never supplied in sufficient quantities and this caused unnecessary hardship to men travelling in such crowded conditions during the heat of the day. In particular, most train parties received no food or water during the last 24 hours of the journey.

Railhead-Bampong

14. On arrival at Bampong the train parties were marched to -the first staging camp, about one mile from the station. The camp was in filthy state having previously been used by native labour gangs. An I.J.A. notice posted at the entrance in English was entitled "Camp Orders for Coolies and Prisoner of War". Accommodation consisted of large sttap roofs resting on the ground, without floors. Latrines, which were merely open trenches about six feet deep, were filthy beyond description and the whole area was as insanitary as it would be. There was no water for washing and a bare sufficiency for cooking.

15. The "gunzoku" guards at Bampong were in an even more excitable state than is usual among them when a move is in progress. Detrainment was carried out to the accompaniment of progress and the usual stream of conflicting orders. In the Camp itself, a gunzoku called "Toyama" on several occasions thrashed prisoners, for no apparent cause, with the steel shaft of a gold club, inflicting more or less serious injuries on a number of officers and men.

16. As each train load arrived it learned for the first time that the rest of the journey was to be made on foot, starting on the evening following arrival. Distance or the number or stages was not stated.
17. All heavy kit and stores, including medical sotres and bools, belonging to the force, were dumped by order of the I.J.A.in an unfenced, open space at the side of the road in Bampong, and no guard was allowed. When Force HQ arrived by Train 7, a further dump consisting of officers boxes and valises and men's kit-bags was in process of being formed at the roadside in front of the staging camp.
18. By this time, therefore, five trains' parties of the A.I.F. had already marched north of Bampong (the head of the column was, in fact, already 100 Kms away) and the sixth party was due to leave that night. Nominally in control of this operation were Lieut. Fukuda and the interpreter, Koriyasu, with their HQ in Bompong. As each train commander and, with the arrival of train 7, the force commander, objected to the march, Lieut Fukuda made the excuse that it was unavoidable.
21. If Force HQ had arrived six days earlier by Train 1, in accordance with the original plan, it is probable that better arrangements could be made, especially as regards medical stores and cooking containers. As it was, previous train commanders had spent only a few hours at Bampong before marching out with their men, so that there had been no continuity of command there and consequently no chance of making proper arrangement for stores left behind. The I.J.A. had available for transport twelve Harmon lorries and one ambulance. On their first run north from Bampong these vehicle carried Japanese stores few of them completed a second run and some a third, as the monsoon trains destroyed long stretches of road, and after May 20 no wheeled vehicle was able to reach from the south the area in which the force was finally concentrated. As a result, all the heavy equipment of the force which had been brought from Singapore be order of the I.J.A. including all heavy cooking gear and many smaller containers, all officers, and other ranks' kit not carried personally, most of the tools and Red Cross stores at reserve clothing including 800 pairs of boots, canteen goods to the value of $ 2,000 (Purchased by order of the I.J.A.) and three quarters of the medical stores, was left permanently at Bampong and was retrieved until the remnant of the force moved back to Kanburi seven months later, by which time a considerable portion had been looted.

The March

22. The march lasted for about 2½ weeks, over a distance of roughly 300 kilometres, covered in 5 stages of about 20 kilometres each. Marching was invariably done by night, between 2000 hrs and 0800 hrs. Except for the first two stages the road was merely a rough jungle track, capable of taking wheeled traffic in dry weather only. Long stretches of it were cordureyed, which with snags and

holes, made marching in the dark difficult and dangerous. Falls, resulting in sprains and even broken legs, were frequent, control on the march was virtually impossible as all torches had been confiscated during a military search at Bompong. At the same time, the fate of stragglers was uncertain, as Thais armed with knives hung on the tail of the column in certain area, ready to strip off the equipment of any man who feel being. It is probable that some at least of the 20 men still missing from the force met their end at the hands of these bandits.

23. Daily thunderstreams started on 30 April and the monsoon proper, broke just after the earlier parties reached their destination. The later parties thus had to contend with even worse marching conditions. The road surface became slippery and treacherous and long stretches were flooded and even totally washed away. The night march now frequently lasted for 14 or 15 hours instead of 12, and during the day's rest exhausted men had nowhere to shelter from the rain except on sodden ground under trees and bushes. It was unfortunately the less fit British parties which had to contend with these worsened conditions and this undoubtedly accentuated their already inferior physical state on reaching their final camps.

24. Even trained infantry in good physical condition would have found a march of this length and in these conditions an arducus one. But this force included men of all services and of every known physical category except. A.1 for even these rated fit among them had for more than a year subsisted on an inadequate diet, with consequent weakness from malnutrition. In addition there were the 2,000 and more unfit, included in the force as a result of the orders of I.J.A. Hundreds of these were convalescents whose sale reason for being there was that the I.J.A. had guaranteed them a journey by rail and motor transport to a comfortable camp where rest and good rations were assured. Among them were men suffering from beri-beri post-diphtheric hearts and other ailments, which rendered their survival impossible from the moment they were sent marching from Bampong. These unfit men, the number of whom steadily increased, proved from the first a great strain on the fit, who had to help and even carry them from camp to camp. In addition, every party was burdened wish as many small (3 and 6 gallen) containers and as much medical gear as it could carry. Thus, even those who were fit at the start of the march were seriously exhausted or themselves unfit at the end of it.

25. The staging camps were jungle clearings at the side of the road, at about- 20 kilometres distance from each other, generally (but not always) near water. Accommodation consisted of a cookhouse and open trench-latrines, and files abounded but of shelter there was none, except in two of the fifteen camps where tents were available for about a hundred men only. These camps were under the command of junior N.C.Os of some I.J.A. movement central organisation, apparently unconnected with either the Malaya or Thailand PW Administration. These men, whose behaviour was often harsh and

unreasonable, evidently had orders to push the marching columns forward as fast as possible, and the greatest difficulty was experienced everywhere in obtaining permission to leave behind even the worst of the sick.

26. Food, which consisted of rice and vegetable stew, was supplied in insufficient quantities to maintain the strength of men engaged on such a march, and water was often short. At Kanburi staging camp drinking water had to be bought by the prisoners from a privately owned well. Lieut-Col Harris tried to get this put right, but the abuse was not stopped until after the last party of "F" Force had passed through. When "H" Force arrived, however, some weeks later, free water had become available there.

    From Kanburi Col Harris sent back a letter to Lieut Fukuda pointing out that a tradegy was in the making. This letter detailed the immediate steps necessary to avert disaster.

27. It was difficult for the men to obtain sufficient rest during the day time halts at these staging camps for, apart from the lack of shelter, parties were often required to carry water or perform fatigues for the Japanese. This could have been avoided if the I.J.A. had detached permanent fatigue parties of sufficient size at each staging camp, all of which had previously been used by coolie gangs and which became progressively worse from day to day.

28. The strain fell particularly heavily on the Medical Officers and orderlies, as they had to attend to casualties on the line of march and hold sick parades during the day's halt, not only for their own sick but also for the steadily increasing numbers left behind by previous parties. Also at every camp the day ended and the march began with an argument with the Japanese N.C.O. as to the number of sick men to be left. The end of this was always that seriously sick men, with blistered and uncreated feet, and such illnesses as dysentery, beri-beri and malaria, were driven out of the camp to join the marching party, often with blows.

31. Similar scenes were being enacted daily at every staging camp along the road. Hundreds of unfit were being rendered seriously ill by this treatment, and the whole force was being rapidly infected with malaria, dysentery and diarrhee In addition, the health and physique of the fit men also was deteriorating under the strain, so that they also were rendered more liable to infection.

32. Finally, at Konkoita staging camp, after a fortnight's marching, every party was quartered in immediate proximity to hundreds of coolies, who were suffering from some intestinal disease, of which numbers died daily. The whole area was heavily fouled and infested with a plague of files. The I.J.A. protended that the deaths were due to dysentery; it soon became certain that it was, in fact, cholera. Konkoita was the facal point of the infection which caused cholera to break out a few days later at all of the working camps to which the force was dispersed.

33. At Konkoita 700 A.I.F. of Parties Nos. 1 and 2, under Lieut-Col S.A.F. Pond, OBE, 2/29 Bn A.I.F. (Lieut-Col Kappe, Comd A.I.F. Contingent was also in the

camp but hoped to move forward), were halted and placed under the command of Lieut Maruyama of the I.J.A. Engineers. This party of 700 was subsequently detached from the I.J.A. Administration of "F" Force and for all practical purposes came under the control of the Engineers until they rejoined the force at Nieke in December. The history of that deatchment will be found in its separate report made by Col Pond.

34. Lieut Col Banno, the I.J.A. Commander of "F" Force, made his first appearance at Tarso on 8 May in a lorry with the British officers of the Rear HQ. On 9 May he took on Col Harris with them, leaving the remaining three officers of Adv. Force HQ to follow on when the last party left Tarso. Two stages beyond Tarso Col Banno suddenly ordered all the officers of the Rear HQ to dismount from the lorry with the medical stores which they were carrying to start a wayside hospital for the marching troops, while he proceeded up the road another 150 kilos to Nieke with Col Harris. This incrediable action had serious results, as the services of Lieut Col Huston were thus denied to the force during the first critical six weeks, together with the consignment of medical stores, which could not be brought up later by road owing to the breakdown of the road in the monsoon and were not brought up even by river.

SHIMO-NIEKE - Dispersal To Working Camps

35. Col Banno arrived at Shimo-Nieke on 10 May by lorry, Col Harris being the only PW, with him. This was to be the HQ camp. It consisted of two partially roofed huts and seven large unroofed huts in a partly cleared hollow in the jungle. There was a small natural stream to provide water for all purposes. The camp had previously been occupied by coolie labour.

During the next few days some I.J.A. stores arrived from Bampong and a small hut was roofed for Col Banno and his office. The roofed huts were occupied by I.J.A. guards.

No shelter whatever was supplied for PWs - not even for a hospital, an M.I. Room or a cookhouse.

The first batch of troops arrived on 13 May (Party 3 and remains of Parties 1 and 2) and thereafter continued to arrive daily.

Thunderstorms by this time were a daily and nightly occurrence untill the monsoon proper broke in Shima-Nieke on 17 May and spread slowly northwards. From then until well on into September rain was incessant and heavy day and night. It was a rarely for more than four hours to pass without rain. There was one break of 24 hours in June and another in July.

Outbreak Of Cholera

38. On 15 May five cases of cholera were diagnosed by Capt. J.L. Taylor, MC, AAMC, a young M.O. who had not previously seen cholera, among the Australian party which had marched in from Konkoita on 14 May, having spent the previous day there. They seriousness of the outbreak was

accentuated because of A.I.F. contingent and part of the British contingent were not protected against cholera.

40 . The force Comd immediately saw Col Banno and stressing the seriousness of the situation urgent:

(a) immediate local arrangements for an isolation hospital.

(b) provision of vaccine to complete anti-cholera inoculation:

(c) absolute necessity for not allowing further uncontaminated parties into Konkoita or Shimo-Nieke camps;

(d) cancellation of move of affected Australian party Shimo-Nieke to Shimo-Senkrai;

(e) Col Huston and his medical stores to be sent for immediately from Kanoi.

Col Banno agreed bo (a) and (b) but did not act on (c), (d) or (e). A definite negative was not given at the time but that evening orders for continuation of the move were issued.

41. As a result, camp to camp movements continued and the infected troops from Shimo-Nieke moved to Shimo-Senkrai on the night 16/17th. One man actually fell out on parade with diarrhoea, and died next day of cholera. Fresh cases arrived with each party from Konkoita and as infected troops moved on to Camps 2,3 and 5 epidemic cholera broke out in each place.

42. As soon as news arrived from Camp 1 that cholera had broken out there the Force Comd got Col Banno to agree:

(a) to send Major Stevens, S.M.O., A.I.F. and Major Bruce Hunt, AAMC, from Konkoita. A similar request was later received from No. 1 Camp.

(b) to send a letter of instruction to Col Huston Ramc telling him to come forward as soon as possible.

The former was acted on at once and both officers arrived at Shimo-Nieke at 10 p.m. Major Hunt with Capt Taylor, AAMC, some medical orderlies and six British soldiers who were fully inoculated and who volunteered for cholera nursing went forward by M.T. at midnight with everything of use for fighting cholera that could be scraped together.

Major Stevens remained at Shimo-Nieke to control the base hospital.

The letter to Col Huston was written by Col Harris and sent by Col Banno, butthe I.J.A. private in charge at Kanio refused to act on it and would not let Col Huston move himself or his medical stores.

43. At another conference with Col Banno the necessity for geting cholera vaccine, medical stores of all kinds, and the need for rest (to recover from the march) and a good protein diet were all re-emphasized. The necessity for getting Col Huston and his stores forward was again stressed.

Col Banno, who was obviously very worried, agreed to all points and produced for the sick six tins of milk from his own private stock; He did, in fact, produce cholera vaccine within about 10 days. In about a fortnight an irregular and inadequate meat issue was begun. Col Huston arrived about six weeks later, but then on foot without medical stores.

Lower NIEKE Hospital

44. Some 400 seriously sick gradually accumulated at Lower Nieke. Some tents were issued, with I.J.A. instructions to put them up on bamboo roof-frames, instead of attap. It was found, however, that in this way they would not keep out the rain. Most of them were old British tentage, badly perished, and the pitch of the roof was, in any case, too flat for using tentage as roofing. Accordingly, they were removed and set up inside the roofless hut frames, in which way they gave reasonable protection. The I.J.A. however, insisted on their being put back on the roofs. The stupidity was later repeated at Nieke, inspite of visual demonstration of rain pouring through, just as if no tents were there at all.

    In spite of difficulties, however, Lower Nieke hospital did good work. Stringent isolation of cholera cases and suspects kept that disease in check and by the time the hospital had been cleared to Nieke at The end of June, deaths from all causes had been only two officers and 32 men, of which 19 were due to cholera - a result achieved through unceasing effort on the part of the mixed British and Australian hospital staff and of Capt A. Barber, RAMC, on whom the bulk of the work fell.

45. On receipt of news that some parties of sick had been left in the neighbourhood of Konkoita, Asst-Surgeon Wolfe, IMD, was sent down to do what he could. A report on what he saw and did is attached at Appx "E".

Later Stages of Cholera Epidemic

46. The cholera epidemic followed its usual course in all working camps. In lower Senkrai, the A.I.F. put out a tremendous effort to overcome their difficulties (especially to overcome the lethargy and weariness following the march) and succeeded in exterminating the disease when they had last 110 men (6 per cent) - a supremely creditable effort, especially on the part of Major Bruce Hunt, AAMC, of which a full report will be found in Major Johnson's report.

    At No. 3 Camp the A.I.F. similarly stamped out the disease reasonably quickly. At Lower Nieke and Nieke (mixed camp' under direct control of Force HQ) the situation was always in hand the deaths from cholera totalled only 26 out of a strength of 1,300.

    At Nieke the I.J.A. provided a small hut about half a mile from camp and an isolated hospital. It was effective, although difficult to supply with food and water. Cases, contacts and suspects were all sergregated and Asst-Surgeon Wolfe took charge and lived there.

    One day without warning two Tamil coolies suffering from cholera were dumped at the isolation hut and left there for us to look after. As we were always attacking the I.J.A. on the international nature of Red Cross. We protested only on the grounds that this was an unfair burden on our already overtaxed medical staff and resources and one which the I.J.A. medical service should properly have borne. Five coolie cases in all were dealt with, two of whom recovered.

At Nos. 2 and 5 Camps (both British) the physical state of the men and the camp conditions were such that losses were more severe. Cholera deaths were:-

in Camp No. 2, strength 1,800 :- 227 (14 per cent)

In Camp No. 5, strength 700 ;- 159 (23 per cent)

The special difficulties of these camps will emerge as the report continues. By the end of June the cholera situation within the force north of Nieke was definitely in hand. Eventually the total deaths from cholera in the whole force were approx 650 (or nearly 10 per cent).

Start of Working Camps

To visualize condition it is necessary to remember that everything described took place in incessant rain, day and night.

Camps when occupied consisted of huts without roofs for prisoners. At no camp were the I.J.A. personnel in charge of prisoners, or the I.J.A. engineers, without roofs to their huts.

At Nos. 3 and 5 Camps, it was found on arrival that part of the accommodation was occupied by coolies who were already suffering from cholera. At those two camps the rations were at first issued to the coolies who cooked both for themselves and the prisoners. Although this was stopped in a few days, there was another certain source of cholera infection. At No. 1 Camp, where Lieut Fukuda was in charge, with an I.J.A. civilian interpreter, Koniyasu, a few days were allowed in which to set the camp in order. The advantage to be gained was largely nullified by lack of tools and the stupid insistence of Lieut Fukuda on priority being given to non-essentials. It did, however, give the men a much needed breathing space.

At Nos 2,3 and 5 camps, no such break was allowed and men put on I.J.A. work at here, once 48 There occurred at this time a minor horror which deserves mention. A party of 20 men under a Warrant Officer were from Shimo-Nieke to Nieke as advance party to form the new camp. These were actually taken off the line of march by the Engineers before arriving at Nieke and put to pile driving in the river. Fourteen days later, when Lieut Col Dillon came across them, it was found that they had been pile-driving near Nieke daily from first-light until 10 p.m. up to their armpits in cold swift-running water, the whole time (except for half an hour for lunch) and driven with blows and sticks. They were then in a terrible state and only three were fit for any work at all. Strong representations resulted in cessation of their work but they were too far gone and all have since dies.

49. In all camps roofing was completed in the first two weeks by native labour, but the roofing material (attap) was so skimped that all the huts in all camp leaked badly.

50. In Nos. 3 (A.I.F.) and 5 (British) camps, no arrangements existed for the isolation of cholera patients. All that could be done was to collect them together into one part of the prisoners huts. In No. 3 Camp an isolation building was provided after about two weeks, but in No. 5 Camp nothing was done until the cholera epidemic had more or less spent itself.

51. In all camps the "hospital" consisted merely of normal huts with always 12, and in some cases (No. 2 Camp) 16 to a bay (Bamboo platform 12' x 13' - see sketch of ulcerward. Appx 'J'). No, other hospital facilities whatever existed. Everything had to be improvised-bed-pans from large bamboos canulars (for intravenous saline injections) from bamboo tips, tables from spill bamboo, water containers from long bamboos, buckets from bamboo strips, bandages and dressings from shirtsleeves, trouser legs, mosquite nets or from banana leaves tied on by with eys, stretchers from bamboo and sacks, and many other necessary articles.

52. No light was provided by the I.J.A. and the best had to be made of light from fires in the gangways of the huts, but these, of course, made extravagant use of wood and gave rise to further difficulties in wood collection.

53. The huts were full of bugs. Lice were prevalent and the overcrowding soon gave rise to scabies which became universal among men and officers. Even those who worked in cam and had opportunity for daily washing were all affected. The spread of all other communicable diseases was also ensured by this overcrowding.

Shortage of Stores

54. Only asmall quantity of the medical stores, Red Cross food (a small balance from the consignment received in Changi in August, 42) and a few cooking utensils and food containers which had arrived at Bampong had been brought up to Shimo-Nieke. Practically no tools were brought up either belonging to prisoners or to the I.J.A. The medical stores and Red Cross food were stored by Force HQ. at Shimo-Nieke and doled out to camps in small quantities on medical recommendation.

55. What cooking utensils and containers did arrive all went with the first parties to No. 1 Camp, in the expectation of the arrival of further lorry loads. Even so, this camp was very poorly provided.

Each party had marched from Bampong carrying some containers and medical stores. As sick accumulated at various staging camps, containers were forcibly taken by the I.J.A. from the later parties to maintain the sick and medical stores were used up in their treatment.

These later parties arrived at Shimo-Nieke therefore with very few or no containers and no medical stores.

56. As a result, Camps Nos. 2,3 and 5 were formed with practically no containers and almost no medical stores. The I.J.A. provided little except rice boilers (Koalis), which are heavy fixtures and therefore useless for food or water distribution to hospital or to outside working parties.

In No. 3 camps (400 Australians), which was small and compact, close to its water supply with a cookhouse near the sleeping quarters, this lack was a serious inconvenience. In Nos. 1 (1,600 British) and 5 (700 British) camps it was a disaster. The former had a cookhouse a quarter of a mile from the camp, and as the sick figure rose there was no efficient means of carrying food these 800 yards to the main hospital and to the isolation hospital yet another 400 yards.

Through the never-ending rain parts of meals were ferried all day by parties of officers and convalescents in the-few buckets and containers available. No containers would be spared for use in the hospital for boiling water for sterilisation of utensils anywhere in camp, thus further ensuring the spread of disease.

In No. 1 camp the special difficulty was not the distance from the cook house but the fact the water had to be carried from one well over a long and bad patch to the hospital cookhouse and the camp the results being much the same as in No. 2 camp. Sufficient containers were never issued by the I.J.A. even up to the end. There were few available in the "F" Force I.J.A. stores, and, in spite of pressure from our side, no attempt was made to obtain them from the Engineers, who had plenty. One hundred ordinary buckets would have eliminated most of our serious difficulties in this regard.

57. As regards cooks, a few were carried by each marching party but, as in the case of containers, the later trains were denuded of these at staging camps. The I.J.A. brought up practically no tools for "F" Force - which greatly hampered improvement work in camp. In come camps it eventually became possible to borrow some tools from the Engineers, but then the process was so hedged with restrictions, that it lost a great deal of its potential value until late September, by which time the damage had been done.

Interpreters

58. Two of our prisoner interpreters with the force were arbitrarily retained by N.C.Os of the I.J.A. organisation controlling the march at unimportant staging camps, and their services were lost to the force until it- re-assembled in Kanburi in December.

Working Parties

59. In all camps the I.J.A. Engineers demanded maximum numbers to work. The I.J.A. prisoners administration adopted as a principle the calculation of figures as follows:-

Other Ranks

A Hospital Patients -

Hospital Staff -

Camp Duties -

Total A -

B. Total Camp Strength -

B. Minus A - figures ordered for outside work.

60. This did not allow for any sick in lines or convalescent. They had therefore to be kept in hospital if they were not to go out to work. The keeping of these men in hospital produced a delicate position; for the I.J.A. would not recognise debility, weakness, malaria, beri-beri and trench feet, as being incapacitating diseases.

It became our task therefore on the one side to struggle to obtain agreement to the lowest possible figure and, on the other, to select men best able to stand a day's work to go out from the convalescents the "lines sick".

66. The duties allowed in camp, apart from a small office, comprised men for cremation or burial, manitatig cookhouse, wood-collecting and cutting. As these were essentially jobs which required a particular aptitude and a considerable proficiency combined with health and strength (especially in view of the minimum numbers allowed) in no camp was it found possible to organise any system of a day to day changeover to relieve men going out to work every day. As a result, men working outside worked on day after day until they fell sick and went to hospital. As already described, there was continual selection from convalescents to replace those going sick. As a result, there was no half-way, in effect a man was ill in bed or out at work, and the deterioration in health was rapid, general and very quickly complete.

67. In camp also, multifarious duties had to be performed both for the I.J.A. and for ourselves. Ration drawing, path making, road construction in camp, latrine digging, fence making, draining, continual building for the I.J.A. and but repairing, (the huts were rotten and constantly collapsing double-bunking basket making, collecting firewood for I.J.A. cookhouse and fuardroom, and many casual tasks. All these had perforce to be done by convalescents and by malaria patients on their better days, thus retarding and indeed often preventing recovery.

The situation would have been desperate enough even if the outside work had been a fair day's work, but the inhuman slave-driving to which the outside working men were continually subjected made the situation hopeless.

Outside Work for I.J.A. Engineers

68. The working day started with reveille and breakfast in darkness at about 0600-0700 hrs. Movement to and from meals and for purposes of nature were all in

pouring rain about the muddy, ill-sited camp. Breakfast consisted of 3/4 pint of plain rice. Parade for work was at first light and then the I.J.A. Engineers took over. If the numbers were not up to demand there was a scene on parade, sometimes ending with the striking of officers in charge. The daily task of selecting the last few men to go out from a number of convalescents really all unfit to go was heartbreaking and a tremendous strain on those to whose lot it fell.

69. The party would be marched off to draw tools and then to the scene of work. This often entailed a considerable march of 5 to 10 kilos. Many men (in June up to 80 per cent) were without usable boots. Marching was always through deep mud with many snags in the way of rocks and sharp bamboo roots. Without boots it was difficult for men to keep their foot in many places.

70. The work itself was mostly very heavy - beyond the strength of an average fully fit man and far beyond the capacity of our starved and debilitated men. Particularly severe was the portaging of logs from the mountain side to the roadway and the pile-driving and tree hauling for the big bridge at SONKRAI, which often entailed working in swift cold water up to the waist, sometimes event to the armpits. Obviously obeying instructions from their officers, the Engineer 0. Rs in change of parties drove the prisoners savagely with blows from fists, boots, sticks and wire whips.

71. Protests by our officers out on the work site often resulted in their being hit too. Visible resentment or objection were treated as mutinous and savagely punished.

72. It is necessary to emphasise that most of this continual war not disciplinary but was used to drive men as beasts to beyond their, strength.

73. All the time rain poured down, making conditions more unpleasant and work more difficult, on some tasks men were often kept actively working (i.e. continually plying shovels, adzes, axes etc) for three hours at a stretch without a second's break. A short interval, sometimes only a few minutes, was allowed for the midday meal-a pint of rice with a few beans.

74. Work continued until long after dark and then tools were collected and the march back began - a nightmare performance in the mud, rain and darkness. Tools had to be checked in and this was frequently made an excuse for further harsh treatment and delay. With the best will in the world it was very difficult to collect or check tools in the darkness at the scene of work where small parties were distributed over a large jungle area.

75. At last the party would arrive back in camp at 2200 hrs or even later, tired, worn out and dispirited. Numbers had again to be checked before they were dismissed to eat their evening meal (1 pint of rice and usually 1/2 pint of some form of vegetable stew) and turn in to their sleeping quarters - 2 ft by 6 ft or less per man-to get what sleep they could before the next day's agony started.

76. These who were sick had to be examined by fire-light. With these working conditions, starvation diet and with cholera, dysentery, diarrhoea, malaria,

beri-beri, tropical ulcers and trench feet rife, it was not long (by the end of June) before the total number of men working outside camps from the whole force (originally 7,000 strong) was 700 men.

In May railway construction was several months behind schedule and the orders from TOKYO for its speedy finish entailed working through the monsoon, mid-May to mid-September.

By 20 May the road south of SHIMO-NIEKE had ceased to be practicable for MT or bullock carts and there was no hope of reestablishing it for use.

In order to maintain a railway labour force of PWs and coolies in "F" Force area it was therefore essential to keep open the road thence northwards into BURMA. In May this road was merely a track cleared through the fungle. Through lack of foresight no steps had been taken to weather proof it before the monsoon broke.

I.J.A. Administration within the Force

85. The I.J.A. Administration within "F" Force attained a standard of inefficiency which is almost beyond description. A cadet officer (ONISHI promoted 2/Lt in Dec 43) who was responsible for "Q" and pay, appeared to us to be mentally deficient. It is probable that much can be put down to the uselessness of this individual, but he was working right under the eye of Col. BANNO and the result of his muddling was plain to see and was continually the subject of complaint by us in all camps. With the exception of Lieut WAKABAYASHI, those in a position to have things put right did not do so. This especially applies to Col. BANNO.

The I.J.A. were entirely dependent on us for records, but it was clear that some effort was directed to obscuring the real position from TOKYO; e.g. all deaths from dysentery were reported as from "diarrhoea" to save office work, the former being a disease that demanded special reports. This interpreter often acted in that capacity at interviews with Col BANNO, Lieut ONISHI and ethers. Sometimes (as in matters of pay) he was most helpful, at other times he took an extreme anti-PW attitude.

86. Again and again we pressed the question of Japanese international obligations under the '06 and '07 agreements and asked how they thought JAPAN would be able to explain things away. The answers always was that a victorious JAPAN would not have to explain to anybody, and this appeared to summarise the attitude of all Japanese officers, except Lieut WAKABAYASHI.

The Burma Hospital Project

87. Shortly after arrival at Shimo-Nieke, Col Harris pointed out that no amenities existed for the establishment of a base hospital and suggested that all sick should be immediately evacuated to Tarso or Bampong. He also pressed to be allowed to visit all camps as soon as they were established. This was refused,

but on 27 May Col Dillon was allowed to accompany Col Banno on a flying visit to Nos. 1, 2 and 5 Camps.

88. As a result of information thus collected and information received from No. 5 camp, Col Harris again saw Col Banno on 2 Jun' and stressed the seriousness of the situation, pressing for the immediate evacuation of the bulk of the seriously sick (about 3,000) to Bampong. Col Banno stated that it was impossible while cholera continued and that it would still be impossible to do such an evacuation by road, even after the monsoon. Col Harris then urged that it should be done by river as soon as the water was high enough.

This project was considered at length by the I.J.A. and on 23 and 24 June Col Harris was allowed to visit all four camps forward to Nieke and reported to Col Banno on his return. His report of the deplorable conditions, especially in No. 5 Camp, is attached Appx "F". The I.J.A. at last produced another project to open a hospital in Burma.

89. Orders were eventually issued for the evacuation of a staff and 1,700 patients to a camp at Tanbaya in Burma by road and rail through three staging camps to be established at Changeraya (No. 5 camp), Kando and Lonsli. The I.J.A. gave assurance that the hospital would be provided with medical stores and good rations. Road and rail movement tables, which were perfect specimens of their kind, were issued by the I.J.A. and on 30 Jul the advance party of staff moved. Thereafter followed the normal Japanese administrative mess. In no single instance were movement tables adhered to and the journey was carried out under most distressing and inhuman conditions, which added greatly to its unavoidable hardships to the sick. These additional hardships were due to no other causes than Japanese inefficiency and callousness and sometimes active and bestial cruelty. Evacuation to Burma dragged on through August and was not completed until September.

90. The selection of patients to go was exceedingly difficult. It was on good sending those who would not survive the journey on the other hand those who were not sent would surely die if retained in our working camps. The patients themselves were almost without exception eager to take their chance and go.

The selection was of course made without pre-knowledge of the unnecessarily evil conditions under which the journey would be made. 43 out of the 1,700 patients died on the journey.

91. The TANBAYA hospital itself consisted of a hutted camp without light or water or any special amenities. The amount of medical stores issued were infinitesimal and rations were at all times poor, being particularly deficient to Vit. B which was vital to the treatment of the patients (debilitated from dysentery malaria and tropical ulcers), practically every one of whom suffered from beri-beri in one in one from or another. Approximately,750 patients died in TANBAYA, or about 45 per cent of the total.

92. This outcome was a bitter disappointment, but at least the remaining 55 per cent were saved from inevitable death in the working camps. On one point the I.J.A. kept their word - TANBAYA was not called upon to supply outside working parties. Convalescents were thus at least given a chance to recover if and when they had managed to survive their actual illnesses.

Reorganisation Noth of Nieke

93. No sooner had the move of the advance party to the BURMA Hospital started than an order was received to close NIEKE, SHIMO-SONKRAI and CHANGARAYA and to re-group at SONKRAI" and KAMI- SONKRAI in such a way that each camp could provide approximately the same number of working men; a figure of 800 from each camp was mentioned. Patients and staff for BURMA were ordered to remain in the old camps until moved. These men who were so ill that they had not been selected for BURMA were also to stay.

Most of these were expected to die. This order was received at 1400 hrs on 2 Aug and the move was ordered to be completed on the following day. It involved marching through rain knee deep in mud. Carrying all personal kit, cooking and medical gear and with all patients other than those booked for the BURMA Hospital or too ill to be sent there.

Col HARRIS protested strongly against the order. He pointed out that the BURMA project catered for only half our sick, the remainder (about 1,700) would be left on our hands and, apart from the difficulty and inhumanity of moving them, the figure of 800 working men from each camp was beyond all possibility; about half that number might with difficulty be found.

In the end we were forced to carry out the move. All sick (except those mentioned above as remaining) had to be got out of had and marched to the next camp. We did obtain the slight concession that these sick should stage at SHIMO-SENKRAI and SONKRAI on successive nights on the journey to KAMI-SONKRAI. This engagement was, however, broken forthwith by the I.J.A. and they were forced to march straight through. There is no doubt that a number of the deaths which occurred subsequently at KAMI-SONKRAI were directly attributable to this march.

94. In order to balance the number of working men available at the two re-organised forward camps it was necessary to create mixed camps of fitter Australians with the less fit British.

95. KAMA-SONKRAI, commanded by Col KAPPE, A.I.F., had as its I.J.A. Commandant Lieut FKUDA. This remained until the end a disgraceful camp from the point of view of I.J.A. responsibility and had during August, September and right through Oct. a very heavy death roll. The other camp, No 2 at SONKRAI, was at first an even worse case, but after the general clearance of the bulk of the worst of the patients by death (averaging 10 a day throughout August), and by transfer to the BURMA Hospital, the situation greacly

improved. To this camp also was posted Lieut WAKABAYASHI, who was the only Japanese officer with whom "F" Force had to deal who showed the slightest glimmerings of humanity or understanding of his responsibility towards the PWs under his charge.

96. About 20 Aug Lieut Wakabayashi came to Col Harris and stated that he had orders from Engineers HQ. that, unless the working figure produced by both camps was doubled, all prisoners, sick as well as fit, would be turned out into the jungle to fend for themselves, thus making room for coolies who could work to be brought in. This threat also applied to Kami-Sonkrai. To his credit must be said that Lieut Wakabayashi was obviously thoroughly ashamed in having to repeat this order.

A few days later the Colonel commanding the Engineers visited Sonkrai and Lieut Wakabayashi created an opportunity for Col Harris, with Col Dillon and Major Wild, to approach, him on the subject direct. The attitude of the Engineer Colonel was at first most unencouraging, but after great perserverance it was decided to retain part, (about two-thirds) of our accommodation, leaving the remainder available for fresh labour. It is emphasized that the project of turning us out into the jungle was a real one and would have been carried out if it had not been for the interview, in spite of the fact that the monsoon was in full flood. It is a grim recollection that we were able to promise to make available a third of our accommodation only by taking into consideration the number of deaths which would inevitably occur in the next few weeks.

97. About 20 Sept, the monsoon started to peter out and condition began to improve, which improvement was maintained at a slow rate until, the force was finally withdrawn to Kanburi enroute to Singapore in November.

Return to Singapore

100. In November the Force was moved back - first to Kanburi ever the Thai railway and later by the Bangkok-Singapore railway to Singapore. The arrangements for the first part of this journey were disgraceful, no attempt being made to provide reasonable amenities, food or water for the fit or sick, and fourteen men perished on this journey. The arrangements for the second part of the journey had not improved since April and were as described in para 13.

Appendix I

3 Extract from Report by U Aung Min on conditions in Coolie Camps during, constructions of the Burma-Siam Railway

Conditions

(a) Hard work with no prospect of returning home, had and insufficient food, lack of clothing, uncomfortable dwellings and no recreational facilities made the life of the labourers miserable while beatings and slappings for the slightest offence added to their misery and resulted in many desertion. Numbers of these deserters were picked up and put to work further down the line.

(b) The buildings in the camps were constructed of bamboo thatch and insofar as accommodation was concerned were adequate. During the rains and cold seasons some buildings, especially those under the charge of Capt Kuwabara, did not provide sufficient shelter as they either leaked badly or were too open to ward off the cold.

(c) The only clothese the coolies had were what they had brought with them and only about one third were suitably clad. During the cold season of 43-44 a small issue of gunny bags was made but this went nowhere. Some months later the clothing position improved and those coolies who had only three days absence from duty in a month were given clothing in form of shorts, vests, shirts or lunggyis.

(d) The food the coolies were given consisted mainly of rice supplemented by a few vegetables, cooking oil, meat or dried fish, but sometimes only rice and vegetables were available and many reports came in of the quantity supplied being far short of that required.

(e) Boiled water was provided where possible for drinking and in some camps wells were dug but in others water from streams was used for all purposes. In general the water supply was bad and inadequate.

(f) The work was heavy and monotonous, digging and carrying earth, constructing bridges, laying mines etc. and the treatment they received at the hands of the Japanese was harsh and cruel. Normally the coolies worked from seven in the morning to five in the evening with an hour off in the middle of the day. Late in 44 the coolies were given a day off per week when they could wash their clothes, but as most had nothing other than the rags they stood in, they could not do so, further, soap was never seen.

Medical

(a) In 43 there were five hospitals along the line located at:

THANBYUZAYAT,	MEZALI
LONSI	SONGKRAI
TADEIN	

In these hospitals there were Japanese and Burmese doctors, appointed and paid by the Burma Govt. The hospital were under the charge of Capt Tagahashi, while the Burmese doctors were under U Ko Gyi, then district Medical Officer, Moulmein. Only very bad cases were admitted to these hospitals and the patients had, in some cases, to walk some considerable distance to reach them. There were no doctors or medical staff attached to the camps along the line. There was no special diet for the sick and irrespective of the patients complaints they were given the same food as those working received. However, there was an occasional issue of coffee, milk and sugar but no wages were given the sick and they could not buy extras which they so much required; the result was that they sold whatever scanty garments they had left in order to supplement their meagre rations.

(b) The Burmese doctors had no say in the treatment of the sick and had to depend on the Japanese for everything. Very few drugs were available; quinine, blace powder for stomach disorders and a lotion for ulcers were all that was available. The diseases most common were malaria, dysentery, scabies, ulcers and beri-beri. Sick had no work assigned to them but one case was reported of some twenty patients being made to cut bamboos and build barracks, this was brought to the notice of the I.J.A. and the Burma Govt. No reports of epidemic diseases were heard except one at the start of the project when cholera broke out and many coolies succumbed.

Action by the Burma Govt.

Early in 44 the Govt. decided that something had to be done for the many thousands of coolies on the line and shops were set up in camps and hospitals which sold tobacco and special Burmese food. A hospital was opened at Mudon and the sick were brought in from outlying hospitals. The hospitals at Tadien, Lonsi, Mezali and Thanbyuzayat were closed. Feeding and the provision of blankets at the Mudon hospital were done by the Govt. Clothes and tobacco were later distributed free in the hospital. Arrangements were made for troops of actors to go up the line to entertain the labourers and encouragements was given by the Govt towards saving by offering an equal sum to that which the labourers saved up to the termination of their employment.

In addition to the above written statement, U Aung Min stated in an interview;- "In the early days the recruitments of coolies was done only in the Moulmein and Thaton areas and each recruit signed an agreement to serve for three months on the Railway. This agreement was never kept as far as the Burmese coolies were concerned but the Chinese Association in Rangoon, who were supplying batches of coolies the same terms, insisted that the men only serve three months and on the expiry of their term they returned to their homes. On one occasion a number of Burmese coolies who had served well ever their term of three months went on strike and although the Japanese were forcing them to stay, the Burmese Govt. advised the Japanese to allow them to go as grave trouble might result.

When the supply of coolies from Moulmein and that on districts diminished, press ganging of coolies started all over Burma. Many were taken from the streets and fields by force and lodged in jail till such time as a party was proceeding up the line".

Appendix J

Medical Report by Major Tagami, Chief Medical Officer, 9 Rly Regt.

I (a) When I was attached to the Regiment on 18 May 43, the Work was in the last phase; about that period, especially with regard to the exact figures, I have no records; so this report relies upon my memory and that of others.

This SIAM - BURMA Railway line, which is the great epoch-making construction of this century, was completed within a time which we scarcely considered possible. I cannot say, however, that the construction was carried out according to any definite plan, nor were through plans made by the Imperial Headquarters, Headquarters Southern Area or the Superintendent of No. 2 Railway Corps and units under its command.

To express it shortly, though a wartime venture and faced with great natural obstacles, too little attention was given to preparation and planning. I believe this to be the cause of the large number of victims among the labourers.

When I arrived at HQ. Regt in WANYAI, SIAM, 9 Railway Regt (Approx 2,600 men) PW (approx 30,000) L of C and Medical units etc. had been employed on work spread over an area of some 240 kms. One battalion took charge of about 50 kilometeres, mountainous and thick with jungle, where no human had ever set goot. Transportation of goods for the hinterland depended upon the road which ran parallel to the projected roadway, and on a tributary of the MEKONG River and the KEONOI River which was at its lowest, making transport by boats useless so the road was mainly used. At that time, also trains were running up to WAMPO.

(b) Connection between 9 Rly Regt and Co-operating Units: 9 Railway Regt was the main operational unit in the construction of the Railway. The PW Cage which was combined to it supplied the manpower required. The L of C was in charge of food supply to 9 Rly Regt and other units. A field hospital, (2 F'd Hospital, 21 Div) followed and was established at WANYAI, KINSAIYOKE, and TARKANUN. This undertook the treatment of soldiers. The Sanitary and Water purification Dept stayed in WANYAI, and TARKANUN and was responsible for sanitation and anti-fever measures.

(c) Increase in Man-Power: Before my arrival, the Chinese Central Association in SIAM had supplied about 4,000 men, Siamese and Chinese, but most of them had run away and had actually done little work.

(d) It became clear that the time of completion of the Railway fixed by Imperial Headquarters would be quite impossible with the man-power available at that time, making it imperative to send some 65,000 men from MALAYA.

While the railhead was moving towards WANYAI, 600 labourers were sent daily from WAMPO and from WANYAI; they had to walk into the hinterland. They were sent to each of the battalions and put under charge of each section, no special organization had been made ready to receive them and they were put under the control of the section's Labour Controlling officer.

(e) In much the same manner as above, about 3,000 men from No. 5 Branch PW Cage, Malaya proceeded to KANNYU and HINTOK. The PW were under the command of our Regt but were under the charge of Capt HACHISUKA, OC PW Cage.

(f) Labour Camps at that Time: For housing purposes, HQ Southern regions and No. 2 Railway Corps sent many tents which were available in the Southern Area, but the supply was insufficient to cater for so large a number of men. Great difficulty was experienced in building an isolation hospital for the workers. During the later stages, on completion of the railway, due to increased transportation of goods there was an improvement in the supply of roofing materials.

(g) Rations at that time: The road having become very muddy as the dry season changed to the wet, it could not be used. At the same time, the water in the river did not rise, so that the supply of rations, especially vegetables, was very poor and for a certain period there was a complete lack.

The areas around KANNYU and HINTOK were very far from the river and the dispatching of rations was very restricted; this scarcity was felt very badly by the Japanese Army as well as PW and other labourers, with the progress of the Railway and the rise in the height of the water in the rivers there was a decided improvement.

On the other hand, to supply milk and fats, 200 to 300 live cattle were sent on foot daily. Summing up; according to my observations for about two months rations were very poor, but improved after that. At the end of construction of the railway,I believe that we could have accomplished our purpose of supplying sufficient nutrition.

I remember that in the PW Camps, especially due to skillful cooking in these camps, the food was tastier and had more nutritive value than the food of the Japanese soldiers.

2. Outbreak of Cholera and Matters Relating: After taking up post, I first received a report of the outbreak of cholera in the section of 5 Railway Regt operating in the NEEKEY area. The Regiment took precautions for the prevention of an epidemic, but suddenly at the end of May, I received a report that some of the PW in the Siam PW Cage at TARKANUN had contracted Cholera. The Regiment, acting in conjunction with its Medical units, tried its best to prevent an epidemic. There are two opinions regarding the cause; one that the source was at NEEKEY, and the other that it originated in SIAM. The opinion that the cholera bacillus was spread through the medium of the KEONOYE River has been refuted as a result of the repeated examination of the cultivation of bacteria. It is believed that the water of the mountain stream was contaminated due to some Siamese who stayed in the hinterland to sell goods.

Further, a case of cholera occurred in the PW Cage, SIAM at WANYAI.

(a) On receipt of this information I reported the matter to my seniors and also informed the authorities concerned, so that medical reinforcements were dispatched to that place, the fear of an epidemic of cholera was experienced by the Japanese army and the labourers in the PW area. The labourers were extremely frightened and ran away, one after the other, and this feeling was passed to the newly arrived labourers also. For this reason an investigation station was opened at Wanyai and labourers who had run away were kept there to prevent the spread of cholera.

The Medical Officer and his four men of the Medical Dept of Railway Regt combined with the Japanese Medical staff of the PW Cage and medically trained members of the PWs under the guidance of the Sanitation and water Purifying Unit tried their best to prevent an epidemic of Cholera.

In the midst of the rainy season, we were much concerned with the deep, muddy, bad road. We devoted all our energies to the isolation of patients, sanitation, treatment and disposal of dead bodies, working all through the night. However, due to the increasing number of patients, disposal of dead bodies became a problem. Antiseptic materials could not be transported by road and boats were used.

I confirmed the plan for the prevention of an epidemic of cholera, gave the necessary instructions to the medical members in the area and returned to HQ.

I reported the state of affairs to the Staff Officers of 2 Railway HQ, the O.C. being absent. I announced that if this condition continued in the future there would be a great many victims. In accordance with my ideas Staff Officers Horimote and Nakamura decided to stop the dispatching of further labourers and refer the matter to Senior Staff Officer Nagasawa, for decision.

The decision to stop further influx of labour was rejected and a supply of antiseptic and additional medical staff was promised. I waited for the return of the O.C. Regt. On his return, I immediately brought the matter to his attention. The O.C. Regiment, ordered the work to be halted for three days during which time everybody was to do whatever was necessary to prevent the spread of cholera. The O.C. understood the problem thoroughly but at the same time he could not ignore the orders of his seniors for the completion of the railway in the required time, and I believe he was forced to issue the above orders.

After this there were outbreaks of cholera in many places and we tried our best with our scanty medical staff to prevent heavy casualties occurring.

(b) Statistics of death show that there were 12,000 deaths out of a total of 45,000 labourers of which 6,400 men died of cholera. Of the 35,000 PW involved, there were, I believe, some 6,000 deaths. In my opinion 30 per cent of the deaths may be attributed to the cholera epidemic.

(c) Concerning the cause of infecting among PW I think it was due to unsuitabl equipment for purifying water. Further, I except that the men, who worked heavily were tired out physically and did not take much care regarding sanitation. In addition there were the poor living conditions already mentioned above, in our regiment of about 2600 men there were only five cases of choleras of which three died. On investigation it was found that these men had been ignorant of hygine.

With the increase in medical staff the cholera epidemic finally died out, due to thorough examination of cases, isolation and preventive inculations and also to improved conditions after the rainy season.

3. Outbreak of Tropical Ulcers: Tropical ulcers became prevalent, especially among the labourers who were bare-footed. HQ Southern Regions sent out some professors from medical universities who set up plans for consultation and treatment. But with the poor medicines available, the treatment laid down in the plans could not be followed. We were forced to treat the patients by using medicines which were comparatively plantiful: potassium permanganate, liquor of cresol soap, and by means of surgical operations. Of the labourers about 50 per-cent were treated for ulcers.

Even after the completion of the railway, there were cases of tropical ulcers and these still continued when 9 Railway Regiment was transferred to Burma. Members of the Burma Construction Service, and labourers supplied by the Burma Govt. also were affected. In case of those suffering from tropical ulcers and complications of malaria the necessary exercise in walking became the more difficult and many of the patients fell and died from general prostration. I believe about 25 per-cent of the deaths were from ulcers.

4. Concerning Malaria: In the area of the Siam-Burma border where the incidence of malaria is high, the presence of many labourers who were germ carriers caused an increase in violence of about 50 per-cent. Even the Japanese forces in this area, when outbreaks of malaria occurred, would have been without ability to carry out operations but for the fact that we had considerable stocks of quinine.

5. Resistance to Disease of Japanese Army, PW and Labourers: In view of my limited knowledge and experience it is useless for me to discuss this subject at any great length. Nevertheless I will offer my humble opinion. I will omit the more scientific and technical descriptions of predisposition and simply divide it into the two parts, cogenital and posterior.

The term cogenital disposition does not differ whether in Japanese, European, Malay-Indian or Malayan, but posterior predisposition will differ according to circumstantial and cultural backgrounds. The resistance to disease of labourers who suffered from chronic malaria was particularly weak. Again, if, like the European PWs if they took too much carbohydrate before their bodies had become adapted to it, they were inclined to become ill and resistance to disease was lowered.

I have heard of cases where PWs had to eat considerable quantities of rice. Having to take quantities of rice and vegetables which were rich in carbohydrate, where formerly they had been accustomed to taking large amounts of albumen and fats, no doubt, caused a lowering of resistance to disease. The fact that there was a temporary shortage of food, especially vegetables, had the effect of lowering resistance even more.

6. Medical Organisation:

(a) In the treatment of PWs everything was done by their own medical officers under the guidance of Japanese medical officer attached to the PW Cage.

The treatment of labourers was carried out by 9 Railway Regiment. There was a total of seven medical officers in 9 Regiment, two in HQ and one in each battalion. In addition there were medical N.C.O.s, temporary assistants and medical orderlies totalling about thirty, so that we were unable to supply even one man to each section. Thus it can be understood the difficulties which facted this small number in serving labourers' camps, which unlike battalions, are sometimes spread as far as 50 kilometres. Moreover, traffic in the rainy season made it more difficult to supply treatment for cholera epidemics. Again and again, I requested senior officers to increase the medical personnel. Finally, the strength of the medical officers was increased to 15 and the number of medical N.C.O.s was also increased. We were still unable to supply even one member to each labour barracks. Moreover, P.O.W. medical personnel, including 13 medical officers, were sent to our regiment in the early part of August 1943. These were sent out to all battalions and put to work giving treatment to the labourers.

But it was our regret that, owing to lack of medical supplies, they could not be employed to the best of their ability. While the Japanese and PW medical personnel understood little of each other's language, they lived, ate and worked hand in hand to give treatment. I perceived that the PW medical officers and their personnel were very sincere in the discharge of their duty. Owing to the existing circumstances, I was unable to supply all their demands regarding treatment. This was a matter of great regret to me.

In the middle of August, 4 Malayan physicians came, but these, with the exception of one, had little ability. Towards the end of September, 27 more Malayan physicians were sent to us and while a few of these were diligent in performing their duties, most of them were unsatisfactory.

(b) After the cholera ended, tropical ulcers increased in violence. Labourers hospitals were hastily built at the order of HQ. and began working. At first these were established at three point: Wanyai, Kinsaiyoke and Tarkanun. Eventually hospitals were also established at Kanburi, Tanmaijo, and Neekey and were placed under charge of 19 Casualty Transport, 2 Field, Hospital, of 21 Division.

In the beginning accommodation in the form of lodgings were poor; there were no tents and grass for roofing could not be sent owing to transportation difficulties. Therefore, we repeatedly advised the senior officers that the patients should be sent back and admitted to the near hospital. But as hospitals for labourers were eventually established, patients were sent to these hospitals.

7. (a) I thought it would be more suitable to adapt the Burmese assistant physicians, who understood the language, for the treatment of Burmese labourers. I began the training of Burmese assistant physicians in support of U Ko GYI, the director of the HOULMEIN Civil Hospital. We first trained 24 men, and continuing through three more installments we trained a total of 63 men but during the difficult situation many ran away, and just before the close of the war only 35 remained.

8. Improvisation: In their leisure time research was carried out by medical personnel with a view to finding substitutes for medical goods. For example, bandaged made out of banana bark served as cotton bandage. Animal charcoal powder was made out of animal bone. Active carbon was made out of coconut shells. Use was made of the bark of "hora leana anti-dysenterica" for amoebic dysentry. Substitute absorbent cotton was made from the bark of the Indian "Lingo" tree. Injection medicine was made from quinine sulphat. Vitamin "B" was made from rice bran etc. We tried and applied these.

9. Shortage of Clothing: Successful operation was also prevented by reason of the lack or shortage of rations and clothese, since financial restrictions could not prevent an abnormal rise in prices. While the labourers were supplied with clothes and funds these were dissipated wither by gambling or exchanged for food and cigrettes or lost by theft, so that they had actually nothing but the clothese on their backs.

At one time shortly after the hospital had been established, blankets were loaned to the labourers, but they either sold them or ran away with them. This caused the hospital to run short of blankets.

10. Numbers and Percentages of Deaths: In BURMA malaria took the highest toll. It was responsible for 50 per cent of the patients. Tropical ulcers took the next 10 per cent, 20 per cent for beri-beri and skin diseases. Still malaria took the highest toll of these diseases for Japanese Army and PW personnel alike.

During the time that 9 Railway Regt was in charge of construction in SIAM, a period of about 1 years the deaths were:

	Total	*Deaths*	*Percentage*
Labourers Approx	45,000	12,000	26
P.Ws. Approx	35,000	6,000	17
Japanese Army Approx	2,000	100	4
Burmese Labourers Approx	45,000	3,500	7

Appendix K

Maltreatment-British Protest to Japanese Government

The following is a copy of the letter dated 4 Dec, 1944 from the Swiss Minister in TOKYO to the Minister of Foreign Affairs (Protest by British and Australian Governments). Tentative translation of the letter dated 4 Dec 1944 from the Swiss Minister to the Minister to the Minister of Foreign Affairs:

I have the honour to acquaint Your Excellency with the fact that the British and Australian Governments have requested my Government to convey the following communication to the Japanese Government.

Some 150 Australian and United Kingdom survivers from the Japanese transport S.S. "RAKUYO MARU" torpedoed in the SOUTH CHINA SEA on September 12th have reached AUSTRALIA and GREAT BRITAIN. Following is a brief summary of the knowledge which has consequently come into possession of His Majesty's Government in the UNITED KINGDOM and AUSTRALIA regarding treatment of British and Australian Prisoners of War by Japanese Military Authorities;

All available Prisoner of War in SINGAPORE and JAVA were moved early in 1942 to BURMA and THAILAND. Australians were sent by sea to BURMA crowded into ships' holds which had been horizentally sub-divided so that the ceilings were no more than four feet high. Prisoners from the UNITED KINGDOM were sent by rail to THAILAND so crowded into steel cattle trucks that they could not even lie down during the journey. They were then marched some 80 miles. All were sent to work on the construction of a railway though primitive disease infested jungle in THAILAND and BURMA. Conditions under which all these men lived and worked were inhuman; such accommodation as was provided gave little or no protection against tropical rains or blazing sun. Worn out clothing was not replaced and soon many lacked clothing, boots and head covering. The only food provided was a panikin of rice and a small quantity of watery stew three times a day but work had to go on without respite whatever the cost in human suffering or life. The inevitable result was a dreadful deathrate, the lowest estimate being 20 per cent. These conditions continued until the railway was finished about October 1943, when those not needed for maintenance work were moved in camps in THAILAND and later to SINGAPORE on route to Japan.

The rescued men were on a ship which left SINGAPORE early in September 1944. There were probably 1300 United Kingdom and Australian prisoners on board. After she was sunk, the Japanese deliberately picked up all Japanese survivers but left the prisoners to their fate. Statements of our men constitute direct and unimpeachable evidence of the outrageous treatment by the Japanese of the defenseless prisoners of war.

I add that I communicated to His Excellency Minister SUZUKI in the letter dated 19 Nov, that the recused men from the "RAKUYO MARU" according to British information, arrived in ENGLAND and AUSTRALIA and that a public announcement would be given in both countries on the basis of the accounts of those men to the maltreatment accorded the Prisoners of War in Thailand and BURMA.

I hereby express my high regard to Your Excellency.

SWISS MINISTER.

Appendix L

A copy of the Charge Sheet in the case of MIZUTANI Totaro, who was probably the worst individual criminal connected with this railway. He was found guilty on all three charges.

Charge Sheet

The Accused

Misutani Totare Major

In the service of the Imperial Japanese Army

Attached to is charged with:—

First Charge	Committing A War Crime in that he between 18 January 1943 and 14 November 1943, in BURMA, in violation of the laws and usages of War, when engaged in the administration of British, American, Australian and Butch Prisoners of War employed in the construction of the BURMA-SIAM Railway, was concerned in the inhuman treatment of the said Prisoners of War resulting in the deaths of hundreds of the said Prisoners of War and Physical suffering of many others of the said Prisoners of War.
Second Charge	Committing A War Crime in that he in the month of July 1943, at the Camp near APALON, in BURMA, known as 83 Kilo Camp, occupied by Japanese and Prisoners of War engaged in the construction of the BURMA-SIAM Railway, in violation of the laws and usageds of War, being in the service of the occupying power, ill treated a Burmese civilian inhabitant of the occupied territory causing physical suffering to the said inhabitant.
Third Charge	Commiting a War Crime in that he on 31 December 1944 at TAMUAN Prisoner of War Camp, SIAM in violation of the laws and usages of War, killed No. 4272350 Fusilier L.W. WANTY, Royal Northumberland Fusiliers, a British Prisoners of war interned in the said camp.

Singapore

46

Commanding.........

To be tried by Military Court

Singapore

46

.............Major General

II
History of "F" Force[1]

An account of the treatment by the Japanese of 7,000 British and Australian Ps. O.W. sent to help construct the Burma/Siam Railway April, 1943-April, 1944.

Part I. History of "F" Force –By Lt. Col. S.W. Harris, O.B.E., R.A.
(Commanding 18 Div. P.O.W. Area, CHANGI)

Appendix A. Report to Military Police.
B. Report on No. 2 Camp (Sonkrai)
C. Report on Nos. 5 and 4 Camps.
D. Report on No. 5 Camp (Changaraya).
E. Statement by Acting Surgeon D. Wolfe on Konkoita.
F. Report by Lt. R.G. Fletcher.
G. Selected correspondence to and from "F" Force HQ.

Part II. Medical Report by Lt. Col. J. Huston, R.A.M.C. with Appendix A, B, C.

Annexure to Part II
Tanbaya Hospital Report
Appendix A. Tanbaya Hospital Staff
Appendix B. Sketch of Tanbaya Hospital
Appendix C. Copy of letter submitted to IJA
Appendix D. Medical Tanbaya Hospital Burma Aug 1.- Nov. 24 1943.
Appendix E. Copies of letters submitted to IJA
Appendix F. Report on Tanbaya Hospital subsequent to the departure of the main body.

1. F. No. 601/7377/Historical Section.

History of "F" Force

Introduction

1. In April 1943 a party of 7,000 P.O.W. was sent from Changi, Singapore, to Thailand. By the end of August 25 per cent were dead and 90 per cent of the remainder were sick. By December, 40 per cent of the whole force were dead and the move of the unfit remainder back to Singapore began: it was completed in April. The total dead was then approximately 3,100 or 45 per cent in the one year.
2. This party was throughout the whole period under the charge of No. 4 Bureau (Comd: Colonel Banno) of the I.J.A. Malayan P.O.W. Administration, whose headquarters were at Changi, Singapore.
3. This account is being written in a P.O.W. camp and is therefore confined to facts sufficient to establish a case and to describe steps taken by us to overcome our difficulties.
4. In order to keep the body of the report reasonably compact sufficient detail has been incluaed only to make the general narrative clear. Further details must be obtained from reports from camps and from the evidence of individuals.

Orders

5. The orders received from the I.J.A. stated that:—
   (a) The reason for the move was that the food situation in Singapore was difficult and would be far better in the new place.
   (b) This was NOT a working party.
   (c) As there were not 7,000 fit combatants in Changi, 30 per cent of the party were to be men unfit to march or work. The unfit men would have a better chance of recovery with good food and in a pleasant hilly placn with good facilities for recreation.
   (d) There would be no marching except for a short distance from the train to a nearby camp and transport would be provided for baggage and men unfit to march.
   (e) Bands were to be taken.
   (f) Gramophones, blankets, clothing and mosquito nets would be issued a the new camps.

(g) All tools and cooking gear and an engine and gear for electric light were to be taken.

(h) A good canteen would be available in each camp after three weeks. Canteen supplies for the first three weeks were to be bought with prisoners money before leaving Singapore.

(i) The party would include a medical party of about 350 with equipment for a central hospital of 400 patients and medical supplies for three months.

(j) The force was to include a H.Q.

(k) No Red Cross representative was to accompany the force nor could any Red Cross money to obtained to take with the force. Facilities would, however, be given be communicate with Singapore for this purpose if need arose.

Preparation

6. Lieut-Col. S.W. Harris, OBE, RA (Commander, 18 Div. P.O.W. Area in Changi), was accordingly appointed by British H.Q. Changi, with concurrency of Comd, A.I.F. to command the force, using 18 Div Area H.Q. as his staff. The A.I.F. contingent was to consist of 27 Inf Bde, A.I.F., plus dets to bring the strength up to the required total, Lieut-Col. C.H. Kappe, AIF, Commanding.

7. The A.I.F. contingent was to total 3,600 and the British 3,400.

8. The Force Comd. with Major Wild had several interviews with Capts. Miyasaki and Tanaka (I.J.A. Offrs i/c Changi) with regard to the force with especial relation to sub-paras (b), (c) and (d) of para 5 above, i.e. work, fitness and marching. There was a special meeting with regard to Red Cross matters. Record copy is in correspondence file. At these interviews the A.I.F. contingent would contain about 30 per cent unfit for full duties. The British contingent, however, would consist of not more than 50 per cent fit for heavy work and marching. It was also pointed out that even the so-called fit men in Changi had nearly all been in hospital as P.O.W. for one reason or another and were all without exception on the border line of disease arising from lack of vitamins (especially B, B_1 and B_1 complex) in the diet and liable to recurrent breakdowns from this cause. This was, in any case, well known to the I.J.A. from continual representations from prisoners H.Q. at CHANGI on the subject of the provision of a balanced diet and from our regular returns.

9. In the light of the above instructions H.Q. A.I.F. re-examined all their men and re-classified as fit to go a number of men previously marked unfit. This classification was, however, made in the light of the Japanese instruction, which made it appear, likely that the men accompanying the force would have a good chance of re-habilitation with good food.

For the British contingent the problem was far more complex, as British Ps.O.W. were spread over four more or less independent areas. There was also to be considered the advantage of keeping units together rather than sending off detachments under strange N.C.Os and officers. The British troops were examined before selection but the inspection did not amount to more than establishing fitness to travel.

10. It is conceivable that the I.J.A. in Changi themselves believed much of what they promised. In one particular item, however, this cannot have been the case. They stated that the purpose of the party was not for work. This must have been to their knowledge untrue and it is on them, therefore, that full responsibility for what followed must lie.

11. Orders were issued by the I.J.A. for the move of the force in thirteen trains, with Force H.Q. and all heavy baggage and medical gear in the first train. Later, at the last minute, this was altered: the first six trains were to be all A.I.F. and the later trains British. This displaced Force H.Q. and heavy baggage to Train 7- a most unfortunate change which had for reaching consequences as will be seen later.

    If the medical and other essential gear had arrived with H.Q. in Bampong on the first train there would have been nothing to prevent it being moved up into the forward area before arrival of the troops and before the rains broke, rendering the roads impassable to M.T. The whole move was also put forward by two days thus making it impossible for the A.I.F. contingent to have their second cholera inoculation before leaving.

12. All ranks were glass-rodded by the I.J.A. and instructions were issued for re-vaccination and inoculation against typhoid, plague, dysentery and cholera.

Owing to alterations in date the whole A.I.F. contingent left Changi after only one cholera inoculation and owing to short issue of anti-cholera vaccine part of the British contingent had no inoculation at all against this disease.

Train Journey

13. The force travelled to Bampong in 13 freight trains, leaving Singapore on successive nights in parties of 500-600. The accommodation was one steel box-car for approx 27 mon. The journey lasted 4-5 days. Cooked rations of rice and vegetable stew, provided at various stations, were generally inadequate, drinking water was never supplied in sufficient quantities and this caused unnecessary hardship to men travellling in such crowded conditions during the heat of the day. In particular, most train parties received no food or water during the last twenty-four hours of the journey.

Railhead-Bampong

14. On arrival at Bampong the train parties were marched to the first staging camp, about one mile from the station. This camp was in a filthy state, having previously been used by native labour gangs. An I.J.A. notice posted at the entrance in English was entitled "Camp Orders for Coolies and Prisoners of War". Accommodation consisted of large attap roofs resting on the ground,

without floors . Latrines, which were merely open trenches about six feet deep, were filthy beyond description and the whole area was insanitary as it could be. There was no water for washing and a bare sufficiency for cooking.

15. The "gunsoku" guards at Bampong were in an even more excitable state than is usual among them when a move is in progress. Detrainment was carried out to the accompaniment of blows and the usual stream of conflicting orders. In the camp itself a "gunsoku" called Toyama on several occasions thrashed prisoners, for no apparent cause, with the steel shaft of a golf club, inflicting more or less serious injuries on a number of officers and men.

16. As each train arrived it learnt for the first time that the rest of the journey was to be made on foot, starting on the evening following arrival. Distance or the number of stages were not stated.

17. All heavy kit and stores, including medical stores and tools, belonging to the force, were dumped by order of the I.J.A. in an unfenced open space at the side of the road in Bampong, and no guard was allowed. When Force H.Q. arrived by Train 7, a further dump consisting of officers; boxes and valises and men's kit-bags was in process of being formed at the roadside in front of the staging camp.

18. By this time, therefore, five train parties of the A.I.F. had already marched north of Bampong (the head of the column was, in fact, already 100 km. away) and the sixth party was due to leave that night. Nominally in control at this operation were Lieut. Fukuda and the interpreter Koriyasu, with their headquarters in Bampong. As each train commander, and, with the arrival of train 7, the force commander, objected to the march, Lieut. Fakuda made excuse that it was unavoidable.

Control on the way would, he said, be exercised by "another unit", and conditions were likely to be "cruel", but at the other end, they said "we shall be able to be your friends again." The distance, however, was not disclosed and the impression given was that it would be about forty miles. Although the ordering of any marching was a breach of faith, the information available at the moment did not in any way foreshadow the rigours of the march to come. A march of 50 miles or so in short stages under reasonable conditions would have entailed hardship for some and some casualties, but it would not have been disastrous or impossible.

19. The maximum concessions which could be obtained following protests by Col. Harris were:—

    (a) A few seriously ill men to be left in a Japanese hospital at Bampong.

    (b) A few more in an extemporised hospital in the camp. Apart from these all men had to march.

    (c) Medical stores and cooking containers were to be sorted out from the dump for priority of dispatch by lorry to destination.

(d) The dump itself to be put under a guard (but this was removed by the I.J.A. shortly afterwards).

(e) Lieut-Cols. Harris, Hutchison and Dillon and Major of Wild of Force H.Q. to go forward by M.T. to overtake the head of the column and take charge at Tarso, which was then understood to be the base camp of the final concentration area.

It was also arranged that a rear party of Force H.Q. should remain at Bampong and come forward by lorry with Lieut-Col Huston, the S.M.O. of the Force, when the last party left.

20. Permission to change Malay currency for Thai was refused. As a result on the march the only means of buying extra food and, at one camp, drinking water, was by means of selling to the Thais or I.J.A. guards personal belongings or kit which could be carried no further.

21. If Force H.Q. had arrived six days earlier by Train 1, in accordance with the original plan, it is probable that better arrangements could have been made, especially as regards medical stores and cooking containers. As it was, previous train commanders had spent only a few hours at Bampong before marching out with their men, so that there had been no continuity of command there and consequently no chance of making proper arrangements for stores left behind. The I.J.A. had available for transport twelve Marmon lorries and one ambulance. On their first run north from Bampong these vehicles carried Japanese stores: few of them completed a second run and none a third, as the monsoon rains destroyed long stretches of the road, and after 20 May no wheeled vehicle was able to reach from the south the area in which the force was finally concentrated. As a result, all the heavy equipment of the force; which had been brought from Singapore by order of the I.J.A., including all heavy cooking gear and many smaller containers, all officers' and other ranks' kit not carried on the man, most of the tools and Red Cross stores, all reserve clothing including 800 pairs of boots, canteen goods to the value of $ 2,000 (purchased by order of the I.J.A.) and three-quarters of the medical stores, was left permanently at Bampong and was not retrieved until the remnant of the force moved back to Kamburi seven months later, by which time a considered portion had been looted.

The March

22. The march lasted for about 2 ½ weeks, over a distance of roughly 300 kilometres, covered in 15 stages of about 20 kilometres each, 'Marching was-invariably done by night, between 2000 hrs and 0800 hrs. Except for the first two stages the road was merely a rough jungle track, capable of taking wheeled traffic in dry weather only. Long stretches of it were corduroyed, which, with snags and holes, made marching in the dark difficult and dangerous. Falls, resulting in sprains and even broken legs, were frequent. Control on the march was virtually impossible as all torches had been confiscated during a military

search at Bampong. At the same time., the fate of stragglers was uncertain, as Thais armed with knives hung on the tail of the column in certain areas, ready to strip off the equipment of any man who fell behind. It is probable that some at least of the 20 men still missing from the force met their end at the hands of these bandits.

23. Daily thunderstorms started on 30 April and the monsoon proper broke just after the earlier parties reached their destination. The later parties thus had to contend with even worse marching conditions. The road surface became slippery and treacherous and long stretches were flooded and oven totally washed away. The night march now frequently lasted for 14 or 15 hours instead of 12, and during the day's rest exhausted men had nowhere to shelter from the rain except on sodden ground under trees and bushes. It was unfortunately the loss fit British parties which had to contend with these worsened conditions and this undoubtedly accentuated their already inferior physical state on reaching their final camps.

24. Even trained infantry in good physical condition would have found a march of this length and in these conditions an arduous one. But this force included men of all services and of every known physical category except A.I., for even these rated fit among them had for more than a year subsisted on an inadequate diet, with consequent weakness from malnutrition. In addition there were the 2,000 and more unfit, included in the force as a result of the orders of the I.J.A. Hundreds of these were convalescents whose sole reason for being there was that the I.J.A. had guaranteed them a journey by rail and "motor-transport to a comfortable camp where rest and good rations were assured. Among them were men suffering from beri-beri, post diphtheric hearts and other ailments, which rendered their sure impossible, from the moment they were sent marching from Bampong. These unfit men, the number of whom steadily increased, proved from the first a great strain on the fit, who had to help, and even carry them from camp to camp. In addition, every party was burdened with as many small (3 and 6 gallon) containers and as much medical gear as it could carry. Thus, even those who were fit at the start of the march were seriously exhausted or themselves unfit at the end of it.

25. The staging camps were jungle clearings at the side of the road, at about 20 kilometres distance from each other, generally (but not always) near water. Accommodation consisted of a cookhouse and open trench-latrines, and flies abounded: but of shelter there was none, except in two of the fifteen camps where tents were available for about a hundred men only. Those camps were under the command of junior N.C.Os of some I.J.A., movement control organization, apparently unconnected with either the Malaya of Thailand P.O.W. Administration. These men, whose behaviour was often harsh and unreasonable, evidently had orders to push the marching columns forward as fast as possible, and the greatest difficulty was experienced everywhere in obtaining permission to leave behind even the worst of the sick.

26. Food, which consisted of rice and vegetable stew, was supplied in insufficient quantities to maintain the strength of men engaged on such a march, and water was often short. At Kanburi staging camp drinking water had to be bought by the prisoners from a privately owned well.

Lieut-Col. Harris tried to get this put right, but the abuse was not stopped until after the last party of "F" Force had passed through. When "H" Force arrived, however, some weeks later free water had become available there.

From Kanburi, Col. Harris sent back a letter to Lieut. Fukuda pointing out that a tragedy was in the making. This letter detailed the immediate steps necessary to avert disaster.

27. It was difficult for the men to obtain sufficient rest during the day time halts at these staging camps; for, apart from the lack of shelter, parties were often required to carry water or perform fatigues for the Japanese. This could have been avoided if the I.J.A. had detached permanent fatigues parties of sufficient size at each staging camp, to close up on the force when the march was completed. Such parties could also have done much to improve the sanitation of the staging camps, all of which had previously been used by coolie gangs and which became progressively worse from day to dry.

28. The strain fell particularly heavily on the Medical Officers and orderlies, as they had to attend to casualties on the line of march and hold sick parades during the day's halt, not only for their own sick but also for the steadily increasing numbers left behind by previous parties. Also at every camp the day ended and the march began with an argument with the Japanese N.C.O. as to the number of sick men to be left. The end of this was always that seriously sick men, with blistered and ulcerated feet, and such illnesses as dysentery, beri-beri and malaria, were driven out of the camp to join the marching party, often with blows.

29. At Tarso the staging camp was of the usual type, but in the vicinity was the headquarters of both the I.J.A. Railway Engineers and the Thailand P.O.W. Administration with a permanent P.O.W. camp and hospital, besides an I.J.A. hospital. Then Advance Force H.Q. reached this staring camp (which, far from being the base camp of the force, proved to be at only one-third of the distance to destination) Col Harris visited the H.Q. of the Thailand P.O.W. Administration; but his reception there was so unfavourable and indeed offensive that it was evident a breach existed between the two administrations, presumably owing to jealousy at Malaya's retention of control over "F" Force during its stay in Thailand. There was ample confirmation later that this jealousy existed, and to it can be attributed some of the misfortunes of the force, (such as the uncompleted state of the working camps—see below).

30. The proximity of the hospitals at Tarao gave rise to hopes that Force H.O. would be able to secure proper attention and accommodation there for the more seriously ill. On the night of our arrival it was necessary to restrain the

I.J.A. Corporal in charge of the staging camp from striking with a stick the sick men whom he had arbitrarily decided to send on the march. From the A.I.F. party which arrived the following morning Major Wild took 50 sick men for inspection by the I.J.A. Medical Officer at Tarso, who told the Corporal that 36 of them were quite unfit to march night. Later, a written order that these men should not be made to march was obtained from the Japanese M,0. and was convoyed by his Sgt-Major to the Corporal: but he chose to ignore it. The same evening the 36 men wore paraded and the Corporal ordered all but 10 of them to march. When Major Wild and Major Hunt, AAMC remonstrated, they were beaten with bamboos in front of the men, and a bone in Major Hunt's hand was broken. Finally 17 of these sick were forced on to the road. Of these, 3 were carried back after covering a few hundred yards, and the remainder were as usual helped or carried by their comrades to the next staging camp. Among the latter was the Rev. Ross-Dean of the A.I.F., who died at the next camp shortly afterwards.

31. Similar scenes were being enacted daily at every staging camp along the road. Hundreds of unfit were being rendered seriously ill by this treatment, and the whole force was being rapidly infected with malaria, dysentry and diarrhoea. In addition, the health and physique of the fit men also was deteriorating under the strain, so that they also were rendered more liable to infection.

32. Finally, at Konkoita staging camp, after a fortnight's marching, every party was quartered in immediate proximity to hundreds of coolies, who were suffering from some intestinal disease, of which numbers died daily. The whole area was heavily fouled and infested with a plague of flies. The I.J.A. pretended that the deaths were due to dysentery; it soon became certain that it was, in fact, cholera. Konkoita was the focal point of the infection which caused cholera to break out a few days later at all of the working crnps to which the force was dispersed.

33. At Konkoita 700 A.I.F. of Parties Nos. 1 and 2, under Lieut-Col.S.A.F. Pond, OBE, 2/29 Bn A.I.F. (Lieut-Col. Kappe, Comd A.I.F. Contingent was also in the camp but hoped to move forward), were halted and placed under the command of Lieut. Maruyama of the I.J.A. Engineers. This party of 700 was subsequently detached from the I.J.A. Administration of "F" Force and for all practical purposes came under the control of the Engineers until they rejoined the force at Nieke in December The history of that detachment will be found in its separate report made by Col. Pond.

34. Lieut-Col. Banno, the I.J.A., Commander of "F" Force, made his first appearance at Tarso on 8 May in a lorry with the British officers of the Rear H.Q. On 9 May he took on Col. Harris with them, leaving the remaining three officers of Adv, Force H.Q. to follow on when the last party left Tarso. Two stages beyond Tarso Col. Banno suddenly ordered all the officers of the Rear H.Q. to dismount from the lorry with the medical stores which they were carrying to start a wayside hospital for the marching troops, while he proceeded up the road

another 150 kilos, to Nieke with Col. Harris, This incredible action had serious results, as the services of Lieut-Col Huston were thus denied to the force during the first critical six weeks, together with the consignment of medical stores, which could not be brought up later by road owing to the breakdown of the road in the monsoon and were not brought up even by river.

Shimo-Nieke-Dispersal to Working Camps

35. Col. Banno arrived at Shimo-Nieke on 10 May by lorry, Col. Harris being the only P.O.W. with him. This was to be the H.Q. camp. It consisted of two partially roofed huts and seven large unroofed huts in a partly cleared hollow in the jungle. There was a small natural stream to provide water for all purposes. The camp had previously been occupied by coolie labour.

During the next few days some I.J.A. stores arrived from Bampong and a small hut was roofed for Col. Banno and his office. The roofed huts were occupied by I.J.A. guards.

No shelter whatever was supplied for Ps.O.W. not even for a hospital, an M.I. Room or a cookhouse.

The first batch of troops arrived on 13 May (Party 3 and remains of Parties 1 and 2) and thereafter continued to arrive daily.

Thunderstorms by this time were a daily and nightly occurrence until the monsoon proper broke in Shimo-Nieke on 17 May and spread slowly northwards. From then until well on into September rain was incessant and heavy day and night a rarity for more than four hours to pass without rain. There was one break of 24 hours in June.

36. The Force Comd protested to Col. Banno against the ircumstances of the March and the lack of roofs. No satisfactory reply was received. The most obvious necessity was for a hospital for the sick as they arrived. It was already clear that the force would arrive heavily infected with malaria, dysentery, diarrhoea and septic sores on feet and legs.

Col. Banno explained that only the H.Q., would remain at Shimo-Nieke. The remainder of the force (excluding the 700 A.I.F. left at Konoita, which was to be known as No. 4 Camp) would be distributed to other camp, which, he stated, were all roofed. Distribution was to be:-

Distribution			*Aust.*	*Brit.*
No. 1 Camp -	SHIMO(Lower)	SONKRAI	2,400	
No. 2 Camp -	SONKRAI			2,000
No. 3 Camp -	KAMI(Upper)	SONKRAI	400	
No. 4 Camp -	KONKOITA		700	
No. 5 Camp -	CHIANGARAYA			1,200
H.Q. Camp & Base Hosp.	SHIMO (Lower)	NIEKE	100	200
(100 H.Q. and 200 Medical))			3,600	3,400

37. Note. (The actual figures which had left Singapore are believed to have been: Australian 3,666; British 3,334.

By the end of May movement had temporarily ceased but the numbers had resulted approx. as follows—

		Aust.	*Brit.*	
No. 1 Camp -	SHIMO-SONKRAI	1,800		Incl dead
No. 2 Camp -	SONKRAI		1,600	Incl dead
No. 3 Camp -	KAMI- SONKRAI	400		Incl dead
No. 4 Camp -	KONKOITA	700		Incl dead
No. 5 Camp -	CHIANGARAYA		700	Incl dead
H.Q. & Hosp.	SHIMO –NIEKE (Nieke in June)	200	200	Incl dead
Still down the road, incl.		566	834	
Drivers, cooks, sick, dead		3, 666	3,334	

Outbreak of Cholera

38. On 15 May five cases of cholera were diagnosed by Capt. J.L. Taylor, MC, AAMC, a young M.O. who had not previously seen cholera, among the Australian party which had marched in from Konkoita on 14 May, having spent the previous day there. The seriousness of the outbreak was accentuated because the A,I,F. contingent and part of the British contingent were not protected against cholera (see para 12).

39. The position at that moment was (from south to north) approx, as follows :-

South of Konkoita	Brit.	3,034)
(but marching north-wards)	Aust.	766)
KONKOITA (Cholera infection centre)	Brit.	300) (Staging)
	Aust.	900) (incl 200 staging)
SHIMO-NIEKE	Aust.	1,000 (incl 5 cholera cases)
SHIMO-SONKRAI	Aust.	1,000
		7,000

Over 800 Australians from the party with the cholera cases were due to move from Shimo-Nieke to Shimo-Sonkrai on the 16th and similarly 300 British and 200 Australian ware due to move from Konkoita to Shimo-Nieke that night, another party automatically moving into Konkoita from the south.

40. The Force Comd immediately saw Col. Banno and stressing the seriousness of the situation urged:-

(a) immediate local arrangements for an isolation hospital;

(b) provision of vaccine to complete anti-cholera inoculation;

(c) absolute necessity for not allowing further uncontaminated parties into Konkoita or Shimo-Nieke camps;

(d) cancellation of move of affected Australian party from Shimo-Nieke to Shimo-Sonkrai;

(e) Col. Huston and his medical stores to be sent for immediately from Kamoi.

Col. Banno agreed to (a) and (b) but did not act on (c), (d) or (e). A definite negative was not given at the time but that evening orders for continuation of the move were issued.

41. As a result, camp to camp movements continued and the infected troops from Shimo-Nieke moved to Shimo-Sonkrai on the night 16/17th. One man actually fell out on parade with diarrhoea and died next day of cholera. Fresh cases arrived with each party from Konkoita and as infected troops moved in to Camps 2, 3 and 5 epidemic cholera broke out in each place.

42. As soon as news arrived from Camp 1 that cholera had broken out there; the Force Comd got Col. Banno to agrees-

(a) to send Major Stevens, S.M.O., A.I.F. and Major Bruce Hunt, AAMC, from Konkoita, A similar request was later received from No. 1 Camp.

(b) to send a letter of instruction to Col. Huston RAMC telling him to come forward as soon as possible.

The former was acted on at once and both officers arrived at Shimo-Nieke at 10 p.m. Major Hunt with Capt. Taylor AAMC, some medical orderlies and six British soldiers who were fully inoculated and who volunteered for cholera nursing went forward by M.T. at midnight with everything of use for fighting cholera that could he scraped together.

Major Stevens remained at Shimo-Nieke to control the base hospital.

The letter to Col. Huston was written by Col. Harris and sent by Col. Banno, but the I.J.A. private in charge at Kanto refused to act on it and would not let Col, Huston move himself or his medical stores.

43. At another conference with Col. Banno the necessity for getting cholera vaccine, medical stores of all kinds, and the need for rest (to recover from the march) and a good protein diet were all re-emphasized. The necessity for getting Col. Huston and his stores forward was again stressed.

Col. Banno, who was obviously very worried, agreed to all points and produced for the sick six tins of milk from his own private stock!

He did, in fact, produce cholera vaccine within about 10 days. In about a fortnight an irregular and inadequate meat issue was begun. Col. Huston arrived about six weeks later, but then on foot without medical stores!

Lower Nieke Hospital

44. Some 400 seriously sick gradually accumulated at Lower Nieke. Some tents were issued, with I.J.A. instructions to put them up on bamboo roof-frames, instead of attap. It was found, however, that in this way they would not keep out the rain. Most of them were old British tentage, badly perished, and the pitch of the roof was, in any case, too flat for using tentage as roofing. Accordingly, they were removed and set up inside the roofless hut frames, in which way they gave reasonable protection. The I.J.A., however, insisted on their being put back on the roofs. This stupidity was later repeated at Nieke, in spite of visual demonstration of rain pouring through, just as if no tents were there at all.

In spite of difficulties, however, Lower Nieke hospital did good work. Stringent isolation of cholera cases and suspects kept that disease in check and by the time the hospital had been cleared to Nieke at the end of June, deaths from all causes had been only two officers and 32 men, of which 19 were due to Cholera - a result achieved tlhrough unceasing effort on the part of the mixed British and Australian hospital staff and of Capt. A Barber, RAMC, on whom the bulk of the work fell.

45. On receipt of news that some parties of sick had been left in the neighbourhood of Konkoita, Asst-Surgeon Wolfe, IMD, was sent down to do what he could. A report on what he saw and did is attached at Appx "E".

Later Stages of Cholera Epidemic

46. The cholera epidemic followed its usual course in all working camps. In Lower Sonkrai, the A.I.F. put out a tremendous effort to overcome their difficulties especially to overcome the lethargy and weariness following the march) and suceeded in exterminating the disease when they had lost 110 men (6 per cent) - a supremely creditable effort, especially on the part of Major Bruce Hunt, AAMC, of which a full report will be found in Major Johnston's report.

At No. 3 Camp the A.I.F. similarly stamped out the disease reasonably quickly. At Lower Nieke and Nieke (mixed camps under direct control of Force HQ), the situation was always in hand and deaths from cholera totalled only 26 out of a strength of 1,300.

At Nieke the I.J.A. provided a small hut about half mile from camp and an isolation hospital. It was effective, although difficult to supply with food and water. Nurses, contacts and suspects were all segregated and Asst-Surgeon Wolfe took charge and lived there.

One day without warning two Tamil coolies suffering from cholera were dumped at the isolation hut and left there for us to look after. As we were always attacking the I.J.A. on the international nature of the Red Cross we protested only on the grounds that this was an unfair burden on our already overtaxed medical staff and resources and one which the I.J.A. medical service should properly have borne. Five coolie cases in all were dealt with, two of whom recovered.

At Nos. 2 and 5 Camps (Both British) the physical state of the men and the camp conditions were such that losses were more severe. Cholera deaths were-

In Camp No. 2, strength 1,600:-	227	(14 per cent)
In Camp No. 5, strength 700:-	159	(23 per cent)

The special difficulties of these camps will emerges as the report continues. By the end of June the Cholera situation within the force north of Nieke was definitely in hand. Eventually the total deaths from Cholera in the whole force were approx. 650 (or nearly 10 per cent).

Start of Working Camps

47. To visualise conditions it is necessary to remember that everything described took place in incessant rain, day and night.

Camps when occupied consisted of huts without roofs for prisoners. At no camp were the I.J.A. personnel in charge of prisoners or the I.J.A. engineers without roofs to their huts.

At Nos. 3 and 5 camps, it was found on arrival that part of the accommodation was occupied by coolies who were already suffering from cholera. At these two camps the rations were at first issued to the coolies who cooked both for themselves and the prisoners. Although this was stopped in a few days, there was another certain source of cholera infection. At No. 1 Camp, where Lieut. Takuda was in charge, with an I.J.A. civilian interpreter, Koryaru, a few days were allowed in which to set the camp in order. The advantage to be gained was largely nullified by lack of tools and the stupid insistence of Lieut. Fakuda on priority being given to non-essentials. It did, however, give to even a much needed breathing space.

At Nos. 2, 3 and 5 camps, no such break was silenced and man were put on I.J.A. work at once.

48. There occurred at this time a minor horror which deserves order. A party of 20 men under a Warrant Officer were sent from Shimo-Nieke to as advance party to from the new camp. These were actually taken off the line of fiver. Fourteen days later, when Lieut-Col. Dillon came across them, it was found that they had been pile-driving near Nieke daily from first-light until 10 p.m. Up to their armpits in cold swift-running water and whole time (except for an hour for launch) and driven with blows and sticks. They were then in a terrible units and only three were fit for any work at all. Strong represented the resulted in cessation of their work but they were too far gone and all have since led.

In all camps roofing was completed in the first two weeks by native labour, but the roofing material (attap) was so skimped that all the huts in all camps leaked sadly.

50. In Nos. 3 (A.I.F.) and 5 (British) camps, no arrangements existed for the isolation of cholera patients. All that could be done was to collect them together into one part of the prisoners huts. In No. 3 camp an isolation building as provided after about two weeks, but in No. 5 camp nothing was done until the cholera epidemic had more or less spent itself.

In all camps the "hospital" consisted merely of normal huts with always, and in some cases (No.2 camp) 16 to a bay (Bamboo plattered see sketch of ulcer ward. Appx. 'J'). No other hospital facilities whatever existed. Everything had to improvised-bed-pans from large bakes (for intravenous saline injection) from bamboo tips, tables from spilt bamboo, containers from bamboos, baskets from bamboo strips, bandages and dressing from shirtsleeves. Trouser legs, mosquito nets or from banana leaves tied on by with, short from bamboo and sacks, and any other necessary articles.

52. No light was provided by the I.J.A. and the best had to be made of light from fires in the gangways of the huts but these, of course, made extravagant use of wood and gave rise to further difficulties in wood collection.

53. The huts were full of bugs. Lice were prevalent and the overcrowding soon gave rise to scabies which became universal among men and officers. Even those who worked in camp and had opportunity for daily washing were all affected. The spread of all other communicable diseases was also ensured by this overcrowding.

Shortage of Stores

54. Only a small quantity of the medical stores, Red Cross food (a small balance from the consignment received in Changi in August 42) and a few cooking utensils and food containers which had arrived at Bampong had been brought up to Shimo-Nieke.

    Practically no tools were brought up - either belonging the prisoners or to the I.J.A. The medical stores and Red Cross food were stored by Force HQ. But Shimo-Nieke and doled out to camps in small quantities on medical recommendation.

55. What cooking utensils and containers did arrive all went with the first parties to No. 1 Camp, in the expectation of the arrival of further lorry loads. Even so, this camp was very poorly provided.

    Each party had marched from Bampong carrying some containers and medical stores. As sick accumulated at various staging camps, containers were forcibly taken by the I.J.A. from the later parties to maintain the sick and medical stores were used up in their treatment.

These later parties arrived at Shimo-Nieke therefore with very few or no containers and no medical stores.

56. As a result, Camps Nos. 2, 3 and 5 were formed with practically no containers and almost no medical stores. The I.J.A. provided little except rice boilers (Koali.), which are heavy fixtures and therefore useless for food or water distribution to hospital or to outside working parties.

In No. 3 Camp (400 Australians), which was small and compact, close to its water supply with a cookhouse near the sleeping quarters, this lack was a serious inconvenience. In No. 2 (1,800 British) and 5 (700 British) Camps it was a disaster. The former had a cookhouse a quarter of a mile from the camp, and the sick figure rose there was of-efficient means of carrying food thence 800 yards to the main hospital and to the isolation hospital yet another 400 yards.

Through the never-ending rain parts of meals were ferried all day by parties of officers and convalescents in the few buckets and containers available. No containers would be spared for use in the hospital for boiling water for sterilization of utensils anywhere in camp, thus further ensuring the spread of disease.

In No. 5 Camp the special difficulty was not the distance from the cookhouse but the fact that water had to be carried from one well over a long-and bad catch to the hospital cookhouse and the camp - the results being much the same as in No. 2 Camp. Sufficient containers were never issued by the I.J.A., even up to the end. There were few available in the "F" Force I.J.A. stores, and, in spite of pressure from cur side/no attempt was made to obtain them from the Engineers, who had plenty. One hundred ordinary buckets would have eliminated most of our serious difficulties in this regard.

57. As regards tools, a few were carried by each marching party but, as in the case of containers, the later trains were denuded of these at staging camps. I.J.A. brought up practically no tools for "F" Force- which greatly hampered-improvement work in camp. In some camps it eventually became possible to borrow some tools from the Engineers but then the process was so hedged with restrictions "that it lost a great deal of its potential value–until late September, by which has the damage, had been done.

Interpreters

58. Two of the four prisoner interpreters with the force were arbitrarily retained by N.C.Os, of the I.J.A. organisation controlling the march at unimportant staging camps, and their services were lost to the force until it re-assembled in Kanburi in December.

Working Parties

59. In all camps the I.J.A., Engineers demanded maximum numbers to work. The I.J.A. prisoners administration adopted as a principal the calculation of figures as follows:-

Other Ranks

A. Hospital Patients -

Hospital Staff -

Camp Duties -

Total A.

B. Total Camp strength -

B, minus A. - figures ordered for outside work.

60. This did not allow for any sick in lines or convalescent. They had therefore to be kept in hospital if they were not to go out to work. The keeping of these men in hospital produced a delicate position; for the I.J.A. would not recognize debility, weakness, malaria, beri-beri and trench feet, as being Incapacitating diseases.

61. If withstood beyond a certain point the I.J.A. would themselves select men at random from the unfit or arbitrarily order out a further total number, e.g.

    (a) Col. Banno himself did this more than once.

    (b) Dr. Tanio allowed men to be sent out though admittedly unfit and incapable of work.

    (c) Capt, Maruyama ordered (in writing) working parties to be augmented by sick.

It became our task therefore on the one side to struggle to obtain agreement to the lowest possible figure and, on the other, to select men best able to stand a day's work to go out from the convalescents and "lines sick."

62. In this matter, although continued and heavy pressure was maintained by us on I.J.A. H.Q, for all-round reductions in working numbers, reasonable hours, and rest days, the struggle was largely an individual one in each camp with varied and constantly varying success.

At headquarters various reports and complaints were received from other camps and were invariably put to I.J.A. headquarters in the strongest possible manner. The interviews were often stormy and threats were frequently used by the I.J.A., mostly on the lines of cutting rations, to drive more men to work.

63. Referring back to the calculation of outside numbers (para 59), it will be seen that a great deal depended in each camp on the number which the I.J.A. would agree to being retained in camp for hospital staff and camp duties.

In one camp (No. 2), the I.J.A. at first insisted on Red Cross personnel going out to work, but an appeal to Col. Banno had this decision over-ridden - one of the few promises he made and kept.

As the number of sick rose it became necessary in each camp to reinforce the Red Cross personnel with combatant personnel to look after the sick.

This was done mainly by using convalescents. No. 1 Camp (A.I.F.) pioneered the use of combatant officers as ward-masters and for hospital registry work. This practice was an unqualified success and spread to all camps.

64. Less happily, No. 1 Camp were forced by their I.J.A. officer into counting the number of combatant; officers in camp against the numbers of all ranks available for camp duties. Ostensibly this was "officers working to save their men." In fact it was to the I.J.A. merely a means to increase the number for outside work."

Once the principle had been established in No. 1 Camp pressure was immediately brought on other camps to fall into line. Previously, in these camps fit officers had been working in camp, but had been available in addition to the number of O.Rs, agreed for camp duties. The change also affected the amount of pay coming into camp.

65. In No. 4 Camp officers were sometimes made to work outside as ordinary labourers (See. Col, Pond's Report). In other camps they accompanied outside working parties only to supervise. There were one or two isolated incidents of officers being made to labour, but this was exceptional. One case occurred where an I.J.A. Engineer officer forced an officer to work at the point of the revolver. In another case an officer was sent to work for some days as punishment after torture (See statement in file. Appx F).

66. The duties allowed in camp, apart from a small office, comprised men for cremation or burial, sanitation, cookhouse, wood-collecting and cutting. As these were essentially jobs which required a particular aptitude and a considerable proficiency combined with health and strength (especially in view of the minimum numbers allowed) in no camp was it found possible to organise any system of a day to day change-over to relieve men going out to work every day. As a result, men working outside worked on day after day until they fell sick and went to hospital. As already described, there was continual selection from convalescents to replace these going sick. As a result, there was no half-way: in effect a man was ill in bed or out at work, and the deterioration in health was rapid, general and very quickly compete.

67. In camp also, multifarious duties had to be performed both for the I.J.A. find for ourselves. Ration drawing, path making, road construction in camp, latrine, logging, fence making, draining, continual building for the I.J.A., hut repairing (the huts were rotten and constantly collapsing), double-bunking, basket making, collecting firewood for I.J.A. cookhouse and guardroom, and many casual tasks. All these had perforce to be done by convalescents and by malaria patients on the days, thus remedies.

The situation would have been desperate enough even if the outside work had been a fair day's work, but the inhuman slave-driving to which the outside working men were continually subjected made the situation hopeless.

Outside Work for I.J.A. Engineers

68. The working day started with reveille and breakfast in darkness at about 0800-0700 hrs. Movement to and from meals and for purposes of nature were all in pouring rain about the muddy, ill-sited camp. Breakfast consisted of ¾ pint of plain rice. Parade for work was at first light and then the I.J.A. Engineers took over. But the members were not up to demand there was a scene on parade, sometimes ending with the striking of officers in charge. The daily task of selecting the land few men to go out from a member of convalescents really all unfit to go was heartbreaking and a tremendous strain and those whose lot it fell.

69. The party would be marched off to draw tools and then to the scene of work. This often entailed a considerable march of 5 to 10 miles. Many men (in June up to 80 per cent) were without usable boots. Marching always through deep mud with many snags in the way of rocks and charge bamboo boots. Without boots it was difficult for men to keep their feet in many places.

70. The work itself was mostly very heavy-beyond the strength of an average fully fit man and for beyond the capacity of our starved and debilitated men. Particularly severe was the portaging of legs from the mountain side to the roadway and the pile-driving and hauling for the big bribed at Sonkrai, which often entailed working in swift cold water up to the waist, sometimes even to the armpits. Obviously obeying instructions from their officers, the Engineers O.Rs. in charge of parties drove the prisoners savagely with blows from fists, boots, sticks and wire whips.

71. Protests by our officers out on the work site often resulted in their, being hit too. Visible resentment or objection were treated as mutinous and savagely punished.

72. It is necessary to emphasise that most of this continual beating was not disciplinary but was used to drive men as beasts to offer beyond their strength.

73. All the time rain poured down, making conditions more unpleasant and work more difficult. On some tasks men were often kept actively working (i.e., continually among shovels, adzes , axes etc) for three hours at a stretch without a second's break. A short interval, sometimes only a few minutes, was allowed for the midday meal–a pint of rice with a few beans.

74. Work continued until long after dark and then tools were collected and the march back began- a nightmare performance in the mud, rain and darkness. Tools had to be checked in and this was frequently made an excuse for further harsh treatment and delay. With the best will in the world, it was very difficult to collect or check tools in the darkness at the scene of work where small parties were distributed over a large jungle area.

75. At last the party would arrive back in camp at 2200 hrs or even later, tired, worn out and displicited. Numbers had again to be checked before they were dismissed to eat their evening meal (1 pint of rice and usually ½ pint of some form of vegetable stew) and turn in to their sleeping quarter-2 fit by 6 ft. or less per man-to get what sleep they could before the next day again started.

76. These who were sick had to be examined by fire-light. With there working conditions, starvation diet and with cholera, dysentery, diarrhoea, malaria, beri-beri, tropical ulcers and trench feet rife, it was not long (by the end of June) before the total number of men working outside camps from the whole force (originally 7,000 strong, was 700 men).

Efforts Towards Amerioration-Failure of I.J.A. Administration

77. The fight to break out of these evil conditions was from our side unceasing, prosecuted with every means in our power, and very slowly met with a measure of success.

78. Basically the I.J.A. attitude depended *on* orders from Tokio (with an alleged message from the Emperor) that the railway was to be finished at all costs. Secondarily, it was generally held that prisoners had no rights whatever and that prisoners from the "unconditional" surrender of Singapore, in particular, were I.J.A. chattels, and were outside the provisions of any international agreement. In addition, the I.J.A. rank and file were pumped full of lying propaganda of the bad treatment of I.J.A. prisoners by the Americans and of all Eastern races by the British, e.g., the Japanese newspapers published illustrated statements:—

(i) that the British cut off the thumbs of all Indian mill workers to prevent competition with Lancashire!

(ii) that the Americans in Guadaleanal laid Japanese wounded out in rows and deliberately ran tanks over them!

79. From our own side action was continually and urgently demanded with regard to:-

(a) Starvation diet. Full details are given in the Medical Report.

(b) Lack of medical supplies except cholera vaccine and a minimum and precarious issue of quinine.

(c) Inhuman working conditions.

(d) Lack of containers, tools and clothing, especially boot? and blankets. Only 60 per cent had blankets on leaving Singapore.

(e) Impossible working numbers.

(f) Bad accommodation, especially for hospitals.

On all these points a continual bombardment was kept up in all camps by letter and interview, and by Col. Harris at Force HQ, to Col. Banno. Appeals were made in writing to General Arimura in Singapore, to the International Red Cross at Tokio, and to the Japanese Government.

80. It is no part of this report to minimise the local Japanese difficulties: the situation was as follows:

In May railway construction was several months behind schedule and the orders from Tokio for its speedy finish entailed working through the monsoon, mid-May to mid-September.

By 20 May the road south of Shimo-Nieke had cessed to be practicable for or bullock carts and there was no hope of re-establishing it for use.

In order to maintain a railway labour force of Ps.O.W. and coolies in "F" Force area it was therefore essential to keep open the road thence northwards into Burma. In May this road was merely a track cleared through the jungle. Through lack of foresight no steps had been taken to weatherproof it before the monsoon broke.

81. The task of keeping it open by corduroy work for about half its length, and the building of bridges and culverts, was therefore essential to the maintenance

of labour for the railway in the area. Even with the work done it remained a precarious means of communication traversable at irregular intervals only by 6-wheeled lorries with non-skid chains.

82. The I.J.A. Administration of "F" Force failed utterly to cope with the situation.

(a) "F" Force itself had in the forward area about six Marmon Harrington lorries in bad condition and without, non-skid chains. These lorries could have been put into good order if the I.J.A. had either allowed us to do so or had done it themselves. They took neither of these courses in spite of much urging. Chains could have been obtained from Bampong, Singapore or Burma, at made up in the big engineers shop at Nieke. This was not done. As a result the lorries were completely wasted. When taken out they broke down and became bogged and hauling by convalescent men, who were called to the rescue. TIvJ of fact on "F" Force was that for transport it remained at the meroy of the . had to subsist on whatever they choeeto spare. As the supply of labour from "F" Force was poor, the engineers made things as difficult as they could and a vicious circle of failure was established, which the I.J.A, administration of "F" Force failed to bre-ilc.

(b) With the seasonal rise the river from Bampong became, by mid-June navigable for motor boats right up to Nieke. This line of supply was used by the I.J.A. engineers and by the local Thai shopkeepers. It could equally well have been used to bring up food, clothing and medical stores and to take down the sick. Nothing was done. In spite of continual urging by us.

(c) With a properly concerted plan they could have been organised so that regular convoys from Burma could be passed through. No such plan existed and labour was frittered away in disjointed work, much of it useless and ill-conceived.

(d) As pointed out earlier, the forcing of convalescents out to work, plus lack of food, clothing and accommodation rapidly reduced the amount of P.O.W. labour available.

(e) The failure to evacuate the sick used up a lot of effort, in all camps, which could have been usefully employed on the road.

(f) The continual brutal treatment of working prisoners by the I.J.A. engineers, long hours and no holidays for months on end, further reduced the labour available.

Responsibility

83. Col. Banno himself always expressed sympathy on the question of brutal treatment and told us again and again that he had seen the Engineer officer and that brutality would cease and shorter hours would be arranged.

In practice, he was overruled and conditions did not improve until September.

He himself, however, personally had a hand in sending unit men to work, and he continually approved of the wicked practice of issuing a starvation ration to sick men in hospital, on the grounds that this would drive them out of hospital quickly– which it did to the cemetery.

84. In Thailand there appeared to be a military command under whom was (amongst others) a Thailand P.O.W. Administration, responsible for other Ps.O.W. already in Thailand. The I.J.A., Engineers appeared to be independent of the Thailand Adm and to be the paramount authority in the "F" Force area.

"F" Force continued to be administered by the Malayan P.O.W. Adm in Singapore, and Col. Banno was the local representative of that organisation.

The Singapore office failed (if they ever tried) to intervene effectively to improve the conditions of "F" Force.

Whether the headquarters was properly informed by Col. Banno is not known but what evidence we have seems to show that it was so informed.

I.J.A. Administration Within the Force

85. The I.J.A. Adm within "F" Force attained a standard of inefficiency which is almost beyond description. A cadet officer (Onishi, promoted 2/Lt in Dec 43) who was responsible for "Q" and pay, appeared to us to be mentally deficient it is probable that much can be put down to the uselessness of this individual, but he was working right under the eye of Col. Banno and the result of his muddling was plain to see and was continually the subject of complaint by us in all camps. With the exception of Lieut. Wakabyashi, those in a position to have things put right did not do so. This especially applies to Col. Banno.

An opportunity occurred to compare Lieut. Onishi's work with that *of* another quartermaster similarly placed. In November, when "F" Force returned to Kanburi, it shared a camp with part of "H" Force - also under Malayan P.O.W. administration. Although Kanburi was a land of plenty, supplies to "F" Force were never more uncertain, and greatly inferior to supplies to "H" Force.

The issue of rations to "F" Force was never on a fixed scale, but was on an iniquitous "present" system, by which we were at the mercy of dishonest storekeepers. Peculation among the Korean gunsoku in charge of stores was universal. This was pointed out again and again to Lieut. Onishi and Col. Banno.

They constantly asserted that the ration issued to the P.O.W. was the same as that issued to the I.J.A. This was a flagrant lie. Very often, and for long periods, the P.O.W. ration was not half that drawn by the I.J.A. in rice, and in other commodities was similarly on a reduced scale. For example, in Nieke (Col. Banno's own camp), when one bullock was killed, half the dead weight was taken for 40 I.J.A., leaving the poorer half, consisting mostly of bones, for 1,000 P.O.W. This was pointed out to Col. Banno and to Lieut. Onishi more than once.

On the "A" side, matters were mainly in the hands of a civilian interpreter, Mr. Saji. His attitude towards the P.O.W, varied from time to time, but his authority derived only from the idleness of the officers over him.

The I.J.A. were entirely dependent on us for records, but it was clear that some effort was directed to obscuring the real position from Tokio; e.g., all deaths from dysentery were reported as from "diarrhoea" to save office work, the former being a disease that demanded special reports. This interpreter often acted in that capacity at interview with Col. Banno, Lieut. Onishi and others. Sometimes (as in matters of pay) he was most helpful; at other times he took an extreme anti-P.O.W. attitude.

86. Again and again we pressed the question of Japanese international obligations under the '06 and '07 agreements and asked how they thought Japan would be able to explain things away. The answer always was that a victorious Japan would not have to explain to anybody, and this appeared to summarise the attitude of all Japanese officers, except Lieut. Wakabyashi.

The Burma Hospital Project

87. Shortly after arrival at Shimo-Nieke, Col. Harris pointed out that no amenities existed for the establishment of a base hospital and suggested that all sick should be immediately evacuated to Tarso or Bampong. He also pressed to be allowed to visit all camps as soon as they were established. This was refused, but on 27 May Col. Dillon was allowed to accompany Col. Banno on a flying visit to No. 1, 2 and 3 Camps.

88. As a result of information then collected and information received from No. 5 camp, Col. Harris again saw Col, Banno on 2 Jun and stressed the seriousness of the situation pressing for the immediate evacuation of the bulk of the seriously sick (about 3,000.) to Bampong. Col. Banno stated that it was impossible while cholera continued and that it would still be impossible to do such an evacuation by road, even after the monsoon. Col. Harris then urged chat it should be done by river as soon as the water was high enough.

This project was considered at length by the I.J.A. and on 23 and 24 Jun Col. Harris was allowed to visit all four camps forward of Nieke and reported to Col. Banno on his return. His report of the deplorable conditions, especially in No. 5 Camp, is attached at Appx "F". The I.J.A., at last produced another project to open a hospital in Burma.

89. Orders were eventually issued for the evacuation of a staff and 1,700 patients to a camp at Tanbaya in Burma by road and rail through three staging camps to be established at Changaraya (No. 5 Camp), Kando and Ronshi. The I.J.A. gave assurances that the hospital would be provided with medical stores and good rations. Road and rail movement tables, which were perfect specimens of their kind, were issued by the I.J.A., and on 30 Jul the advance party of staff moved. Thereafter followed the normal Japanese administrative mess. In

no single instance were the movement tables adhered to and the journey was carried out under most distressing and inhuman conditions, which added greatly to its unavoidable hardships to the sick. These additional hardships were due to no other causes than Japanese inefficiency and callousness and sometimes active and bestial courtesy. Evacuation to Burma dragged on through August and was not completed until September.

90. The selection of patients to go was exceedingly difficult. It was no good sending these who would not survive the journey; on the other hand those who were not sent would surely die if retained in our working camps. The patients themselves were almost without exception eager to take their chance and go.

The selection was of course made without pre-knowledge of the unnecessarily evil conditions under which the journey would be made. 43 out of the 1,700 patients died on the journey.

91. The Tanbaya hospital itself consisted of a hutted camp without light or water or any special amenities. The amount of medical stores issued were infinitesimal and rations were at all times poor, being particularly deficient in Vit.B, which was vital to the treatment of the patients (debilitated from dysentery malaria and tropical ulcers), practically every one of whom, suffered from beri-beri in one form or another.

Approximately 750 patients died in Tanbaya, or about 45 per cent of the total.

92. The outcome was a bitter disappointment, but at least the remaining 55 per cent were saved from inevitable death in the working camps. On one point the I.J.A. kept their word-Tanbaya was not called upon to supply outside working parties. Convalescents were thus at least given a chance to recover if and when they had managed to survive their actual illnesses.

The story of the hard struggle against disease and death at Tanbaya by the medical staff, headed by Major Bruce Hunt, AAMC, is given in detail in the report on Tanbaya Hospital (Annexure).

Lieut. Col. G.T. Hutchison, NC, RA (GSOI18 Div) was appointed Adm Commandant of the hospital camp and his report is appended (Part II Annexure Appendix F).

Reorganisation North of Nieke

93. No sooner had the move of the advance party to the Burma Hospital started then an order was received to close Nieke, Shimo-Sonkrai and Changaraya and to re-group at Sonkrai and Kami-Sonkrai in such a way that each camp could provide approximately the same number of working men: a figure of 800 from each camp was mentioned. Patients and staff for Burma were ordered to remain in the old camps until moved. The men who-were so ill that they had not been selected for Buma were also to stay. Most of these were expected to die. This order was received at 1400 mtrs on 2 Aug. and the move was ordered

to be completed on the following day. It involved marching through rain knee-deep in ...mud, carrying all personal kit, cooking and medical and, with all patients other than those booked for the Burma Hospital or too ill to be sent there.

Col. Harris protested strongly against the order. He pointed out that the Burma project catered for only half our sick, the remainder (about 1,700) would be left on our hands and, apart from the difficult and inhumanity of moving them, the figure of 800 working men from each camp was beyond all possibility: about half that number might with difficulty be found.

In the end we were forced to carry out the move. All sick (except those mentioned above as remaining) had to be get out of bed and, marched to the next camp. We did obtain the slight concession that these sick should stage at Shimo-Sonkrai and Sonkrai on successive nights on the journey to Kami-Sonkrai. This engagement was, however, broken forthwith by the I.J.A., and they were forced to march straight through. There is no doubt that a number of the deaths which occurred subsequently at Kami-Sonkrai were directly attributable to this march.

94. In order to balance the number of working men available at the two re-organised forward camps it was necessary to create mixed camps of fitter Australians with the less fit British.

95. Kami-Sonkrai, commanded by Col. Kappe, A.I.F., had as its I.J.A. Commandant Lieut. Fukuda. This remained until the end a disgraceful camp from the point of view of I.J.A. responsibility and had during August, September and right through October a very heavy death roll (See Col. Kappe's report, Appendix "C", and the report to Military Police (Appx "A"). The other camp, No. 2 at Sonkrai, was at first in even worse case, but after the general clearance of the bulk of the worse of the patients by death (averaging 10 a day throughout August), and by transfer to the Burma Hospital, the situation greatly improved. To this camp also was posted Lieut. Wakabyashi, who was the only Japanese Officer with whom "F" Force had to deal who showed the slightest glimmerings of humanity or understanding of his responsibility towards the Ps.O.W. under his charge.

96. About 20 Aug. Lieut. Wakabyashi came to Col. Harris and stated that he had orders from Engineers H.Q. that unless the working figure produced by both camps was doubled all prisoners, sick as well as fit, would be turned out into the jungle to fend for themselves, thus making room for coolies who could work to be brought in. This threat also applied to Kami-Sonkrai. To his credit must be said that Lieut. Wakabyshi was obviously thoroughly ashamed in having to repeat this order.

A few days later the Colonel commanding the Engineers visited Sonkrai and Lieut. Wakabyashi created an opportunity for Col. Harris, with Col. Dillon end Major Wild, to approach him on the subject direct. The attitude of the Engineer Colonel was at first most unencouraging, but after great perseverance Major Wild, speaking for Col. Harris, managed to persuade him into allowing us to retain part (about two-thirds) of our accommodation, leaving the remainder available for fresh labour. It is emphasized that the project of turning us out into the jungle was a real one and would have been carried out if it had not been for the interview, in spite of the fact that the monsoon was in full flood. It is a grim recollection that we were able to promise to make available a third of our accommodation only by taking into consideration the number of deaths which would inevitably occur in the next few weeks.

97. About 20 Sep. the monsoon started to peter out and conditions began to improve, which improvement was maintained at a slow rate until, the force was finally withdrawn to Kanburi en route to Singapore in November.

Canteen Supplies

98. Canteen supplies were at all times in very short supply. There was one small shop across the main river from Nieke, from whence the goods had to be ordered and brought up by elephant to Sonkrai. They were distributed to the two forward camps, volunteer parties of officers and men carrying for the goods the remaining four miles to Kami-Sonkrai.

Finance

99. (a) **Officers.** When the Force left Singapore the officer had been paid up to the end of February. They did not receive pay for March, April and May until well on into June. In the meantime the only money possessed by the Force was its central, fund, amounting to some $ 12,000, but, as none of this was changed into Thai currency, it was useless. Throughout the period in Thailand officers continued to receive pay at $ 40 or $ 50 a month, forty per cent being deducted for the purchase of extra food for hospitals under schemes which varied as the situation altered.

(b) **Combatant O. Rs.** Working pay was paid to men who worked. It averaged about twenty per day per-working man, or one-fifth of the prevailing rate to coolies working under identical conditions. Here again the practice varied from time to time and in different camps, but as a general rule some system of pooling by camps was in force.

(c) **Red Cross O. Rs.** These drew rates varying from $ 10 to $ 20 per month. They were allowed to draw their full pay, as the burden on the hospital staffs was tremendous and it was felt that the little they could purchase with this money helped to keep them fit to work and thus the camps benefited more than if the money had been pooled.

Return to Singapore

100. In November the Force was moved back - first to Kanburi over the Thai railway and later by Bangkok-Singapore railway to Singapore. The arrangements for the first part of this journey were disgraceful, no attempt being made to provide reasonable amenities, food or water for the fit or sick,

and fourteen men perished on this journey. The arrangements for the second part of the journey had not improved since April and were as described in para 13.

Residue hospitals were left in Burma and Kanburi and finally returned to Singapore in May 44.

Morale

101. As may be imagined, under the terrible circumstances displayed in the foregoing report the bonds of discipline and morale were stretched to breaking point - but they never quite broke. If they had, probably not one man would have returned alive. The Australian half of the Force suffered 28 per cent, deaths while the British half suffered 61 per cent. The reasons for this difference may be summarised as follows:-

(a) The Australian officers and men were all members of one volunteer force with a common emblem and outlook. The British portion was heterogeneous collection of men of all races and units, many of whom found themselves together for the first time.

(b) The average physical standard of the small volunteer Australian force was incomparably higher than that of the mixed force of regular soldiers, territorials, militiamen, conscripts and local volunteers who formed the British half. As will be noted from the earlier paras, referring t o selection, it was possible for the A.I.F., to maintain a far higher standard of fitness for selection for this particular force than could the British half.

(c) The A.I.F. had among them a higher proportion of men who were used to looking after themselves under "jungle" or "bush" conditions.

(d) The Australian contingent was fortunate in completing its march and occupying its working camps before the monsoon broke.

(e) It so happened that at the main Australian camp there was a Japanese officer of the P.O.W. Adm in charge, whereas at Sonkrai and Changaraya there were only military auxiliaries of Private rank and in the latter cases therefore the local engineers were able to give free rein to their brutality.

Report to Military Police

102. At Kanburi the Military Police visited the camp after Col. Harris had left for Singapore and demanded a report on conditions in Thailand. The P.O.W. Adm. represented at that moment in Kanburi by Lieut. Fukuda, were aware that request had been made and demanded that a copy should also be given to them.

Col. Dillon and Major Wild prepared the report at Appx "A" and handed it over. This report has never been answered or challenged. We did, however, receive orders to destroy all copies of it; which, of course, was not done. It will be noticed that it is stressed in the opening para, that it is neither a complaint nor a protest, but a statement of fact. These were included only to evade the rule which the P.O.W. Adm had made that complaints and protests would only be handed to them.

103. At Appx "G" is a selection of letters written by the Force Comd, Col. Harris, to I.J.A. Camp Comd, Col. Banno, Gen. Arimura, the International Red Cross at Tokio, and one to the Tokio Government. This last letter may or may not have been sent to Japan, but the officers concerned were not in fact shot. They were court-martialled and imprisoned in Outram Road Gaol, Singapore.

Appendix A

Report on Conditions of Prisoners of War in Thailand May to December, 1943

Introduction

The representative of the I.J.A. Military Police has required a frank report to be made on the recent conditions of Ps.O.W. in Thailand with suggestion for the improvement of conditions for Ps.O.W. generally.

Accordingly, this report is made in two parts: I. Facts and II. Suggestions.

Part I is neither a complaint nor a protest, but a statement of facts, all of which can be substantiated by officers who were present.

The suggestions in Part II are made in the sincere hope that the conditions of Ps. O.W. will improve in future, since it is our firm belief that our recent experiences have not been in accordance with the policy or intentions of the Imperial Japanese Government in Tokyo or of the Japanese Red Cross, who cannot have been aware of the actual state of affairs in Thailand.

I. Facts

1. Early in April orders were issued to prepare 7,000 Ps. O.W. for a move by train. The orders stated that:—
   - (a) The reason for the move was that the food situation in Singapore was difficult and would be far better in the new place.
   - (b) This was NOT a working party.
   - (c) As there were not 7,000 fit combatants in Changi, 30 per cent of the party were to be men unfit to march or work. The unfit men would have a better chance of recovery with good food and in a pleasant hilly place with good facilities for recreation.
   - (d) There would be no marching except for a short distance from the train to a near-by camp and transport would be provided for baggage and men unfit to march.
   - (e) Bands were to be taken.
   - (f) All tools and cooking gear and an engine and gear for electric light were to be taken.

(g) Gramphones, blankets, clothing and mosquito nets would be issued at the new camps.

(h) A good canteen would be available in each camp after three weeks. Canteen supplies for the first three weeks were to be bought with prisoners' money before leaving Singapore.

(i) The party would include

This amounted to the equivalent of about 15 railway truck loads of stores and baggage.

3. The march, in fact, was one of 300 kilometres in 15 stages and lasted 2 ½ weeks. Marching was at night along a rough jungle track (except for the first two stages) and as all torches had been taken from all P.O.W. during at Bampong, control by P.O.W. officers and N.C.Os. was difficult or.

4. After the first stage the unfit men became increasingly ill and were a heavy handicap to the other men, who were first fairly fit but rapidly themselves became ill and exhausted as they had to help and even carry the increasing number of men who were unable to walk unaided.

5. Conditions at the staging camps were:

(a) At no stage was overhead cover provided except for a few tents (for 100 men) at one camp. The weather was variable and the rainy season started while the march was in progress.

(b) Food supplied was generally very poor and in many camps consisted of rice only.

(c) Water was short at many camps and at Kanburi drinking water had to be brought by the prisoners from a privately owned well. Col. Harris protested but the matter was not put right.

(d) No proper arrangements existed for retaining sick at these Camps and men who were absolutely unfit to march (owing to disease and weakness) were beaten and driven from camp to camp. Officers, including medical officer who begged and prayed for sick men to be left behind were themselves beaten at many camps. In one particular case a Japanese medical officer (Lieutenant) ordered the I.J.A. corporal in charge of Tarso staging camp to leave 36 sick men behind as they were too ill to move. The corporal refused to obey this order, although it was repeated in writing, and a British officer interpreter (Major) and an Australian doctor (Major) were severally beaten when they protested. A bone in the doctor's was broken. Of these sick men who were compelled to march nearly all have since died, including an Australian chaplain who died at the next camp. (The Japanese Medical Officer had particularly said that the chaplain should not march as he was an elderly man with a weak heart and was already at the end of his strength.

(e) The men marched all night, as a rule from 7 p.m. to 7 a.m. They had to perform camp duties, get their meals and wash during the day and so had very little rest.

6. **Medical**

(a) Such medical stores as had been hastily selected at Bampong and carried by hand with the marching parties were rapidly used up and the march continued with no medicine at all.

(b) Dysentry and diarrhoea broke out in all parties and exhaustion was general. Ulcerated feet occurred in large numbers, due to sick men with blistered feet being forced to march on day after day.

7. At Konkoita the marching parties were quartered in the same camp as a Thai labour corps, who were suffering from cholera. The infection was picked up by each of the thirteen parties of marching prisoners.

8. On 15 May cholera broke out at Shimo-Nieke

Col. Harris (Commander of the Ps.O.W.) immediately reported to Col. Banno, the I.J.A. commander, and requested that movement should cease until the outbreak was under control and that Konkoita Camp should at all costs not be used for further parties. Unfortunately Col. Banno was unable to comply with this request and, as a result, cholera was spread into all five camps occupied by the force.

9. Only a very small quantity of the medical stores at Bampong was later brought up by lorry (over three-quarters of it was still in Bampong when the force returned to Kamburi in December). The I.J.A. were unable at this time to produce any medical supplies whatever but Col. Banno gave as six tins of milk of his own property.

10. By the end of May about 5,000 men had been distributed to several different camps. These camps consisted of huts without roofing, although the rainy season had now fully started and rain was falling heavily every day and night. The camps were not fully roofed for some weeks, during which time the men had no proper shelters; consequently deaths from pneumonia were numerous.

11. In spite of the above conditions, the general state of exhaustion of the men, the presence of epidemic cholera in all camps and practically universal malaria, diarrhea and dysentery, the men were put to work by the Engineer at once.

12. Maximum numbers of men were taken out to work every day. This left insufficient men in camp for sanitary duties and for nursing the sick, while disease of every kind increased rapidly. In some camps Red Cross personnel were forced to go out to work on the road, but this was quickly stopped by Col. Banno.

13. In several camps a great scarcity of tools made improvements to sanitation difficult or impossible. The tools which the prisoners had brought from Changi, and which were part of the heavy baggage in Bampong, were never brought up.

14. It was clear to all prisoners officers that if the Engineers continued to take all fit and convalescent men to work every day there would be no men at all fit to work. In fact, the Engineers were rapidly discouraging their only available source of labour.

This aspect was explained to our own I.J.A. Headquarters, who clearly agreed that they were apparently unable to prevent the Engineers doing as they liked.

The task in front of the Engineers and the need for speed were fully understood by us, but the destruction by the Engineers of their only available labour was just as bad from their point of view as from ours.

A little common-sense on the part of the Engineers could, early in June, have saved the situation for us and for themselves.

Unfortunately for us this short-sighted policy continued, and by the end of June only about 700 of the 6,000 men north of Nieke were at work daily, and of those at least half were unfit and useless for heavy work. Of the remainder, except for Red Cross personnel, and a small number of administrative personnel (including officers), all men were lying ill in the camp hospitals.

15. By ths time the road from the South was impassable and to the North was difficult, and the scale of rations fell to below the level required to keep fit men in health and far below the level required to help sick men back to health. It has been said that we were on the same rations as I.J.A. soldiers, this is not true as can very easily to proved.

The rations of men in hospital were fixed at far too low a scale except cholera vaccine and quinine, which were always supplied as repaired..In our opinion this was a great mistake and we continually said so to the I.J.A.

There seemed to be an idea that the lack of pay and rations would drive men out of hospital, but this, of course, would happen only if the men were not really ill. There was, however, no deception about the illness of our men and men were dying in large numbers.

The work was often beyond what could reasonably be expected of fit men and it was certainly beyond the strength of our weakened men. This especially relates to the carriage of heavy logs. It was noticed that where Thai or Burmese labour was used two and three times the number of men were used.

It became common for our men to be literally driven with wire whips and bamboo sticks throughout the whole working day. Hitting with the fist and kicking also occurred frequently throughout the day. It is emphasised that this beating was not for disciplinary purposes but was intended to drive unfit men to efforts beyond their strength.

17. The hours of work were also excessive. Fourteen hours a day was a common occurrence and work went on day after day without a break for months. Many men never saw their camp in daylight for weeks on end and never had a chance to wash themselves or their clothes.

18. In some camps where the number of fit men fell below the Engineers demands, the Engineers themselves came into the camp and forced prisoners out of hospital to work.

Except in isolated instances officers were not made to work outside camps but the Engineers often used the threat that officers would be taken for work if more men were not turned out from hospital.

19. At Sonkrai, where conditions were probably worse than anywhere else, the I.J.A. Engineer Officer Lieutenant Abe, himself came into the officers' quarters and, asking to see the six officers who were most seriously ill (of whom three subsequently died), said "unless 150 more men are produced for work tomorrow I will send my soldiers to take these officers out to work". This Engineer Officer was conscious at all times infailing to stop brutal treatment of prisoners by his men even when it happened in his presence.

Of the 1,600 men who originally went to Sonkrai Camp in May 1,200 are already dead and 200 more, are still in hospital, of whom many are not expected to recover. Many petitions and appeals were made to Lieut. Abe, but he treated them with contempt.

The result would have been worse if it had not been for the arrival of Lieutenant Wakabayashi (of the Malaya Prisoner of war administration in Sonkrai camp at the beginning of August. From the date of his arrival the situation in that camp gradually improved.

20. By July more than half the force were without boots and this caused a large number of poisoned feet, and "trench foot", from continual work in the wet.

Blankets were not issued as promised (at Changri) to the men without them. (Later in August some blankets and sacks were issued and more in Kamburi in November).

Clothing issues were negligible. Issues of medical stores were totally inadequate. Bandages and dressings "were seldom issued, and only in very small quantities. For hundreds of tropical ulcer cases, dressings were improvised from banana leaves, and bandages from the sleeves and legs cut from men's shirts and trousers. Consequently many limbs had to be amputated unnecessarily and many patients died.

21. By the end of July the road from Bampong was still impassable but although the river was open to traffic and was in use by the I.J.A., and Thai shopkeepers, our medical and other, stores at Bampong were still not brought up and, in the end, were never brought up. This was in spite of our repeated requests.

22. It was during the foregoing period-that several men, sometimes alone, sometimes in groups, disappeared into the jungle. Some probably had some idea of escaping, some undoubtedly only left so as to die in freedom rather than in captivity by disease and ill-treatment. The men on the whole in despair. The choice in front of them seemed to be death from disease, or never ending toil and brutal treatment at the hands of the Engineers...

Their officers were unable to protect them in spirt of all their efforts. One party of officers, seeing their men dying and ill-treated all around them, and in despair of being able to get any redress from the I.J.A., attempted to escape so as to let the world know what ws happening to the prisoners and obtain help from the International Red Cross.

The party failed, as was inevitable. Five perished from privation in the Jungle and the remaining four were recaptured.

23. In August a hospital ws established in Burma and about 2,000 men were sent there. Unfortunately the rations were still deficient of the necessary vitamins and 800 men died. Nevertheless, the Burma hospital did great good for there was not Engineer work and therefore many men had a chance toget well slowly.

24. From August onwards things improved at Sonkari, but did not imporve much at Kami-Conkari. As late as October, for instance, the Engineers there were blasting in a quarry just behind the prisoners hospital in such a way that rocks and stones fell on the hospital huts at each blast. The huts were crammed full of patients, many of whom were in a dying condition. (About 8 a day were dying). All patients were terrorised, many were hit and more or less seriously injured, and one man had his arm broken and subsequently died from the combination of the injury and his previous sickness. This went on for over a week before representations by the I.J.A. officer in charge of the camp were successful in stopping it. Blasting continued but in such a way that rocks did not fall on the hospitals, thus showing that the previous practice had been avoidable.

In this camp also the latrine used by several hundred Tamil labourers was within ten yards of the prisoner officers' quarter. The Tamils had suspected cholera and small pox at the time.

25. In all camps accommodation was totally inadequate. Men slept actually touching each other and as a result skin disease infection was 100 per cent throughout the force. Except in Sonkari most officers were as badly off as the men.

26. The move back to Kanburi took place in November but the men were in such a state that (although the worst cases were left in Burma) 46 died on the train journey and 186 more in the first three weeks in Kanburi, in spite of better food and liver conditions.

It is certain that several hundreds more will die in the next month or two from the results of their treatment in Thailand.

27. Our guards on the whole treated us well.

Face slapping of prisoners of all ranks was discouraged by our I.J.A. officers, but ws still fairly common. It nearly always arose from a language misunderstanding and was not in itself serious, although it makes the maintence of discipline very difficult for the prisoner-officers when their men see them slapped by young Japanese privates. Similarly, when the men are slapped and beaten it merely breeds resentment and bad felling, which will last long after the war.

There are some guards, however, who seem incapable of being put in sharge of any task without losing their tempers and hitting prisoners.

The most flagrant case is that of a Gunsoku, Toyama, who claims to be a well-educated men. At Bampong he hit officers and men of every party with a heavy steel-shafted golf-culb. He cut one Major's head open, badly damaged another Major's arm and severely hurt many others. The causes of these assaults was never known. Later at Shimo-Sonkrai and at Kami-Sonkrai camps he habitually hit officers and men on every possible occasion for no just cause. He had an ungovernable temper and is apparently uncontrollable by his own officer. Apart from actual striking, he was always at pains to be insulting officers, especially senior officers. Such a man should never be allowed to be in charge of prisoners.

28. There were many cases latterly in which our own guards prevented Engineers from maltreating prisoners.

29. It may be thought that some of the above report is exaggerated. It is, however, only the barest outline of a period of intense hardship suffered by a party of prisoners. of war.

If proof is wanted it is surely sufficient to point to the fact that of the 7,000 prisoners who left changi, in April, now; in December, about 3,000 are dead. 3,000 more are hospital patients or convalescents, of whom hundreds more will die in the next few months from the result of the hardships they have undergone.

30. We know from letters received from England and Australia that it is believed there that prisoners-of-war are being well treated by the Japanese. If the actual facts regarding Thailand were known abroad, the news would be greeted with indignation and amazement.

II. Suggestions

General

We ask firstly that we should be treated in accordance with the letter and spirit of the Geneva and Hague Convention, particularly those of 1906 and 1907, both of which were ratified both by Britain and Japan.

It has been suggested that the unconditional surrender of Singapore places the prisoners from Singapore outside the terms of the Hague Convention. This is obviously not so.

The position of any prisoner who is captured on the field of battle is clearly that of unconditional surrender, but no one would suggest that he is not covered by the Convention. How then can the nature of Singapore's surrender (which was correctly made at the written request of General Yamashita "in order to avoid the further useless loss of life on both sides and especially the lives of civilians in the city") put the garrison of Singapore outside the terms of the Convention?

Detailed Suggestions

The following detailed suggestions are all consequent on this general one.

1. "Doctors and Red Cross personnel are not prisoners of war and should not be treated as prisoners". (Geneva Convention, 1906, Article 9).
2. "Prisoners should be humanely treated". (Annex to Hague Convention, 1907, Article 4).
3. "Work should not be excessive. (Annex to Hague Convention, 1907, Article 6).
4. "Prisoners should be treated as regards rations, quarters and clothing on the same footing as the troops of the government which capture them". (Annex to Hague Convention 1907, Article 7).

Note 1. All the above Articles were broken in Thailand.

Note 2. As regards rations, it is not enough to fix a scale of rations: the essential is that the rations should reach the prisoners. It is suggested that the military police undertakes the duty of seeing that the scale of issue allowed does in fact reach the prisoners.

Note 3. As regards quarters and clothing it should be remembered that officer prisoners pay for their quarters.

5. "Officers must not be employed for labour". (This equally applies to being threatened with labour). (Annex to Hague Convention, 1907, Article 6).

   There were not many occasions when officers of this party were made to labour, but it was known to all of us that many hundreds of officers in other parties were forced to work as labourers on road and railway construction in organized gangs. This treatment of officer prisoners of war is without precedent in the whole history of modern war, besides being a direct breach of the Hague Convention. It will not be forgotten or forgiven for a hundred years.
6. "Red Cross representative should be allowed to visit POW camps". (Annex to Hague Convention, 1907, Article 15).

   No representative were allowed to visit us in Thailand.
7. "Proper arrangement should be made to collect deceaseds' effects". (Annex to Eague Convention, 1907, Article 14).

   This has not been done and many effects have, as a result been lost.
8. "Soldiers should be respected and taken care of when sick". (Geneva Convention, 1906, Article 1).

   This was often broken in Thailand when sick men were forced to go to work.
9. Games, entertainments, reading, educational classes and lectures should be encouraged to keep up morale.

10. Arrangements for letters to and from home should be improved. Letters arriving are a year old and we have not been allowed to write a single letter home, but only a few lines on a postcard twice in two years.

    Prisoners of war in all belligerent countries in Europe are allowed to write as follows:

    Officer: Two letter and two postcard each month.

    Other ranks: One letter and one postcard each month.

Appendix B

Report on No. 2 Camp (Sonkrai)

Trains Nos. 7, 8 and 9, totaling 900 all ranks, arrived at SONKRAI on the morning of 20 May 1943 after a march of 315 km.

The camp consisted of three huts, approximately 150, 200 and 250 ft. long. The I.J.A. gaurds, P.O.W. officers and W.Os. were quartered in the smallest hut; the other two, which were roofless, being occupied by ORs. Adequate latrines were already in existence, as was also a cookhouse, but "Kawalis" had to be installed before a meal could be prepared. Only twelve containers (six gallon) were brought up, this shortage, which was never remedied, caused endless difficulties.

The 21 May was spent in clearing up the camp. Large quantities of tree toppings and scrub being removed from between huts.

On the 22 May 600 men sent out to work on the railway. On the final stage of the march the men had marched for five consecutive nights, becoming in most cases quite exhausted, and had the I.J.A., given the men a few days rest or arrival there is no doubt that the subsequent death rate would not have been nearly so high.

On the 23 May, Lt-Col. Pope with 700 men of Trains Nos. 10 and 11 arrived, bringing the camp strength up to 1,600. Lt. Col. Pope assumed command of the camp, but on 6 Jun relinquished it owing to ill health to Lt. Col., A.T. Bangston. Lt-Col. Pope subsequently died in Burma.

Cholera broke out on 23 May and by the end of the month 63 deaths had occurred. The monsoon was approaching and rain was increasing daily, but it was over a fortnight after arrival before the Burmese finished roofing the large huts. This lack of roofing caused great hardship to the men, who, coming wet from working parties, were never to dry their clothes and this constant living and sleeping in wet clothes and bedding, reduced their resistance to disease.

As more and more men fell sick from Cholera, dysentery, beri-beri, fever and a form of trench foot, it became increasingly difficult to find the number demanded sick men had to be turned out for work until finally 65 to 70 per cent of working parties consisted of sick men. Repeated representations were made for the reductions of working parties without effect, the difficulty being that there was only a sergent i/c I.J.A. administrative party, whereas there was a Lieutenant i/c Engineers, who overruled all objections, flatly refused reductions and threatened that if working figures demanded were not produced, his men would go into the huts and fetch the sick out themselves.

By mid-June the ration situations, never good (the main ration being rice and onion or bean stew) had deteriorated to such an extent that a party of 50 men had to be sent to No. 5 Camp to collect rations, the bullock carts used having to be pulled by the men themselves as the bullock were exhausted and the road was impassable to lorries. The I.J.A. also ordered that sick men were to be reduced to two meals daily, the working men continuing to receive full rations. This was done partly in an endeavour to force more men out to work and partly due to ration shortage.

On 7 June two parties of five respectively escaped. The larger party was recaptured in September, but nothing has since been heard of smaller party. Little excitement was shown by the I.J.A. over this escape.

The last, and 20st, death from cholera occurred on 16 June, but as the cholera cases decreased the dysentery, fever and ulcer cases increased until there were over a thousand men sick in lines of hospital, which figure remained constant until the evacuation of sick to Burma. On 20 June Lieut. Fakuda addressed the officers and informed them that the high death and sickness rote were due to bad camp sanitation and to the fact that the men did no P.T. From the beginning of July Lieut. ABE and an I.J.A. medical officer inspected the hospital, and, inspite of protestations by M.O. ordered 50 more sick men to be sent out on working parties. The death rate then was 230.

A camp duties figure of 171 had been agreed to by the I.J.A., but, owing to their excessive demands for working parties, some of this total, which included sanitation squad, cooks, water carriers etc., had to be sent on I.J.A. work and replaced by sick men, until finally, except for a few cooks, the camp was worked entirely by sick men. The position finally became so acute that for some weeks officers were carrying all rations to the hospital and isolation camps, no fit men or sick men strong enough to carry full containers being available.

On 5 July eight officers and one O.R. escaped, four being subsequently recaptured, the others dying in the jungle. All officers had their kits searched, their money confisated and were confined, under guard, to their quarters without food for thirty-six hours. The O.C. Camp was told that if another escape occurred he would be shot, as he was considered responsible by the I.J.A.

Cases of ill-treatment of men by I.J.A. engineers were frequent, representations to Lieut. ABE being totally ignored, as also were requests for the reduction of the number of men demanded for work and of the number of working hours the men leaving for work at daybreak and invariably returning soaking wet after dark.

The rations improved slightly in the latter half of July, but were always inadequate, except for rice, for working or sick man. The container and cooking pot situation steadily deteriorated as "kawalis" were out and were not replaced by the I.J.A.

On 2 Aug, Force H.Q. moved up from NIEKE and Lieut-Col. Dillon took over command of the camp. On 25 Aug the first party of sick left for the Burma Hospital at TANBAYA, by which date the death roll numbered 562 and had risen to 620 by the time the last party of sick had left for Burma.

That the death rate in No. 2 Camp was so much higher than in other camps may be attributed to the following reasons:—

1. Exhaustion of the men from the long march up and the failure of the I.J.A. to allow any time for them to recuperate before being made to work. Many of them were sick or on light duty before leaving CHANGI. No "rest days" were allowed, work going on for seven days out of seven days for month after month, plus constant ill-treatment by the I.J.A. engineers whilst at work.
2. **Living conditions:**— Overcrowding in unroofed huts; insufficient rations; no canteen for the first 2 ½ months and men's clothes wet for days on end.
3. **Working conditions:**—Men often worked up to their waists in water long hours, being made to excessive weights and the forcing out of sick men to work.
4. Absence of drugs, antiseptics and dressings; men's shirt sleeves, old clothes and even banana leaves being used for the latter.
5. That an I.J.A. Sergeant only i/c Administrative party, whereas in all other camps there was an officer. This sergeant, although he did his best, was unable to obtain any relief or concession from the Engineer officer, who insisted on his demands for men being met, which prevented much-needed work on latrines, cookhouse, camp improvement etc. being carried out.
6. **Tools:**— These were in the hands of the engineers. Cutting tools for cookhouse and cremation wood were often unobtainable and were issued late and had to be returned early.

It is not yet possible to obtain complete figures of the number of deaths, but it is estimated that between 1,200 and 1,800 out of the original 1,600 all ranks forming this camp are now dead-their deaths being entirely due to the conditions under which they were forced to live and work by the I.J.A.

Report On Camp No. 3	*3rd June 1943*
Strength	392
Sick	
Cholera	2
Dysentary & Diarrhoea	97
Fever	49
Beri-Beri	5
Septic Sores	15
Others	2
	170

2. **Site.** A very bad site; water runs into camp from all sides and lies there. There is no drainage.
3. **Cholera.** There has been one death and there are now two cases. No building exists for segregation, and the two cases are in the hut with the rest of the men.

There is no medicine or medical equipment to deal with the sick. The following are urgently required:

A building in which cholera cases can be segregated. Buckets for use with cholera and other patients. 4 bottles of cholera vaccine to complete first inocculation. 10 bottles of cholera vaccine to complete second inoculation. Hypodermic syringe to give oculations, Disinfectants. Quick Lime.

It is reported that the coolies cholera hospital is using as a latrine a small stream which flows into the one used by the prisoners for washing. Coolies are dying every day of cholera.

4. **Accommodation.** In addition to a building for cholera patients, more accommodation is required for the main party. There are now 9 men to each bay on each side of the hut. There are 8 officers who are paying a large sum for this accommodation. More attap is urgently required to roof more huts.
5. **Mosquito Nets, Mats and Blankets.** None have yet been issued. As a result malaria is rife.
6. **Clothing.** Many men are without boots with soles. 150 pairs are required at once and 200 more pajama within a month. Shorts and socks are now beyond repair and a general issue is necessary, need their suit-cases and bed-rolls left behind at Bampong.
7. **Food.** Adequate on the whole but lacking vitamin B. Rice polishings, vitamin B tablets or injections must be produced to make good the deficiency. More cooking pots and a big container for boiling water is needed.
8. **Containers.** Extra cooking pots are also required to enable separate cooking for the sick.
9. **Canteen.** No facilities exist for purchase of local supplies,
10. No arrangements have yet been made to change Malayan-Japanese money. No arrangements have yet been made for working pay.
11. **Office.** No office facilities, paper or pencils are available. Keeping of rolls properly is impossible.
12. **Relations with IJA.** Good. The IJA NCO in charge gives all assistance but has little or nothing with which to help.
13. **Work.** All fit men except 11 cooks and duty men, 4 cowmen, the commanding officer, elector and half the non-combatant personnel go out to work daily.

    At least 4 men are required for camp sanitation all day.

    Non-combatants should not be sent out to work

    A system is required by which every fit man gets one day's rest in seven,

14. **Conclusion**

(a) Unless immediate action is taken today a general outbreak of cholera will occur in this camp.

(b) Unless the other points noted are all carried out, no men in this camp will be fit for work in a few days.

(c) If the IJA are unable to meet requirements then help should be sought from the neutral representative of the International Red Cross, quickly.

(signed) F.J. Dillon.

Lieut. Colonel

Afternote 5th June 1943

Since writing the above, six cases of cholera have developed, and there has been another death, with two more expected,

(a) The IJA NCO in charge has promised to arrange for segregation of cholera patients.

(b) All work has been stopped.

(c) Col. Banno has delivered some lime and disinfectants.

Appendix-C

Headquarters Camp,
10th June 1943.

Sir,

The following report from Mr. WOLFE on conditions at No. 4 P.O.W. Camp is submitted as requested. I should be grateful if the remaining British personnel at KONKOITA, which I understand consists of 11 cooks, could be transferred as soon as possible to No. 4 Camp, as the conditions at KONKOITA seem deplorable.

I am most grateful for the prompt delivery of quinine yesterday, which will do much to assist the malaria patients at No. 4 Camp.

I have the horour to be, Sir

Yours faithfully,
Lieut. Colonel
Commander

The Commander,
Prisoner of War Camp,
Imperial Japanese Army

Report

1. Konkoita

On 26 May 10 sick men were brought by lorry from Konkoita to this Headquarters Camp, Of these, one man died on the way and two men died soon after admission to hospital. As the report of these men was that the other sick left at Konkoita were in a terrible condition without medical attention of any kind. Colonel Banno kindly permission for Assistan-Surgeon Wolfe to go to Konkoita with a mail party. Mr. Wolfe arrived at Konkoita on the evening of 28 May. The Japanese guard did not allow him to see the sick until the morning of 29 May; there were 3 cases of Cholera, 1 case of Malaria, 3 of Dysentery and 3 of Diarrhoea. These 10 men had been lying helpless for several days in one tent. They had had no medical attention whatever. There were no sanitary arrangements of any kind. The cholera patients were vomiting; and defecating on the ground and flies were everywhere. Hundreds of coolies were isolated in neighbouring huts, and numbers of the so were dying every day, apparently from Cholera. Mr. Wolfe saw the Medical Major of the Imperial

Japanese Army at Konkoita immediately to report the three cases of cholera. He asked for a truck to bring the sick to Headquarters Camp, but this was refused. He offered to hire bullock-carts with the patients' money, but this was not permitted. He asked the Medical Major on three separate days for medical supplies, but was given nothing except a little disinfectant for his hands. He was told, "If they die, they die". Finally on 2 June Mr. Wolfe and his party carried the sick away from Konkoita in the rain, and put them in a bomboo-grove beside the road, while he sent an urgent message to No. 4 Camp. A party of 40 Australians then came and carried the 10 sick (also 5 sick cooks who had been working at Konkoita) to No. 4 Camp where they received proper treatment.

2. No. 4 Camp

All men who could work marched out on June, except 30 fit men left for camp duties. Lieut-Colonel POND has stayed behind in command. Malaria has been rampant, 25/30 now cases daily. Sick left behind are approximately:- Malaria 140, dysentery & Diarrhoea 65, Cholera 11 cases (in isolation). In addition to the 30 fit men, there remain 1 Medical Officer and about 17 medical personnel. Total about 350 men.

Medical supplies should be sufficient, thanks to the very prompt delivery of quinine tablets yesterday.

Rations are the great problem, as meals recently had been reduced to two, of thin rice gruel, daily.

Appendix D

General Report on Conditions at No. 5 Camp (Changaraya)

1. Before leaving NIEKE Camp I was told by Major Wild, the interpreter, that the I.J.A. Colonel was fully alive to the state of health of the men and to the necessity for three days complete rest on arrival at the new camp, in order to settle in and rest the men before working parties would be expected.
2. On the evening of the 27 May the first party – "A" Group (383) under the command of Major reached the camp and were housed in No. 1 Hut, with the officers in a small room in the I.J.A. N.C.Os hut next door. These huts were fully roofed. At 2100 hrs "B" Group (318) under my command arrived in the pitch dark, having been held up for one hour at No. 1 Camp. Accommodation was eventually found under what roofing existed by putting 200 men into 7 bays, 12' x 15' and the remaining 110 in with "A" Group.
3. Cookhouse. This was found to be in use by 500 Burmese Coolies, with whom we were expected to share - which turned out to mean that we were allowed to us, it when the Burmese did not want it, the natural result being that the mid-day meal on the first day was eventually served at 1700 hrs.
4. Rations. These were drawn from the IJA NCO i/c Burmese Cookhouse, and it as found that both our own and the Burmese rations were issued in bulk to this Cookhouse, so that we were given what they did not want.
5. Cocking Utensils. No utensils of any sort were issued to us on arrival and all our cooking had to be done in the Burmese containers and rice "qualies".
6. Well. There are two wells, the one near the Cookhouse containing very dirty water fit only for washing the body and clothes. This was being used by the Burmese cookhouse for cooking water. The other is some 500 yds away by a very bad track, but excellent water.
7. Containers. Only 4x6 gallon containers managed to arrive in camp with the two parties and these were the only means of drawing water and cooking stews.
8. On the morning of 28 May I made immediate representations to the I.J.A. For- (a) Separate Cookhouse (b) Water containers and buckets (c) Two 65 gallon oil drums, of which I could see several not in use in the camp (d) Better accommodation for the men (e) Blankets (f) Other cookhouse utensils and (g) Lime for the cookhouse and latrines

9. As a result of these representations I was given permission to build myself a cookhouse alongside that of the Burmese and was issued with 12 qualies (two broken) aid some wicker rice baskets and have since received a few wooden buckets which can be used for issues to the troops. Rations are now drawn separately but are« issued to the cookhouse at the discretion and whim of a completely incompetent I.J.A. Korean 3rd Class private. 18 bullocks were also issued for the week, which have been consumed and have been a godsend. The rations to date have consisted otherwise of rice, onions and salt fish and we have been assured for the past ten days that onions were the only vegetable available. However, yesterday our man was sick and the was surprised when we said we did not want only onions. He told us that he had plenty of beans, peas etc, which we could have had all along if he had known we liked them. These are now being received. Although they admit that there are plenty of buckets in the camp they are on charge to a different unit and cannot therefore be issued to us. We have received one 65-gallon drum which has a leak in the seam one-third of the way up. This is now used as a reservoir at the hospital, catching rainwater.

10. Over a period of the next five days further accommodation was attapped, and the men were able to spread out to about 10 to a bay. Incidentally, as an example of their inconsideration, at mid-day on the day following our arrival the officers were ordered out of their present quarters into one of the barrack blocks, which was still roofless and the attap was actually put on the roof while and after the officers moved in a downpour of rain. The following morning when 400 men were out on a working party, I was ordered to move the whole of 'A' Group and one Coy. of 'B' Group out of their quarters at five minutes notice, again into quarters which had not been roofed. A certain amount of roofing had by now been done, but for the next two days we were again squashed up to about 15 to a bay. The roofing in accommodation for 200 men is still not completed.

11. As regards all other stores, I invariably get the same answer that they are coming up from the rear and we will have to wait.

12. In spite of the assurance I received before leaving NIEKE, I was ordered to send out on a working party all fit men of 'A' Group the morning after arrival at 0900 hrs. 300 paraded and were worked until 2000 hrs.

13. That night (the second in camp) we had our first case of cholera. This resulted in an issue of five mail bags of lime and a visit from an I.J.A. doctor, also the erection of an isolation hut to accommodate about eight cases.

14. The general sanitation of the camp when we arrived was nothing, short of unbelievable filth. The Burmese had thrown all their unwanted rice and other food all over the camp and particularly near their own huts. Incidentally, there were parties of Burmese in every hut in our area, including those occupied by my men, and had "shat" indiscriminately everywhere. The flies were a menace;

remains of slaughtered animals and skins were in the undergrowth all around the cookhouse in every degree of decomposition.

Latrines are on the whole good, but shortage of lime renders it difficult to keep them clean. They are some way from the huts and have had path to them, which makes it difficult to got to them on these very dark nights.

It must be remembered that 80 of the men arrived in camp with diarrhoea. This resulted in a further menace of the men following the example of the Burmese and shitting indiscriminately in the undergrowth at night. Some undoubtedly could not get to the latrines in time, others were just lazy, as they have been throughout this crisis.

The following steps have, however, been taken to improve conditions and marked improvement has resulted throughout:—

(a) All undergrowth has been cleared between huts and in the vicinity of the cookhouse.

(b) The Burmese have been made to clear up the mess in their area and are firmly dealt with by the I.J.A. when seen throwing food about.

(c) A limited amount of lime is now available for the latrines and cookhouse.

(d) A railed path has been made to one latrine.

(e) Night latrines are erected between the two huts and are being used by the men.

(f) General drainage of huts and paths is in progress as and when men are available.

15. Representations were made the third day to the engineer officers of the I.J.A. to give me two days off working parties, partly to give the men a rest and partly to get the camp in order. I was told that they would get a rest later on but not yet. However, after the fifth day of work, I was given the men for one day. This did help enormously in the camp but I am afraid was little or nearest for the men.

16. Meanwhile, cholera was getting a grip and my other sick were increasing at an alarming face rate it came to the time when I could put only 200 men on working parties.

17. I again appealed to the engineer officers to let me have some of the fit men for work in camp and the reply I received was that I was not producing enough for him, and I would have to turn out the sick 'B' men as well the next day.

18. That day (4th June) the I.J.A. Colonel i/c P.O.W. Camps arrived with two sacks of lime and some other disinfectants. I told the interpreter of our requirements, such as buckets lime and Blankets – also another M.O. The Colonel ordered that all work out side camp would cease until all the men in camp were fit again. I also sent down to the base and to Lt. Col. Harris which I had written two days before and was therefore rather out of date, but had no time to rewrite, by the British driver.

That nilght at 11 p.m. I was sent for by the I.J. A. engineer officer and told that the Colonel had only referred to work on the railway and not to work on the road which must continue and that I might keep 15 fit men in camp next day but that the rest must work. I appealed against this order as it did not fit in with the spirit of the Clonol's remarks. However he compromised my making me give him 80 O. R.S. the following day he took 30 and today 100.

19. On the 3rd June the I.J.A. Doctors again arrived complete with glass rods and stabbed all Diarrhoea and Dysentery cases. On the 4th a list of 61 names was sent in of men they said were cholera positives and were to be isolated immediately. This was done but only three of these have so far been admitted to the Cholera Ward.

20. There were only 4 R.A.M.C. personnel in the party on arrival, of whom 2 have since died of Cholera. Seven other orderlies from Roberts Hospital were with the unit. This was the basis with which we had to start, since when over 80 O.Rs have volunteered to help in the wards, of which through sickness death and complete exhaustion only 20 are now available for work. No further volunteers can be obtained even after continued appeal by Company Commanders and others, and I have now been reduced to ordering the Cholera suspects to act as orderlies. The work done by the Medical Staff and volunteers cannot be too highly praised. They worked themselves to a standstill cheerfully expecting any moment to be a case themselves. The M.O., Capt. Emery, has been suffering for the past 4 days from Malaria and diarrhoea but has carried on throughout, even on one day from his bed in the M.I. Room next to the Dysentery Ward. A convalescent bay has new been established, which is rapidly filling up – which speaks for itself.

21. Disposal of dead has been a great difficulty, owing to the weather and complete absence of petrol. However, up to yesterday all bodies were disposed of by fire, but yesterday 10 bodies had to be buried. Burial again has its difficulties as graves fill with water at two foot and it is lucky if rock also is not encountered. Yesterday a pit three foot deep was dug, the bodies put in and then a high mound of earth and rock raised above it. This was the only method found to be feasible.

22. Four officers have been taken with Cholera, one, Lieut. Furzo R.E., has died, two are well on the way to recovery and the fourth, Capt. Turner A. & S. H. is still in the balance. Of the other fifteen officers, with the exception of myself and Adjt. (Lieut. Fletcher), only two officers are really fit to do any heavy work, malaria and diarrhoea being the main causes of trouble. Similarly very few are still at work.

7 June 1943. (Sgd) Gairdner, Major,

Commanding, No. 5 Camp.

23. **Miscellaneous.** A box of medical stores was received from force H.Q. on the 3rd, containing anti-cholera serum and some antiseptics and bandages, all most useful. The serum was given as injections to medical orderlies who asked for it. A further box was received on the 6th, brought on foot by an A.I.F.

O.R., who also brought a reply to my letter to Col. Harris. He took back with him a further report from me, stating my immediate requirements. Although a second M.O. has been promised, he has not yet turned up.

24. A bottle containing an anti-septic solution is kept in each Coy. for disinfecting hands after any chance of contamination. Also two troughs of antiseptic solution are placed in each hut for use at any time, particularly after Benjo by the troops.

25. A steriliser is situated near the cookhouse, which is useful when it is in action, but great difficulty seems to be met in keeping the thing going.

7 June 1943. (Sgd) Gairdner, Major,

Commanding, No. 5 Camp.

9 June 1943

A further stool examination was carried out this morning by the I.J. A. 480 men were examined.

At last after almost daily application permission has been given for us to keep and use as water containers empty oil tins from the ration issue. Three are now in use, two in the cholera ward and one in the dysentery ward. Also ten rice sacks have been given to us permanently. These have been issued to the convalescent cholera ward. All further sacks emptied from rations may be retained on loan, to be returned when a blanket issue is made. Similarly a second 55 gallen oil drum has been received and is kept at the cookhouse for boiling drinking water. A marked decrease in cholera admissions over the past three days looks hopeful.

Although a second doctor was promised four days ago, none has yet materialise. One more bag of lime was received last night. 50 men daily are still going out on working parties.

An issue of pumpkin has been received, sufficient for four meals, also more head of cattle.

Rain has averaged between 18 and 20 hours of the 24 since our arrival, mud is everywhere and our drainage is only in its infancy. Far more men are required for making paths than I can produce.

Permanent daily fatigues are required as under, which eat up men:—

Cremation	12
Hospital water	8
Hospital ward	6
Cookhouse water	8
Cookhouse ward	6
Sanitation	6
Herdmen	5
Cooks	20
Medical	46

9 June 1945 Gairdner, Major,

Commanding, No. 5 Camp

Appendix E

Statement by Assistant-Surgeon on P. WOLFE, on Konkoita

Three to four days after the completion of the march and arrival at Shimo-Nieko, I proceeded under instructions from Lieut-Col. S.M. Harris, with four medical orderlies, to Konkoita.

After marching all night in heavy rain, through mud and without food, the party arrived at Konkoita the following morning. There I found nineteen patients crowded into one tent on the river tank. Of these, nine were cholera cases and the remainder untreated malaria and had ulcer cases. These personnel had been without attendants or treatment for some days and the tent was in a filthy condition and full of files; the cholera cases defecating and vomiting where they lay, their comrades being unable to help them.

My party commenced work immediately segregating the patients, cleaning up and giving, what little treatment was available, and I went and interviewed the Senior I.J.A. H.Q. at the camp, pleading for drugs, food shelter and/or conveyance to our own camp. He gave no help even refusing conveyance, and when I remonstrated with him, pointing out that all the patients would die if no assistance was forthcoming he said "we must all die some day" or words to that effect.

The party remained at Konkoita for some days, the Japanese giving us plain rice only during that time, and refusing us permission to communicate with P.O.W. drivers passing the camp daily.

With the aid of a common metal funnel provided by a Tamil coolie, the rubber tube of my stethescope and needle I had in my possession, I managed to keep the patients alive by administering intravenous saline.

Eventually I obtained permission, after refusal by the Japanese to make bullock carts available, on the grounds that they would become contaminated, for myself and the four orderlies to move the nineteen patients to one of our own camps. The Japanese, however, still refused permission for me to communicate first with such camp.

To left the camp with five stretcher cases, cholera patients having to be half dragged along by men who were already carrying stretchers, and others doing their best to hobble along on their own. The Japanese sent no guards as they were too afraid of becoming infected through contact with the party.

In stages of about one hundred yards, we eventually reached a point about one kilo from the camp, and out of sight of it, where I hid the party in the jungle and improvised shelter for patients, and sent an orderly to obtain assistance from the nearest Camp which was under the command of Lieut-Col. C.M. Kappe, A.I.F.

On reaching this camp, the orderly made his way in stealthily through the back of the camp, as admission to the camp was prohibited. He contacted Lieut-Col. Kappe, Lieut-Col. Pond and Capt. R.M. Mills, who immediately made available one officer and fifty men with stretchers, food, water and a few drugs, and they managed to bring my patients on the camp where they were cared for.

I am greatly indebted to these officers and men. Were it not for their prompt assistance we would have been completely stranded.

(Signed) P. Wolfe,
Asst. Surgn, I.M.D.

Appendix F

Report of Beating up of Interpretor of No. 5 P.O.W. Camp, Thailand-27 Jun, 1943

On the evening of June 27 while at the 115 Mile Camp I and Lieut. Raw were invited by the No. 1 Nipponese Engineer to come to his hut for coffee and a hot bath. This hut was about 50 yards from the British Officer's hut and there had never been any question of its being out of bounds. While there I received a message from the P.O.W. Camp Commandant, 2/Lt Kanada, to report at his H.Q. when I returned. This I duly did. Asked where I had been I said that I had been having a bath in the Engineers hut. I was at once accused of being out of bound and without more ado beaten ferociously with sticks by 2/Lieut. Kanada and other Nipponese soldiers. The Nipponese interpreter told me that I had been trying to escape. After about half an hour of this bashing I was made to stand at attention with my left foot right up against the fire and was told I would have to stand there for five hours. Every now and then I received further blows and if I staggered was always made to resume my position with my left foot touching the fire. I fell once or twice but was always beaten to my feet again. Lieut. Raw was summoned, but no action was taken against him. Major Gairdner (British C.O.) was summoned and confirmed that no word had been said placing this hut out of bounds. After some two hours I was permitted to depart (at 2400 hrs). Both my eyes were black and swollen and I had several cuts and bruises over the head and shoulders. My left leg had burns on the foot and all up the calf.

Following on this I was made to work for four days, axing trees, carrying stores and digging latrines in spite of the Medical Officers declaring me unfit for it. At the end of that time I could not put my left feet to the ground without very great pain and was allowed to be admitted to hospital. The ulcers developing from my burns healed up at the beginning of September.

(Signed) R.G. Fletcher,

Lieut.

Appendix G

Correspondence and Report from "F" Force HQ to IJA HQ

Letter No.	*Subject*	*Date*
1	Letter and report on conditions in Forward POW camps	31. 6. 43
2	Report on Camps 1, 2, 3, and 5	26. 6. 43
3	Copy of Daily Detail	7. 7. 43
4	Report by Major Stevens-food situation	12. 7. 43
5	Representation to Imperial Government Tokio on behalf of officers due to be executed	19. 7. 43
6	Duplicate copies of Nominal Rolls	4. 8.43
7	Covering leter and Medical Report of SMO	8. 8. 73
8	Inventory of medical equipment on Changi	undated
9	Medical requirements No. 2 Camp for 1 month	13. 9. 43
10	Letter concerning forward move of certain officers	8. 9. 43
11	Appeal to General Animura	18. 8. 43
12	No. 2 Camp. Pay	30. 8. 43
13	Immediate medical requirements	2. 9. 43
14	Supply of medical stores	1. 10. 43
15	Lists of medical requirements for Tanbaya Hospital	undated
16	Guarantee of good behaviour	7. 10. 43
17	Suggested distribution of prisoners HQ during return move to Changi	12. 11. 43
18	Letter to Malayan Prisoners of War Administration. Health of "F" Force	29. 11. 43
19	Medical supplies for Kanburi Hospital	undated
20	Dressings for No. 1 Camp	19. 10. 43
21	Details of medical supplies	1. 11. 43
22	Letter from SMO to Imperial Japanese Army Medical equipment	1. 12. 43

Selection of Correspondance to and from "F" Force H.Q.

To,

Colonel Banno,

Officer Commanding,

British and Malayan POW. Camp,

Thailand,

Sir,

I have the honour to enclose a report on the four forward, POW Camps I visited on 23 and 24 June 1943.

While I fully appreciate the difficulties our local I. J. A. administration are faced with, and appreciate the fact that Colonel Banno and his administration are doing everything they can on our behalf, at the same time there are certain outstanding needs that are of vital necessity fo the health and welfare to the troops under my command. Unless immediate action is taken to deal with these needs the opinion of my senior medical officers is that a great number of the lives of these POW will be unnecessarily sacrificed.

I found in all camps that the morale of the POW troops was good and was improving

I wish to press for:-

1. An increased ration scale to contain more vitamin B content i.e. towgay and bean, and also for an issue of cooking fats. (Also for the supplementation of rations by the establishment of canteens and local purchase.) The medical officers consider this the most immediate need and state that unless this is done there will be a high incidence of deficiency diseases, and men recuperating from cholera, dysentery, malaria and debility diseases generally will have no chance of recovery and of becoming fit for work.
2. Shorter working hours for the road parties so that the men can have an opportunity of washing themselves and their clothes. If working parties could return by 1830 hours this would meet the case. A regular holiday for working parties in all camps is also a necessity.
3. A stoppage of boating and ill-treatment of working parties by the I. J. A. Engineers. At No. I Camp this is particularly in evidence. Every day men are being beaten and there are constant cases of face-slapping of officers.
4. No ill or unfit men to be included in outside working parties.
5. A sufficient number of tools to be made available for Camps Hygiene purposes.
6. The supply of buckets and containers for all camps and particularly for Camps Nos 5 and 2, where they are most un-gently needed.
7. I am most grateful for the supply of quinine which has been made available for all camps as malaria is greatly on the increase. Mosquito nets are a crying necessity.

Recently I put forward a consolidated request for drugs and medicines. I trust that steps are being taken to produce these as they are of vital necessity.

I also put forward a written request to allowed to got in touch with the nearest representative of the International Red Cross. I should be glad if you would advise me what is being done in this matter as we are in urgent need of his assistance. I have a prescriptive right to apply for access to an International representative under the Hague Convention.

The increase of rations in Headquarter Camp is greatly appreciated.

I have the honour to be , Sir.

A Report on POW Camps 1, 2, 3, and 5 Visited 23 and 24 June 1943

Camps No.1

Morale of the troops is good and Camp Hygiene and sanitation satisfactory. The Camp Commandant presses for:-

1 A fuller ration scale, supplemented by a canteen.

2 Shorter working hours for road working parties and a regular holiday.

3 Cessation of ill-treatment by the I.J.A. Engineers of officers and men on road parties.

4 Road parties in this camp were tested on "piece work" by the I.J.A. Engineers, and their work found satisfactory. Could this principle be established and the men be allowed to work under their own officers?

Camps No. 2

Morale of troops good. Camp Hygiene and sanitation fair.

The Camp Commandant would be grateful for:-

1 An increased scale of rations supplemented by canteen.

2 The attapped hut across the roadway from his camp (at present occupied by about 50 natives) to be made available for 200 of his troops, as accommodation in his camp is badly overcrowded.

3 The river to be made available again for bathing and washing purposes. At present the water carry is a long one and there are only a few men and containers available for this duty.

4 The I. J. A. Administrative Sergeant is constantly overruled by the I. J. A. Engineer Officer. Could this be remedied please.

Camps No. 3

Morale of the troops very good and the Camp Commandant expressed satisfaction with his working conditions.

Camps No. 5

Conditions in this camp are deplorable. British POW are living in close proximity to Burman labourers and Camp Hygiene is impossible. The ground is waterlogged and it is not possible to construct adequate latrines and refuse pits.

The I.J.A. Engineers insist on every available man going out on working parties, men who are convalescing from cholera and who are actually suffering from malaria and dysentery are being forced on to working parties. There are insufficient men for carrying out hygiene and sanitation. The water carry in this Camp is a long one and there are NO buckets or water containers available.

I feel strongly that this camp needs all the help possible from our own I.J.A. Administration . There is high incidence of sickness, disease and death in this camp. This high incidence of disease will continue unless conditions are improved.

I wish to make the strongest representation that in all camps but this one in particular, only fit men are taken out on working parties, and that buckets and containers be supplied to them as soon as possible.

TRUE COPY

Notice

1 The hour of daily work is stipulated as belows:

1	Get up	7.00
2	Breakfast	7.30
3	Morning Roll Call	8.20
4	Set to work	8.30
5	Consulation to Surgeon	10.00
6	Tiffin	12.30
7	Resume work of afternoon	14.00
8	Evening Roll Call	18.30
9	Supper	19.00
10	Consulation to Surgeon	20.00
11	Go to bed	21.00

2. The Captive who can go out of fence in the daytime are as belows;

   I. Water-drawer, Firewood-carrier, Waterman around the Camp, and persons in charge of the dead.

   II. The Captive who take bath after work. But the time limit is till 21 O'clock (9 p.m.)

   All the Captive with the exception of items mentioned above should ask for permission of the Chief of this Prisoners' quarters.

3. The Captives who disobey or oppose to the orders of the Nippon Army are strictly punished or condemned to Capital Crime.

4. Measures to the Deserter:

   I. The Captives who devised to run away and were captured are condemned to Capital Crime.

   II. The Chief of Section on which produced the Deserter and concerned officer are severely punished in joint.

III. When the Deserter can not be found within two days from the day of desertion, the chief of Section concerned officer will be punished to Capital owing to their Responsibility to Soldier-men.

7|th July 2603 (1943)

Chief of the 5th Detachment of Malaya

Prisoners' Quarters
Headquarters Camps
NIEKH.
12th July, 1943

Sir,

Food

Further to my interviews with you on this subject, I now forward a report by my senior medical officer, which summarises the situation and shows its extreme seriousness.

I have the honour to be, Sir,

Your Faithfully,
Sgd/ F.W.H
Lieut-Colonel,
Commander

Commander,
P.O.W. Camps,
Imperial Japanese Army

Commander,
'F' Force

The present ration scale for this Force is viewed with the utmost concern by the medical officers attached to this force. The present scale is entirely deficient in Vitamin B, Fat, protein and calcium and if persisted in will result in the rapid deterioration of health of the, at present, moderately fit men, and the impossibility of recovery of the already sick.

My appreciation is that on the present scale the force will be totally incapacitated in one month's time and that the death rate will be extremely heavy.

Most alarming is the very rapid increase in diseases caused by the absence of Vitamin B in the diet Beri-Beri, Follagra failing eyesight and in some cases blindness, Asthenia and general weakness. The entire force is on the verge of Beri-Beri, and most men are already showing mild symptoms. These will increase at an alarming rate in the near future and many deaths and total invalidity will be the result.

The additions necessary to make the present ration a suitable one are as follows:-

1	**Vitamin B.**	Rice polishings Towgay Beans	2 ozs per man per day. 3 ozs per man per day. 3 ozs per man per day
2	**Fat** (Which is not only necessary as a food, but conserves Vitamin B) Cooking oil		1 ozs per man day.
3	**Protein**	Meat or Fish	4 ozs per man per day
4	**Calcium**	Whitebait	2 ozs per man per day.

The above additions would constitute a diet on which steady improvement of health and working capacity of this force could be confidently predicted.

(Signed) R.H. Stevens, Major

S. N. O. A. I. F. 'F' Force

12 July 1943

NIEKE

19th July, 1943

Sir,

I have the honour to inform you that yesterday I was told by Lieut. YAMADA that some British officers had been arrested for escape, that they would probably be condemned to death and that I must hold myself in readiness to witness their execution.

If this is so, then as senior British Officer and therefore the representative of the British Government on the spot, I wish to make a formal appeal to the Imperial Japanese Government (on behalf of the British Government) not to exact the death penalty.

While I have no information as to the reasons that impelled these officers to escape, the basis of this appeal is:-

(a) It is contrary to the Laws and Usages of War to exact the death penalty from prisoners of war who escape, nor is capital punishment imposed by other Great Powers.

(b) There is a feeling of despair among some officers at their continued inability to mitigate the severe and unprecedented hardships of the men of whom they have been put in command by the Imperial Japanese Army. These hardships have already caused in the space of three months the deaths of over 600 men and sickness of 90 per cent out of this force of 7,000 men. I have no doubt that this feeling of responsibility weighed heavily on the minds of these officers.

In the meantime I urge that immediate action be taken to postpone execution until such time as a reply to this appeal is received.

I have the honour to be, Sir,

Yours faithfully,
Lieut-Colonel.
Commander

Colonel Banno,
Commanding Malayan P. of. W.
Thailand

No. 2 Camp.
4 Aug 43

Sir,

Now that the HQ of this force is situated away from your own HQ, it would be of great assistance in ensuring the accuracy of the various reports submitted to you if you would allow the duplicate copies of the Force Nominal Rolls at present in your office to be retained by this HQ.

If this could be arranged, and No. 3 Camp could be instructed to send all death notifications and other reports through this HQ, it will be possible in future to avoid mistakes in making reports to you.

The roll of NIEKE personnel has been amended to date to show movements of all troops. As this HQ will not know when hospital are moved from NIEKE to the Burma Hospital, could Lieut. Wing please be instructed to keep a record of these movements so that the roll may be kept up-to-date.

Sgd/ Dillon
Lieut-Colonel
Commander.

Mr. Saji.
Headquarters,

Headquarters,
"F" Force.
8th August 1943.

Dear Colonel Banno,

I regret to have to forward this report as I know and appreciate all that you and your administration have tried to do on our behalf. However, the present situations is so scandalous and its consequence in less of life is improving so widespread that it is bound to be made the subject of an official enquiry by the British Government after the war with serious and lasting diplomatic repercussions between our two countries.

I feel, therefore, in the interests of all concerned that there should be no delay in forwarding this statement through His Excellency General Aripur, to the highest quarters.

Your faithfully,

Sgd/ Lieut-Colonel,
Commander,
"F" Force

Colonel Banno,
Commanding Malayan P.O.W.
Thailand

Colonel Banno,
Imperial Japanese Army,
Commanding,
Malaya Prisoners of War in Thailand

Headquarters, "F" Force
8th August 1943

Sir,

I have the honour to submit a report from my Senior Medical Officer on the medical situation at this camp. This report fills me with the gravest concern as 25 per cent of the original strength of the camp are already dead and the remainder are dying at the rate of 2,800 a year, which is an appalling state of affairs.

Col. Huston in his report points out the possible remedies, and I should be grateful if immediate steps could be taken to implement them. To my mind our most urgent and pressing needs are

(i) no unfit men to be forced to ge on working parties, and working men to be allowed one day off in seven to wash themselves and their clothes.

(ii) The cessation of ill-treatment by the I.J.A. engineers. Cases are occurring every day of severe beatings of prisoners of war. Men have been knocked unconscious and left to lie in the mud.

(iii) Improvement of rations particularly for the sick and the provision of the foods enumerated in Col Huston's report, rice polishings, cooking fats, sugar and flour being the most urgent.

(iv) The provision of medical stores, antiseptics and disinfectants.

Present conditions are so disgraceful that they are stadily and rapidly killing the men of this force and will undoubtedly grossly undermine the health of any survivors. None of the other belligerents in this war are treating their prisoners in this manner, and it was to save prisoners of war from suffering such treatment that the Great Powers became party to the Geneva Convention, numerous clauses of which are now being glagrantly disregarded here. It is my belief that if the Japanese Government in Tokyo were made aware of the present situation and if the Japanese representatives of the International Red Cross Society could see the disgraceful conditions in which our sick are perishing in the so-called hospital in this camp immediate steps would be taken to come to our rescue.

The establishment of the hospital in Burma for 1,250 patients is much appreciated but it only touches the fringe of the problem, as there are over 1,400 sick in this camp alone, of whom only 350 will be sent to Burma.

I therefore request that this letter be forwarded as soon as possible to His Excellency General Arihura for transmission to the Imperial Japanese Government.

Sgt/
Lieut-Colonel,
Commander,
"F" Force

Colonel Banno,
Commanding Malayan P.O.W.

* (However urgent their work may be)

Medical report by Lt-Col J. Huston, Senior Medical Officer

Lt-Col S.W. Harris, BE, RA,
commanding "F" Force, Thailand.

The high death rate and the medical situation generally in this camp is causing me the gravest anxiety, and unless stringent and immediate steps are taken to remedy existing conditions the death rate, which is now at the rate of 100 per cent annum, will continue in an increasing ratio.

The following report on this situation is submitted for your information and possible action:-

1. Availability on 6 Aug 43 (excluding officers).

	Fit	*Light Duties*	*In Hosp*	*Red Cross Non-Combatants*	*Total*
On road	214	83	-	-	297
In Camp	70	35	1463	86	1654
Total	284	118	1463	86	1951

2. Deaths (out of an original total of 1,600)

Cholera-209	Starvation and Dysentry-119
Beri-Beri-28	Malaria-17. Diphtheria-14.
Tropical Ulcers-7.	Misc Causes-5

Making a total of **399**

3. Causes of Ill Health and High Death Rate
   (a) Defective diet during the past 2.5 months, the present ration for sick men contains 1400 calories only, which is not sufficient to maintain life much less to enable desperately sick men to recuperate.
   (b) The prolonged march here of a force in which there were 30 per cent unfit men. Excessively long working hours and ill treatment of men on road and rail working parties.
   (c) Sick men being forced to work on outside working parties. After working long hours some of these men have been found dead in their huts
   (d) A lack of medical supplies and hospital equipment.
   (e) Inadequate rations and non-payment of unfit men.
4. Suggested remedies
   (a) Immediate improvement of camp conditions, sanitation, cooking facilities and hygiene generally. (This is now being the orders of Lieut. Wakadyashi and we very grateful for this dispensation).
   (b) Only fit men to be allowed to work on the roads and railway. At present sick men are forced to work-men suffering from malnutrition, beri-beri, sore feet and malaria. If it is true that the daily working party is to be increased from 300 to 700, then I anticipate that the number of sick will steadily increase and there will be a rapid rise in the death rate.
   (c) Supply of a good mixed diet containing rice polishings, fresh vegetables, and cooking fats to produce 3,500 calories daily for all men whether sick or fit. As I have already stated the present ration for sick men contains only 1,400 calories, which is not sufficient to support life, with a consequence that unfit men are dying in large numbers and the number will undoubtedly increase unless the rations are improved.
   (d) Supply of medical equipment which was brought from Changi with this force. This has been dumped at Bamtong, Kanu (Headquarters of 'H' Force) and Tarkanan. We are also in urgent need of dressings, cotton wool, gauze, Emetine, Vitamin B tablets, Magnesium Sulphate tablets, Bismuth and Opium for diarrhoea, Iodoform and Sulphur for treating ulcers and skin disease.
   (e) Invalid foods are urgently needed, fish oil, milk eggs, sugar and flour.

(f) Antiseptics are also urgently needed for disinfecting hands and preventing the spread of disease, (Creosol Lysol and Xylenol).

(g) A supply of tools, utensils, basins, buckets, and scrubbing brushes are also needed for keeping the sick and their quarters clean.

Finally in particular I must warn you that at present without disinfectants and with inadequate food the whole camp is defenceless against another outbreak of cholera.

Sgd/

Lieut-Colonel, R.A.M.C.

S.M. O. 'F' Force

8 Aug 43.

Herewith completed pro formae in respect of paragraphs 1, 2 and 3 of your letter dated 1. 11. 43 . It will be seen that only a very small amount of medical stores arrived in Neike which had proviously reached Bang Pong (See answers to para 2 and para 3)

J. Huston

SMO. "F" Force

Answer to Paragraph 3.

List of medical supplies and equipment ex Changi which arrived at Bangpong.

This list is an approximation from memory about 1/4th of the total arrived at Nieke. About 1/3 th of these arrived at Nieke. It is impossible to give a list of the drugs etc but they comprised at least 1,500 separate items. Receipts at Nieke are listed in answer to question 2. About ½ of this arrived at Nieke.

In addition plates, knives, and other accessories were packed.

Starch of Talc Powder–G2000. Lint-G2000

Gauze-G2000 (20 pkts). Bandages various-100.

Wool absorbent-G1000. Adhesive surgical tape-10 rolls

Field Dressings-100.

For Diarrhoea and Dysentery (Albasil (Yamanouchi Co Ltd)

Emetine–Tabs 1000. Yatren –6250 (or Sulphopyridine-Tabs 1000)

Mag Sulph or Sod. Sulph- G2000. Tinct Opium-G250.

For Malaria and suppressive treatment

Quinine Sulph Gr 3-4-150,000 Atebrin tabs-1000.

Plasmoquin tabs-4000.

Item	*No*	*Remarks*
Medical Pannies and boxes	69	These were numbered consecutively and contained dressings and appliances of all kinds.
Cotton Wool bales	1	50 lbs each
Lint bala	2	--
Sod. Sulph. Exsice	1	28 lbs
Soap 60	1	15 lbs
Red Cross Food	42	Miscellaneous invalid foods meat, soups, pineapple, milk
Clarifying Powder Cartons	1	Containing 11 oz tins
Water Sterilsing Powder boxes	2	Containing 96 oz tins each
Medical boxes	12	Unnumbered
Operating Table	1	In separate parts
Cresiol Crude drum	4	5 gals each
Chloride or lime drum	6	112 lbs each
Magnes. Sulphas	1	56 lbs
Kaolin	1	56 lbs
Salt lbs	36	packed in box
Stretchers	250	As beds
Faillasse cases	250	For filling with grass
Warmers stomach	24	Use as air rings
Hurricane Lamps	10	Lighting
Kerosine Gals	20	----
Thomas splints	25	Treatment of fractures
Diesel Lighting Set	1	Complete with oil engine, switchboard, storage batteries, cable, bulbs, accessory tools.
Blankets	40	For Patient's
Sheets	12	-----
Pyjama suits	12	-------
Hospital clothing	20	-------
Balkan Beams	1	--- Fractures
Shovels, picks, kals	12 each	
Axes hand	4	
Axes felling	4	
Spyer stoves	4	
Farmhouse cookers	2	
Containers 6 gal	12	
Buckets asserted	24	
Oven Field Pattern	1	For General Hospital use
Primus stoves	3	
Tables complete	20	

For Beri-Beri

Ebios yeast tabs- 50 bottles. Vit B1 amps for injection

Vitamin B Tabs (10 Milligrams)-Amps 200.

Rice Polishings-KG 100.

For Skin Diseases

Sulphur powder –G500. Vaseline-G4000 Boric Acid-G1000.

Calamin pulv-G1000. Tinct Benz Co-G1000.

For General use with sick

Thermometers clinical- 4. Morphine 1 per cent Ice-Amps 100.

Iron and Ammonium Citrate-G2000. Soda Bicarb-G2000.

Aspirin- 1000. Tr. Ipecacacuanha- G1000.

Ammon. Carbonate-G500. Coramine or Anacardone for the heart-Amps 50.

Cod Liver Oil- G400. Pot. Cit-G1000. Cresol or Liq. Xylenol for cleanliness of wards and disinfection of hands, bowls, etc.

13.9.43

Sgd/ J. Huston

Lt-Col RAMC

To:- Colonel Banho, No. 2 Camp, Sonkrai.
Commanding Malaya Prisoners of War,
Thailand 8 September 1943.

Sir

Now that road conditions are improving I shall be grateful if you would arrange for certain individuals to be brought up to the forward area. Details are as follows:-

Chaplain Rev. A. Jackson now at Tamaran Pat to be sent to Burma Hospital,

Chaplain Rev E. Cordingley now at Kanchanabri to be sent to Burma Hospital.

Interpreter Capt. Waller now at kanchanabri to be sent to Kami-Sonkrai.

Dentist Capt. Mannion now at Tamaran Pat to be sent to Kami-Sonkrai.

2. I have in a previous letter already asked for two doctors, Major Rogers from Kancha Kanchanabri and Capt. Brand from Tamaran Pat, to be sent forward or, alternatively, to be exchanged for Capts. Brown and Frew now at Shimo-Sonkrai and Nieke in charge of Tamil labors groups. My request in that letter for Capt. Mannion to be sent to the Burma Hospital is now cancelled, as another dentist, Capt. Dix, has been sent to the Hospital.

3. All except the interpreter are Red Cross non-Combatants.

Yours Faithfully,
Lt-Col.
Commander, "F" Force

Commanding Malaya Prisoners of War,
Thailand

No. 2.P.O.W. Camp
Sonkrai
18 th August, 1943.

Sir,

Knowing your goodwill and sincerity, and since you are entrusted by His Excellency General Arimura with the responsibility for this force of 7,000 prisoners of war (Now unhappily reduced by death to less than 6,000), I must make this further personal appeal on behalf of these men, of whom I am the senior British officer.

As anticipated in my letter of 8 Aug 43 the position is steadily worsening, as the sickness and death rate is accelerating day by day. Since my arrival in this camp about two weeks ago 120 men have died (12 during the last 24 hours) and this is not due to an epidemic but to diseases mainly caused by overwork, ill-treatment and malnutrition.

Lieut. Wakabayashi has always done his utmost to help us and with his kind assistance we have been able to improve greatly the sanitation, hygiene and cooking facilities in this camp. In spite, however, of these and other measures our 1,400 sick grow weaker and more men fall ill every day; until now we have only 160 fit men to send out to work, with 250 others who should be excused duty on account of illness to make up the daily working parties of 400. The causes of this disastrous situation are:-

(I) The lack of suitable food apart from rice (see Colonel Huston's report of 8 Aug 43) which weakens all men and causes actual starvation among the sick.

(II) Excessively long hours and ill treatment at work.

(III) Lack of drugs and suitable nourishment for these in hospital.

I must therefore implore you to take suitable measures immediately to prevent this situation developing into an overwhelming tragedy. I should also welcome the chance of an early interview with you.

Your faithfully,
Lieut-Colonel, Commanding,
"F" Force.

No. 2 Camp,
Sonkrai,
30 Aug 1943.

1. Lieut. Wakabyashi advised me to write to you with reference to the following difficulties about pay:-
   (a) When are the other ranks going to be paid for the period of the march up, especially the various camp cooks, who were promised heavy duty rates?

   Amount required –approx $ 15,000

   (b) When are the other ranks going to be paid for the working period 10 May to 20 June? Camps 1, 2, 3, 4 and 5 were all at work by 23 May. Camp 4 (Konkoita) started work on 10 May and the others in between these dates.

   Amount involved –approx $ 16,000.

   (c) When are the officers and Red Cross personnel going to be paid for
2 From the above it will be seen that the force has been owed $ 45,000 for more than one month.
3. We expected that all these matters would be put right with this month's pay, it did not happen.
4. In addition to the above, officers and Red Cross personnel are now due for pay for August (approx $ 14,000), which brings the total amount now owing to $ 59,000.
5. Our total capital is about $ 10,000 and so we cannot support this big debt owing to us.
6. In spite of Changi promises we cannot get Malay money changed. Can anything by done about this? I have here $ 2,000 and Col. Kappe and Col. Hutchison have similar amounts or more.
7. We will be glad to help in any way we can to clean up this mess.
8. Lastly, there is the matter of Red Cross W. OsI, which explain in the attached note. What can be done to have this mistake put right?

I hoped to see you up here one day.

Your sincerely,
?????

Mr. Saji,
P.O.W. Headquarters,
Nieke.

To:- Colonel Banno,
Commanding Malaya Prisoners of War,
Thailand.

No. 2 Camp,
Sonkrai
4 Sep 43.

Sir,

The attached letter from Colonel Huston, Senior Medical Officer to this force, is forwarded for your consideration I shall be grateful if you could see your way to granting his requests.

May permission be given please to Colonel Huston and myself to visit the Burma Hospital and the new Light Sick Camp, which is being established in Burma.

Your faithfully,
Sgd/ J.W.H.
Lieut-Colonel,
Commander,
"F" Force.

Subject:- Immediate Medical Requirements. No. 2 Camp,
To:- Commander, "F" Force. 2 September 1943

Sir,

It is requested that the following needs of the force be brought to the notice of the I.J.A. as soon as possible:-

1. **Medical Officers**- to be moved as soon as they can be spared:-

Capt. A. Earber RAMC from Nieke to No. 2 Camp.

Capt. Lloya Cahill AAMC from No. 1 to No. 2 Camp.

Capt. J. Taylor AAMC from No. 1 to No. 3 Camp.

Major D.G. Gillies RAMC from No. 5 to No. 3 Camp.

Major P.E. Routley RAMC from No. 5 to No. 3 Camp.

Capt. Mannion, Australian Dental Officer from Tamaran Pat to Burma Hospital.

Capt. J. Frew AAMC and Capt. R. Brown RAMC-These two officers do not belong to "F" Force, but owing to the heavy sick rate their services are required as the Thailand administration has depleted the number of medical officers of "F" Force by two (Major Rogers AAMC at Kamburi, Major Brank AAMC at Tamaran Pat). Capt Frew is required at the Burma Hospital and Capt Brown at New Light Sick Camp.

2. **Medical Equipment**. It is requested that Dental Equipment (one gray box marked "F. D. O. Capt. Dix, Dental Stores") thought to be at Tamaran Pat be sent to New Light Sick Camp.

3. The following are most urgently needed for the camp hospitals of this Force:-

Dressing for wounds and ulcers-Lint; Gauze, Cotton Wool, Field Dressings, Adhesive tape or plaster, bandages, Iodine, Alcohol, Iodoform, Starch Powder.

For Dysentery and Diarrhoea—Emetine, Yatren of Emetine-Bismuth-Iodine. Sulphopyridine (M.&B. 693). Tinct. Opium. Kaolin. Chalk, Bismuth, Magnesium Sulphate, Sodium sulphate.

For malaria—Soluble quinine in glass ampoules for injection.

For Beri-Beri—Large amounts of yeast tablets, or vitamin B tablets. Ampoules of concentrated Vitamin B. I. for injection (10 milligrams per ampoule).

For Skin Diseases—Sulphur, Simple ointment or Vaseline.

for general use in hospitals—Clinical Thermometers (Centigrade or Fahrenheit). Cresol, Xylenol, or other crude antiseptic for cleanliness of wards and hands and to keep down infectious disease.

Invalid Foods urgently needed—Fish oil, or Butter or Ghi, Wheat flour or Barley, Milk, Sugar, Meet, Eggs, Unhusked rice or a large supply of Rice Polishings (Silver Fleece).

I have the honour to remain, Sir,

Your obedient servant.

????

Lt-Col. RAMC

To: Colonel Banno, No. 2 Camp
Commanding, Malayan P.O.W. Thailand Sonkrai

1 Oct 1943

In view of the impending move of this force southwards, it is earnestly requested that any of these stores that are available should be supplied as soon as possible to enable the sick to recuperate sufficiently to stand the strain of the train journey.

Rice Polishings are the most urgent food requirement as one-third of the patients in the hospital are suffering from Beri-Beri as will be seen from the attached medical statistics of Tanbaya Hospital.

A list of medical requirements for Camps 1 and 2 for one month was submitted to your Headquarters about two weeks ago and no supplies have as yet reached these camps. Dressings are very urgently required.

Lieut-Colonel,
Commanding,
"F" Force

Tanbaya Hospital	Current Medical Statistic
Camp Total	1535
Malaria (Active)	350
Malaria (Convalescent)	219
Beri-Beri	554
Dysentery	512
Scabies	900
Ulcers	329

Fit Workers (including Medical & Administrative Officers and O.Rs) 182

(Signed) Bruce Hunt,
Major, AAMA,
Commanding, Tanbaya Hosp.

Lt-Col S.W. Harris, OBE, RA,

Commanding, "F" Force

The attached list of food and medical requirements for the Hospital at Tanbaya has been received from Major Hunt, Medical Officer in charge. It is strongly recommanded that the Imperial Japanese Army be asked for the above food, drugs and dressings, which urgently needed. These supplies are not available from our own resources.

Licut –Colonel, RAMC
S.M.O., "F" Force

Oct 43

List of Medical Requirements at Tanbaya Hospital

1. **Foods.** Rice Polishings
   Beans-especially Towgay (Rachang Kyan), at least 4.5 ozs per men daily
   Fats and Oils, Meat—increased ration

2. Medicines.
   B1 Vitamin Tablets and Injections. C Vitamin Tablets.
   A Vitamin Tablets.
   Sulphur-for Scabies.
   Emetine, Emetine Bismuth Iodide,) –for Amoebic
   Yatren, Stovarsol, Rivanol.) Dysentery
   Sulphonamide, Iodoform , Eusol-for ulcers.
   Ointments of all sorts, ospecially Hyd. Ammon. Dil,
   Boric and Plain Vaseline.
   Chlorodyne or Tinct Opii- for Dysentery.
   Morphine – to relieve pain
   Alcohol & Iodine, Salicylic Acid-for Ringwrom.
   Creosote Pills-for dysentery.
   Adhesive plaster, Bandages, Gauze, Lint.
   Surgical Catgut.
   Local Anaesthetic (Novocain)
   General Anaesthetic (Ether-Chloroform)

Dental Drugs and Instruments (See List)

Plasmoquine-to prevent malarial relapses.

Cresol or Xylenol-for disinfection of hands of nurses, and patients, and antiseptic sprays.

(Signed) Bruce Hunt,

Major, AAMC,

Commanding, Tanbaya Hospital

Dental Requirements

1. Local Anaesthetic (Novocain or Novatex)
2. Pair of Lower Universal forceps
3. Excavators
4. Sealers
5. 42 mm Hypodermic needles

October 7th, 1943.

To:- Lieut. Wakabyashi, Imperial Japanese Army,

Commanding Sonkrai P.O.W. Camp

On the occasion of my visit to Tanbaya Hospital in Burma with Major R.H. Anderson, A.I. F. and four other ranks, I voluntarily guarantee the good behaviour of this party and in particular I promise that no attempt will be to escape by myself or any member of it.

S.W.H.

No. 2 Camp

12 Nov 43

Sir,

In accordance with instructions received from Lieut. Wakabyashi Commandant of No. 2 Camp noted below is the suggested distribution of the Prisoners HQ during the move with which I hope you can agree.

Singapore to proceed with Ist Party:-

Lt. Col. S.W. Harris and 1 Orderly,

Kanburi to proceed with Ist Party and remain at Kanburi until move is completed.

Lt. Col. F. J. Dillon

Major Hild

Capt. Anderson

Capt. Dyer

S.S.M. Blinch

Adjutant

In charge of stores and Dump from

Nominal Rolls and Records works and 2 orderlies at Tanbaya until that Hospital is reduced to a very small figures.

F. Dillon
Lieut. Colonel,
Commander

Mr. Saji,

Headquarters,

I.J.A. H.Q.

To:- Headquarters, Kanchanabri Camp,

Malaya Prisoners of War Adminstration, 29 Nov. 1943

Malaya

Sir,

Subject:- Health of "F" Force

The attached report on the medical situation of "F" Force is submitted for your information. The departure of the party of 1, 000 prisoners of war who are due to leave for Singapore in the near future will leave the following position here:-

2,000 Ill in Hospital

1,500 Fit for light camp duties only.

These 3,500 men are broken in health and suffering from malnutrition and vitamin deficiencies. To remedy this it is essential that they receive extra food such as milk, eggs, sugar, flour and cooking oil.

At a meeting between the I.J.A. representatives (captain Hachisuka and Mr. Fujibayashi) and the British Red Cross representatives at Changi on 13 April 1943 it was agreed that when things settled down, if the force urgently required money it could apply for a grant from the International Red Cross through the I.J.A. administration, which would be the same as at Changi.

Money is urgently required by "F" Force for the purchase of special food and drugs for the 3,500 P.O.W. renaining here. This amount is estimated at $ 50,000 for a period of three months. At present hospital pationts and sick men are not paid by the I.J.A. and during the past seven months the sick of the Force have been financed by blustery contributions from the officers, who contribute 3/8th of the limited pay they receive in cash to this purpose. I do feel that the provision of extra food and medical requirements for the Force should not be the responsibility of the officers, and in any case their contributions (although, of course, these will still continue) are now totally inadequate to meet this urgent situation.

It would be greatly appreciated if the I.J.A. would allow the International Red Cross Society to:-

(1) Supply the necessary drugs and dressings for this Force which the local I.J.A. administration is unable to provide.

(2) Furnish the Force with a sum of money ($ 50,000) to purchase extra food and necessities for the sick.

The clothing of this Force is in a deplorable condition, a big proportion of the men are without boots and are literally in rags. It would be appreciated if an issue of clothing be made at the earliest opportunity.

Although the 1,000 Prisoners of War that have been selected to go to Singapore from this Force in the near future are the fittest avaible, nevertheless 200 are unfit and of the remaining 800 over 90 per cent have suffered during the past seven months from malaria and dysentery and they are bound to have freduent relapses. It is respectfully requested therefore that which ever work is allotted to this detachment should not be of too arduous a nature.

Lieut-Colonel, R.A.
Commander

To: Commander "F" Force.

Kanburi Camp,
November 28th, 1943.

Sir,

Subject: Health of "F" Force

Of the 7000 P.O.W.'s who left Changhi at the end of April 1943, about 2500 are dead of disease, 2000 are ill and in hospitals, 1500 are fit only for light camp duties and, not more than 1000 are fit for work. The principal causes of death have been Chronic dysentery, with Malnutrition, Beri-Beri, Cholera, arid Tropical ulcers, and Malaria.

Measures which will lesson disease and unfitness, (a) supply of a good mixed diet with rice polishings, fresh vegetables or fruit and cooking fats to produce 1000 calories daily for all men whether in hospital, light duties or working, (b) supply of sufficient tools to maintain a good standard of camp sanitation, buckets and scrubbing brushes, cresol and lime are essential to keep quarters etc. clean, (c) only fit men to be allowed to do heavy work such as road and railway construction, and those for not more than eight hours a day, six days a week, (d) supply of medical stores in sufficient quantity to all camps. Appendix shows the amount required monthly for 2000 hospital sick and the particular drugs etc., needed, (e) supply of boots and other clothing as required. At present many men lack boots and suffer from skin troubles of the foot, (f) It is suggested that invalid foods such as cooking oil, milk, eggs, sugar, flour be provided for the hospitals and camp sick.

It would be appreciated if the I.J.A. would allow the International Red Cross Society to supply any items (e.g. Emetine, which is the drug of greatest value in the treatment of Amoebic Dysentery, which at present appears to affect some sixty per cent of the Force), which are difficult to obtain. I have the honour to be, Sir, Your obedient servant,

J. Huston

J. Huston, Lt. Col. R.A.M.C.

S.M.O. "F" Force

Medical Supplies Required for 2000 Sick per month at Kanburi Hospital

For treatment of Malaria	In addition to Quinine, Sulphate Tablets now being supplied by the I.J.A.:—	
	Quinine ampoules for injection	100 ccs.
	Atebrine - .1 gm.	1000 tablets
	Plasmoquine - .01 gms	2000 tablets
	Atebrin mucnate ampoules	20
For Beri Beri	Rice Polishings (for treatment and prophylaxis)	100 kilos daily
	Vitamin B-1 ampoules	150
For Amebic Dysentery	Emetine Hydrochloride	400 gm.
	Tablets – Rivanol) Yatron) Rimioni)	5000 of each
	Kaolin	2 Kilos
	Tincture of Opium or Opium Tablets	1000
	Stevarsol (3 grs)	1000
	Bismuth Subnitrate	1 Kilo
For Bacillary Dysentery	Sulphopyridine .5 gm	1000
	ol. Ricini	4 kilos
	Sodium of Magnesium Sulphate	10 Kilos
For Tropical Ulcers	Fish oil (e.g. crude cod liver)	10 Kilos
	Vitamin A & C preparations Iodoform	1 kilo
	Tincture Iodine 5 per cent	2 kilos
	Sulphonilamine .5 gm.	2000
For Dressings	Adhesive Plaster	30 Reels
	Bandages, Cotton Wool, Gauze, Lint, Jaconet or Rubber Sheeting.	Sufficient for 500 daily.

For Skin Diseases	Unguentum simplex	2 kilos
	Sulphur	6 kilos
	Potassium permanganate	500 gms.
	Glycerine	2 kilos
	Calamine	1 kilo
	Zinc Oxide	1 kilo
	Acriflavine	50 gms
	Dichloride of mercury	3 bottles of 500 gms.
	Gentian Violet	50 gms.
	Alcohol	5 litres
	Boracic powder	1 kilos
	Dusting powder	2 kilos
	Salicylic acid	50 gms.
For Eye Diseases	Protargol Silver proteinate	50 gms.
	Zinc sulphate	50 gms.
For General purposes	Clinical thermometers	20
	Small brushes for paintings, lotions	10
	Scrub brushes	20
	Soap	10 Kilos
	Safety pins	500
	Cresol or other crude antiseptic	10 kilos
	Morphine for injection, 1%	100 ccs
	Bicarbonate of soda.	2 kilos
	Air or Sorborubber cushions	20 (non-recurring items)
Anaesthetics	Novocaine 5% or other local anaesthetics	500 ccs
	Anaesthetic Ether	25 kilos
	Chloroform	4 kilos

To: Lieutenant TANIO,
Medical Officer,
HQ. Malaya,
P.O.W. Camps,
NIEKE

No. 2 Camp,
Sonkrai,
19 Oct., 43.

Sir,

I have just visited the P.O.W. Hospital at No. 1 Camp, KAMI-SONKRAI, where the Medical Officers are deeply concerned by the lack of dressings for the many ulcers and for the amputations which have been caused through these. I am sorry to say that they now have to make dressings by cutting off the arms and legs of men's shirts and trousers and by cutting up officers' private-mosquito nets.

Please do your best for as by providing dressings or any material from which to make them, us this is now absolutely essential for both No.1 Camp and the Burma Hospital.

J. Huston,
Lieut-Colonel, RAMC
S.M.O., "F" Force.

I.J.A. Headquarters,
"F" Force P.O.W.
Nieke.

To: Lt-Col J. Huston, RAMC
Senior Medical Officer,
"F" Force P.O.W.,
Sonkrai Camp.

1. Please submit on the attached form the approximate monthly quantities of medical supplies received by "F" Force from the I.J.A. only, as from and including May 1943. If exact details of amounts received by staging camps and hospitals below Nieke are not known these figures should be excluded and your remarks regarding this added.
2. Details of all medical supplies and equipment which was brought up from Changi and arrived at Nieke, both from British and I.J.A. sources.
3. Details of all medical supplies and equipment brought up from Changi which arrived at Bampong.
4. The above information is required as soon as possible.

Sgd: S. Tanio, Lieut,
Senior I.J.A. Medical Officer,
"F" Force P.O.W.

1st November, 1943

To:- Commander,
"F" Force

KANCHANABRI CAMP
1 Dec 43.

Subject:- Medical Equipment "F" Force

It is requested that permission be obtained from Imperial Japanese Army for the transfer of the medical equipment, drugs and dressings and stretchers belonging to the Force at the Staging Camp nearby this camp for use in Kanchanabri Hospital. This refers to the conversation between Mr. Saji and myself yesterday.

To: Imperial Japanese Army
(Malayan Administration)

(Sgd) J. Huston.
Lieutenant-Colonel,
Royal Army Medical Corps,
Senior Medical Officer,
"F" Force.

Permission is respectfully requested for the move of the above equipment.

Lt. Col. "Royal Artillery.

Commanding "F" Force.

To: —Lieutenant Tanio | No. 2 Camp,
Medical Officer, | SONKRAI,
HQ, Malaya P.O.W.
NIEKE. | 12 Oct., 1943

Sir,

I wish to express my appreciation of your interest and help in our difficulties in the past.

I have heard from Major Hunt, Medical Officer in charge TANBAYA Hospital. He states that Beri-Beri cases have increased in number and that there are over 500 B-Beri patients in the hospital. He would like a daily supply of Vitamin B containing food, and, as Rice Polishings seem to be unobtainable, he suggests Beans or Towgay. The hospital would require 4 bags daily and we hope this would lessen Beri-Beri.

Another supply urgently needed is dressings for the Tropical Ulcers and amputations at TANBAYA and Camp No. 1. If prepared dressings are not obtainable, perhaps you could supply us with white cotton cloth (Calico or Latta) or old bed sheets for this purpose.

I know we can rely on your help to obtain these supplies to help the sick problem.

Once again thanking you,

Yours faithfully,

J. Huston, Lieut-Colonel, RAMC, S.M.O., "F" Force

Part-II

Medical Report by Lieutenant Colonel J. Huston (Sino "F" Force)

Introduction

The following Medical Report deals with conditions leading to the Death of over 3,000 British and Australian Army Prisoners of War between April 1943 and April 1944. These belonged to "F" Force, A party of approximately 7,000 men - half Australian, half British. It was taken under the care of Lieut. Colonel Banno Imperial Japanese Army, from Changi, Singapore Island, to work on the construction of the Burma-Thailand Road and Railway in the vicinity of three-pagodas pass. The main body of survivors returned to Changi in December 1943 leaving only the very Sick with their attendants, at Tanbaya Burma, and at Kanburl, (Kanchanabrui) Thailand The Survivors of these "Hospitals" rejoined at Changi at the end of April.

Appendices

App. Table I. " F" Force deaths by months, camps and main diseases.

Table II. Summary of above, total Australian and British deaths and death rate per mile per annum.

Table III. Australian and British combined rate of death by months and diseases.

Table IV. Combined death by diseases for the various camps. Table V. Deaths by diseases summarised in three 4-monthly period.

App. 'B' Nominal roll of medical Officers with "F" Force and numbers of medical other ranks.

App. 'C' Samples of letters addressed to I.J.A.

Two I.J.A. notes Illustrating different Ideologies and the difficulties In dealing with the Nippon viewpoints.

App. 'D' Two reports from officer wardmasters inserted to illustrate the difficulties in nursing.

App. 'E' Sketch Map of South Burma and Upper Thailand illustrating working area of 'F' Force.

App. 'F' Report on Tropical Ulcers as seen in "F" Force.

App. 'G' Details of "F" Force Thailand Camp Diets with an analysis and extracts from this report of Capt. T. Wilson, R.A.M.C. (Nutrition Expert).

Medical Report "F" Force

Prisoners of War for period April 1943 - April 1944

Preliminary Information

At the beginning of April 1943 information was received at Changi, Singapore, that a force of 7,000 P.O.W. would move by train at an early date. The orders stated that the food situation at Changi was difficult, but this would be better at the new destination, that it was not to be a working party and that it would include 30 per cent unfit men who would have better chances of recovery as the new place would be situated In low hills with good facilities for improving their health. Bands, lighting sets, all tools and cooking gear were to be taken. Canteens would be available after the first three weeks. There was to be no marching except from trains to adjoining camps and transport for baggage and unfit would be provided. A medical party (for composition, see Appendix B.) with equipment for 400 patients and medical supplies were to be included.

The personnel had been P.O.W. since the capitulation of Singapore to the Japanese on 15.2.42. The anticipated effects of the ration supplies to prisoners by the I.J.A. had been reported to their Headquarters in writing by the British and Australian Medical authorities at Changi at the beginning of March 1942. It was then pointed out that the diet was deficient in proteins, fats and vitamins, that it was too low in quality to support health and that serious diseases such as Beri-Beri and Pellagra would follow if the defects were not remedied. These ill effects had appeared for many months at Changi before departure of "F" Force, a large majority of whose personnel had been in hospital once or many times with dysentery or pellagroid manifestations (glossitis, stamatitis, serotal dermatitis, pellagra skin, burning feet, partial ambylopia, granular cornea) or scabies and infected skin conditions. Diptheria was rife. Many men were thin and undernourished after periods in hospital. Diet centres where better food was provided from Canteen and Red Cross sources, had improved the condition of these sick men, and many of the recovered were included in the force. They were fit enough to move by train to the better conditions promised.

The Medical Store at Changi was already depleted of many useful stores because of supplying forces of P.O.W. who had left previously and the consumption of large hospital populations there and in working camps at Singapore. Consequently Emetine (100 grains), Diphtheria antiserum, Sulphonamide drugs, Sulphar, Magnesium sulphate all very important drugs were produced in negligible quantity. Blankets (20 very old and worn) Mattress covers, bedpans and urine bottles were inadequate. Small quantities of meat extract, tinned milk and meat were taken. Units of the force took their carefully saved Red Cross rations where these existed.

The force consisted of approximately, 3,500 Australian and 3,500 British troops. The whole party was submitted to anal swabbings and blood (thick drop) examination before departure by I.J.A. Vaccimnation against Smallpox, inoculation against Dysentery, Plague, Cholera and Enteric were given in 2 doses at weekly intervals under Area managements. In some cases these were not completed owing to alterations in the train programme.

Train Move: Personnel was moved by lorries from Changi, and entrained in all metal rice trucks at Singapore. 28-29 men were packed in each truck. A Medical party including or more Medical officers and a box of Medical requirements were taken with each train. These were adequate for the Journey which lasted 5 days. Thirteen trains moved the parties. As each train load of 600 arrived Bampong Thailand, Kit which could not be carried was dumped. Each party was reached to a nearby transit camp and was detailed to march, the same night or following night carrying all that could be carried. The camp at Bampong was insalubrious, the forerunner of worse places to come. No troops staged more than 24 hours and all were fatigued after 5 days cramped in hot truck with poor meals at infrequent intervals. Medical parties moved with each trainload, leaving the sick in a bamboo hut to be taken care of by the next incoming party until the following day. On orders of O.C. 'F' Force Lt. Col. S.N. Harris O.B.E. R.A. I stayed after arrival in Train 9 to see to the disposal of the sick unable to march up the road.

When the whole force had passed through, there remained some 50 seriously ill men. Much negotiation resulted in 5 of the worst dysentery patients being removed to a Japanese Hospital in the neighbourhood (these were well treated) and the others were carried in loaded ration lorries two marches up the road to Kanchanabri (KANBURI). These Included acute-pleurisy and pneumonia, a fractured femur etc., and all were ill. They were cared for by Major Rogers AAMC and party who remained behind at this camp until the return of 'F'. Force at the end of November 1943 when a total mortality of one for the whole period was reported. These were Fortunes Favourites, the mortality of the upcountry camps exceeded this figure.

The Medical stores of the Force were dumped with all other equipment at Bampong; it was difficult to locate the most important articles. I was able to get hands on about 12 panniers of drugs and equipment and move these in the two lorries with the sick when the last party left. Meanwhile each road party took such essentials as were at hand and could be carried. Valiant efforts were made to take as such as possible.

At Bampong I represented the great necessity of getting forward the main medical equipment to Lt. Col. Banno, the Japanese Officer i/c 'F' Force, he said it would be sent on within a few days. He accompanied the two lorries and after leaving the 50 sick at Kanburi, we went on to Tarsu and spent the night. Next morning we were joined by Lt. Col. Harris, O.C. 'F' Force who had proceeded us, when some 15 Km. beyond Tarsu, near Kanu, Col. Banno stopped and ordered me to take the medical panniers and form a wayside hospital for the marching men of the force. It was pointed out by Col. Harris and myself, through an interpreter that as S.M.O. it would be better for me to go ahead to sake medical arrangements at our final destination. Major W.J.E. Phillips R.A.M.C. who had been ill at Bampong was with us, and we told Col. Banno that we could leave him there to make a Hospital. Col. Banno's mind was made up. Both Major Phillips and I were left with the Medical Panniers and a Japanese medical orderly who produced a very rat-eaten Inner lining of a small marquee this was to house the hospital for the sick. We carried the equipment to a bamboo patch beside a stream by the road and dealt as best we could with the sick arriving each morning after their night-long march. Rations were poor, marching parties were exhausted and had to sleep in the open, and there were many sick with dysentery, diarrhoea and an enormous number of the blisters and sores on feet and legs. There was a daily battle with the accompanying guards who wanted to make the maximum possible numbers march up the road. Between preparation and taking of food, having feet attended to, muster and roll-call, the marchers averaged 3 hours sleep at thle camp. There was no shelter except the hospital 'tent' which sheltered the men -most of them were raised upon with monotonous regularity as the monsoon had broken. Major Phillips was sent off with one of the later parties these were men who had been sick at other stages on the road and were being hurried forwards to catch up with the main body. Officers and men were for the most pert unfit—many of them wretchedly so.

By the end of May I received a note from Col. Harris that Cholera had broken out in the camps where "F" Force were located and that the I.J.A. ordered movements to camps to continue. He asked me to come up as quickly as possible as Col. Banno now sanctioned this, and to send up any stores suitable for dealing with Cholera. I packed a pannier with such funnels, tubing, needles, Sodium chloride, camphorodyae, and Pot. Permanganate as were with me and despatched them with directions by an on going lorry. I repeatedly asked all Japanese in the vicinity assisted by tha interpreter with "H" Force H.Q. nearby; but nobody would or could allow me to proceed. The excuses were that the roads were impossible or it was not within their jurisdiction to allow the move. Had Col. Banno or his staff sent a written order, this useless delay would have been avoided. Finally at the beginning of July, 2 months after arrival, I was allowed to go back to Tarsu by Garge with 30 sick men who had been in the camp for weeks, they were left i/c Major Aguew and after 2 days interrogation by the Japanese P.M.O. on Cholera, Indian Epidemics etc., I was sent to Tunknun by boat, delayed 6 days there, and marched to Nieke by Korean guards, arriving at "F" Force H.Q. in mid-July.

9 Medical panniers were taken from me by I.J.A. at Kanu, those contained among other stores tinned milk, soup, beef etc., for invalids. I was allowed the 9 remaining Panniers as far as Tarkanun and arrived at Nieke without there. (those finally arrived a month later).

It may be mentioned that conditions in Tamil and British camps in the Kanua area were utterly distressing. Coolies stricken with Cholera or dysentery were ordered out into the Jungle by their guards and there left to die. A British camp (O.C. Lt. Col. Warren, Royal Marines) was almost knee deep in mud, including the hospital huts; their employers made neferious demands for labour, there was a shocking sick rate. The mortality for June 1943 was 104 out of proximately 650 strength (including only 2 cases of cholera).

These two notes describe conditions of the march. The reports of other medical officers relate to similar experiences.

Extract from a Report by Major B.A. Hunt RAMC

The march was long and extremely arduous - It laid the foundations for the widespread debilitation of the force which played a major part in increasing the death rate from infectious diseases (Cholera Malaria and dysentery). The march was always one done at night. The average distance covered was about 23 K.M. and the majority of the troops covered 14 such stages aggregating it about 300 k. "Rest nights" were given at Camp 2, Camp 4, and Camp 9, but many men who had been left behind for a night on account of illness were unable to take advantage of these, being compelled to press on and endeavour to join their parties. After the first two marches which were along a highway the roads were bad and usually very bad—the moon gave no assistance or most of the march-rain was frequent and conditions on really wet nights were nightmarish. Owing to the appalling road conditions many of the marches lasted 10-14 hours with only very short halts. Little rest could be obtained at the staging camps, specially by the medical personnel, most of whose tme was taken up in attending to the sick from their own and previous parties, and in dressing the hundreds of injured and ulcerated feet which were brought to them for attention. There was no shelter at any of the camps apart from improvised bivuaos, and heavy rain frequently made these ineffective. Every possible endeavour was made by M.Os. to protect the sick against the weather, with, however, only moderate success.

Food was poor—it consisted almost solely of rice and onion water. At the first three staging camps it was possible to purchase supplementary food but thereafter these facilities ceased.

Treatment of the troops, and in particular the sick, by the I.J.A. guards varied from march to march and from camp to camp. At some camp, the M.O. of the party was allowed to leave behind without interference, such men as he considered unfit to march. On other occasions the M.O. was subject to much interference, and at several places man with active malaria or dysentery or with large infected ulcers on their feet were compelled to do a whole night's march, to the great detriment of their health. One such episode, the details of which are still fresh in my mind, is worth recording. At Camp 5 (Tarso) I was informed that all sick had to be submitted for inspection to the I.J.A. M.O. who was stationed about ½ mile away. The total of sick on this occasion, derived from men from my own and previous parties, was 37-27 with infected feet, 10 with malaria and dysentry. The Japanese officer agreed that none of these men were fit to march but the corporal of the guard only gave permission for 10 to remain. A further interview with the I.J.A. M.O. by Major Wild (interpreter) and myself confirmed the previous advice and produced a letter of instruction from the MO/also to the corporal. This was resultless as was a further visit from Major Wild to the H.O. later that afternoon.

At the time sheduled for parade I fell in the 37 sick men apart from the main parade, and Major Wild and I stood in front of them. The corporal approached with a large bamboo in his hand and spoke menacingly to Major Wild who answered in placetory fashion. The corporals only reply was to hit Major Wild in the face. Another guard followed suit and as Major Wild staggered back the corporal thrust at the Major's gentalis with his bamboo. I was left standing in front of the patients and was immediately set upon by the Corporal and two other guards - one tripped me while two others pushed me to the ground. The three then set about me with bamboos, causing extensive bruising of skull, back hands and arms, and a fractured left 5th metacarpal bone. This episode took place in front of the whole parade of the troops. After I was disposed of the corporal then made the majority of the sick men march with the rest of the troops.

At camp 6 I was again struck and some of my patients rejected - these were the only occasions on which I persennally received violence at the hands of the guards. It was the general practice of M.O.'s to march at the rear of the column to succour the stragglers and to endeavour to prevent any possible molestation of these by the guards - I saw such threatened on a number of occasions as sick men were hurried along, but the intervention was usually successful, and I never saw a blow struck under these circumstances.

The chief disabilities which manifested themselves during march were:-

(1) *Senility and Cardiac weaknesses.* All these cases were left behind at Camp 2, and I believe that many of them were forced along the road with fatal results.

(2) *Dysentery.* Became increasingly common as the march progressed (I myself was held up for a day at Camp 9 by a very acute attack of Bacillary Dysentery.

(3) *Septic abrasions of the feet.* Many of the boots were fitting and very many of the men wire totally unaccustomed to marching.

(4) *Fever.* Were of lesser frequency and importance until arrival in worker camps.

Report by Assistant - Surgean Woolf M.D.

Left Singapore on No. 7 Train. On March from Bampong carried out duties of M.O. as Capt. Sillon was ill and remained behind at about fourth halt Medical duties were difficult owing to

1. Shortage of drugs, dressings and orderlies (only 2 untrained orderlies were available owing to others having dropped out).
2. Arduous conditions on the march. Medical personnel had to treat sick left

behind by former party soon after arrival at camp. On completion of this they had to attend to the sick of their own party. In addition had to treat sick all along the route of march and consequently had little time to rest between marches.

Arrived lower Nikki late May. The following day Cholera broke out and an isolation ward was immediately established. I worked in this ward until the arrival of two more medical officers. The next day, under orders from Col. Dillon and Col. Harris, I and four nursing orderlies proceeded to Konkoita. On arrival there I saw a horrible scene. In one tent on the bank of the river fifteen patients were lying helpless. Eight of these were suffering from Cholera with nobody to attend to them. The whole area was polluted with infectious stools and vomit, and full of flies. A report was made to the Japanese Medical Officer (Major) who removed us to the coolies'. Cholera camp. In spite of repeated requests this Officer refused to give any transport to move these patients to hospital. He also refused to give any drugs or adequate accommodation (most of us were left out in the rain). I treated these cases with M & B Em No 4. and saline by a transfusion set improvised from stetheccope rubber and funnel. These drugs were soon exhausted and I sent an orderly with an urgent appeal for help to 2/29 Bn. A.I.F. camped at Timonta, 7 Miles away. An officer was sent next day with necessary drugs etc., I then received orders from Col Harris to proceed to Timonta to relieve Capt. Mills (M) who was ill. I could not leave my patients and go to Timonta, so I suggested that all of us, including patients, should go to Timonta. The Japanese M.O. refused permission for the move.

On 5.6.43 eventually after a great deal of representations from 2/29 Bn., I was told I could take all my patients to Toimonta. No transport was provided. I raised subscriptions amongst ourselves and promised to pay for the hire of 2 or 3 bullock carts. This was refused. We improvised bamboo stretchers and carried 5 strectcher cases, two men carrying a stretcher. The rest of the patients had to struggle along somehow. It was impossible to carry the patients very far in the heavy rains and boggy roads. Col. Dillon had told me that on the authority of Col. Banno, I would get all the necessary help at Konkoita from the Japanese hospital. The Japanese MO not only refused to give me any help but treated me most callously and only smiled when I remonstrated to him that we would all die there if we were not given drugs, help and transport. He did not seem to care. Fortunately, there were no sentries and we managed to get out of the camp area and hide ourselves in the jungle. I then sent an orderly to Timonta with an appeal for the help. The 2/29 Bn, immediately sent an officer and 50 men with stretchers and food and carried all our sick to their camp. Through an act of Providence, we did not lose a single patient. I owe great thanks to Col. Kappe, Col. Pond and Capt. Mills for their great kindness and prompt help, otherwise we would have been stranded. I must also mention the great and unselfish work, under the most trying conditions, that was done by the orderlies, particularly by 1,Cpt Somerfield R. and Pte. Carlton of the A.A.M.C.

On my arrival at Timonta I found the MO (Capt. Mills) sick and still working very hard. He was forced to go on leave and I carried out his duties. This unit was under great hardships, on half rations and more were about 400 sick including Cholera cases. After a weeks stay here, I left with half 2/29 Bn. to Nikki, Capt. Mills remaining behind with patients and unfit men. This march was one of the worst I have experienced I reported to Col. Harris on my arrival at Lower Nikki hospital and marched with Col. Harris and patients to Upper Nikki.

After a few days work in Upper Nikki hospital Cholera broke out again and I was detailed by Major Phillips to be, i.c., of Cholera Isolation Hospital, furlongs away from the main hospital. In addition to our troops I was obliged to treat Burmese patients here. One incident here is worth mentioning. When under orders from Col. Dillon, I objected to admitting Burmese collies to our Hospital, the Japanese threatened to hit me and gave as a long lecture about "superiority complex" and about our being fed and paid by the Japanese Govt. and as such we have to obey and work for them. The little success I have had in treating cholera was I think due to the following treatment. Large saline transfusions (about 4- pints on the first day, 2 or 3 pints on subsequent days depending upon the condition of pulse, dehydration, vomiting, diorrhoea etc.) M & B tablets, Fn No 4 (weak solutions orally), cordise stimulents when necessary, plenty of fluids, rest nursing, etc.

At the end of the cholera epidemic, I worked a few days in the malaria ward at Nikki. On 1.8.43. I proceeded to Ronchi there I stayed for about 20 days, i/c of staging section, Burma Hospital, I then went to Tanbaya where I was in charge of Dysentary Ward and did other small jobs such as M.I. Room and Isolation Ward at times. On final evacuation of Tanbaya Hospital, I came along with patients to Kanburi.

I owe thanks to all my superior officers particularly to Major Hunt and Cols. Huston Harris, Dillon and Hutchison for the encouragement and help they gave me in my work and for their kindness to us.

Health of 'F' Force—May to November 1943

The staple article of diet was rice, supplemented by small and varying quantites of dried "Chinese radish", beans, whitebait, dried meat oil, and in certain camps (e.g No. 2 during June and July) some lean local beef. During 4 months at No 2 Camp one bag of Rice Polishings was supplied. Rice polishlngs was also supplied to Tanbaya Hospital, Burma after repeated requests from 15 October 1943 until its closing down with very beneficial results in the health of the patients and staff there. The amount of rice issued for the men working was slightly deficient in per cent total calories, that for Camp staff more so, that for the sick was totally inadequate for the maintenance of body weight, and the recovery of health. Efforts were made in all camps to use local produce, e.g., wild pumpkin leaves to build up deficiencies. There is a report from Capt. T. Wilson. R.A.M.O. Dietetic with F Force which gives an accurate picture of this diet, its intended distribution and its effects.

No. 2, Camp.
31.7.1943

"**Diet**. Major Dobson R.A.S.C. has supplied figures for the rations actually received for the 16 day period 6-21st July 1943, of different amounts to seperate groups, such as working parties, camp duty men and the sick, but the main difference is in the amount of rice supplied to each group. Assuming that items such as onions, beans, potatoes, whitbait, dried meat and oil were supplied and divided equally I estimate that these supply only 340 Calories per man per day.

The remainder of the energy requirements have to be made up from rice issue. Rice provides approximately 360 Calories per 100 gms. (dry weight). Sick men receive roughly 300 gms. of rice per day, so that their diet only give about 1420 Calories. This is below the amount needed for basal metabolism and maintenance of the body weight even in health, and quite inadequate to help a patient through an attack of disease or to enable him to recuperate afterwards. In other words once a man goes sick he either dies of disease or is gradually starved to death. I consider the present very high death rate, in the absence of acute opidemic disease, most be largely a result of this very poor diet.

The energy values for the camp duty men, assuming 600 gms. of rice is 2500 calories, and for working parties, assuming 700 gms. rice and 100 gms. dried fish, is 3,000 calories. These figures are better though still well below normal requirements for the types of work done, but the diet of all groups is seriously lacking in Vitamins, particularly these of the B Compex; Beri-beri is already prevalent and increasing. The diet is also lacking in fat and protein.

I consider it esentlal that the ration for sick and convalescents - should be increased to at least 400 gms. rice per day and that an essestial, Rice pollshlngs, more towgay, peanuts, potatoes, green leaf vegetables and fats should be provided for everyone to make good the existing deficiencies. There is sufficient pumpkin leaf growing in the isolation area camp with green leaf vegetables for quite a long time. The leàves have been pointed out to several people ıcluding officers".

The poor diet, especially defective in Vitamins A & B was, in my opinion the most important factor in producing the enormous sick and death rates which prevailed in 'F' Force during the whole period. The ration of the sick was supplemented by deductions from that of the fitter personnel whilist local purchases from Camp Funds, of tinned fish, milk, sugar, the only articles purchasable were used to make the diet of the very sick a little more nourishing aud attractive. This could only be done in a very small way and only in some camps. No sick man could lose in single day's feeding without the direct consequences. With the sources of Malaria or the flux of dysentary upon them, eating was difficult and sometimes impossible. Thus died many prisoners.

Working Conditions

The working hours were lond and ardous. Men arose at 7 a.m. had breakfast and wer mirchal out at 8 a.m., they returned from work 12 to 19 hours later. They worked seven days a week.

Here are the figures for the camp, (of the time prebably the fittest on lest bed time) for the first 9 days after their arrival on the evening of the 25th may 1943.

	Working	*Sick*	*Camp duties*
May. 27th	330	50	13
28th	285	90	18
29th	282	93	18
30th	271	103 (1 death)	18
31th	267	107	18
June. 1 st	260	113 (1 death)	18
2nd	215	160	18
3rd	215	160	18
4th	182	193	18

That the Engineers were quickly destroying their source of labour was repeatedly explained to our own I.J.A. Headquarters by the Force Commander. Even Col. Banno understood this, but the, state of affairs continued.

The conditions of the sick was demonstrated to the local Engineers. They would rush out of the sick huts rather than endure the sight of the results of their inhumun treatment. Numbers were demanded and if they were not supplied they were taken out of the hospital huts in camps, despite the utmost protests of our officers and Doctors. The 3 a.m. parade was generally known as "the murder parade" and not without foundation.

By the end of June of 5,000 men North of Nieke, 700 were at work daily and at least half of this 700 were unfit and useless for heavy work. Apart from the Red Cross men and the small camp staff and the remainder were lying ill camp hospitals. Working conditions continued in this way until the railway was completed at the end of October.

Our own administration and camp staffs made repeated pleas and suggestions to ameliorate working conditions with slight or no success. The Engineers appeared to have complete control of working conditions and were insensible to any of our requests. The I.J.A. Administrative Staff on the other hand, appeared in certain camps, to be concerned about the condition of their prisoners. Camps at Nieke, Shimo Sonkurai, (from early August) managed to improve conotatlon and accommodation by getting a proportion of working men off for outside work for short periods.

At Tanbaya Hospital (August 1943-January 1944) and at Kanburi Hospitals December 1943-April 1944) men were only required to maintaining their own camps.

Accommodation: Accommodation was always totally inadequate. Prisoners, whether in hospital or fit lay closely packed, touching each other, on platforms made of split bamboo. In many huts there were two docks of platforms so that men had to climb ladders to get to bed. These added to the difficulties of reaching the latrines in the dark. Scabies was universal owing to the crowding. Louse infestation was widespread. At No.2. Camp these conditions were so bad that epidemic typhus seemed likely to occur. Fortunately the transference of large numbers of sick to Tanbaya Hospital in August removed the threat. The huts were made of bamboo, roofed with attap. (At Timonta and Tarkanun only (camp 4) men were accommodated in tents. Huts were partially or completely roofless for the first week or two, the roofs leaked and gullies of storm water ran through them during rainstorms.

Bugs were universal. They added to lack of sleep and to septic skin conditions. Accommodation to segregate cholera patients from others was not provided at Camp 5 until mid-June though the epidemic started in mid-May. The same happened at Tarkanun. At the hospital in Kanburi (Dec. 43 - April 44) where conditions had improved enormously accommodation was still tight. Huts 132' x 21' held 120 patients.

Water: At all camps water was available from adjoining streams or the river, except at Tanbaya where there were 2 wells (which dried) and a river 800 yards away. At Kanburi II there were two small wells and a water cart service from the river 1 mile away. At no camp or hospital was there a piped supply.

Drinking Water had to be boiled before use in mess tins and eating utensils had to be sterilized for each meal. Shortage of containers for water storage and sterilization was a most difficult problem (except at Kanburi where containers brought from Changi were available). 44 galloon drums were used (extensively) where they could be procured. In some camps e.g. Camp 5.', although there were plenty of drums, we were not allowed to use them. Our own water sterilising powder and tablets was conserved for use during moves.

Ablution. Man bathed in the river when opportunity occurred. Bathing parades were allowed at most camps—the difficulty was that the working parties did not get back to camp until after dark—when bathing was prohibited. At Camp 3 the only bathing place available was a small creek which ran through the middle of the camp. It drained the seepage of the area and was most foul.

Cooking. This was done in saucer-like metal bowls (kuelas) holding 12 galloons heated over open trench fires or built up on mud platforms. Cooking was done in the open with a light bamboo and attap superstructure. Working conditions were difficult in the rains.

Latrines. At halts on the march and at camps on arrival latrines were open trenches of varying depths 92' to 4' as a rule. These were foul and teeming with fly larvae. Dysentery was rife. On pointing this out to I.J.A. I was told that flies made no difference, all men had been anal swabbed at Changi, and there were no dysentery carriers. At most camps that latrines were on higher ground owing to fouled areas of the camps. Efforts were made to improve matters by making deep trench latrines (12 ft to 14ft) with solid wooden covers and lids making the structure flyproof.

Where this was done for sufficient numbers (as in Camp No. 1) it was successful. The difficulties in obtaining tools and labour were enormous. More of the trenches were left semi-open with bamboo straddle slats. All latrines were of the squatting type. Separate places were kept for dysentery patients. Bamboo bedpans and later improvised commodes, made from oil tins were used for the lying sick. Apart from a scanty supply of lime there were no crude anti-septics except a few bottles of our own stock of cresol which were used diluted in bamboo drop bottles for disinfection of hands. Latrine paper was not supplied except later in Burma. Fouling of ground by demoralised men suffering from diarrhoea and dysentery was common. Corduroy tracks to latrines were made gradually from bamboo to aid men in their journey through the mud which was difficult to negotiate in the darkness. Strong disciplinary action had usually to be taken to prevent fouling of the ground. Sanitary squads at all camps worked hard and some showed amazing ingenuity in overcoming difficulties.

Medical Stores issued by the I.J.A. Until the return of "F" Force to Kanburl, the amount of drugs and dressings Issued was minute. Upcountry small issues of drugs were made (so far as I am aware) on three occasions. For months camp hospitals had no drugs to treat dysentery or diarrhoea except charcoal made locally. Tom up shirt sleeves, mosquito netting and banana leaves were used to cover the thousands of ulcers. It was difficult to preserve sufficient wool and gauze to cover the stumps of freshly amputated limbs. Considered carefully it is probable that 70 per cent of the Force was (and still is) infected with Amoebic Dysentery. Yet the only issue off freshly amputated limbs. Considered carefully it is probable that 70 per cent of the Forces was (and still is) infected with Amoebic Dysentery. Yet the only issue of specific drug was 100 1/3 grains Emetine Ampoules to the Tanbaya Hospital where there were 1500 men in hospital, hundreds of them in need of this paritcular drug. (The amount received was sufficient for 3 patients judged by normal British standards). Two other camps received smaller quantities and the remainder, none. I implored Col. Banno to inform the International Red Cross of our urgent needs of drugs and invalid foods, if the I.J.A. could not supply them. He said I was a theorist.

On the return of the Force to Kanburi, the supply of drugs was much better and the I.J.A. Commandant (Lieut Wakabyashi) did everything he could to help us.

Quinine and Anti-Cholera vaccine (given every 3 months) were supplied more liberally Quinine tablets (3½ gr) were, however, much short of our requirements suppressive quinine could rarely be used as it was required for treatment purposes of Malaria which continually affected some 50 per cent of the Force. Even then it too frequently fell short of normal treatment requirements. At Kanburi it was possible to provide adequate treatment aid adequate suppressive dosage during the greater part of the period with the resulting improvement in the malarial sick rate. (50 per cent reduced to 10 per cent). Sulphur was urgently needed for the specific treatment of scabies which affected the whole Force. A few grammes only were ever supplied. Our own Administration purchased small quantities through the Canteen supplier at funtastically high prices from September onwards. The supply of this drug was sufficient at Kanburi. Constant demands were made for concentrated Vitamin B extracts or Rice polishings to treat and prevent Beri-beri. From September onwards a supply of Ebios (Yeast) tablets was issued to Camp 3, and Rice polishings was issued to Tanbaya only. At Kanburi it was purchased out of Camp funds. Small quantities of Vitamin B1 ampoules for injection were issued by the I.J.A. These were most useful in the acute cardiac emergencies of Beri-Beri.

It is hard to conceive why Rice Polishings, which would have saved many hundreds of cases of Beri-beri, should be difficult to obtain in Burma, Thailand or Malaya, countries with many rice mills. The only answer given as at Kanburi—"They are difficult to obtain because we use them to feed our Cavalry horses".

Conditions during movement of prisoners. Presumably in order to reinforce labour at various points, or to make room for coolies frequent movement took place. Conditions then were generally night-marish. Only a few examples need be quoted (note necessarily the worst).

Camp 4 (400 strength) moved from Timonta on 21/6/43 carrying by hand their tents, cooking gear, kits and sick about 50 kms., arriving near tartanun. The road was a muddy moress entailing an enormous expenditure of energy; it also entailed walking men over a skeleton bridge 50 above a river torrent and across a preapitious cliff force. When this party eventually marched back to Nieke at the beginning of November their number were reduced to 100 fit men.

At the end of July orders were received to remove now all sick and fit men from Nieke to No. 2 and No. 3 Camps apart from those earmarked go to Tanbaya Hospital. No transport was to be provided. Force Administration eventually prevailed on Col. Banno to leave the very ill and dying men (about 120). The remaining hospital sick had to march 12 kms to Camp 2. We were allowed frequent halts as the men were pathetically weak and ill and road extremely broken and muddy.

The move of men unlikely to recover under 2 months to Tanbaya Burma (see Appendix D) commenced at the end of July and continued piece-meal for the following 6 weeks. Transport provided was open lorries on roads and the usual metal rice trucks on rail. At all camps involved there was always complete uncertainty of the time and number to move the I.J.A. guards were excitable at these times. The sick would be laid out on the sides of the road for hours on I.J.A. orders awaiting lorries; they were frequently taken back to their huts in the evening owing to them not arriving. There was never bedding or straw on the metal floors of the lorries or railway trucks. We had not been able to bring more than half a dozen service stretchers from Bampong (where 200 were left) so bamboo stretchers made with matting or rice sacks were used, to carry the lying. The I.J.A. were kind enough to provide a quantity of rice, sacks in lieu of blankets or bedding. The sick on this move were passed through one or more staging camps at camp 5 Kandu, Ronahi, on their Journey (Nieke-Tanbaya was 83 Kms) The trouble was that no extra accommodation was provided. Camp 5 had shockingly inadequate facilities. One of our Medical Officers with a small medical party was at each of the above camps but arrangements were bad. Only part of the railway in Burma was completed at the time. Guards jabbed ulcerated buttocks to make the sick 'speedo' in their climb into the railtrucke and stoned them to 'speedo' the unfortunates out again. A party of ulcers patients had to walk 4 Kms from Ronchi to the railway. Their ulcers poured blood over their ankles as they stumbled along. Accommodation in rail trucks varied, the worst case reported was 54 men plus panniers and containers (these trucks measure 19'3" × 7'3").

There were 50 deaths on the move to Tanbaya and hosts of men died soon after arrival there. This table of deaths at Tanbaya speaks for itself:—

	British		*Australian*	
Camp	*Died*	*Arrived*	*Died*	*Arrived*
Nieke	71	160	35	143
No.1			81	342
No.2	408	751	109	380
No.5	70	133		
	549	1044	225	865

Last death 20 January 1944.

The move from the Burma-Thailand border to Kanburi was carried out by rail. At the end of November all fit and sick were moved to Kanburl except 316 of the very sick and small staff left at Tanbaya. The latter party moved down at the end of January 1944, their move was well arranged and they were not too over-crowded in the usual metal trucks. There were two deaths on the journey.

The main body, at the end of November was not fortunate. All heavy sick from Nieke No. 2 & 3 Camps—some of them moribund, were ordered to move. Trains were loaded in a bhrry sometimes at night. The guards were sometimes excited. Accommodation average 30-40 per truck-including very ill men. Our own I.J.A. administration did try to get more transport and Lt. Wakabyashi and Dr.Tanio were obviously distressed by conditions, when the parties commenced this journey. 46 men died during the move and 186 during the first three weeks at Kanburi

· **Camp Hospitals**. The conditions described in the foregoing paragraphs applied to all camp Hospitals. Patients were accommodated in tent and huts in the same way as the fit men. There were no special hospital facilities anywhere. The nursing staff consisted of RAMC, AAMC (and voluntour orderlies among there was heavy upcountry these was an average rich rate of 6 per cent) and men had to work like the outsider workers when ill, a high proputroned died. There were many outstanding workers, who gave of their best without stint; others were of poorer quality, and suffered from lowered morale, medical officers and assistant surgeons were overworked and many were sick (about 60 per cent). It was found that the Wardmaster system—the placing of Combatant officers incharge of discipline and detailed administrative arrangements in each hut had great advantages and helped to make things work more smoothly and efficiently. The method was adopted at No. 1, 2 and 3 Camps and Tanbaya and Kanburi Hospitals. Advantages were:—

(a) It relieved the medical staff of much non-medical work, e.g., wood, water feeding, discipline, returns, disposal effects.

(b) ensured continuous supervision-which medical officers were unable to do.

(c) shared the heavy responsibilities of the care of the sick with Medical officers and kept the whole camp informed of current difficulties and the progress of patients.

Details of wardmasters duties are well described in Appendix E in the reports of H.D. Price, R.C. of Signals, and Capt. G. Gwyne; 2, 4 M.G. Bn AIF.

This system was first adopted by Major B. Hunt at No.1 Camp and such praise is due to his energy and enthusiasm in training many officers in this work. Officers wardmasters needed to be strong characters, with the wisdom of Solomon and the patience of Job. Their adoption must not be taken to infer criticism of as medical colleagues nor of the others ranks, nursing. They worked endlessly and under as miserable conditions as anyone can imagine. Attending to incontinent and dying men in the darkness of long nights with only the light of a fire or bamboo flares to guide them, required stamine and endless patience, Maintaining the strength of men suffering froa disease, on the rations preparation of rice etc., and patients held to be forced to eat to enable them to maintain their weight which once lost could not be regained on the ration. Cooking facilities and the rations did not permit much variety. Rice pep and tea for breakfast, Rice and thin stew for dinner, rice and riseple or vegetable has and tea for supper was the usual fare. Lest it be thought that the subject of food has been laboured this was the I.J.A. ration at Kanburi Hospital (we were fortunate enough to be able to supplement it there with peanuts, eggs, fish and rice polishings bought with officers subscriptions and Canteen profits).

Daily Average of Goods Supplied by I.J.A. Kanburi Hospital-Period 17 Dec. '43 - 31 Mar. '44

Average Strength	*Rice*	*Sugar*	*Tea*	*Salt*	*Oil*	*Curry Powder*	*Pepper*
708.329	676.5 ozs	518.1 ozs	123.1	210.3	29.5	3 ozs	25 ozs
Average Rst. p. man per day	15.28 ozs	.678 ozs	.173 ozs	.282 ozs	.818 ozs	.004 ozs	.035 ozs
Extimated Weights	801 lbs per bag	100 lbs per bag	90 lbs cases	80 lbs per bag	4 Gal Tin	lbs 5 ozs	1 lbs 5 ozs per tin

Average Strengt	*Vegetable*	*Meat*	*Pork*	*Eggs*	*Fish*	*Poultry*	*Cheese*	*Butter*
708.329	3821 lbs 4.5 ozs	39.62 ozs	197. 285 ozs	221. 18 ozs	91. 429 ozs	137 only	6.5 ozs	8 ozs
Average Rat. p. man per day	8.63 ozs	.056 ozs	.278 ozs	.62 ozs	.129 ozs	.02 ozs	.009 ozs	.011 ozs
Estimated weights	601 lbs per Basket			2 ozs per egg	40 lbs per case	for 105 days	12 ozs tins	16 ozs tins

12. Main diseases: The predisposing factors—previous illness, poor quality and quantity for food, hardship and exposure have been described.

The main diseases were of one general pattern. Most patients suffered from two, three or more conditions at the same time, i.e., Malaria, dysentery, ulcers, beriberi, in any combination.

Cholera epidemic: I.J.A. Medical authorities diagnosed among Thai labourers in huts at Konkoits on Prisoners from Train parties 1-6 had passed this Camp and occupied its huts. Movement was to continue by the I.J.A. 2 cases of Cholera appeared at No.1 Camp on 17.5.43 and further cases on 18th, and following lays, appeared at Shino-Nieke on 15th May at No. 2 Camp on 21 May at No. 3, 4 and 5 on 26th May. It should be noted that there were great numbers of Tami! Thai and Burmese labourers in or close to all the same huts had been used by them until our arrival (e.g. in Camp 3).

The disease presented no unusual features. The main wave of the epidemic was over by Mid-June, but carriers and cases occurred in Camp 3 as late as August and September. The mortality varied from 66 per cent to 15 per cent (Nieke and Camp 1). There was a much heavier preponderance of cases and deaths among British Troops than among Australian. This seems to have been due to the fact (a) that the A.I.F. were a fitter body of men when we left Changi (b) they had been left intact in main units, e.g., 28th, 29th and 30th Bns. whereas the British were composed of bits and pieces of many units who had supplied previous Forces from Singapore (c) there were a number of British and Volunteers who had been on Asiatic service for years before the war, without a break (d) conditions at Camp 5, a wholly British Camp, were deplorable, accommodation, medical suppliers and local I.J.A. Administration were worse than anywhere in our Area (e) Australian troops were better at adapting themselves to strange conditions, e.g., many of our British troops after generations of living in towns, were at a disadvantage in fending for themselves under these primitive and stark realities (f) The A.I.F. troops in general were more healthy and hygiene minded. They seemed to have been taught and learnt the fact that the rules of hygiene are one of the most important essentials in soldiers training and not merely "the doctors' fad" (g) The A.I.F.part of "F" Force had made considerable progress on the road march before the main force of the monsoon struck.

Treatment was difficult and medical equipment extremely limited. Nevertheless intravenous saline made from kitchen salt and foiled creek water and often given by improvised bamboo cannulae, was employed widely and with success. Free fluids-tea, rice, water, nutrine when available. Potass-Permang, drinks and morphine were the mamslays. Sulphanamides were tried in a very few cases with no apparent result but the cases were too few to any way determine its value.

Isolation measures were only very partially possible at No. 5 and No. 4 Camps, at the former no separate accommodation was provided until mid-June despite repeated representations and these highly infectious patients had to be nursed at one end of the hospital hut. There was much sadism in the earlier days of this camp which left 140 of 240 cases of cholera out of an original camp strength of 690.

Anal swabbing in the search for carriers was done by the I.J.A. Carriers were placed in such isolation as they could be provided. Carriers and recovered cases were declared non-infectious after three negative swabbings at weekly intervals. The Force was inoculated with Cholera vaccine at the onset. In several places the supply was short and this was not completed until mid-June. Men were subsequently inoculated at three monthly intervals.

Malaria : There had been relatively little Malaria at Singapore. Heavy infections occurred on the march. Nieke, Camp 1 and Tanbaya were heavy breeding areas (sectors A minimus and A malalatus) and practically 100 per cent of the population of these camps contracted the infection. As mentioned under medical supplies, the supply of quinine, while more liberal than any other drug, was inadequate for suppressive and therapeutic use. The supply of atebrin was very small until arrival at Kanburi at the end of November, when it was possible to place men who had chronic relapsing malaria, on suppressive Atebrin with marked benefit. Plasmoquin supply was unsatisfactory but when available was used with quinine in the treatment courses; the recommended course for M.T. and B.T. cases was quinine Sulp. grs. 30 (in three doses) with plasmoquin .03 or .04 gramme (in two doses) for 14 days. Often the amount of Quinine available up-country allowed of only a 7 or 10 day course of 24 grains of quinine daily. The I.J.A. supplied Begnon ampoules (soluble quinine) for parenteral use. It was found satisfactory. The incidence of B.T. and M.T. infections was almost equal. There were many mixed infections. As there was only one microscope available for the Force, detailed observations were impossible. Many case of prolonged resistance to oral Quinine were substantiated in undoubted malaria cases in Burma and Thailand. Intra-muscular or Intra-venous quinine was given in these usually with success but all medical officers observed cases which relapsed on 7th to 10th or 12th day of malaria while on full doses of quinine. Plasmoquin added to the quinine throughout a course definitely lengthened the interval between relapses.

Most of the clinical variations of malignant malaria were seen. The most common and dangerous being cerebral. It yielded satisfactorily to parenteral quinine as a general rule but there were fatal outcome.

The small supply of atebrin at our disposal was used suppressively with success on personnel e.g. Interpreters, Medical Officers, Cookhouse superintendent, but in a proportion of these (taking two Atebrin tablets twice weekly regularly) Overt M.T. or B.T. infections appeared. Suppressive Quinine was largely ineffective unless used in doses of 10 grains daily - given on parade. We could only afford this for a period at Kanburi, (January-February 1944.)

Mosquito nets were supplied by the I.J.A.; they were eventually taken out of use as they effectively trapped mosquitoes entering through the bamboo slats on which we slept.

Where an attack of malaria supervened in another disease there was rapid deterioration and in the very emaciated it frequently heralded the end of the struggle.

Dysentery : Troops of this force suffered heavily from this diseases prior to leaving Changi - more especially the British element. Conditions on trains the march and the insanitary state of all camps in the early days produced an enormous amount of acute uysentery - with insufficient treatment and the incessent demand for labour relapses were very common even among those who made a satisfactory recovery the heavy labour and prodigious hours almost inevitably brought a return of the condition.

The clinical features were frequent copious stools especially at night and in the morning hours, with tremendous urgency, severe abdominal colic and generally little tenesmus (unless it was an acute attach). The stools contained undigested food and thin mucus or traces of blood and muco-pus. In time practically the whole force suffered from the disease. At the end of the period under review one cannot meet any officer or man who has not had it—most of them had it for many months.

There were few drugs to treat dysentery. The very limited amount of sulphuraphyridine was successful in acute bacillary cases used in 0-8 gm. doses for the first 24 hours. It was much less successful in the chronic conditions. Homemade charcoal, and some I.J.A. preparations of the same element (e.g. ALSYLIN) were palliatives, Mag. Sulphate was limited and used for tenesmus and toxaemis, spirocid etc., were useful but very scaree. It is probable that a high proportion of chronic cases had a mixed bacillary and amoebic infection. Their histories often suggested it. From the use of Emetine the clinical features, the results of a limited number of microscopic examinations of stools and from sigmodioscopic observations (by Major Hunt, at Kanburi) it appears certain that 70 per cent-80 per cent were infected with E.histolytica.

Incessant requests for specific drugs to the I.J.A. resulted in enough Emetine to treat 8 cases.

In a wasting disease such as this, with food of limited caloric values, it was essential to use all means to make patients eat every grain of rice procurable for them otherwise they consumed their body proteins which on the diet could not be replaced. Where attention to this principle was successfully enforced, results were decidedly less deplorable than where the orthodox doctrine of "initial starvation" to enable the bowel to rest lingered in the minds of certain medical officers.

The incidence of Amoebic hepatitis and Liver abscess was very low as would be expected in overtdysentery.

Tropical Ulcers: The prolonged march with blistered and sore feet, lack of footwear, wet muddy camps and roads, debility and lowered body resistance to local infection was the soil in which ulcers were sown. The condition rapidly became one of the "big four" diseases. We might add starvation or malnutrition to make a "big five", as it was the solid background of all serious diseases in the force—a sort of Bank of England to the Commercial Banks.

Ulcers affected the parts of the body most exposed to injury, commonest sites were (a) the region of the ankle, the front of the leg and dorsum of the foot especially over the bases of the toes, (all these from knocks and abrasions). (b) The buttacks, back and are over the crests of Illum and great Trochanters (due to pressure sores from sleeping on split bamboo platforms acute abscesses often preceeded these. (c) The skin creases of the body - flexures of the elbow, knee and groin (caused by abrasion the result of scratching scabies areas.

These ulcers commenced as small abscesses and infected abrasions and spread superficially involving increasing areas of skin and deeply involving subcutaneous tissues, deep fascia tend on sheaths and muscle, and finally bone in the progressive case.

In severe odematuos Beri-Beri the origin of the ulcer was frequently a blob on the skin of the dordum of the foot. In consequence of ulcers, every break of the skin, however, minute was suspect and had to be meticulously treated until and if, healing took place.

The subject of Tropical Ulcers in "F" Force is well dealt with by Capt. F. Cahill. F.R.C.S. (Surgical Specialist with the Force in Appendix F). The conditions he describes prevailed in all camps and the facilities for treatment were approximately the same with the important exception that rice polishings were not available except after the return of the patients to Kanburi. The better results and decreased incidence of new ulcers after rice polishings were given at Tanbaya was more than borne out in the rapid and marked improvement in ulcers in December - April at Kanburi, where a reasonable quantity of Vitamin B foods were obtained (at our own expense).

As regards amputation results - and amputation was resorted to was the last means of saving a patient's life, of 53, amputations done in our camps in the Burma Thailand area there are only 5 survivers in April 1944. The vast majority lost their lives from other diseases—beri-beri, malaria, dysentery, subsequent to operation. Results of the few amputations done after reaching Kanburi gave much better results by reason of better nutrition.

An authority on Tropical diseases (monson-Buhr) showed some knowledge of the disease in writing that "sloushing phagodens is apt to attack the half starved, malaria stricken prisoners in jungle lands, overdriven slaye gangs and soldiers campaigning in the tropics". Whether or not the prisoners of the Force belonged to any or all of these categories is left to the reader.

Beri-Beri: The state of nutrition prior to leaving Changi has been noted. Conditions which affected "F" Force subsequently have been described. A number of Beri-Beri cases developed on the march, mostly contanotous. The supply of beans in the I.J.A. ration appeared to prevent rapid development, but this supply unfortunately fluctuated very considerably. The disease lags beind the deficiency of thismis and so we found that there were 5 death ascribed to Beri-Beri in June, 20, in July, 87 in August, 156 in September. Lack of the necessary vitamins was all the more felt because the resting disease cholera and dysentery, and the hard physical toil used the body reserve which could not be made good from the existing diet.

Nouritic beri-beri was relatively rare but cases of wrist drop, foot drop, ensesthesis of the lips, etc. were seen. Cedematons Beri-Beri was the commonest variety seen, it affected the feet and legs in the milder degrees, but by July camps had patients resembling water-beds, so swollen were they. Despite strenous efforts to make good the diet deficiency in these by giving extra beans from the ration of the fit melany liver procurable, and Yeast Tablets (I.J.A. supply, but very scarce) most of them succumbed to Cardiac Beri-Beri, Dysentery, Chest Conditions malaria and Ulcers. Tapping of ascites and hydrotheraces gave no more than temporary relief. Efficient mereurial uiuretice were unobtainable (execept 10 ampoules of Neptal purchased by ourselves at Kanburi in February 1944) Parenteral vitamin B was supplied in very small quantities and was reserved for the acute cardiac emergencies of this disease, and was useful here.

Sudden passing of faeces during sleep or temporary mental aberration followed by epileptiform fits were seen occasionally. These fits were, mere often than not, fatal. They were afebrite and previous routine examination of this central nervous system was usually negative. Cardiac abnormalities in association with Beri-Beri were common and became more so as general health deteriorated. The usual "Sohosin" attacks were seen and many ended fatally. But Medical officer noted the prevalence of conditions not usually attributed to this disease. The left side of the heart was affected more often than the right, there was bradycardia rather than trochycardia. A forcible slapping cardiac impulse could be seen and felt. The apical first sound was loud and banging and often split, with or without a systolic murmur. The pulmonary second sound was usually accentuated and often duplicated. Abnormalities of rythm were more often extra systolos than suricular fibrillations (though the latter were often enough soon as a terminal event).

The subject of Beri-Beri and cardiac disorders were much in the minds of medical officers. A history of beri-beri was found in a very high percentage of our population as was that as recurrent malarial attacks with major degrees of secondary anornia. One hesitates to dogmatise on the actiology of these heart condition- they were abnormal and were heated by as complete recombency as passible and extra B1 contain in diet were this was procurable.

So far as our experience goes, Beri-Beri takes longer to recover than to develope. At Kanburi after 4 months treatment with an adequate thiamin intake, some oedematous cases show only moderate improvement, meuritic show a slight improvement and cardiac cases have been slower still, prognosis is doubtful and permanent damage is likely in some of them.

The longer the period of deprivation the slower the recovery seems to emerge from our study of this syndroms.

Skin Diseases: Scabies and the difficulties in treating it owing to lack of sulphur and facilities for preventing re-infection has been mentioned. The great importance was that the heions became infected, and were common originating foot of ulcers. Severe secondary infection affecting the legs, thighs and buttocks was very common and required prolonged treatment with weak antiseptic lotions. Tropical pemphigus and chiere-neupholya were also common. The lesions required constant attention with perchieride Mercury for choice as a cleansing agent-followed by boric or other powder. Tinea was common. The shoulders, body and crutch being of the most affected. The warm moist climate made cure difficult. There was great shortage of iodize or salicyclic acid for it. Tines of the external auditory meatus, was common and resistant to treatment.

Pellagra: The manifestations of vitamin B complex deficiency seen very commonly at Changi were less noticeable in Thailand. This may have been due to the supply of beans and vegetables which fluctuated considerably. Camps and individuals made use of wild pumpkin leaves etc., to make good this deficiency. By the middle of the period more serious pellagra cases were seen with typical extensive skin lesions, loss of muscle tissue, and mental deterioration. It was often associated with chronic dysentery, beri-beri and ulcers. In our observation persons who had lived a number of years in the tropics were more prone. Deaths due to this disease have been recorded under beri-beri or miscellaneous diseases.

Tropical Typhus: A number of undoubted cases occurred at Tanbaya, Camps 1. and 2. Serological tests were imoossible.

Diptheria: The disease was present at Changi and the infection remained in "F" Force mainly among British Troops. (who were much more effected than the Australians at Changi) No specific anti-sera were available. It accounted for 26 deaths. The course and sequale presented no unusual features.

Small-pox: Appeared in No. 2 & No.4 Camp later at the end of the period in No.3 Camp. Cases from the latter Camp were transferred to Nieke during the move to Kunburi and a small outbreak of 6 cases occurred there. The force was vaccinated prior to leaving Changi and again where cases occurred.

Jaundice: There was almost constantly considerable amount of what appeared to be ordinary catarrhal jaundice in most camps. The intensity and duration were very variable. They lasted anything from 10-30 days. An attack did not confer immunity. Two fatal cases of what may well have been Well's disease were reported from Tanbaya Hospital and room No.4 Camp. One had 26 days of fever with intense jaundice.

Surgical conditions : Facilities for operating were most primitive. A large I.J.A. mosquite net used in the open or where space could be spared at the end of a hut, was the operating room. Three small sets of instruments were brought from Changi. The difficulty was dividing these among Camps. Among major conditions dealt with in addition to the amputations, were perinephric abscess, suppurative chelceystitis, appendicitis, fracture femur, empyeme thoracis. A case of mesemtaris venous thrombosis in an advanced beri-beri case died during induction with Ether. Anaesthetics were sarce and full use was made of local novocaine. Closed E & C.E. mixtures given by improvised shipway apparatus were used as a routine.

Sickness and Death Rates (This section is taken from the report by Capt. T. Wilson, RAMC).

Lack of Medical Records makes it impossible to compute accurately either the amount of sickness caused by the different diseases or the total amount of sickness from all diseases. The best that can be done is to make rough estimates based on information supplied by our own observations and by observations of other M.O.'s.

(a) Incidence of diseases : Cholera attacked about 1300 persons with an immediate mortality of about 50 per cent but the ultimate mortality may have been 80-90 per cent. Few of the cholera convalesce made a complete recovery and many eventually succumbed to other diseases. Malaria attacked about 80 per cent and tthere were a few cases of blackwater fever. Dysentery and diarrhoea were widespread throughout, and almost everyone developed a state of incipient beri-ber. Bugs, lice and scabies affected practically everyone. These pests were responsible for much loss of sleep, and infected scratches were frequently the starting points of septic sores and ulcers.

Lung diseases like bronchitis and pneumonia were surprisingly rare considering the living and working conditions.

(b) Total sickness: Certain records still exist showing daily number of sick and number at work. Here are a few examples:

Camp	*Date*	*Total Camp Population*	*Numbe rsick*	*Number demanded for I.J.A. work*
Shimo-Sonkurai	19th July	1850	1350	343
Kami-Sonkurai	16th Aug	1670	1075	450
Takanun	Mid July	564	464	160
Sonkurai	25th July	1300	1050	280

Remembering that the prisoners themselves supplied all the labour for the cookhouse (including water carrying and firewood cutting and collection in the surrounding jungles) and for camp maintenance and also all medical staff required to deal with such large numbers of sick, one can readily perceive from these figures that the I.J.A. demands for workers were indeed excessive. But the records do not show the true position in other respects. Had the medical standards of unfit for work been anything like normal, the proportion of sick to workers would have been very much higher than that records above.

A progressively deterioration in physical-condition occurred as the month went by. This deterioration was noticeable at the time, but it became strikingly obvious when one was able to compare the returned men of "F" Force with the men who had remained at Changi. Some idea of it is given by the results of an inspection made by I.J.A. medical officers in February, 1944. 1420 Australian troops (excluding those in hospital) were examined two months after their return to Changi, and only 125 of them are classified as fit for heavy duty.

One may conclude that only an insignificant fraction of the "F" Force survivers can have remained free from disease; the overwhelming majority suffered from several diseases either in succession or in conjunction.

(c) Deaths and Death Rates : Of the 6998 men who left Singapore in the second half of April 1943, 3087 died during the twelve months May 1943 - April 1944, giving a crude death rate of 441 per mile per annum. Analysis and discussion of individual causes of death must be prefaced by a reminder of the prevalance of diarrhoea, beri-beri, malaria and ulcers. Failure to mention any one of the diseases in the actual death report may mean that it was not an immediate cause of death, but certainly does not exclude the possibility of it contributing thereto. This fact has influenced the remarks that follow and has to be borne in mind when studying the tables of causes of death.

The tables (see appendix A) have been prepared from the official records. The only deaths not based on medical officers reports are some of those occurring in transmit camps and about 20 escapees who are presumed to have died in the jungle. About 30 death reports gave three or more causes, and these have been listed under the first two causes mentioned. Apart from these exceptions, diseases were classified according to the records. The heading 'Dysentery' includes diarrhoea, gastro-enteritis and colitis. 'Malaria' includes fevers unspecified. Movements of populations make it useless to attempt comparison of the health of different camps by months. Thus the sudden drop in the deaths at Sonkurai from 275 in August to 12 in September, was due far more to the removal of all the sickmen to Tanbaya and their replacement by fit men from Shimo-Sonkurai. And Neike, than to any miraculous improvement in conditions at the camp itself. We will deal then, mainly with the time sequence of deaths in the force as a whole.

Grouping of the deaths into three periods of four months each, to correspond with the distinct phases of the force's existence, helps to bring out the main points. This has been done in Table IX and we quote here only the figures of the chief single causes of deaths.

Period	*Population of beginning of period*	*Cholera*	*Dysentery and Diarrhoea*	*Beri-Beri*	*Malaria*	*Ulcers*	*Total all diseases*
		Death Rate Per Mille Per Annum					
1943 May, June, July, Au	6998	269	176	38	27	10	595
Sept., Oct., Nov., Dec.	5613	5	213	163	31	77	841
1944 Jan, Feb, Mar, April	4037	--	10	15	7	2	93

The first period, May, June, July, August, 1943, covers the March and the greater part of the monsoon; by the end of it the move to Tanbaya Hospital in Burma was practically completed.

Cholera was the great killer, causing half of the total deaths, with dysentery a close second, and all other diseases lagging well behind.

The second period, September, October, November, December, 1943,' includes the last month of the monsoon, the finishing of the railroad and the return move to Kanburi and Singapore. By the end of it 3200 men were back in Singapore, 500 were at Kanburi and only 300 still in Burma. Cholera had become negligible as a direct cause of death, and dysentary, beri-beri and ulcers were all powerful. The total death rate had increased by 246 and averaged 841 per mille per annum over this four month period.

The third period, January, February, March, April 1944, was the period of recuperation. All I.J.A. work had ceased, and living conditions, food and drug supplies were better for everyone. The death rate fell rapidly and averaged 93 per mille per annum over the period, although this was still very high in comparison with the Singapore rate of 13 per mille for the first twelve months of imprisonment.

Some additional information can be gleaned from the records of deaths by months detailed in Table VII. The crude death rate from all causes per mille per annum for each month was:-

1943								1944			
May	June	July	Aug	Sep	Oct	Nov	Dec	Jan	Feb	Mar	April
314	748	451	1048	1082	928	1006	778	226	79	37	37

Reference to the table will show a rough time sequence of diseases with cholera as the prime cause of death in May and June; dysentery deaths increasing rapidly in July with a sharp peak in August; ulcer deaths at a maximum in September; and deaths from beri-beri alone at their highest in November, but those from beri-beri combined with other diseases remaining at a high level from August to December.

The very high rates for August and September must to some extent be attributable to the movement of sick to the Tanbaya Hospital camp in Burma. About 1900 men participated in this move, which started at the beginning of August and was completed by the second week in September. The journey a trying one even for the more or less fit men of the hospital staff, its effect on the sick can be judged by the fact that a considerable number died at various places during the journey and that, out of a total of 748 deaths occurring at Tanbaya during the six months of its occupation, 310 deaths took place during September. There was a much smaller step up in the death rate at the time of the return move to Kanburi in November.

Our impression however, was that the men who died during a move or shortly afterwards would almost certainly have died later on, i.e. that the moves acted mainly as accelerators of the fatal ending. The records for Kami-Sonkurai, the one camp north of Neike which did not send patients to Burma, tend to confirm this impression. This camp had originally consisted of 396 Australians, and up to the end of July they had lost 23 men, 14 of them from cholera. It was filled up to a strength of 1685 in the first week of August with batches of men from Neike, Shimo-Sonkurai and Changaraya. Many of these men were unfit and would have been sent to Tanbaya Hospital had it not been that the number to go there had been fixed by the I.J.A. some time beforehand and could not be increased. At Kami-Sonkurai it will be noted that the food was sufficient in quantity but just as unbalanced dietetically as elsewhere; while working conditions were among the worst experienced. The only change in population were the losses from deaths and the arrival of a small party of women from Changaraya in September. From the first of August until the 28th of November, when the camp was finally vacated, there occurred 490 deaths. The transformation of deaths per month into death rates per mille per annum exaggerates the figures considerably when dealing with figures in general. The death rates from all causes were:- August 481, September 787, October 1150, November 1399; with a steady increase from month to month in the death rate from dysentery, beri-beri and ulcers.

One can only wonder what December death rate might have been; it is certainly not surprising that everyone in the camp was convinced that their one hope lay in a speedy removal to the more cultivated areas near Kanburi, and that morale fell to a very low level when this removal was repeatedly deferred.

We think it quite probable that, had it not been for the mass move to Burma,the deaths for the Force as a whole would have followed a similar course to those at Kami-Sonkurai. We can express our opinion of the total deaths by saying that about 73 per cent could well be grouped together under the composite heading of Dysentery, Beri-Beri, Ulcers and Malaria (with cholera as an additional-contributory cause in about one-fifth of these); with 21 per cent being put down as directly due to cholera, and 6 per cent being caused by small -pox, diphtheria, pneumonia and 'other diseases'.

Reports to Improve Conditions

To become prisoners of war is a considerable error of judgement. It will be realised that we were not our own masters. Every effort was made by the "F" Force Commander and his staff from the onset, and by the officers of each marching party and working camp, to help to get big and little things put right. A heavy strain was put upon them and upon the interpreters. Stereotyped methods such as letters produced little or no result (Appendix 'C' gives some samples) and verbal and very diplomatic means were tried, varying from "a firm stand" to trading one's cigaratte case or fountain pen, or giving English lessons to Korean guards — all with the same end in view and with regretably little result. Two notes, from Nippon sources, are included in Appendix 'C' to illustrate the difficulty of getting amelioration. One is a written order to send out even sick men in hospital to work; the other, it is supposed, puts forward a simple explanation of our troubles according to the tenets of Shintoism.

The S.N.O's visits to other camps to attempt to co-ordinate or improve medical work were almost impossible to achieve and, when permission was granted, they were so brief as to be valueless. During the whole period I saw Camps 1 and 4 once, Tanbaya Hospital twice, Caup 3 four times, Camp 5 never. The S.N.O. worked at Neike, Sonkurai and Kanchanabri (Kanburi) for varying periods.

Acknowledgements

In this sombre report it is pleasant to record the immense help and support received from the Force Commander (Lieut-Colonel G.W. Harris, O.B.E., R.A.) who used every resource to improve our lot. To Lieut-Colonel F.J. Dillon, M.C., R.A.S.C, who commanded Neike and later No. 2 Camp and who managed financial aid for our Camps and the Hospitals at Kanburi and Tanbaya. To his diplomacy, ingenuity and energy, the members of this Force are under a heavy debt. I am indebted to Lieut-Colonel C.T. Hutchison, R.A., for much good advise and for his work as Administrative Commandant, Tanbaya Hospital. The whole Force owes much to the efforts of the Interpreters, Major C.Wild, Oxf. & Bucks L.T., Captain G.G. Waller, F. S.V.F., Lieut. Fletcher, Gordons; large demands were made upon their courage and ability. Many Combatant officers worked as Wardmasters under the exceptional conditions prevailing in Thailand and were of the utmost use, special mention should be made of Lieut R. Eaton, A.I.F., Lieut A. Ellerman, A.I.F., Lieut. Geikie, A.I.F., Capt. Gibson, A.I.F., Major W. Auld, R.A.O.C. Major M.D. Price, R. Sigs, Capt. J. Ainger, R. Sigs, for their valuable services. Capt. T. Wilson, R.A.O.C., who was the expert in Nutrition with "F" Force has been good enough to collect from many sources the figures for rations issued by the I.J.A. and to make an analysis of the food values therein. On return to Changi he also re-checked these figures and the figures for deaths by diseases. This has been work of great complexity and magnitude and every credit is due to him for the results obtained.

I am also indebted to officers i/c 2nd schelon, British and Australian Troops, and the Staff of the B.R.E. at Changi, and also to R.S.M.J. Blinch (18 Div H.Q,) for their help in checking up figures in this report, and to Cpts Skippen and Berry, R.A.O.C, for their patience and care in typing this report.

Not least, the Medical Officers of this dismal expedition gave of their best to their patients and loyally supported me, I am indeed grateful to them for their sustained and unfortunately often unavoiding efforts against appalling odds.

Salary

The main factors which contributed to the appalling sickness and death rates in "F" Force have been mentioned in this report. The apportionment of blame for the conditions described is a matter for consideration by higher authority. Those factors may be very briefly ricapitulated:—

1. Wrong information was given at the onset to the effect that the party would have light work amid pleasant surroundings and that food would be better than at Changi. This led to the inclusion in the force of a large number of delicate men suffering from the effects of previous disease and dietary deficiency.
2. Almost complete lack of transport and general organisation to get the force to its working camps in Thailand. This led to the forced march under shocking conditions, to the loss of practically all our own medical supplies, and to the breaking down of the strength of even the fittest elements in the parties as they had to overtax themselves with carriage of stores and sick comrades.
3. Failure to provide provisioned staging camps on the way.
4. Setting of camps in malarious and insanitary areas often in the closest proximity to disease infected coolies.
5. Not stopping all movement on the first information that cholera had broken out.
6. Lack of provisions of adequate rations and accommodation (during monsoon weather) on arrival at working area. Bad siting of camps. No time or personnel allowed to get the camps in order when the parties had arrived.
7. Excessive demands for labour and excessive hours under cruel conditions resulting in a heavy sick rate and inadequate camp maintenance staffs.
8. The pernicious system of reducing the ration scale for the sick far below basal metabolic requirements.
9. Failure to call a halt to the above conditions even when the results were blatantly apparent to the most ignorant and stupid of our guardians.

10. Lack of provision of special transport or accommodation for the sick. (Ambulance cars were used for transporting rations and the sick were carried by their less sick comrades).

Summary on Return to Changi

British

Departed April 1943		3,336
Died in Burma and Thailand and earlier parties	2012	
on return to Changi up to 27.4.44	17	2,029
Escapees (fate unknown)	5	
Missing	1	
Unconfirmed death report	1	7
Alive 27.4.44		1,300
		3,336

A.I.F.*

Departed April 1943	3,662
Died in Burma and Thailand and earlier parties	
on return to Changi up to 25.4.44	1,058
Alive	2,604
	3,662

(J. HUSTON)
Lieut-Colonel, R.A.M.C.
S.M.O. "F" Force

Appendix A-Table 1.

"F" Force Deaths

May 1943

(A = Australian), (B = British)

	Cholara		*Dys & Diarr*		*Dys & Beri-beri*		*Dys & malaria*		*Dys & Ulcers*		*Beri-beri*		*Beri-beri & Malaria*		*Beri-beri & Ulcers*		*Malaria Fever Unspec.*		*Malaria & Ulcers*	
	A	*B*	*A*	*B*	*A*	*B*	*A*	*B*	*A*	*B*	*A*	*B*	*A*	*B*	*A*	*B*	*A*	*B*	*A*	*B*
Changaraya	–	24	–	–	–	–	–	–	–	–	–	–	–	–	–	–	–	–	–	–
Kame-Sonkuari	–	–	–	–	–	–	–	–	–	–	–	–	–	–	1	–	–	–	–	–
Sonkurai	–	66	–	–	–	–	–	–	–	–	–	–	–	–	–	–	–	–	–	–
Shino-Sonkurai	53	1	–	–	–	–	–	–	–	–	–	–	–	–	–	–	–	–	–	–
Neike & Shimo-Neika	6	3	–	3	–	–	–	1	–	–	–	–	–	–	1	–	–	–	–	–
Konkoita; Taimonta; Takanun; Tamarand Pat.	5	–	–	1	–	–	–	–	–	–	–	–	–	–	–	–	–	–	–	–
Transit Camps	–	–	–	5	–	–	–	–	–	–	–	–	–	–	–	1	–	–	–	–
Total	64	94	–	9	–	–	–	1	–	–	–	–	–	–	2	1	–	–	–	–
	159		9		–		1		–		–		–		3		–		–	

(Table Cont..)

(Table Cont..)

	Ulcers		*Diphthoria*		*Small pox*		*Pneum-onia*		*Other Diseases*		*Total*		*Combined Total*
	A	*B*	*A*	*B*	*A*	*B*	*A*	*B*	*A*	*B*	*A*	*B*	*A*
Changaraya	–	–	–	–	–	–	–	–	–	1	–	25	25
Kame-Sonkuari	–	–	–	–	–	–	–	–	–	–	1	–	1
Sonkurai	–	–	–	–	–	–	–	–	–	–	–	66	66
Shino-Sonkurai	–	–	–	–	–	–	–	–	1	–	54	1	55
Neike & Shimo-Neika	–	–	–	2	–	–	–	–	–	–	7	9	16
Konkoita; Taimonta; Takanun; Tamarand Pat.	–	–	–	–	–	–	–	–	–	–	5	1	6
Transit Camps	–	–	–	1	–	–	–	–	7	–	7	7	14
Total	–	–	–	1	–	–	–	–	8	1	74	109	
	–		3		–		–		9		183		183

June 1943

	Cholara		*Dys & Diarr*		*Dys & Beri-beri*		*Dys & malaria*		*Dys & Ulcers*		*Beri-beri*		*Beri-beri & Malaria*		*Beri-beri & Ulcers*		*Malaria Fever Unspec.*		*Malaria & Ulcers*	
	A	*B*	*A*	*B*	*A*	*B*	*A*	*B*	*A*	*B*	*A*	*B*	*A*	*B*	*A*	*B*	*A*	*B*	*A*	*B*
Changaraya	–	124	–	4	–	–	–	–	–	1	–	–	–	–	–	–	–	–	–	–
Kame-Sonkuari	14	–	–	–	–	–	–	–	–	–	–	–	–	–	–	–	–	–	–	–
Sonkurai	–	150	–	4	–	–	–	–	–	–	–	1	–	–	–	–	–	1	–	–
Shino-Sonkurai	49	–	5	–	–	–	2	–	–	–	1	–	2	–	–	–	4	–	–	–
Neike & Shimo-Neika	1	14	1	1	–	–	–	–	–	–	–	1	–	–	–	–	–	–	–	–
Konkoita; Taimonta; Takanun; Tamarand Pat.	7	–	–	3	–	–	–	–	–	–	–	–	–	–	–	–	1	–	–	–
Transit Camps	–	–	2	6	1	–	1	–	–	–	–	2	–	–	–	–	–	–	–	–
Total	71	280	8	18	1	–	3	–	–	1	1	4	2	–	–	–	5	1	–	–
	359		26		1		3		1		5		2		3		6		–	
Carried forward	135	382	8	27	1	–	3	1	–	1	1	4	2	–	–	–	7	2	–	–
	517		35		1		4		1		5		2		–		9		–	

(Table Cont.)

(Table Cont..)

	Ulcers		Diphthoria		Small pox		Pneum-onia		Other Diseases		Total		Combined Total
	A	B	A	B	A	B	A	B	A	B	A	B	A
Changaraya	–	–	–	1	–	–	–	–	–	1	–	130	130
Kame-Sonkuari	–	–	–	–	–	–	–	–	1	–	15	–	15
Sonkurai	–	–	–	3	–	1	–	–	–	–	–	160	160
Shino-Sonkurai	–	–	–	–	–	–	–	–	2	–	65	–	65
Neike & Shimo-Neika	–	–	–	1	–	–	–	1	3	–	5	18	23
Konkoita; Taimonta; Takanun; Tamarand Pat.	–	–	–	–	–	–	–	–	1	1	9	4	13
Transit Camps	–	–	–	–	–	–	–	–	6	1	10	9	19
Totals	–	–	–	5	–	1	–	1	13	2	104	321	
	–		5		1		1		15		425		425
Carried Forward	–	–	–	8	–	1	–	1	21	3	178	430	
	–		6		1		1		24		608		608

July 1943

	Cholara		*Dys & Diarr*		*Dys & Beri-beri*		*Dys & malaria*		*Dys & Ulcers*		*Beri-beri*		*Beri-beri & Malaria*		*Beri-beri & Ulcers*		*Malaria Fever Unspec.*		*Malaria & Ulcers*	
	A	*B*	*A*	*B*	*A*	*B*	*A*	*B*	*A*	*B*	*A*	*B*	*A*	*B*	*A*	*B*	*A*	*B*	*A*	*B*
B./F May to June 1943.	135	382	8	27	1	–	3	1	–	1	1	4	2	–	–	–	7	2	–	–
	517		35		1		4		1		5		2		–		9		–	
Changaraya	–	10	–	13	–	–	–	–	–	–	–	1	–	–	–	–	–	–	–	–
Kame-Sonkuari	–	–	1	–	–	–	–	–	–	–	–	–	1	–	–	–	3	–	–	–
Sonkurai	–	11	–	30	–	–	–	5	–	–	–	13	–	–	–	–	1	12	–	–
Shino-Sonkurai	–	–	3	–	2	–	1	–	–	–	–	–	–	–	–	–	3	–	–	–
Neike & Shimo-Neika	–	–	–	–	–	–	1	–	–	–	–	1	–	–	–	–	–	–	–	–
Konkoita; Taimonta; Takanun; Tamarand Pat.	28	–	1	–	–	–	–	–	–	–	3	–	–	–	–	–	2	–	–	–
Transit Camps	–	1	2	14	–	–	1	–	–	–	–	1	–	–	–	–	–	–	–	–
Total	28	22	7	107	2	–	3	5	–	–	3	16	1	–	–	–	9	12	–	–
	50		114		2		8		–		19		1		–		21		–	

(Table Cont..)

(Table Cont..)

	Ulcers		*Diphthoria*		*Small pox*		*Pneum-onia*		*Other Diseases*		*Total*		*Combined Total*
	A	*B*	*A*	*B*	*A*	*B*	*A*	*B*	*A*	*B*	*A*	*B*	*A*
B/F May to June 1943.	–	–	–	8	–	1	–	1	21	3	178	430	
	–		8		1		1		24		608		608
Changaraya	–	–	–	2	–	–	–	–	–	–	–	26	26
Kame-Sonkuari	–	–	–	–	–	–	2	–	–	–	7	–	7
Sonkurai	–	2	–	6	–	2	–	–	–	2	1	133	134
Shino-Sonkurai	–	–	–	–	–	–	–	–	–	–	9	–	9
Neike & Shimo-Neika	–	–	–	–	–	–	–	–	1	–	2	1	3
Konkoita; Taimonta; Takanun; Tamarand Pat.	–	–	–	–	–	–	–	–	3	1	37	1	38
Transit Camps	–	–	–	–	–	–	–	–	2	2	5	18	23
Totals	–	2	–	8	–	2	2	–	6	5	61	179	–
	2		8		2		2		11		240		240

August 1943

	Cholara		*Dys & Diarr*		*Dys & Beri-beri*		*Dys & malaria*		*Dys & Ulcers*		*Beri-beri*		*Beri-beri & Malaria*		*Beri-beri & Ulcers*		*Malaria Fever Unspec.*		*Malaria & Ulcers*	
	A	*B*	*A*	*B*	*A*	*B*	*A*	*B*	*A*	*B*	*A*	*B*	*A*	*B*	*A*	*B*	*A*	*B*	*A*	*B*
Changaraya	–	2	2	22	–	–	–	–	–	5	–	2	–	–	–	–	–	1	–	–
Kame-Sonkuari	9	27	6	10	3	1	–	–	–	–	3	6	1	–	–	–	2	–	–	–
Sonkurai	5	–	3	156	–	15	4	5	–	1	1	33	1	3	–	1	6	15	–	–
Shino-Sonkurai	–	–	5	–	9	–	3	–	–	–	1	–	1	–	–	–	2	–	–	–
Neike & Shimo-Neika	–	–	6	12	2	2	1	–	–	–	1	3	–	–	–	–	1	–	–	–
Konkoita; Taimonta; Takanun; Tamarand Pat.	10	5	6	4	–	–	–	–	–	–	3	–	1	–	–	–	2	3	–	–
Transit Camps	1	–	6	10	–	1	2	–	–	1	1	3	2	–	–	–	–	1	–	–
Tanbaya Hos.	1	–	–	1	1	2	1	3	–	1	1	6	–	1	–	–	–	1	–	–
Total	26	34	32	289	15	19	11	8	–	8	11	53	6	4	–	1	13	21	–	–
	60		261		34		19		8		64		10		1		34		–	
Carried forward	189	438	47	363	18	19	17	14	–	9	15	73	9	4	–	1	29	35	–	–
	627		410		37		31		9		88		13		1		64		–	

(Table Cont..)

(Table Cont..)

	Ulcers		*Diphthoria*		*Small pox*		*Pneum-onia*		*Other Diseases*		*Total*		*Combined Total*
	A	*B*	*A*	*B*	*A*	*B*	*A*	*B*	*A*	*B*	*A*	*B*	*A*
Changaraya	–	–	–	–	–	–	–	–	–	–	–	32	32
Kame-Sonkuari	–	–	–	1	–	–	–	–	–	–	24	45	69
Sonkurai	–	18	–	5	–	1	–	–	3	1	23	252	275
Shino-Sonkurai	–	–	–	–	–	–	–	–	–	–	21	–	21
Neike & Shimo-Neika	–	–	–	1	–	–	–	–	1	2	12	20	32
Konkoita; Taimonta; Takanun; Tamarand Pat.	–	–	–	–	–	–	–	–	1	–	23	12	35
Transit Camps	–	–	–	1	–	–	–	–	2	5	14	30	44
Tanbaya Hosp.	–	3	–	–	–	–	–	–	–	1	4	25	29
Totals	–	21	–	8	–	1	–	–	7	9	121	415	
	21		8		1		–		19		537		537
Carried Forward	–	23	–	16	–	4	2	1	34	17	360	1025	
	23		16		4		3		51		1385		1385

September 1943

	Cholara		Dys & Diarr		Dys & Beri-beri		Dys & malaria		Dys & Ulcers		Beri-beri		Beri-beri & Malaria		Beri-beri & Ulcers		Malaria Fever Unspec.		Malaria & Ulcers	
	A	*B*	*A*	*B*	*A*	*B*	*A*	*B*	*A*	*B*	*A*	*B*	*A*	*B*	*A*	*B*	*A*	*B*	*A*	*B*
B./F May to August 1943.	189	438	4	368	18	19	17	14	–	9	15	73	9	4	–	1	29	35	–	–
	627		410		37		32		9		88		13		1		34		–	
Changaraya	–	–	–	2	–	–	–	–	–	–	–	–	–	–	–	–	–	–	–	–
Kame-Sonkuari	3	6	9	28	7	2	–	–	3	2	6	15	–	2	–	1	4	2	2	1
Sonkurai	–	–	2	2	–	–	–	–	–	–	–	1	–	1	–	–	–	–	–	–
Shino-Sonkurai	–	–	2	–	1	–	–	–	–	–	1	–	–	–	–	–	–	–	–	–
Neike & Shimo-Neika	–	–	–	1	–	–	–	–	–	–	–	–	–	–	–	–	–	–	–	–
Konkoita; Taimonta; Takanun; Tamarand Pat.	1	–	–	–	–	–	–	–	–	–	–	–	–	–	–	–	–	–	–	–
Transit Camps	–	–	3	21	–	–	–	–	–	–	–	5	–	–	–	–	1	5	–	–
Tanbays Hos.	–	–	11	5	22	45	5	26	3	18	4	23	4	9	7	12	2	2	–	8
Kanburi Hos.	–	–	3	2	4	–	3	–	–	–	4	2	–	–	–	–	–	3	–	–
Total	4	6	30	107	34	48	8	26	6	20	15	46	4	12	7	13	7	12	2	9
	10		137		82		34		26		61		16		20		19		11	

(Table Cont..)

(Table Cont..)

	Ulcers		*Diphthoria*		*Small pox*		*Pneum-onia*		*Other Diseases*		*Total*		*Combined Total*
	A	*B*	*A*	*B*	*A*	*B*	*A*	*B*	*A*	*B*	*A*	*B*	*A*
B/F May to August. 1943.	–	23	–	16	–	4	2	1	34	17	360	1025	
	23		16		4		3		51		1385		1385
Changaraya	–	–	–	–	–	–	–	–	–	–	–	2	2
Kame-Sonkuari	2	3	–	–	–	–	8	–	–	–	–	62	106
Sonkurai	–	1	–	2	–	–	1	1	1	–	4	8	12
Shino-Sonkurai	–	–	–	–	–	–	–	–	2	–	6	–	6
Neike & Shimo-Neika	–	–	–	–	–	–	–	–	–	1	–	2	2
Konkoita; Taimonta; Takanun; Tamarand Pat.	–	–	–	–	–	–	1	–	1	–	–	–	3
Transit Camps	–	2	–	–	–	–	–	–	4	2	8	55	43
Tanbays Hosp.	3	51	–	–	–	–	–	2	–	1	61	249	310
Kanburi Hosp.	–	–	–	–	–	–	–	–	–	1	14	8	22
Totals	5	57	–	2	–	–	10	3	8	5	140	366	–
	62		2		–		13		13		506		506

October 1943

	Cholara		*Dys & Diarr*		*Dys & Beri-beri*		*Dys & malaria*		*Dys & Ulcers*		*Beri-beri*		*Beri-beri & Malaria*		*Beri-beri & Ulcers*		*Malaria Fever Unspec.*		*Malaria & Ulcers*	
	A	*B*	*A*	*B*	*A*	*B*	*A*	*B*	*A*	*B*	*A*	*B*	*A*	*B*	*A*	*B*	*A*	*B*	*A*	*B*
Kame-Sonkuari	–	–	14	39	5	9	3	2	1	4	15	15	1	2	–	1	2	6	10	1
Sonkurai	–	–	2	6	1	–	–	–	–	–	2	3	1	1	1	–	–	–	–	–
Nieko	–	–	–	–	–	–	–	–	–	–	–	–	–	–	–	–	–	–	–	–
Konkoita; Taimonta; Takanun; Tamarand Pat.	–	–	–	1	1	–	1	–	–	–	–	–	–	–	–	–	–	–	–	–
Transit Camps	–	–	1	–	–	–	1	–	–	–	–	–	–	–	–	–	1	–	–	–
Tanbaya Hos.	–	–	6	22	33	42	8	4	14	7	6	14	–	3	3	4	1	2	–	–
Kanburi Hos.	–	–	1	–	–	–	4	–	2	–	5	3	1	–	–	–	–	–	–	–
Total	–	–	24	68	40	51	17	6	17	11	28	35	3	6	4	5	4	8	10	1
	–		92		91		23		28		63		9		9		12		11	
Carried forward	193	444	101	538	92	118	42	46	23	40	58	154	16	22	11	19	40	55	12	10
	637		639		210		88		63		212		38		30		95		22	

(Table Cont..)

(Table Cont..)

	Ulcers		Diphthoria		Small pox		Pneum-onia		Other Diseases		Total		Combined Total
	A	B	A	B	A	B	A	B	A	B	A	B	A
Kame-Sonkuari	8	7	1	–	–	–	3	–	1	–	64	86	150
Sonkurai	–	1	–	1	–	–	–	–	–	–	7	12	19
Neiko	–	–	–	–	–	–	–	–	–	–	–	–	–
Konkoita; Taimonta; Takanun; Tamarand Pat.	–	–	–	–	–	–	1	–	–	–	3	1	4
Transit Camps	–	–	–	–	–	–	–	–	–	4	3	4	7
Tanbaya Hosp.	6	13	–	–	–	–	1	1	–	3	78	115	193
Kanburi Hosp.	–	1	–	–	–	–	–	–	–	5	13	9	22
Totals	14	22	1	1	–	–	5	1	1	12	168	227	
	36		2		–		6		13		395		395
Carried Forward	19	102	1	27	–	4	17	5	43	34	668	1618	
	121		28		4		22		77		2886		2886

November 1943

	Cholara		Dys & Diarr		Dys & Beri-beri		Dys & malaria		Dys & Ulcers		Beri-beri		Beri-beri & Malaria		Beri-beri & Ulcers		Malaria Fever Unspec.		Malaria & Ulcers	
	A	*B*	*A*	*B*	*A*	*B*	*A*	*B*	*A*	*B*	*A*	*B*	*A*	*B*	*A*	*B*	*A*	*B*	*A*	*B*
B./F May to October 1943.	189	444	101	538	92	118	42	46	23	40	58	154	16	22	11	19	40	55	12	10
	637		639		210		88		63		212		38		30		95		22	
Kame-Sonkuari	–	–	27	25	–	2	2	–	5	2	11	55	2	–	3	3	2	2	1	–
Sonkurai	–	–	1	–	2	–	–	–	–	–	1	4	–	–	1	–	–	–	–	–
Neike	–	–	2	–	1	1	1	–	2	–	1	1	–	–	–	–	1	–	–	–
Konkoita; Taimonta; Takanun; Tamarand Pat.	–	–	2	–	1	–	–	–	–	–	–	–	–	–	–	–	–	–	–	–
Transit Camps	–	–	5	3	2	4	1	–	2	–	3	11	–	–	–	–	–	–	–	–
Tanbays Hos.	–	–	9	47	17	18	2	1	11	1	1	15	1	–	–	–	–	2	–	–
Kanburi Hos.	–	–	3	3	1	–	2	1	1	1	4	4	–	–	–	–	–	–	–	–
Total	–	–	49	78	24	25	8	2	21	4	21	90	3	–	4	3	3	4	1	–
	–		127		49		10		25		111		3		7		7		1	

(Table Cont..)

(Table Cont..)

	Ulcers		*Diphthoria*		*Small pox*		*Pneum-onia*		*Other Diseases*		*Total*		*Combined Total*
	A	*B*	*A*	*B*	*A*	*B*	*A*	*B*	*A*	*B*	*A*	*B*	*A*
B/F May to October 1943.	19	102	1	27	–	4	17	5	43	34	668	1618	
	121		28		4		22		77		2286		2286
Kame-Sonkuari	5	13	–	–	–	–	1	1	1	2	60	105	165
Sonkurai	–	1	–	–	–	–	–	–	2	–	7	5	12
Neike	–	–	–	–	–	1	–	–	1	–	9	3	12
Konkoita; Taimonta; Takanun; Tamarand Pat.	–	–	–	–	–	–	–	–	–	–	3	–	3
Transit Camps	1	–	–	–	–	–	–	1	3	1	17	20	37
Tanbays Hosp.	5	9	–	–	–	–	–	–	–	1	46	94	140
Kanburi Hosp.	3	–	–	–	–	–	–	–	3	–	17	9	26
Totals	14	23	–	–	–	1	1	2	10	4	159	263	
	37		–		1		3		14		395		395

December 1943

	Cholara		*Dys & Diarr*		*Dys & Beri-beri*		*Dys & malaria*		*Dys & Ulcers*		*Beri-beri*		*Beri-beri & Malaria*		*Beri-beri & Ulcers*		*Malaria Fever Unspec.*		*Malaria & Ulcers*	
	A	*B*	*A*	*B*	*A*	*B*	*A*	*B*	*A*	*B*	*A*	*B*	*A*	*B*	*A*	*B*	*A*	*B*	*A*	*B*
Neike	–	–	–	–	–	1	–	–	–	–	–	–	–	–	–	–	–	–	–	–
Transit Camp	–	–	2	–	1	–	–	–	–	–	2	1	–	–	–	–	–	–	–	–
Tanbaya Hosp.	–	–	–	2	7	16	1	–	3	3	5	6	1	2	4	2	–	–	–	–
Kanburi Hosp.	–	–	31	15	15	11	2	2	2	2	34	22	4	3	3	8	13	6	2	–
Changi	–	–	–	3	1	–	1	–	–	–	–	–	1	–	–	–	–	1	1	–
Total	–	–	33	20	24	28	4	2	5	5	41	29	6	5	7	10	13	7	3	–
	–		53		52		6		10		70		11		17		20		3	
Carried Forward	193	414	113	636	140	171	54	50	45	49	120	275	25	27	22	32	56	66	16	10
	637		819		311		104		98		393		52		54		122		26	

(Table Cont.)

(Table Cont..)

	Ulcers		*Diphthoria*		*Small pox*		*Pneum-onia*		*Other Diseases*		*Total*		*Combined Total*
	A	*B*	*A*	*B*	*A*	*B*	*A*	*B*	*A*	*B*	*A*	*B*	*A*
Neike	–	–	–	–	–	–	–	–	–	–	–	1	1
Transit Camp	–	–	–	–	–	–	–	–	1	–	6	1	7
Tanbaya Hosp.	–	1	–	–	–	–	–	1	–	2	21	35	56
Kanburi Hosp.	4	4	–	–	–	2	5	4	4	6	119	58	204
Changi	–	–	–	1	–	–	1	1	–	1	5	7	12
Totals	4	5	–	1	–	2	6	6	4	9	151	129	
	9		1		2		12		14		280		280
Carried Forward	37	130	1	28	–	7	24	13	58	47	978	1983	
	167		29		7		37		105		2961		2961

January 1943

	Cholara		*Dys & Diarr*		*Dys & Beri-beri*		*Dys & malaria*		*Dys & Ulcers*		*Beri-beri*		*Beri-beri & Malaria*		*Beri-beri & Ulcers*		*Malaria Fever Unspec.*		*Malaria & Ulcers*	
	A	*B*	*A*	*B*	*A*	*B*	*A*	*B*	*A*	*B*	*A*	*B*	*A*	*B*	*A*	*B*	*A*	*B*	*A*	*B*
B./F May to December 1943.	193	444	153	636	140	171	54	50	49	49	120	273	25	27	22	32	56	66	16	10
	637		819		311		104		98		393		52		54		122		26	
Tanbays Hos.	–	–	–	–	5	5	–	1	1	–	1	1	–	–	1	–	–	–	–	–
Kanburi Hos.	–	–	6	2	3	2	2	–	–	–	7	2	3	2	–	1	4	–	–	–
Changi	–	–	–	–	–	–	3	–	–	–	–	–	1	–	1	–	2	2	2	–
Total	–	–	6	5	8	7	5	1	1	–	8	3	4	2	2	1	6	2	2	–
	–		9		15		6		1		11		6		3		8		2	

	Ulcers		*Diphthoria*		*Small pox*		*Pneum-onia*		*Other Diseases*		*Total*		*Combined Total*
	A	*B*	*A*	*B*	*A*	*B*	*A*	*B*	*A*	*B*	*A*	*B*	*A*
B/F May to December 1943.	37	130	1	28	–	7	24	13	58	47	976	1983	
	167		29		7		37		105		2961		2961
Tanbays Hos.	–	1	–	–	–	–	–	–	1	3	9	11	20
Kanburi Hos.	–	–	–	–	–	–	1	2	1	1	27	12	39
Changi	–	–	–	–	1	–	–	2	1	1	11	6	17
Totals	–	1	–	–	1	–	1	4	3	5	47	29	
	1		–		1		5		8		76		76

February 1944

	Cholara		*Dys & Diarr*		*Dys & Beri-beri*		*Dys & malaria*		*Dys & Ulcers*		*Beri-beri*		*Beri-beri & Malaria*		*Beri-beri & Ulcers*		*Malaria Fever Unspec.*		*Malaria & Ulcers*	
	A	*B*	*A*	*B*	*A*	*B*	*A*	*B*	*A*	*B*	*A*	*B*	*A*	*B*	*A*	*B*	*A*	*B*	*A*	*B*
Kanburi Hos.	–	–	1	1	2	1	1	–	2	–	6	3	1	2	–	–	–	–	1	–
Changi	–	–	–	–	3	–	2	–	–	–	–	–	–	–	–	–	–	–	–	–
Total	–	–	1	1	5	1	3	–	2	–	6	3	1	2	–	–	–	–	1	–
	–		2		6		3		2		9		3		–		–		1	

	Ulcers		*Diphthoria*		*Small pox*		*Pneum-onia*		*Other Diseases*		*Total*		*Combined Total*
	A	*B*	*A*	*B*	*A*	*B*	*A*	*B*	*A*	*B*	*A*	*B*	*A*
Kanburi Hos.	–	–	–	–	–	–	–	1	–	–	14	8	22
Changi	–	–	–	–	–	–	–	–	2	–	4	–	4
Totals	–	–	–	–	–	–	–	1	2	–	18	8	
	–		–		–		1		2		26		26

March 1944

	Cholara		*Dys & Diarr*		*Dys & Beri-beri*		*Dys & malaria*		*Dys & Ulcers*		*Beri-beri*		*Beri-beri & Malaria*		*Beri-beri & Ulcers*		*Malaria Fever Unspec.*		*Malaria & Ulcers*	
	A	*B*	*A*	*B*	*A*	*B*	*A*	*B*	*A*	*B*	*A*	*B*	*A*	*B*	*A*	*B*	*A*	*B*	*A*	*B*
Kanburi Hos.	–	–	–	–	–	1	1	–	–	–	–	–	–	–	–	–	–	–	–	–
Changi	–	–	1	–	–	–	–	–	–	–	–	–	1	–	–	–	–	1	–	–
Total	–	–	1	–	1	1	1	–	–	–	–	–	1	–	–	–	–	1	–	–
	–		1		2		1		–		–		1		–		1		–	
Carried	193	444	191	640	151	180	63	51	52	49	134	279	31	31	24	33	62	69	19	10
	637		831		331		114		101		413		62		57		131		39	

	Ulcers		*Diphthoria*		*Small pox*		*Pneum-onia*		*Other Diseases*		*Total*		*Combined Total*
	A	*B*	*A*	*B*	*A*	*B*	*A*	*B*	*A*	*B*	*A*	*B*	*A*
Kanburi Hos.	–	–	–	–	–	–	–	–	–	2	2	3	5
Changi	–	–	–	–	–	–	–	–	4	–	6	1	7
Totals	–	–	–	–	–	–	–	–	4	2	8	4	
	–		–		–		–		6		12		12
Carried	37	131	1	28	1	7	25	18	67	54	1051	2024	
	168		29		8		43		121		3075		3075

April 1944

	Cholara		Dys & Diarr		Dys & Beri-beri		Dys & malaria		Dys & Ulcers		Beri-beri		Beri-beri & Malaria		Beri-beri & Ulcers		Malaria Fever Unspec.		Malaria & Ulcers	
	A	B	A	B	A	B	A	B	A	B	A	B	A	B	A	B	A	B	A	B
Carried	193	444	191	640	151	180	63	51	52	49	134	279	31	31	24	33	62	69	19	10
	637		831		331		114		101		413		62		57		131		29	
Kanburi Hos.	–	–	1	–	–	1	–	–	–	–	–	–	–	–	–	–	–	–	–	–
Changi	–	–	–	–	–	–	1	–	–	–	–	–	–	–	–	–	–	1	–	–
Total	–	–	1	–	–	1	1	–	–	–	–	–		–	–	–	–	1	–	–
	–		1		1		1		–		–		–		–		1		–	
Grand Total	193	444	192	640	151	181	64	51	52	49	134	279	31	31	24	33	62	70	19	10
	637		832		332		115		101		413		62		57		132		29	

	Ulcers		Diphthoria		Small pox		Pneum-onia		Other Diseases		Total		Combined Total
	A	B	A	B	A	B	A	B	A	B	A	B	A
Carried	37	131	1	28	1	7	25	18	67	54	1051	2024	
	168		29		8		43		121		3075		3075
Kanburi Hos.	1	–	–	–	–	–	–	–	–	1	2	2	4
Changi	–	–	–	–	–	–	–	–	4	2	5	3	8
Totals	1	–	–	–	–	–	–	–	4	3	7	5	
	1		–		–		–		7		12		12
Grand total	38	131	1	28	1	7	25	18	71	57	1058	2029	
	169		29		8		43		120		3087		3087

Appendix 'A' Table II

	Australian	*British*	*Total*
Left Changi April 1943	3662	3336	6998
Died in 12 months May 1943-April, 1944.	1058	2029	3084
Death rate per mille per annum	289	608	441

Appendix 'A' Table III **Summary of "F" Force Deaths** **British and Austrian combined**

	Cholara	*Dys & Diarr*	*Dys & Beri-beri*	*Dys & malaria*	*Dys & Ulcers*	*Beri-beri*	*Beri-beri & Malaria*	*Beri-beri & Ulcers*	*Malaria Fever Unspec.*	*Malaria & Ulcers*
May 1943	158	9	–	1	–	–	–	3	–	–
June 1943	359	26	1	3	1	15	2	–	6	–
July 1943	50	114	2	8	–	19	1	–	21	–
Aug. 1943	60	231	34	19	8	64	10	1	34	–
Sept. 1943	10	137	82	34	26	61	16	20	19	11
Oct. 1943	–	92	91	23	28	63	9	9	12	11
Nov. 1943	–	127	49	10	25	111	3	7	7	1
Dec. 1943	–	53	52	6	10	70	11	7	20	3
Jan. 1944	–	9	15	6	1	11	6	3	8	2
Feb. 1944	–	2	3	3	2	9	3	–	–	1
Mar. 1944	–	1	2	1	–	–	1	–	1	–
April. 1944	–	1	1	1	–	–	–	–	1	
12 month total	637	832	332	115	101	413	62	57	132	29
Expressed as percentage of total	21%	27%	11%			13%	2%	2%	4%	1%

(Table Cont.)

(Table Cont..)

	Ulcers	Diphthoria	Small pox	Pneum-onia	Other Diseases	Total	Strangth at Beginning of period	Death rate per killed per annum
May 1943	–	3	–	–	9	183	6998	314
June 1943	–	5	1	1	15	425	6815	748
July 1943	2	8	2	2	11	240	6390	451
Aug. 1943	21	8	1	–	16	537	6150	1048
Sept. 1943	62	2	–	13	13	506	5613	1082
Oct. 1943	36	2	–	6	13	359	5107	928
Nov. 1943	37	–	1	3	14	385	4712	1006
Dec. 1943	9	1	2	12	14	280	4317	778
Jan. 1944	1	–	1	5	8	76	4037	226
Feb. 1944	–	–	–	1	2	26	3961	79
Mar. 1944	–	–	–	–	6	12	3935	37
April. 1944	1	–	–	–	7	12	3923	37
12 month total	169	39	8	43	128	3087	6998	441
Expressed as percentage of total		1%	–	3%	4%	100		

Appendix 'A' Table IV

	Cholara	*Dys & Diarr*	*Dys & Beri-beri*	*Dys & malaria*	*Dys & Ulcers*	*Beri-beri*	*Beri-beri & Malaria*	*Beri-beri & Ulcers*	*Malaria Fever Unspec.*	*Malaria & Ulcers*
Changaraya	160	41	–	–	6	3	–	–	1	–
Kame-Sonkuari	59	159	29	7	17	126	9	8	24	15
Sonkurai	232	259	16	14	1	59	7	3	35	–
Shino-Sonkurai	103	15	12	6	–	3	3	–	9	–
Neike & Shimo-Neika	24	26	7	4	2	6	–	–	3	–
Konkoita; Taimonta; Takanun; Tamarand Pat.	56	18	2	1	–	6	1	–	8	–
Transit Camps and other	2	88	9	6	3	29	2	–	9	–
Tanbays Hosp.	1	155	214	52	62	83	21	53	10	8
Kanburi Hosp.	–	9	42	18	10	96	16	12	26	3
Changi	–	5	1	7	–	–	3	1	7	3
Total	637	832	332	115	101	413	62	57	132	29

(Table Cont..)

(Table Cont..)

	Ulcers	*Diphthoria*	*Small pox*	*Pneum-onia*	*Other Diseases*	*Total*
Changaraya	–	3	–	–	1	215
Kame-Sonkuari	38	2	–	15	5	513
Sonkurai	23	17	4	2	9	678
Shino-Sonkurai	–	–	–	–	5	156
Neike & Shimo-Neika	–	4	1	1	9	89
Konkoita; Taimonta; Takanun; Tamarand Pat.	–	–	–	–	–	102
Transit Camps and other	3	2	–	1	10	194
Tanbays Hosp.	52	–	–	5	12	748
Kanburi Hosp.	13	–	2	13	24	344
Changi	–	1	1	4	15	48
Total	169	29	8	43	128	3087

Appendix 'A' Table IV

Deaths (Australian and British combined)
Grouped in 4 Monthly Periods

Month	*Population at beginning of period*	*Cholara*	*Dys & Diarr*	*Dys & Beri-beri*	*Dys & malaria*	*Dys & Ulcers*	*Beri-beri*	*Beri-beri & Malaria*	*Beri-beri & Ulcers*	*Malaria*	*Malaria & Ulcers*	*Ulcers*	*Other Diseases*	*Total*
1943 May; June; July; August	6998	627	410	37	31	9	88	13	1	64	–	23	82	1385
September; October; November; December	5643	10	409	274	73	89	305	39	53	58	26	144	96	1576
1944 January; February; March; April	4037	–	13	21	11	3	20	10	3	10	3	2	30	126
Total	16648	637	832	332	115	101	413	62	57	138	29	169	208	3087

Appendix B

Medical Personnel

British	Australian
Lt. Col. J. Huston, R.A.M.C. S.M.O.	Major R. Stevens. R.A.M.C. S.M.O. A.I.F.
Major J. H. Phillips, R.A.M.C.	Major B.A. Hunt, Medical Specialise.
Major D.G. Gillies, R.A.M.C.	Major. Rogers, A.A.M.C.
Major D.A. Kambury, R.A.M.C.	Capt. C. Juttner, A.A.M.C.
Major I.F. Routley, R.A.M.C.	Capt. T.L. Cuhill, A.A.M.C.
Capt/ M/ Sialman, P.A.M.C.	Capt. J.L. Tayler, MC A.A.MC.
Capt. J.F. Partridge, MC. R.A.M.C.	Capt. R. Mill A.A.M.C.
Capt. Wilson, R.A.M.C.	Capt. M.I.A. Hendry, A.A.M.C.
Capt. N.J. Emery,	Capt. V. Brand, MC, A.A.M.C.
Lieut. L.H. Turrer, FMSVF.	
A/S. P. Wolbe I.M.D. A/S D.A. Plamers I.M.D.	A/s M. Gama, I.M.D.
	A/S J. James I.M.D.
Major. J. Reid, R.A.M.C.	Entomologist
Capt. R.J. Dix. A.D. Corps.	Capt. Mannion. A.A. Dental Corps.
Lieut. Ff. Sinden R.A.M.C. (Q.M.)	Lietu Vietch. Q.M.
144 B.O.Rs. (RSM. E.G. Childs)	225 A.O.Rs (W.O.1. B. MeGlym.)

Appendix C

Instructions Given To P.O.W. on My Assuming Command

I have the pleasure to lead you on the charge of last stretch of Railway Construction Wardoom. In examination of various reports as well as to the result of my partial inspection of the present conditions, I am pleased to find you in general keeping discipline and working diligently.

At the same time I regret to find seriousness in health matters. It is evident that there are various causes inevitable for this and but to my opinion, due mainly to the fact of absence of firm belief as Japanese.

Health follows will and lease only when the enemy is annihilitated.

Those who fail to reach objective in charge by lack of health or spirit is considered in the Japanese Army most shameful deed.

Devotion to Death is good. Yet still we have the spirit of Devotion to the Imperial Cause even to the 7th of life in reincarnation the Spirit which cannot become void by death.

You are in act of charge in colleague with the I.J.A. You are expected to charge to the last stage of this work in good spirit by taking good care of your own health. Besides you are to remember that your welfare is guaranteed only by obedience to the order of the Imperial Japanese Army.

Imperial Japanese Army will not be unfair to those who are honest and obey them, but protect such.

You are to understand this fundamental Japanese spirit and carry out the task given you with perfect ease of mind under protection to the Japanese Army.

Given in Kanchanabri June 26th 1943 by Col. Sijuo Nakamura, Comm. P.O.W. Camps in Thailand.

Kanchanabri Camp

29 Nov. 1943

To: Headquarters,
Malaya Prisoners of War Administration,
Malaya
Sir,

Subject : Health of "F" Force

The attached report on the medical situation of "F" Force is submitted for your information. The departure of the party of 1,000 prisoners of war who are due to leave for Singapore in the near future will leave the following position here :-

2,000 ill in hospital

1,500 fit for light camp duties only.

These 3,500 men are broken in health and suffering from malnutrition and vitamin deficiencies. To remedy this it is essential that they receive extra food such as milk, eggs, sugar, flour and cooking oil.

At a meeting between the I.J.A. representatives (Captain Hachisuka and Mr. Fujibayashi) and the British Red Cross representatives at Changi on 13 April 1943 it was agreed that when things settled down, if the force urgently required money it could apply for a grant from the International Red Cross through the I.J.A. administration, which would be the same as at Changi.

Money is urgently required by "F" Force for the purchase of special food and drugs for the 3,500 P.O.W. remaining here. This amount is estimated at $50,000 for a period of three months. At present hospital patients and sick men are not paid by the I.J.A. and during the past seven months the sick of the Force have been financed by voluntary contributions from the officers, who contribute 3/8ths of the limited pay they receive in cash to this purpose. I do feel that the provision of extra food and medical requirements for the Force should not be the responsibility of the officers, and in any case their contributions (although, of course, these will still continue) are now totally inadequate to meet this urgent situation.

It would be greatly appreciated if the I.J.A. would allow the International Red Cross Society to:

(1) Supply the necessary drugs and dressings for this Force which the local I.J.A. administration is unable to provide-

(2) Furnish the Force with a sum of money ($50,000) to purchase extra food and necessities for the sick.

The clothing of this Force is in a deplorables condition, a big proportion of the men are without boots and are literally in rags. It would be appreciated if an issue of clothing could be made at the earliest opportunity.

Although the 1,000 Prisoners of War that have been selected to go to Singapore from this Force in the near future are the fittest available, nevertheless 200 are unfit and of the remaining 800 over 90 per cent have suffered during the past several months from malaria and dysentery and they are bound to have frequent relapses. It is respectfully requested therefore that whatever work is allotted to this detachment should not be of too arduous a nature.

(Signed) S.W. Harris
Lieut-Colonel,R.A.,
Commander "F" Force P.O.W.

To : Commander, "F" Force Kanburi Camp,
November 28th 1943
Sir,

Subject : Health of "F" Force

Of the 7,000 P.O.W.s who left Changi at the end of April, 1943, about 2,500 are dead of disease, 2,000 are ill and in hospitals, 1,500 are fit only for light camp duties and not more than 1,000 are fit for work. The principal causes of death have been Chronic Dysentery, with Malnutrition, Beri-Beri, Cholera, Tropical Ulcers and Malaria.

Measures which will lessen disease and unfitness, (a) supply of a good mixed diet with rice polishings, fresh vegetables or fruit and cooking fats to produce 3,000 calories daily for all men whether in hospital, light duties or working (b) Supply of sufficient tools to maintain a good standard of camp sanitation: Buckets and scrubbing brushes, cresol, and lime 'are essential to keep quarters etc. clean (c) Only fit men to be allowed to do heavy work such as road and railway construction, and these for not more than eight hours a day, six days a week. (d) Supply of medical stores in sufficient quantity to all camps. Appendix shows the amount required monthly for 2000 hospital sick and the particular drugs etc. needed (e) supply of boots and other clothing as required. At present many men lack boots and suffer from skin troubles of the feet. (f) It is suggested that invailid foods such as cooking oil, milk, eggs, sugar, flour be provided for the hospitals and camp sick.

It would be appreciated if the I.J.A. would allow the International Red Cross Society to supply any items (e.g. Emetine, which is the drug of greatest value in the treatment of Amoebic Dysentery, which at present appears to affect some sixty per cent of the Force) which are difficult to obtain.

I have the honour to be, Sir, Your obedient servant,

J.Huston, Lt.Col.R.A.M.C,
S.M.O. "F" Force

Medical Report by Lt. Col. J. HUSTON, Senior Medical Officer

Lt.Col. W.W. Harris, OBE, R.A.
Commanding "F" Force

The high death rate and the medical situation generally in this camp is causing me the gravest anxiety, and unless stringent and immediate steps are taken to remedy existing conditions the death rate, which is now at the rate of over 100 per cent per annum, will continue in an increasing ratio.

The following report on this situation is submitted for your information and possible action:

1. Availability on 6 Aug 43 (excluding Officers Red Cross)

	Fit	*Light Duties*	*In Hosp.*	*Non-Combatants*	*Total*
On road	214	83	—	—	297
In Camp	70	35	1463	86	1654
Total	284	118	1463	86	1951

2. Deaths (Out of an original 1,000)

Cholera – 209 — Starvation and Dysentery - 119

Beri-Beri-28 — Malaria-Diptheria-14

Tropical Ulcers-7 — Misc. Causes-5

making a total of 399.

3. Causes of Ill Health and High Death Rate

(a) Defective diet during the past 2 months the present situation regarding rations for sick men contains 1400 calories, only, which is not sufficient to maintain less to enable desperately sick men to recuperate.

(b) The prolonged march here of a force in which there were 30 per cent unfit men. Exclussively long working hours and ill treatment of men on road and rail working parties.

(c) Sick men being forced to work on outside working parties. After working long hours some of these men have been found dead in their huts.

(d) Lack of medical supplies and hospital equipment.

(e) Inadequate rations and non-payment of unfit men.

4. Suggested Remedies

(a) Immediate improvement of camp conditions, sanitation, cooking facilities and hygiene generally. (This is now being done under the orders of Lieut. WAKABYASHI and we are very grateful for this dispensation).

(b) Only fit men to be allowed to work on the roads and railway. At present sick men are being forced to work - men suffering from Malaria, malnutritution, beri-beri and sore feet. If it is true that the daily working party is to be increased from 300 to 700, then I anticipate that the number of sick will steadily increase and there will be a rapid rise in the death rate.

(c) Supply of a good mixed diet containing rice polishings, fresh vegetables, and cooking fats to produce 3,500 calories daily for all men whether sick or fit. As I have already stated the present ration for sick men contains only 1,400 calories which is not sufficient to support life, with a consequence that unfit men are dying in large number and this number will undoubtedly increase unless the rations are improved.

(d) Supply of medical equipment which was brought from CHANGI with this force. This has been dumped at BAMPONG, KANU (HQ of "H" Force) and TARKANAN. We are also in urgent need of dressings, cotton wool, gauze, Emetine, Vitamic B tablets, Magnesium Sulphate tablets, Bismuth and Opium for Diarrhoea, Iodoform and Sulphur for treating ulcers and skin diseases.

(e) Invalid foods are urgently needed, fish, oil, milk, eggs, sugar and flour.

(f) Antiseptics are also urgently needed for disinfecting hands and preventing the spread . of disease. (Creosol, lysol and kylenol).

(g) A supply of tools, utensils, basins, buckets, and scrubbing brushes are also needed for keeping the sick and their quarters clean.

Finally in particular I must warn you that at present without disinfectants and with inadequate food the whole camp is defenceless against another outbreak of cholera.

Sid. J. Huston,
Lieut-Colonel RAMC SMO, "F" Force

8 Aug 1943.

.....

To : Officer in Charge
Sonkrai Camp

The medical situation in this camp is extremely grave and is becoming worse every hour. At the present moment cholera is raging - there have been 37 deaths and there are over 90 patients in hospital-new cases are occurring at the rate of 25 or more daily.

Dysentery is still a very serious problem and many men are so debilitated from prolonged dysentery or diarrhoea that it will be many weeks before they are fit for any form of work, - meantime their resistance to cholera or any other diseases is seriously impaired.

Malaria is rapidly increasing and we anticipate that within a week or two there will be hundreds of sufferers.

Taking the situation as a whole it is our anticipation that within one month there will NOT be 250 men in this camp fit to do a day's work.

The reasons for this situation are that the men in this camp have been subjected to treatment which it is wrong for any civilized nations to inflict on its prisoners of war In detail :-

1. The men before leaving CHANGI were weekend by dysentery and deficiency diseases (beri-beri and pellagra) and were in no condition to withstand infections.
2. An assurance was given by the I.J.A. at CHANGI to the Commander A. I.F., at Changi that food would be better here than in CHANGI and that troops would not have to march from the train to their destination. Neither of these promises have been kept. Replying on the second promise many men totally unfit to march were included in the Force : very many of these are now in hospitals - some have died.
3. The hygiene of the camps on the road was appalling and hundreds of men were successively infected by dysentery, by malaria, and finally by cholera, the present tragedy is the result.
4. The condition on marching were extremely arduous and in some cases unwarrantably cruel. Sick men were driven out on to the road night after night in some cases with high fever of active dysentery. As a result men arrived here completely exhausted.
5. After arrival men were put in an unhygienic, badly situated camp, roofless and with very bad latrine accommodation; all conditions ideal for the spread of disease were present and disease has, in consequence, rapidly spread - your own report that 53 positive reports for cholera were found in about 500 apparently healthy men showed how rapidly and widely the spread took place.
6. No adequate rest was given to men, nor any assistance given to requests for help. On the contrary men were sent out to work and kept out of camp 12-13 hours a day in pouring rain - conditions typical NOT of the honourable treatment of prisoners of war, but of slave labour.

   At the present moment : (approx.)

37 men are dead of cholera 95 men are in hospital with cholera, 250 men are in hospital with other diseases 140 men are excused all duty on account of sickness, and many of these would be in hospital if there were enough room, or drugs, or nurses. 150 men are so weakened by illness that they are only fit for light duties. 120 men are being used (or have been used) in the care of the sick and of these 30 have always become so sick as to have been already admitted to hospital.

About 800 men out of 2000 have become invalid or have been required to nurse the sick within fourteen days of the arrival in this camp:- and the number is likely to increase rapidly.

In view of the above facts we demand :-

That this document be forwarded ›› the Representative of the International Red Cross in Bangkok and Rangoon.

2. That all work shall cease, not for three days, but indefinitely until the present cholera epidemic has been fully got under control. In this circumstances we

seek your attention to the promise given on 27th May 1943 that all work would cease after three days. This promise was broken the day after it was given.

The reasons for asking for all work to cease are : -

(a) To enable all necessary constructive work around the camp on latrines, roofing and drainage to be done.

(b) To enable hundreds of debilitated men to rest and recover their health.

(c) To permit enough men to be allotted to nursing work, to give adequate treatment to the hundreds of sick and rest to the present overworked and exhausted nursing staff.

3. The supplies of adequate drugs, disinfectants, soap, lights and other medical supplies.
4. The supply of blankets for the sick.
5. The supply of invalid foods, soup and tea and sugar for the sick.
6. The improvement of the camp diet by extra vitamin-containing food, e.g., rice polishings, towgay, meat, oil and fats.
7. The supply of suppressive atebrin for the whole of the camp- the present small quinine dosage is quite inadequate and without effect.
8. The supply of water containers, especially 44 gallons drums, to enable water to be used on a large scale, and also smaller containers for water boiling, to make sterilization possible.
9. The supply of a large number of tents (waterproof) for the cholera area which is extending daily. At least 30 large tents are required apart from what is new in the camp.
10. The supply of oil for dealing with mosquito- breeding places in the camp a visit from Captain Wilson, Malarial Expert, at H.Q. Camp is urgently necessary to locate those.
11. The supply of protective clothing - white coats for nurses handling cholera.
12. As soon as the health of the camp has been improved, which may NOT be for several months, the evacuation of the area by troops and their subsequent treatment in a manner be fitting the honourable Japanese Nation whose reputation must suffer gravely if the present conditions continue.

We demand that this document be laid before Lt. Col. Banno and the senior Japanese Medical Officer for the area, and also before Lt.Col. Harris at the earliest possible moment - preferably tonight.

Signed: W.Mc Johnston,Major

Comd. IF Troops,Shimo Sombrei Camp

Bruce Hunte,S.M.O.Major S.M.O.Camp,A.A.M.O.

C.Tracey, Major Commander, No. 1 Bn

R.H. Anderson, Major Commander, No. 2 Bn

Dear Capt. Barnet,

From this morning I order to you the working number because the work is very hurry. Therefore of course you must select and collect this number from the same sick party.

Today - soldier 130 men, the officer 8 men,

(Sgd) Capt. H. Maruyama

Received at Tarkunnun, Thailand on 19th July 1943.

Annexure to Part II

Tanbaya Hospital Report

1. At the end of June a project for the establishment of a hospital in some locality where food was readily available was put up to the I.J.A. This was examined and a reconnaissance in Burma was carried out by the I.J.A. Medical Officer. However, nothing materialised and the project was shelved indefinitely. Nevertheless at the end of July it was suddenly rosuscitated and became a "fait accompli" almost immediately.

The hospital was to accommodate twelve hundred and fifty patients who were to be drawn from two categories:

(i) Men who would not recover from their present illness within two months, and

(ii) old men with a permanent disability or unsuited for heavy work on the "road". The allotment of patients to camps was :-

Nieke	250
Shimo-Sonkrai	500
Sonkrai	350
Kami-Sonkrai	50
Changaraya	100

The move was to be carried out by M.L. in flights of 250 with nightly stage at Changanya, Kando and Ronshi. The I.J.A. would allow a medical staff of only 8 Officer (including one assistant-surgeon) and 130 O.Rs with an administrative staff of 4 Officers and 51 O.Rs. Any additional personnel required were to be drawn from the convalescent patients. The advanced party moved off at a bare 12 hours notice and the patients were to follow the next day. As will be seen later neither the move nor allotment of patients to camps went according to schedule.

2. On 30 July 43 the advanced party, consisting of all the administrative staff and eight officers and thirty-six other ranks of the medical staff, assembled at Changaraya, which they reached by march route. The remainder of the medical staff was to be spread over the flights of patients whom they accompanied. Both the administrative and medical staffs were drawn from all the camps (The names of the Officer staff are given in appendix "A"). The advanced

party had to drop off at the staging camps- Kando and Ronshi—one medical officer, three medical orderlies and administrative personnel to look after the patients in transit.

The executive order for the advanced party to move was delayed and did not reach camps some time after the working parties had left. Consequently there was some difficulty in collecting the ear-marked personnel. In fact, the detachment from Sonkrai had to be completed from semi-fit men who were in camp and two of them collapsed on arrival at Changaraya and eventually died.

Next day the move to Kando was made by M.T. Here the party were housed for the night in a hut already occupied by coolies. The move to Ronshi was carried out by march route and M.T. The staging party was dropped off and six men including the two men mentioned in the previous paragraph had to be left behind sick. The march a distance of fourteen kms- began at 0430 hours in the pouring rain and pitch darkness and was most arduous. Eventually Ronshi was reached and here the party stayed for thirty-six hours and were occupied on repairing a hut, which was to house the patients in transit. Tanbaya was reached on 3 Aug by march route as the railway was not working owing to a bridge having collapsed in the floods. During the march which was along the railway line, it poured the whole time.

3. It had been decided to adopt a somewhat navel system of command, which is practice turned out very satisfactively Lt. Col. C. T. Hutchison Mc, R.A. was appointed Administrative Commander, while Major Bruce Hunt, AAMC was nominated O.C. Hospital. The former was responsible roughly for all outside activities and personnel employed outside the hospital, also for roll call returns and finance, while the latter's domain was inside the hospital, including the discipline of the medical personnel and patients. To assist the O.C. Hospital combatant officers were appointed to act as wardmasters.

4. The camp, which was adjacent to the railway had been an old camp which hand been allowed to fall into a bad state of disrepair, Secondary jungle had grown up all round. The actual site itself was dry considering it was the middle of the monsoon. One hut and the cookhouse were roofed in, the remaining huts were in the process of being roofed and otherwise repaired. In the roofed hut the advanced party, together with the I.J.A. guards, were housed. Other huts were occupied by coolies employed on the railway and on the repair of huts.

The camp (for plan see Appendix "B") consisted of seven huts each a hundred meters long, with attap sides and roof and a wide bamboo platform to take two men, with a gangway along one side. Each of these huts was scheduled to accommodate two hundred patients. In addition, there was a smaller hut to hold eighty patients and this had two platforms with the gangway down the centre. Later, when the establishment of the hospital was increased, a small camp the other side of the railway line and occupied by I.J.A. railway personnel and coolies was made available. Here there were two big huts, a smaller hut and, in addition, a small hut, which was used as an operating theatre and chapel. When the hospital was finally established the layout was:-

Ward	I	Administrative personnel
Ward	II	Malaria and beri-beri patients.
Ward	III	Dysentery patients.
Ward	IV	Malaria and beri-beri patients.
Ward	V	Malaria and dysentery patients.
Ward	VI	Dysentery patients.
Ward	VII	Medical (non-dysentery) patients.
Ward	VIII	H.Q. officers and stores (H.Q. dispensary etc)
Ward	IX	Tropical ulcer patients
Ward	X	Tropical ulcer patients
Ward	XI	Officer patients.

Latrines were of the usual open trench type and the majority were old existing ones, only two new ones being provided.

The camp lay on either side of the railway line and about hundred yards from it. The actual precincts of the camp was fairly clear of trees though the jungle was quickly reached. It did not, however, have that confined feeling prevalent in the working camps. An outcrop of low hills a mile and a half to two miles away made a pleasant view. The camp was bounded on three sides by two small streams, which eventually joined at the north-east corner of the camp. One flowed almost past the cookhouse and provided the water supply for the camp. The fourth side of the camp was boarded by the Thailand-Moulmein road. Towards the outcrops of hills and a thousand yrads from the camp was larges stream flowing in a north-westerly direction.

5. As soon as the advanced party arrived the usual administrative difficulties began. There were no tools available for camp maintence, let alone camp improvement had it been possible to start on it. Indeed, the only wood cutting tool available for the first few days was an axe carried all the way from Thailand by one of the advanced party. The coolies living in the camp fouled the whole area and that added to the difficulties of the hygiene squad. Requests to have the coolies moved to the other end of the camp were negatived. Malaria took its toll and, in order to provide the fatigues required by the I.J.A., the officers, including medical officers, had to be employed on carrying and chopping wood for the cookhouse, which was shared by the I.J.A. The fatigues on which medical personnel had also to be employed consisted of ration drawing and carrying, construction of a hut for the I.J.A. guard and even clearing ground to make a thirty yard rifle range. The carrying of sacks of rice was a heavy physical strain on the men.

I.J.A. pattern two-handed saw was permitted. Apart from what was brought by Ps. O.W. the maximum tools available were on cross-cut, part use of another two axes, two shovels, one pick and eight chunkels. Nothing in the way of wire or wire cutters for the maintenance of huts or latrines was forthcoming. The shortage of cutting tools was most acute when the daily death rate was high, as all bodies had to be cremated.

Cooking utensils too were always a difficulty, especially containers for cooked food, which were never sufficient. As water had to be boiled for drinking, sterilization of eating utensils and for medical purposes, each ward had to be issued with some containers. This reacted unfavorably on the distribution of food, so much so that at one time meals were being served continuously from 0730 hours to 2130 hours and sometimes later. About the middle of September Force HQ sent down a number of containers of various descriptions and it was then possible to feed the camp in two shifts for each meal. At one time the rice qualies were each being used to cook eighteen boils.

Water was obviously to be the problem of the camp. The stream at the south-east corner of the camp was originally allotted for all purposes. When it was pointed out that as soon as the rains stopped this stream would quickly dry up, the I.J.A. replied "You won't be here then." However, on 13 Oct. the supply suddenly dried up and the cookhouse had to be moved to the other stream to the north of the camp. This source of supply also failed a week later and again the cookhouse had to be moved, this time to the big stream. Although both these moves meant a longer carry for the cooks food and uncooked rations, the manpower and containers involved were less than these necessary to carry the water to the cookhouse. There was at this big stream a pump house with a gravity tank, which was connected to a stand pipe in the camp. All that was required was a lift and force pump. This, however, was now available. To save the long carry of water to the wards two wells were brought into use, but for these the I.J.A. could supply neither buckets nor ropes. Requests to purchase these on behalf of the camp met with the reply that they were unprocurable. Again Ps.O.W property was employed.

6. The basic ration lacked Vitamin B content, and this was clearly proved by the increase in beri-beri, amongst both the patients and fit men. Representations resulted in an improvement and the bean ration was increased somewhat. It was not until 13 Oct, when it was pointed out that a hospital camp five kilos away drawing from the same supply depot was recieving a surfeit of beans, that the supply could be considered as adequate. On 19 Oct rice polishings were issued –at first on a scale sufficient only for beri-beri patients, but later the issue was increased to allow for a good ration to be made to each individual. Incidentally it might be added in passing that these polishings were the best ever seen to date in any camp. The meat issue was on the hoof,

though latterly dried meat in boxes was issued. From time to time prawns were issued in lieu of meat. These scalded made a pleasant variety in the tins. The meat issue was spasmodic and averaged out at about two ounces per head at time could a ration scale be obtained from the I.J.A. Odd quantities of sugar, flour and cooking oil were received, but these commodities were so small that they could be used only for the special diets. Tea was insufficient for a general issue, in the first place were mainly runner beans, and egg-fruit, but latterly sweet fat an ordinary potato were issued. The amounts received varied, at times there was almost glut, so much so that it was possible to produce a rice less meal occasionally by making a big issue of potatoes. At other times again there was almost a shortage. The various representations on rations were usually verbally, though they were referred to in letters on medical subjects. In Appendix "C" is a copy of a letter dealing with the subject. Traders were allowed to come to the camp, but their visits were spasmodic and their supplies limited to smokes, gula and bananas. Eggs in sufficient quantities were unobtainable and cost of cooking oil was prohibitive being over two hundred rupees for four gallons, and beans, if procurable, were about 80 rupees a 100 pound sack.

In the evenings talks, sing-song and general knowledge were organized in the wards. There was no site suitable, if it had been desirable, to hold any centralized form of entertainment. To the speakers and organizers a tribute is due and their efforts were greatly appreciated.

8. Patients began to arrive on 8 Aug. The first batch had staged at Ronshi and, owing to damage to a railway bridge, were forced to trek over two kilometers to where the trains were operating. This in itself was sheer cruelty, as the majority of cases were suffering from tropical ulcers. No further patients arrived until 21 Aug. When the railway was through again. Parties then arrived daily in catches of varying numbers, the smallest being thirty odd while the largest was over a hundred and eighty. Parties staged at Changaraya and Kando, Ronshi was not used after the first party. The journey was made by M.T. and rail and was a severes train on the patients. The trip from Kando took anything between twelve and eighteen hours, with long periods without food and long waits at the debussing and entraining point, where there was no shelter from the rain or shade from the sun. Patients were herded into closed or open tracks and as many as fifty-four is one closed truck is recorded. As the majority of these cases were suffering from tropical ulcers and/or dysentery the atmosphere in the truck bears no description. on route were not infrequent and as many as eight in one party were found to to be dead on arrival. Patients arrived in a sorry state and the lack of clothing and bedding was appalling. Some had only a cloth round their waists.

The time of arrival of parties varied between 2000 hours and 0800 hours. As the only light in wards was from fires the organization for reception was distinctly hampered.

The last party arrived on 7 Sep, bringing the strength of the camp, including staff, up to 1,776, while during the intervening period there has been 148 death. The number of patients from working camps bore no relation to the original plan since to the high death and sickness rate at Sonkrai, the I.J.A. changed the allotment. The numbers from each camp worked out at:-

	British	*A.I.F.*	*Total*
Ex Nieke	159	138	279
Ex Shimo-Sonkrai	3	320	323
Ex Sonkrai	752	406	1,158
Ex Changaraya	146	—	146
	1,060	864	1,924

In these figures the staff has been included.

A detailed medical report is given in Appendix "D". Patients were suffering from a combination of dysentery, recurrent malaria, tropical ulcers, beri-beri and scabies.

The change of environment and the belief that better food would be available coupled with the knowledge that no "work on the road" was awaiting them as soon as they convalescent, did a lot to improve the morale of the patients. Alas, the disillusionment that followed quite neutralized any good that may have been done. True there was no work awaiting convalescents, but the knowledge that no drugs to cure dysentery were available, that there were no dressings for tropical ulcers and drug to combat beri-beri had an advance psychological influence on the patients. Circumstances is to their undying credit. The unselfishness and willingness to help each other in any capacity was most marked.

There was no attempt made to segregate British and Australians. The camp was treated as a single unit and personnel put in where they best fitted, irrespective of whether they were "English" or "Aussie." The harmonious co-operation between orderlies and patients was most marked. If any reorganization of wards was necessary requests were frequently made that a party of "cobbers", invariably containing some British and same Australians, be allowed to remain together, Indeed it would be true to say that many lasting friendships have been made.

A number of patients arrived at Tanbaya undernourished and debilitated. Some suffered from the delusion that they could not eat rice. In view of the small calorific value of the ration it was essential that every scrap of food should be got into the patients. Consequently an "Eat your rice" compaign was started, in which everyone was encouraged, and indeed forced, to eat all their meals—time being no object.

Malaria was prevalent and many primary infections were recorded. The frequency with which relapses occurred was alarming and had a debilitating affect on patients, especially sufferers from dysentery and tropical ulcers. It also had a serious affect on the personnel available for camp labour. Owing to overcrowding in huts there was a general distribution of skin diseases, especially scabies. The resultant irritation caused loss of sleep and also secondary ulcer formations. Iodematic beri-beri was prevalent and severe cardiac beri-beri caused many sudden deaths. With the lack of emetine, the gradual distressing and inevitable warring away of the dysentery patients was pathetic.

Owing to the change of plan for the dispatch of patients the surgical did not arrive till the middle of September. Prior to this some emergency utations had to be carried out with certain instruments loaned by an A.I.F. Hospital kilos away and an ordinary hand-saw borrowed from the I.J.A. In all, about forty amputations were performed. The results were most disappointing, only about four surviving. This low figure can in no way be attributed to medical skill, but to the fact that patients, vitality was low and that they lacked any power of resistance.

Copies of written representations on the medical situation are given in Appendix “E”.

Drugs were always inadequate and repeated representations were of no avail. Quinine was short for a period and at the beginning a full treatment could not be given. Later this was improved and sufficient was always available. When a suspected cholera case died the I.J.A. issued sufficient sorum to inoculate all the prominent staff and other key-men against cholera and pledue. No sulphur was available for treatment of scabies and no drugs or dressings for the tropical ulcers. Emetine and B.I. were, of course, not forthcoming except on one occasion and in minutequantities.

A Colonel of the I.J.A. Medical Service visited the camp on 25 Sep and a plea for drugs brought forth a promise of sulphur and potassium permanganate for the tropical ulcers. These, however, were not forth coming. In addition a prescription of powdered charred yak bones for the dysentery patients was given.

At the beginning of November a small supply of drugs was received, including twelve lbs. of sulphur and sufficient emetine to treat six patients. The former proved a godsend and had a marked effect on the incidence of scabies. The I.J.A. produced on repayment a quantity of muslin which was of the greatest value for bandages.

Eventually the I.J.A. ruled that no stretcher cases were to be moved and that a plan for the organization of the hospital with those remaining was to be prepared. It was then made known that the destination was to be Kanburi and, later, Singapore.

The move began on 19 Nov in parties of 200 on consecutive nights till the night of 24 Nov, when the final party of 132 left. The journey varied from 72 hours to 132 hours, with long halts en route. Like all other journeys it was most uncomfortable. Closed and open trucks at a scale of thirty-three to a truck were used. Food as usual was spasmodic and insufficient.

Major M.D. Price, R. Sigs, was left in command with Capts. E.J. Emery RAMC and F.J. Cahill AAMC, as medical officers. The details were:-

		British		A.I.F.		Total	
		Offrs.	*O.Rs*	*Offrs.*	*O. Rs*	*Offrs.*	*O.Rs*
Staff	(medical)	2*	23	1	29	3	52
	(Administrative)	2	16	2	27	4	43
Patient		3	139	-	76	3	215
		7	178	3	132	10	310

*includes one Assistant Surgeon.

Of the patients approximately 85 were suffering primarily from dysentery and approximately 85 primarily from tropical ulcers. The predominant disease amongst the remainder was beri-beri. Medical opinion considered that the deaths within the ensuing two months would be approximately 90-100.

A short report up to the closing of Tanbaya Hospital is given in Appendix "F"

12. The total, number of death, including dead on arrival, up to 1430 hours on 24 November was 665, representing about 45 per cent of the British and 21 per cent of the A.I.F. population of the camp. Deaths in the main were attributable to dysentery, both amoebic and bacillary, tropical ulcers, beri-beri and malaria. Undernutrition, and lack of essential vitamins very greatly increased the mortality rate from these diseases.

Full details of the dead, together with a plan of the cemetery, have been handed to the respective records branches.

13. The I.J.A. Administration after the arrival of Lieut. Iraiwa, I.J.A., about 22 Aug was in the main sympathetic and helpful within the limits of its power. The hospital was still under the control of Colonel Banno at Nieke. The British method of paying compliments was accepted and this had a marked effect on the morale of the prisoner. A gift of cigarettes with tea and margarine was most acceptable.

14. On the whole Tanbaya Hospital was not the success that it was hoped it would be for the two reas ons : (i) lack of well-balanced diet and (ii) complete lack of drugs. A tribute must be paid to the zeal and energy of Major Bruce Hunt and all his medical staff—both officers and other ranks. With their professional knowledge the task set them to cure the patients must have seemed hopeless, but never for one instant did they despair and were always at pains to do anything in their power at any time of day or night to alleviate suffering.

It must also be placed on record that the patients themselves bore their illness with great fortitude, helped both themselves and their comrades in a thousand and one small ways and, when the end came, expressed their gratitude for what had been done for them and passed on like heroes.

Appendix A

Tanbaya Hospital - Staff

Administrative Commander-	Lt-Col C.T. Hutchison, MC, RA.
O.C Hospital.	Major B.A. Hunt, AAMC

Administrative Officers

Adjutant-	Capt. F.E. Stahl, A.I.F.
Quartermaster-	Major G.D. MCK. Sutherland R.E.
Messing Officer-	Capt. S.S. Roberts, A.I.F.
R.S.M.	R.S.M. neild att'd SSVF

Medical Officers

Major W.J.E Phillips, R.A.M.C.

Major P.B. Hanbury. R.A.M.C.

Capt. F.J. Cahill, A.A.M.C.

Capt. E.J. Emery, R.A.M.C.

Capt. G.H. Lowe, F.M.S.V.F.

Capt. J. F. Pantridge, R.A.M.C.

Capt. H. Silman, R.A.M.C.

Lieut. L.H.Turner, S.S.V.F.

Assistant-Surgeon (WOI) P. Wolfe, I.M.D.

Hospital R.S.S. – R.S.M. Childs, R.A.M.C.

Appendix B

SKETCH OF TANBAYA HOSPITAL

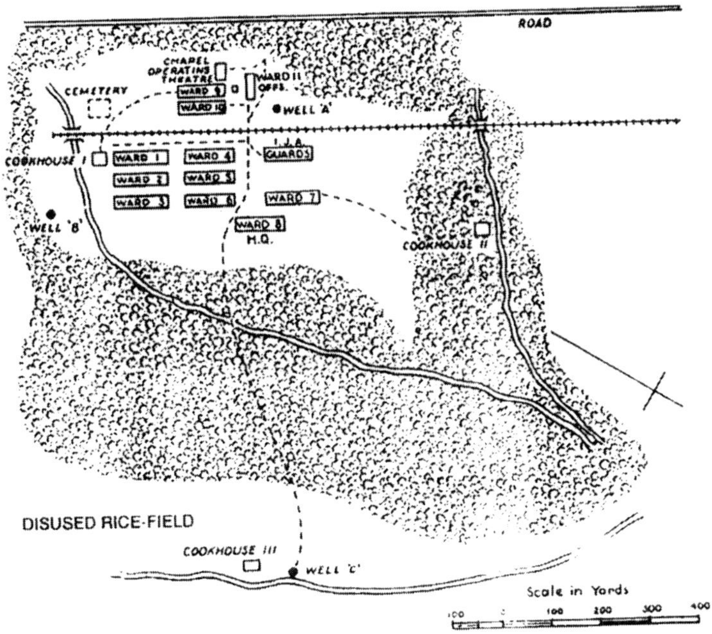

Appendix C

Copy of Letter Submitted to I.J.A.

To :- I.J.A. Officer Commanding Tanbaya Hospital Camp.

From:- Major B.A. Hunt, Commanding Tanbaya Hospital.

Date:- 20 Sep 43.

Sir,

I regret be have to inform you that the health of the men in this camp, instead of improving, is steadily getting worse. This is in spite of all efforts on your side and on ours to make things better. The number of men well enough to carry on the essential services to the camp—nursing, cooking, woodcutting,hygiene—is becoming daily smaller and very few are well enough to be discharged from Hospital to take their place. Seventeen of the working staff were admitted to hospital this morning. It is much to be feared that unless a marked improvement takes place at an early date the whole camp service may break down.

The diseases which are causing the present appalling death rats and the large number of admissions to hospital are:-

I. **Beri-Beri.** Although we know that you are doing your utmost to increase the vegetable supply, the green vegetables and potatoes which are being supplied contain very little Vitamin B, so that Beri-Beri is steadily increasing. Many patients, already sick from other diseases, are suddenly developing acute cardiac beri-beri and dying from it. Many of the camp hard workers-cooks, woodcutters and such—who naturally require a larger supply of Vitamin B and are not receiving it—are becoming attacked by beri-beri each day. The beri-beri patients already in hospital - between 500 and 600—are getting no better, and in many cases are actually becoming worse despite complete rest.

II. **Dysentery.** No medical treatment or drugs are available for this disease. In the absence of such treatment there seems little hope of saving more than a very small number of the 450 (approx) patients now suffering from dysentery.

III. **Malaria.** The malaria in this region is particularly virulent and responds very slowly to quinine. It is hoped that the recent increase in the supply of quinine may effect some improvement in this respect, but this is not to be expected for several weeks to come and in the meantime the replace rate is very high.

IV. **Ulcers.** In many patients these are rapidly spreading in the vitalised skin of the patients, where vitamin lack is so great that they can offer no resistance to the infection. Blood poisoning from ulcers occurs and ulcer patients are dying at the rate of 2 or 3 daily.

V. **Typhus and Typhus like fever.** A persistent fever lasting 2 or 3 weeks resembling typhus (tsussngamushi fever) in many respects but not quite typical of that disease is occurring in increasing numbers. It is extremely weakening and shows no response whatever to quinine. Three medical officers are suffering from this fever at present.

Medical Officers

1. **Australian**

   Major Hunt-Still weak after cardiac beri-beri and malaria.

   Capt. Chiall-Well

2. **British**

   Major Phillips- Very ill for the past 21 days with typhus. Not Improving-Condition serious and in bed.

   Capt. Silman – Ill for the past 9 days with typhus-not improving and in bed.

   Capt. Lowe- Ill for the past 5 weeks with typhus-now-improving but very weak and unable to work.

   Capt. Pantridge- Suffering from cardiac beri-beri working only half time.

   Lieut.Turner- suffering from dysentery and working half time. (Both these officers would, if the need for doctors were not so urgent be kept in bed, as would also Major-Hanbury.

   Major Hanbury- Suffering from cardiac beri-beri-working half time.

   Capt Eaery- Well.

   W. O. Wolfe- Ill with malaria.

Thus only two of the ten medical officers are at present capable of a full day's work.

Future Prospects

(1) If present circumstances continue I anticipate at least 400 deaths in the next 6 weeks and possibly more.

(2) If for any reason it were suddenly decided to move camp population and considerable distance by train (for example, five or six favourable circumstances of weather, food and the like.

Suggestions

The only suggestions for improvement I can offer—and I realise that most of these are beyond your immediate control—are set out below.

In spite of the possible difficulty in obtaining supplies it is by obvious duty to set them out.

1. **Beans.** At least 3, preferably 4, bags daily.

2. **Vitamin B.** Very large supplies of tablets and ampoules for injection.
3. **Drugs, for Dysentery**. Large supply for both bacillary and amoebic dysentery.
4. **Vitamin C.** Either in tablet or in fresh fruit form for the ulcer cases.
5. **Quinine.** Maintenance of the present rate of supply.
6. Iodoform sulphonamide, and dressings for ulcers.
7. **Medical Officers.** A further two medical officers. In this connection I am informed that Capt. Frew, a highly efficient Australian medical officer, is at present employed loading and unloading barges at Nieke.

I have the honors to submit the above report regarding the present state of the Health of the camp for your information in the hope that you will be able to help us to save the lives of many of the pitiable invalids now in hospital.

(Sgd) Bruce Hunt,

Major A.A.M.C.

Commanding Tanbaya Hospital.

Appendix D

Medical Report Tanbaya Hospital-Burma Aug 1-Nov 24, 1943

I. Introduction

It was on 29th June that the I.J.A. first intimated that it intended to establish a hospital in Burma to receive men of "F" Force who would be incapable of work for atleast two months. Rolls for a 2,000 bed hospital were prepared, but on the 8th July it was announced that the idea had been abandoned. On 21st July fresh orders were issued to prepare rolls, this time for a 1,250 bed hospital. Lt.Col. S. Harris commanding 'F' Force had appointed me OC Hospital on 1st July and on 24th July I was sent into Burma with Lt. SAITO to examine the Hospital site. I returned on 23th July and on 30th July left with the advance party for Burma.

II. General Comment

When the proposal for a Hospital camp was first mooted hopes ran high that this would be the means of saving hundreds of lives. This was particularly the case amongst hospital patients who by reason of their illnesses might be regarded as eligible for selection for Burma. There seemed reasonable grounds for this enthusiasm, as the I.J.A. had given assurances that no work would be demanded from the camp and that the dietary would be a good deal better than it was in the working camps. Moreover, a further statement had been made that necessary drugs and dressings would probably be supplied.

The records contained in the war diary indicate that the hopes at first entertained for the success of the camp were not realised. A death rate of 660 (with a probability of a further 90 - 100) out of a total camp entry of 1,924 is a profoundly disappointing result. The reasons for the huge death rate are set out below. It is a melancholy reflection that in November there was almost as much enhusiasm to leave Burma as there had been in July to go there.

III. Factors Concerned in the High Death Rate

A. (i) *State of disease.* Very many patients were in such an advanced state of their disease on their arrival in Burma that even with the best hospital facilities in the world recovery would have been impossible. This applied particularly to patient from Sonkurai Camp (No.2), from which it is believed that evacuation of all very sick patients was practically compulsory.

(ii) *State of nutrition.* Apart from the state of their diseases, the emaciation of many of the patients gravely prejudiced their chance of recovery. In part this was due to poor rations at the working camps but in part it arose from the failure of the medical officers in certain of these camps to insist on the consumption by their sick patients of the full daily ration. In many cases of dysentery liquid diet had been presented over an unconscienably long period, resulting in practical starvation of the unfortunate patient. Apart from the emaciation, long-standing deficiency in intake of vitamins A, B_1 and B_2 and C also greatly lowered the patients ability to combat his disease.

(iii) *Effects of Journey.* The journey was made under very arduous conditions, an inadequate number of fit men was available to help sick patients on the way. Bed was poor and long exposure to rainstorms and severe jolting for hours on end were the lot of all. Under these circumstances many patients whose fate hung in the balance had their last chance of survival taken away from them by the strain of the journey.

Factors Operative at Tanbaya

(i) *Diet.* So far from the diet being better in Burma than at the working camps it was for a long period considerably worse, as will be seen from a study of the ration issues set out in the war diary. Rice was in general adequate, but every other essential for a balanced diet was grossly deficient. In particular, until the bean ration was raised from 1/3 bag to 1 bag on 22nd September, the diet contained practically no vitamin B whatever. Innumerable protests and request for rice polishings and for more beans were made to the I.J.A. but always met the reply that rice polishings were quite unobtainable, and that there was a great shortage of beans, which were being reserved for the camps further from rail. In this connection it is interesting to note that when on the 10th October, we learned that "A" Force Hospital camp 5 kms away had been received an adequacy beans since its formation in July, and pointed this fact out to the I.J.A. camp commander he raised the bean issue from 1 bag to 2.5 bags forthwith. It is also interesting to note that from 26th October onwards regular issues of rice polishing were made to the camp. Had these two steps been taken earlier in the camp's history, it is my considered opinion that upwards of 100 lives would have been saved.

The deficiency in vitamins A and C undoubtedly produced a marked lowering in the resistance of tissues to infection, thereby increasing the frequency and severity of ulcers, furuncles, impetigo, pemphygus and other cutaneous infections. Deficiency in protein produced a lowering of general vitality as also did the deficiency in calcium.

(ii) Drug Shortage. Until 5th November no drugs were received from the I.J.A., and then the supply was pitifully small and inadequate. In particular no

specific therapy was available for the treatment of amoebic or bacillary dysentery, the major killing diseases in the camp. There was no iodoform or other drugs suitable for local treatment of the numerous tropical ulcers. No sulphur (solution cheap and easily procurable product), was available to treat scabies untill 6th November, by which time the whole camp was infected, with much secondary superation and ulcer formation. Dressings were also woefully deficient and many mosquito nets had to be sacrified to dress the enormous ulcers. No iron was available to build up the anaemic patients and no concentrated B_1 was available for the numerous severe beri-beri.

(iii) *Malaria.* Tanbaya was an area where malaria of a particularly severe type was heyperendemic. Eighty deaths are shown as being due either wholly or partially to malaria, but beyond this the disease had a debilitating effect throughout the camp, where its incidence reached practically 100 per cent. In particular malaria caused marked deterioration in the condition of patients suffering from ulcers or dysentery.

IV. System of Administration

The system of administration adopted at Tanbaya differed in several respect from that customary in military hospitals. In part these differences were dictated by local necessity, in part they were devised as possible improvements. Lt.Col. Hutchinson, as Administrative Commmandant of the camp, was responsible for such services as cooking, securing of wood and water, hygiene, canteen and pay. Major Hunt OC Hospital was responsible for all medical treatment and for the administrative control of all medical personnel, whether professional or amateur and of all patients. This subdivision of authority worked very smoothy and I should like here to pay my tribute to Lt. Col. Hutchinson, for his loyalty, his smiling tact and his untiring efforts in the interests of the patients and of humans as a whole.

Details of medical administration were as follows: Patients were segregated so for as possible according to their complaints; this facilitated treatment and prevented much cross-infection. Thus no ward was devoted solely to dysentary, another ward to pure dysentery and ulcers combined with dysentery, two wards to ulcers another wards to general medical diseases, chiefly malaria and beri-beri. Each ward contained in the earlier stages approx. 190 patients and was under the control of a wardmaster. The wardmaster was a combatant officer, usually of company commander status or above; he had as assistants an assistant wardmaster, usually a subaltern two NCOs who acted as C.S.H. and C.G.M.S. respectively and a clerk. The Wardmaster was responsible for nominal rolls, for discipline, for hut cleanliness for missing, for canteen supplies and in general for everything which took place in the ward except such matters as involved technical medical knowledge or skill. We had in addition, through the medical officers or senior nursing N.C.O. supervisery control over tne activities of the nursing orderlies in regard to their non-technical functions.

This system of wardmaster control, first devised in Shimo Sonkurai camp and further extended in Burma, proved of the greatest possible assistance in running the Hospital. Discipline and general ward efficiency were very much better than they usually are under N.C.O. control, in particular messing functioned much more efficiently and with much less complaint than is usually the case. I was particularly fortunate in having a very able body of wardmasters; they worked, ate and slept in their wards and were completely devoted to their duties and to the interests of their patients. I should like here to express formally my appreciation of their valuable services. Wardmasters were (in numerical order of their wards) Lt. I. Perry (2/1 Heavy bty AIF), Capt. R. Walker (2/96 Bn AIF), Maj. R. Hodgkinson (RASC), Maj. Auld (RAOC), Capt. B. Berry (2/10 Fd Regt AIF) Majo. D. Price (RCOS), Capt. G.W. Gwynee (2/4 MG Bn AIF) and Lt. Col. Ferguson. (18 Div-HQ).

The wardmaster's conference, attended also by OC Hospital, Registrar and Messing Officer, was held daily at 1530 hours: this proved the most satisfactory means of keeping the wards in close touch with camp policy.

In view of the shortage of drugs all drug requisitions were checked and countersigned by OC Hospital before completion. This took place at 1500 hrs and permitted of a just distribution of drugs between the various wards and also of the conservation of necessary supplies.

As patients in the various wards improved and became fit for camp duties they were sent to the 'labour exchange' where they were vetted by OC Hospital and then assigned to various sections of the Hospital according to the requirements of the different departments.

V. Staff

Although the number of RAMC and AAMC personnel at Tanbaya was at its highest 14 2, very many of these men arrived as patients and either died at Tanbaya or remained as patients throughout their stay in Burma. Nine members of the RAMC and eight members of the AAMC died at Tanbaya, and five RAMC and nine AAMC men were left behind as seriously ill patients, when the bulk of the camp moved in November. The maximum number of the Medical Corps personnel available for duty at any one time was 62 and the number generally varied between 40 and 50. Under these circumstances it was necessary for the greater part of the nursing work to be done by volunteers from non-medical units, and the steadfast devotion to duty of these men under circumstances of much difficulty and discomfort is worthy of the highest praise. Many of the volunteers showed a marked aptitude for the more technical branches of nursing and in some cases were as good as if not better than the majority of the professional.

VI Disease

Four diseases dominated the clinical pictures. There were the order of mortality which they produced, dysentery tropical ulcers, Beri-Beri and malaria.

(i) *Dysentery.* In the absence of facilities for bacteriological or sigmoidoscopic examination it was impossible in most cases to differentiate between Amoebic and bacillary dysentery. Clinically, however, I formed the impression that the formed disease predominated, and autopsy and the results of treatment of five cases by emetine in November (this was all the emetine we ever received) tended to confirm this impression. The dysentery wards were amongst the most tragic places in the camp. Many of the patients put up a most gallant struggle, forcing their rice down day after day and week after week in a heroic effort to stay alive until adequate facilities for treatment arrived. Dysentery alone caused 114 deaths and in association with other diseases played a part in killing 334 men. In many cases an attack or a recurrence of dysentery was the terminal factor in carrying off patients suffering from beri-beri or ulcers.

(ii) *Tropical Ulcers.* These were of very great frequency and in many cases of horrifying severity. Huge areas of skin, flesh and in some cases bone were eaten away and the skin appeared to possess little or no resistance to the infecting organisms. Ulcers followed small scratches or cuts with distressing frequency and not a few patients died of ulcers which actually developed in the camp. Capt. F.J. Cahill, who was in charge of the ulcer wards throughout, has prepared a detailed memorandum on the subject of these ulcers.

The lower extremity and in particular the region of the tibia was the site of selection for the formation of ulcers. They could and did, however, occur in almost any area of the body, as for example over the great trochanter, over the lower spine, in the groin, over the scapula, on the elbows, wrist and fingers. A few cases responded strikingly to the application of sulphanilamide or iodoform, and had these drugs been available in anything like adequate amounts much life could have been saved. In the absence of these drugs simple dressings with eusol or saline two or three times a day provided the best results, which, however, in many cases were bitterly disappointing. Amputations were performed in about 60 cases (for details see Capt. Cahill's memorandum) but here also the results were in general disappointing owing to the poor general condition of the patients and to the frequency occurrence of severe secondary sepsis in the stump. It was noticeable that an attack of dysentery or malaria caused considerable deterioration in the conditions of the ulcer which hitherto had progressed quite favourably. Ninety two patients died of ulcers alone, and one hundred and five of ulcers complicated by other diseases.

(iii) *Beri-Beri.* Beri-Beri was widespread throughout the camp. At one time there were upwards of 600 patients showing clinical manifestations of the disease. It was also more severe than any which I had previously seen in a P.O.W. experience of 2 years.

A further complication which caused much loss of life in beri-beri patients was the frequency with which the grossly oedematous patients developed a rapidly spreading gangrene in their water-logged extremities. This complication was almost invariably fatal. Many patients remained oedematous for several weeks and in such cases cardiac deterioration generally accompanied or followed on the oedema.

Cardiac beri-beri was both common and severe. Practically every clinical abnormality ever recorded in cardiac beri-beri was observed at Tanbaya. Hearts were enlarged both to the right and to the left, chiefly the latter. The rates varied both upwards and downwards: brady cardia was very common. Abnormalities of rhythm were relatively frequent. These generally took the form of extra systeles, although aurichular fibrillation was observed on a number of occasions, frequently just before death. Variations in pulse volume were not infrequent and generally of poor pregnostic significance. Abnormalities in heart sounds were frequent. A splitting of the first sound was the most characteristic change systolic murmurs occurred frequently. Gallop rhythm was noticed sometimes. The pulmonary second sund was frequently leud and bargain. Cyanosis and other signs of congested heart failure were relatively infrequent. Sudden death, frequently occurring in the middle of the night, was not uncommon.

Administration of Vit B. intravenously saved a certain number of lives when cardiac emergencies occurred but of this as of all other valuable drugs supplies were grossly inadequate. Beri-Beri alone killed 68 men in a further 260 cases beri-beri was one of the causes of death.

(iv) *Malaria.* Malaria was practically universal throughout the compand in August and September relapses were very frequent as owing to shortage of quinine supplies it was not possible to give quinine treatment for longer than 7 days. After the end of September supplies increased considerably and it was possible to increase the course from gr 24 daily for 7 days to gr 32 daily for 12 days, accompaning the latter with plasmoquene 0.02 gm daily. After this step was taken there was a marked fall in the incidence of malarial relapses. Microscopic examination conducted by the I.J.A. showed the relative frequency of B.T. and M.T. infection to be approx. 2:1:.One of the outstanding clinical features of the malaria at Tanbaya was the high degree of resistance to quinine. In many cases undoubted malaria the fever did not come under control until 6, 7 or 8 days after the commencement of treatment. A number of patients was observed to relapse on the 10th or 11th day of treatment while still taking gr 32 of quinine daily. Finally every person who had either been protected from Malaria in Thailand by suppressive atebrin had clinical malaria in Burma, although continuing to take atebrin regularly. Ten people were thus affected.

Cerebral malaria occurred in about thirty cases, many of which responded satisfactorily to parenteral quinine. Haemoglobinuria was seen half-a-dozen times, but no true case of blackwater fever occurred.

(v) *Typhus.* A 14-day fever clinically resembling typhus in many respects was observed in about 40 cases. No rash and no escher were seen, but previous experience of this disease left me in little doubt as to the nature of the fever. Serological confirmation of the diagnosis was of course impossible. The typhus was in general relatively mild and only two or three cases succumbed.

(vi) *Catarrhal Jaundice.* About fifty cases of this disease were seen, all mild and none fatal.

(vii) *Respiratory Disease.* Coryzas were frequent but only about half-a-dozen pneumonias were seen, two of which were followed by empyaemia.

(viii) *Scabies.* Scabies spread steadily from the formation of the camp onwards and by November when the first supplies of sulphur arrived it was almost universal. Scabies, of course, had a high nuisance value but in addition to this it gave rise to much secondary infection and in some cases to severe ulcers which resulted fatally. Treatment was instituted immediately on the arrival of the sulphur in early November, cooking oil being used as a base. Much improvement naturally occurred in the scabies, but the sulphur came for too late to prevent the hundreds of cases of impetigo which caused much distress throughout the camp.

VII. Records

The register of deaths is contained in the War Diary. The camp roll contains an entry of the diseases from which the various patients suffered during their stay at Tanbaya with a view to giving each individual patient some record of his ailments, and entries made by medical officer were made in both British and Australian paybooks. Where paybooks had been lost cards or bamboo slips were issued on which the appropriate particulars were inserted. Every man who left Tanbaya should have with him a full record of the illnesses from which he suffered in that camp.

VIII. Evacuation

As early as September strong representations were made to the I.J.A. that many hundreds of patients would not survive a long railway journey (see letters from Major Hunt quoted in extense in War Diary). As a result of these representations considerable leniency was allowed in the selection of patients to travel. Much care was taken with this selection and, as a result, of the 900-odd patients who left Tanbaya for Kamburi only two failed to survive the arduous five or six days journey.

A staff of 102 was left behind in Burma to look after 210 patients. Of these patients approx. 85 were suffering from dysentery and approx. 65 from ulcers; the majority of the remainder had beri-beri. If conditions prevailing in November persist, and if patients are evacuated in February, as seems probable, I anticipate a mortality of 90-100. This would include about 60 dysenteries, about 5 ulcers and about 15 beri-beri.

XI. Conclusioin

The Burma Hospital camp, for reasons stated above, could not be regarded as a success. Its partial failure, however, was much mitigated by the efficient work of the administrative staff, by the devotion to duty of he wardmasters and by the professional skill and knowledge displayed by same of the medical staff. In this connection I would mention particularly Maj. W.J.E. Phillips, RAMC, Capt. Emery, RAMC, Capt. F.J. Cahill, RAMC and Asstt. Surgeon Wolfe, IMD. Outstanding nursing performed by Corporals Skippen and Sutton, RAMC

Kamburi Dec.1943

Sigd. Bruce Hunt, Major
R.A.M.C. Formerly Cmd.
Tanbaya Hospital

Appendix E

Copies of Letters Submitted to I.J.A.

(For copy of letter dated 20 Sep 43, see Appendix "C")

Copy of letter from Major. Hunt which was handed to I.J.A. Colonel (Medical) on 25 Sep 43 -

Total Patients in Camp - 1632

Admin. Staff	Pern. Admn. Staff-	4 Offrs	51 P.Rs.
	Sick-working -	—	17
		4	34
	Working patients		52
		4 Offrs	86 O.Rs.
Med. Staff	Perm.Med. Staff	10 Offrs	109 O.Rs.
	Sick-working	4	60
	Working patients	6	49
		6 Offrs	130 O.Rs.

Chief Diseases

Malaria -	573	Very virulent and resistant to quinine. High relapse rate.
Beri-Beri-	492	Increasing daily especially in working staff. More than half of cases contracted in this camp. Much heart involvement -many recent deaths.
Dysentery	521	All cases getting steadily worse in the complete absence of drugs for treatment.
Ulcers –	317	Most getting works in absence of vits. A., B and C drugs and dressings.
General Health		The health of the camp as a whole is getting worse, not better, everyday. The increase in Beri-Beri being the chief cause, under present circumstances and in the absence of immediate supply of very large quantities of vitamin containing foods, drugs and dressings. I anticipate not less than 500 deaths in 6 weeks. To these must be added over 280 deaths which have occurred in the past six weeks. The patients are extremely debilited and all come from "F" Foree, a body of 7,000 which left SINGAPORE in April and has already had about 2,000 deaths.

In 20 years of medical practice and after extensive experience of two wars, I have never seen men in a more pitiable condition of health than the men in this camp. The real tragedy lies in the fact that much of the diseases is really curable if proper Vitamin containing foodstuffs such as beans and proper drugs are made available in sufficient quantity, and I earnestly impress upon whatever authority this may reach, that through no fault of their own, men are dying in hundreds and will continue to die until help comes.

(Sgd.) Bruce Hunt, Major AAMC
Commanding TANBAYA Hospital.

Copy of letter submitted by Major B.A. Hunt, AAMC to O.C. TANBAYA HOSPITAL CAMP, dated 14 October 43.

Sir,

I wish to draw your attention to certain facts and figures concerning disease and sickness the body of 7,000 Ps.O.W., British and Australian which left SINGAPORE at the end of April, 1943. In particular I shall detail certain facts and figures concerning the men of that force who are now patients in this camp. I should be grateful if you would, after reading this document forward it to the General responsible for the administration and care of Ps.O.W.

When the original order for the dispatch of this force was issued, no indication that long marching would be required was given (the contrary was implied). As a result many old men and men otherwise unsuitable for marching were sent. These men naturally broke down very early on the march and many of them have been in hospital ever since, or have died of other diseases contracted in Thailand.

2. The force has been in Thailand and Burma for just over 5 months. During that period over 2,000 men have lost their lives from disease - approx. 30 per cent.

3. The chief causes of death have been :-

(i) Cholera. This arose from the troops being herded together in camps in close proximity to Tamil and Thai coolies amongst whom cholera was widespread. The essential article in the treatment of cholera is intravenous saline - none was provided.

(ii) Dysentery. Chiefly AMOEBIC. It is a matter of common medical knowledge throughout the world that Thailand is the most heavily amoeba-infected country in the world. Yet no effort was made to protect the troops at the Staging Camps, where the sanitary arrangements were filthy, and where many hundreds of men became infected. It is again universally recognised that the only treatments of any value in amoebic dysentery are emetine, yatren and asttrovarsol. Despite innumerable requests none of these drugs have been supplied, and as a result hundreds of innocent men have died unnecessarily.

(iii) Beri-Beri. The causes of beri-beri are very well known, especially to Japanese scientists, who have done much valuable work in the treatment of this disease. Yet, on many occasions, and especially in this camp, for no apparent reason a diet has been supplied which was certain to produce, which we informed the I.J.A. would produce, and which has in actual fact produced, many hundreds of cases of beri-beri and caused many deaths. Why his camp should have been receiving a small and inadequate bean ration for over two months, while the hospital camp at 55 km. has throughout this period been getting all the beans it needed, passes our comprehension. In this connection we are most grateful to you for increasing our bean ration to 2.5 bags daily, and hope that it may soon be possible to increase this ration still further to 4 bags. A small supply of B_1 tablets and ampales was given in July - only adequate for a few cases - no official supply since.

(iv) Malaria. It is well known that Thailand is very highly Malarial, yet troops were not supplied with nets until most of them were infected, and quinine supplies were never adequate to give long enough courses of treatment to check relapses.

(v) Tropical Ulcers. The very gross deficiency Fn Vitamins A and C in our diet has so lowered the resistance of the skin to even the most trifling infection that huge ulcers have developed in hundreds of cases, causing loss of legs or loss of life. The only satisfactory local treatment are iodoform and sulphonomide-very small supplies of these drugs were made available in July, enough to last only for two to three days-none before or since.

4. In addition to the above fatal diseases, scabies has spread rapidly throughout the force, and especially through this camp. The only possible treatment for scaies is sulphur, a common and cheap product, yet all our appeals for sulphur have produced no results and over 1,100 men in this camp are now infected with scabies. Infected scabies often goes on to the formation of ulcers.

Tanbaya Hospital Camp

This camp was established at the beginning of August to accommodate between 1,500 and 2,000 of the sick men of "F" Force. We were informed before the camp was formed that the food here would certainly be better than it was in the working camps and that medical supplies would possibly by available. In actual fact the food has not been better than in the working camps and in the particular item of beans has been much worse, so that instead of improving from Beri-Beri, they have actually become worse, and in many cases died. These were several hundred new cases of beri-beri have developed, particularly amongst the working men of the camp, more than half of whom are now in hospital. Apart from what trifling quantities we had left from our own British and Australian supplies at CHANGI no medical stores whatever have come into this camp despite very frequent representations on this matter by every possible channel.

Present Medical Situation

The diseases are Malaria 275, Dysentery 426, Beri-Beri 630, Ulcers 265, scabies about 1,150. In general the health of the camp is not improving, but rather is getting steadily worse - chiefly on account of the poor diet. Fewer and fewer really fit men are available to perform camp work and men are not well enough to come out of hospital to take the place of the fit men as they fall ill is an example - of the total of 142 RAMC and AAMC personnel in this camp (including Barbers and hygiene men as well as nurses) 63 are actually working the moment, the remainder being sick in hospital.

Future Move

We have been informed that a move of part or the whole of this Hospital camp is likely at an early date, and we have been asked to give certain figures. As Hospital Commander the prospect of this move fills me with horror. During the past two days I have completely surveyed all the wards in the hospital, the health of the patients so bad that in my considered opinion not less than 530 men will probably lose their lives during or shortly after a move of any duration (say 3 to 4 days). Above and beyond these, about 400 men will require to be taken by stretcher.

If it is decided to leave many or most of these very sick men behind, the staff of fit men to look after them will be just as numerous as is required at present because there will not be the supply of semi-fit patients who are able to help their fellow sufferers by doing light jobs in the wards.

Since there will be no men whatever available for carrying the stretcher unto and off the trains, if these men are to be moved, the only possible solution of the problem which I can see, will be bring some fit men down from the working camp to help with the move.

So far as the future is concerned, the only possible means of getting away of these desperately sick men sufficiently well to enable them to travel in safety will be improve camp rations, especially as regards beans and meat, very considerably and to make available at a very early date full and adequate supplies of the necessary drugs.

Summary

If we had been taken prisoner by a barbarous race unaccustomed to the wayes of welfare between civilised nations, complete lack of medical precautions and the failure to supply to the sick the drugs which they so urgently need, would be readily understandable. But we find it very difficult to understand why such treatment be meted out to its prisoners by a great and powerful nation like Japan, whose doctors and scientists are amongst the best in the world and whose proud boast is of chivalry to the vanquished. Is it too much to hope that even at this late date these poor, helpless, suffering prisoners may receive the consideration, the food and the medical supplies which they so badly need and which I know - because I have personally inspected many P.O.W. Camps - are always supplied by Great Britain and Australia to the Ps.O.W. who are under their care?

(Signed) Bruce Hunt,
Major AAMC
Commanding Tanbaya Hospital

Wardmastering

It is assumed that this monograph will be read in conjunction with that of Capt. Gywne and in consequence some detail being omitted.

1. My only experience of Wardmastering was at Tanbaya where I had a general medical ward, the majority of the patients being, by comparison with other wards, convalescent. The problems of this ward were similar to these in Capt. Gwynne's with less emphasis on nursing and more on morale and discipline.

2. The ward was of 25 bays, each to hold 8 men. The hut was of attap and bamboo of the type built for coolies and designed for a life of 6 months. Water had to be carried from a stream approx. 300 yards away Wood was initially easy to come by but became increasingly difficult to find and carrying distance increased.

(b) The morale and discipline of the men was nonexistent at the start. Defecating and urinating indiscriminately in and around the hut was normal. Many men had to be bullied into washing. Theft from the quick, dead and dying was common-place and almost impossible to stop as was the subsequent 'black market'[1] selling of the proceeds to local natives.

In such conditions and with Medical Officers in charge of 200 patients each it was obvious that administrative assistance was essential.

3. The definite administrative duties of a wardmaster, with his assistant, Ward C.S.M. and Clerk were as follows :-

(a) *Water.* Water had to be carried and boiled for 170-190 mens, water bottled and for the sterilization and washing up of their mess rear. It was also required for dressing and the washing of bed patient and those not fit to walk to the river, were used for carrying and a total of 7 gallons only of metal containers was available for boiling (In this ward about 80 gallons were carried daily.)

(b) *Food.* Owing to the acute shortage of containers it was essential that there should be no delay in the collection and serving of food and in returning containers. This involved one 'lift' and when the cookhouse was 600 yards away required fairly fit carriers. Every man that could walk drew his food from outside messing patients leaving the ward clear for the mess orderlies to serve bed patients.

(c) *Wood.* Though living in secondary jungle with no cutting restrictions this was a serious problem as tools were scarce. On the average a ward got axe or saw for about 3 hours a week late in the evening. This meant that wood collected had to be of a size for immediate burning or light enough for carriage and subsequent cutting up during an 'axe period'.

(d) *Maintenance.* Again without tools, or with a tomahawk borrowed for a matter of minutes, bay-flooring. Walls and roof had to be kept in the best state of repair possible and clothes rails, messing points etc. constructed. No materials other than those from the jungle were available and there was no spare attap.

(e) *Records.* All administrative and medical records and returning were the wardmasters responsibility. He still experienced, the difficulty of keeping detailed records for 180 men of which the maximum dimension across is about 4" cannot be visualised and the ingenuity of ward clerks was sometimes strained.

(f) *Canteen.* The essence of this was speed in distribution Wing to its high morale effect.

The basis of all here problems, except the last two, is labour. A wars such as mine had to be self-supporting. The ward M.O. was in the first place responsible for the decision as to who was fit for the various jobs but the wardmaster had to watch his selections carefully and assist him in sorting out scrims hankers. Ration and water carriers had to be fairly fit mess and caused some anxiety.

To run this ward of 18 with 'one lift' ration carrying the following labour was a minimum :-

Water 4 (fit or near fit), Ration 12 (50 per cent fit), Wood 6 (usually helped by ration carriers) Ward and area cleaning 2 ward maintenance (Permanent) 1, Bed pan orderlies 3 C.S.H Clerk, Orderly 3, Total 31

While on the subject of labour would state definitely that, particularly when morale is low to get a man fit he has to be put to work to his fullest capacity as soon as he is convalescent.

4. Of other wardmaster duties the most difficult in a convalescent ward was to allow men the maximum of freedom in every respect without equal encouraging crime. The less restriction placed on the convalescent the quicker he got better, mentally and physically. The question of punishment under POW conditions was a difficult one. At Tanbaya the wardmaster had complete powers to cope with crime on the spot. For theft flogging was the only possible punishment, however much donor and recipient disapproved of it A smart clip under the jaw was effective when applied to indiscriminate evacuators caught in the act. Other activities included a ward fattening upon by which rice as converted into some other semblance by backing and flavoured with juri, prawns or anything else which could be come by. The results were fed to those who were unable to eat boiled rice and to 'debilities'.

'Boverin' was encouraged to give convalescents something to do and think about. Many weird dishes were produced.

The administration of rice polishings had to be carefully supervised.

The most intangible and by no means the least ardous of the wardmasters duties was that of philosopher and friend to all his ward and retail reliable camp gossip.

5. When Medical Officers are few and conditions difficult they cannot hope to complete with the thousand and one problems of running a ward. Even when plentiful in my experience the need assistance. When I went to hospital after we had been and month at Changi I was sent to the dysentery ward where for the four days

I was there I had no opportunity to wash my hands although there ward at least fifty men of working parties sent in from other areas sitting doing nothing just outside. Sheets, supposedly washed were filthy and stank of faces. Such things required only organisation and supervision as the water shortage was not as acute as that.

The Wardmaster job in addition to including that of Ward-sister and hospital secretary is really that of POON*BAN.

(Sgd.) M. PRICE MAJOR R. Singnals

RE: The Wardmaster System

The Wardmaster system came into operation in Thailand and Burma through forces of circumstances. The conditions which prompted its inception were unusual and difficult in the extreme. It will therefore be necessary to deal with these conditions in considerable detail in order to demonstrate fully the difficulties of hospital control which resulted in the inauguration of this system.

I am writing this as a combatant officer with no previous knowledge of hospitals or medical services; however, I have seen such services operation at Shimo Sankurai, No. 5 Camp, Kendo, Tanbaya (Burma) and Kanchanbari. At Shimo Sankurai my experience was that of a patient, at No. 5 Camp and Kando as O.C. of a party of sick personnel en route to Tanbaya, and at Tanbaya and Kanchanbari as a wardmaster. I am thus writing on a subject of which I have first hand experience.

Generally speaking descriptions of conditions appertaining will apply to both Thailand and Burma, whereas particular instances will have occurred at Tanbaya which was a hospital only. All other hospital with the exception of that at Kanchanbari were working camp hospitals.

Hospitals. To the average person the word 'Hospital' conjures up the picture of a substantial building, adequately illuminated with iron bedsteads and white sheets staffed by sisters in spotless uniforms and clean cheerful orderlies anxious to satisfy the requests and to attend to the comfort of their patients. The ward also presupposes reasonably pleasant surroundings.

Imagine instead Thailand in the wet weather. If one has no experience of a wet season in the tropics let him picture himself living for weeks on end in a bath tub and shower running full strength and instead of a granolithic floor a mud one. If this impression one be registered it is easy to realise the initial major problems with which hospitals administrations were confronted - roofing and drainage.

When the troops arrived at their respective destination having marched under appelling conditions distances varying from 180 to 300 miles without adequate footwear, rest or food, they were met with the sight of numbers of skeleton huts.

Those huts were constructed of bamboo in their entirety with a passage way approx. 6 feet wide down the centre and contained 30 bays 10 feet in width and 12 feet in depth on each side of the passage. Outside entrances appeared at intervals of ten bays each, thus sub- diving the large hut into three blocks of 20 bays each. The huts were constructed in the main on the sides of hills consequently the bays were high on one side necessitiating the use of ladders for ingrees and agrees while the other side was correspondingly low. The stagings were made of spite bamboo mets were provided but not in sufficient quantity to make more than 30 per cent of the troops to any degree comfortable.

The passage ways were obstructed at irregular intervals by root of bamboo outcrops, roots and stumps of large trees which had been hastily felled during construction and water courses running through. At night it was only possible with the greatest difficulty to move from one end to the other. To add intention of the I.J.A. to cover the roofs with attap nut this did not become available for some weeks and then was laid by our own troops. Some tents and tent flys were provided after a few days but in the majority of cases they were perished and the protection they afforded was in inverse ratio to their nuisance value.

At Tanbaya the hut were constructed on a slightly different pattern each hut contained one length of 25 bays of similar dimensions with a passage in one side only. On the opposite side of the passage was an attap wall with doorways every four bays. The huts were roofed with attap which was in the majority of the huts the roofing afforded practically no proction. The flooring of the bays was also in very bad condition large gaps appeared in tearly every bay rendering it almost impossible for patients to make themselves comfortable. Some mats and some bags were provided but again insufficient to go around. It was in these circumstances that hospital were established.

The first troops arrived at Shimo Sankurai on 15th May and on that day the hospital opened at the extreme northern end of the camp and at first occupied a portion of one hut only. On 30th May the hospital admissions had increased to 400 and on the following day they increased to 800 when all smbulint dysentery patients were admitted.

Cholera broke out on 17th May necessitating the construction of an isolation hospital just north of a stream which bounded the camp.

Almost from the commitment there were insufficient A.A.M.C. orderlies to cope with the increasing numbers of patients. Volunteers were called for with immediate response from members of combatant units. Consequently, at Shimo Sankurai nursing was performed by A.A.M.C. orderlies and Volunteers working side by side.

At Shimo Sankurai there were 4 Medical Officers who were working practical 24 hours a day on medical duties alone, and had very little time to give the ward administration. As a result of this Major B.A. Hunt the camp S.M.C. obtained the services of combatant to menge words thus inaugurating the Wardmaster system which has so successfully operated there are Kemi Sonkurai at Tanbaya and at Kanchansabri.

Wardmaster. It was quite clear to me from the commenecment of my association with hospitals that the secret of successful management was careful and intelligent organization. How essential this was at Shimo Sonkurai can be judged by the fact that containers for the issue of food were as scarce that only two wards could be fed at a time. This is just an instance to show how rigorously a timed programme for meals had to be followed. In the wards the wardmaster was in the position of a Company Commander own Nursing sister. He has to watch carefully and organise his domestic duties paying particular attention to sterilization of mess area provision of boiling water for drinking and cleanliness of quarters. Strange as it may seem it took weeks to create troops to sterilize their mess gear, as a precaution against cholera, and to drink boiled water only with the aid of a Ward C.S.M. and clerk - Both Ward inmates - the maintenance of trees the obtaining of wood and the carrying boiling and issuing of water was organised. At the time of writing this I almost wonder why such ordinary and apparently simple things should be mentioned but at the time the presented very real difficulties owing to the shortage of manpower. The wardmaster who failed at any time to have such services running smoothly soon saw the failure reflected in the mental and physical condition of his patients.

Messing. With a ward largely consisting of bed patients messing presented a difficulty which required careful attention. Firstly all mess gear had to be collected, sterilized and returned to the rightful owners. This necessitated in itself a considerable quantity of Boiling water which was kept at the boil during the process of sterilization. Mess was the served with the maximum of speed under the supervision of an M.C.O. preferably an experienced man. Speed was essential so that containers should be returned for other wards. When the meal was concluded any swill was collected mess gear washed up and returned to patients. With a ward of 180 finishing a meal to everyone's satisfaction was a big job. It was probably the most essential of many in a wardmaster day because so much depended on the complete consumption of all suitable food, to live, patied had to eat but if left to themselves a very large proportion would not look at food much less eat it. They complained that food nauseated them they could not eat rice anyway and all sort of other excuses, many of them quite understandable in view of their physical condition but they had to be compelled to eat. The Wardmaster soon get to know the fenicky eaters and then spent each meal time in persuading cajoling begging or fullying those particular patients. On occasions I have had to resort to forced feeding and have had to hold men's noses to make them open their mouths. It was often necessary to make nursing orderlies feed people who refused to do so themselves but eat they must and eat they did. I believe that considerable number of men on this force died of starvation alone I am equally certain that the wardmaster system saved many lives in this way alone. You wili probably say what about nursing staff was this way their job. I will deal with that aspect later when discussing staff. It was very noticeable at Tanbaya that the most difficult patients to fed came from camps such as Sankurai No 5 Camp Nieke, where wardmasters were not operating. A great many of these troops were lamentably delibuted through self starvation and resented force to eat. To my mind the strongest argument in favour of the system was a comparison of the physical condition of patients from Shimo Sankurai with these from other camps.

Certain patients were in receipt of special diets and it was always necessary to check on the special orderly to see that the patient received his extra food. It was not uncommon for a patient to say he did not feel like food and to endeavour to give away the very food which would probably save his life.

Treatment

Although the wardmaster had no medical training he was vested with absolute authority in his ward and everyone in that ward was responsible to him, including the medical N.C.O. in charge of medical-staff. In the average ward treatment were many and varied. Admittedly patients with similar diseases were inmates of the same ward but even so their treatment differed. It was primarily the duty of the medical N.C.O. to keep his treatment records up to date each day after the M.O.s round and to administer in due course any treatment required. The wardmaster had continually to satisfy himself that the correct treatment was laid down was being carried out. It was surprising the number of times that patients were overlooked or neglected particularly in busy wards. They would have not received adequate treatment in the absence of the wardmaster.

Hygiene

Absolute cleanliness of wards was one of the few safeguards against the spread of disease particularly dysentery which would have resulted very easily in a more appalling death rate that actually happened. The greatest difficulty was experienced at Tanbaya in the initial stages in training patients in ordinary domestic cleanliness and in preventing them from defaecating and urinating just where ever and whenever they felt inclined. Bed patients were often too lazy to call for a bedpan or at any rate to call early enough and would defaecate through the slats of the bay. Others - sometimes light duty personnel - would again through laziness - defaecating in the passage way or through the slats without any though of their health or that of anyone else. At Tanbaya this filthy and dangerous practice was so bad at first that picqets with bamboo canes were mounted in latrines and with wards during the hours of darkness in an endeavour to compel troops to use the latrines and not the adjacent surroundings. The most extraordinary aspect of this serious state of affairs was the disinclination or the point-blank refusal of other patients to name the culprits who must have been known to some of them.

Some of the language used by me in explaining to the ward what I thought of these people and what would happen to them if they were apprehended was neither printable or creditable, nor did it have much effect. However I caught a light duty man on the act of urinating between the slats of the bay one morning and promptly knocked him down. The condition of the ward improved overnight and eventually the average patient became hygiene minded. The lack of the Wardmaster's influence was clearly reflected in the personnel from camps other than Shimo Sankurai. Indiscriminate defecation and urination as well as general lack of ward discipline were characteristic of their behaviour.

Personal cleanliness also came within the purview of the wardmaster. The medical staff attended to the washing of the bed patients but walking patients had in many instances to be driven to wash themselves and their clothing.

At Shimo Sankurai M.O.s. were available and as many as 1456 patients while at Tanbaya 10 (of which no more than 5 were ever available for duty) attended to 1750. That it was impossible for P.O.W's to take part in Ward Administration is self evident.

The objects of the system depended upon the Wardmaster being vested with absolute authority and he most receive full support from his S.M.O. As it was unpopular with medical staff generally who resent non-medical interference.

It is the only system which ensures the patient receiving the best possible treatment.

It is the only possible means of enforcing ward discipline immediately and effectively.

Morale

Apart from looking after and attending to the physical requirements of the patients, the wardmasters primary object was the maintenance of morale. The most affective way of doing this was by personally visiting every men at least once a day listening to his troubles end discussing with him any subject as for removed as possible from his complaint; also keeping him advised of any camp gossip. Food and the iniquities of the kitchen staff were a constant source of conversation. The patience of job were required. The same stories were told day after day and the same answer given. Another visit was devisable after dark because I consider a cheerful ward at that time of day when things always appear worse, very helpful.

Entertainment at night was also the wardmaster's responsibility - lectures and talks generally - and was found to be of the greatest help in the bolseering up of morale. It must be remembered that there was no illumination of any kind - except of course fires - and the hours between 2100 and 2230 were pretty miserable without something to distract the patient's thoughts from his ailments.

Canteens came under this heading. At Shimo Sonkurai and Tanbaya canteen supplies were neither regular adequate but were of tremendous importance to troops when they did arrive. Tobacco was in particular request, and the immediate distribution made a great difference. If for instance tobacco was held overnight when it could have been issued late in the evening, the spirits of the average ward showed a marked decline.

Staff

The handling of a ward staff, particularly in a very sick ward was the most difficult task a wardmaster has to perform. As proviously stated, for the system to work properly he must have absolute control over the medical N.C.C. who is nominally in charge of the nursing side of the ward under the supervision of the ward medical officer otherwise if his common sense suggests to him that patients are not being properly handled he is powerless to act.

At Tanbaya the medical personnel were drawn from N.C.O.s and man of the R.A.M.C. and A.O.M.C. who had previously worked at various camps from No. 3 camp to Neike, excluding Kami Sankurai from which no personnel sick otherwise were sent to Tanbaya. I do not know how or by whom those medical personnel were detailed for Burma but I do know from personal experience that they were not truly representative of their units. Many were singularly lacking in those attributes which are normally associated with Army Medical Units.

As regards R.A.M.C. personnel generally I found a lack of adaptability which I am only attribute to their training. They were slow to improvise where improvisation meant existance. Their were a number of particularly able and consciotious dressers among them but a greater proportion were lazy. If a number of the R.A.M.C. was to excellent if not he was useless in a technical sense.

The R.A.M.C. personnel were not at home in the difficult and uncomfortable conditions in which they were compelled to work but they were often unreliable and on occasions their attitude to patients left a lot to be desired.

There were however some outstanding N.C.O.'s from both Corps. Chronic illness was of course rife amongst medical personnel. One small medical unit last 29 N.C.O.'s and men by illness.

The volunteer orderlies often N.C.O.'s were by and large a long way ahead of the personnel of the medical units. They were enthusiastic in the extreme and individually took a personnel interest in their patients. They never hesitated to perform the most unpleasant and dirty jobs, and very soon acquired the art of dressing. Procaratinatic so evident in medical personnel, was not one of their faults.

Deaths

The death rate during the cholera epidemic and later at Tanbaya was naturally high and every individual death required the immediate attention of the wardmaster to take possession of any kit. It was not possible to trust anyone - again with the exception of a few N.C.O's - to take charge of a dead man's kit which if not immediately taken over by the wardmaster rarely contained anything of value. At night it was not possible to do this but often men died during the night without being discovered till dawn. Consequently the Wardmaster first duty at reveille was to collect what was left of the gear of men then discovered. The neighbourers of the dead were often less trustworthy than the orderlies. If a sick man was in procession of a watch, the wardmaster usually endeavoured to obtain possession of this by some suberfuge or other, rarely was a watch discovered in the prossession of a dead man.

Paper

The duties of a wardmaster were not any easier by the complete lack of paper. He became accustomed to writing on bamboo in Thailand but in Burma suitable bamboo was unavailable and it was necessary to use long narrow strips. Cemete rolling leeping was consequently a work of art. Ones patients was tried to its limits when a suddem delage of rain swamped the administration bay making all bamboo records unreadable.

General System

Once a day all the Wardmasters attended conference called by the G.M.O. hut which one subject of meeting the general running of the hospital was considered. This resulted in a Wardmaster being kept right up to date in all hospital affairs, likewise the administration was fully aware of what was going on in the wards.

Conclusions

The system is an excellent one anywhere and is absolutely essential in hospitals where M.O.'s owing to pressure of work cannot possibly control the internal organisation of wards. Understand the normal establishment for a 600 bed hospital provided for at least 15 M.O.'s

A wardmaster is on duty 24 hours a day. He must be even-tempered but willing and able to hit hard if necessary.

I am satisfied that no one can eulogise sufficiently the work of the Medical Officers who staffed the Hospitals at Shimo Sankurai, Tanbaya, and Kanchanabari, particularly the two former where conditions were at their worst. Never have I seen such untiring efforts made to save life and relieve pain at all hours of the day or night.

Only first class organisation and daily attention to detail prevented Tanbaya from becoming a place of death and misery.

(Sgd) George W. Gwynne

Captain 2/4 M.G. Bn. A.L.F.

Appendix E

Diagram of March Route and Camps

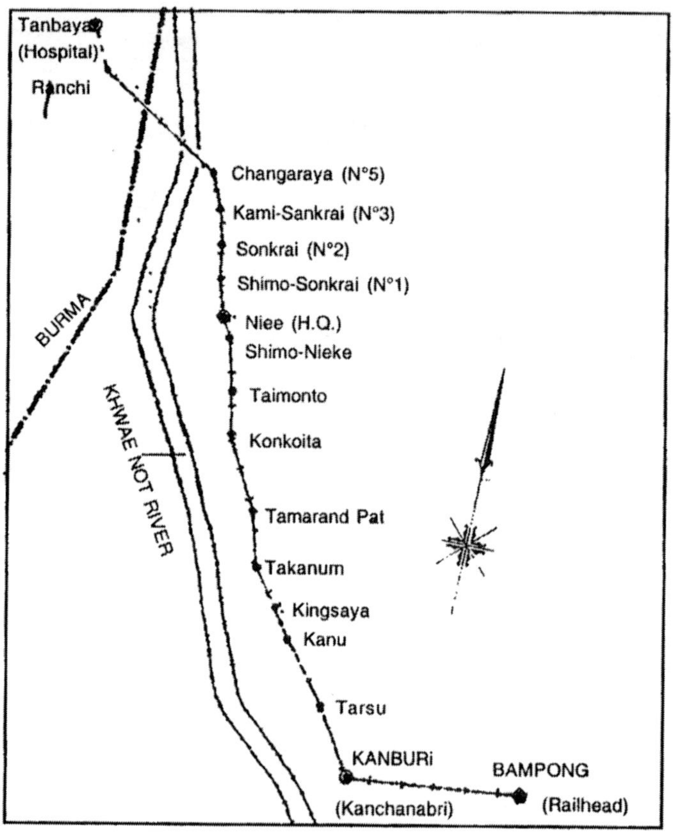

Appendix F

Report on Tanbaya Hospital Subsequent to Departure of Main Body 24 November 43

The I.J.A. ordered the occupation of huts 4, 5, 6, 7 and 8 and the move of patients was carried out before the main body left. No. 8 Hut remained the HQ Hut.

The administrative problems were the same as before - shortage of labour (in the initial stages), lack of tools 'and shortage of water being the main ones. With the smaller numbers to cook for a more varied form of meals was possible. Canteen supplies became more readily obtainable and eggs at a reasonable prior became almost plentiful.

About 16 December it was realised that the water supply would present a serious problem in the near future and water for the cook house had to be obtained from the well (Well C) beside the stream, a lift and force pump being provided. A month later washing points had to be established at the well. Towards the end of January the well on the west side of the railway Well "A") went dry and the well on the east side (Well "B") showed signs of doing so and it was therefore necessary to impose restrictions on washing for a couple of days or so.

The rations had to be collected from ANAQUIN by a yak cart, which was manhandled. This required a minimum of six men and was an every other day fatigue, which was initially a strain on the manpower situation. At first the rations were good but at the end of December the rice was reduced to a ration of 600 gms per day, seldom though were more than 550 gms received; some extra vegetables were issued. After about three weeks the rice ration was increased a little. On the whole, however, the ration was adequate, though of course not properly balanced. The issue of rice polishings continued all the time. Special Xmas Day fare was put on by the cooks and a free issue if cheroots, eggs and bananas was made to the patients. Great credit is due to Lieut. Dean and his cookhouse staff for their herculean efforts, which were appreciated to the fall.

On 31 January 1944 the move back to KANBURI began, a total of 5 Officers and 109 other ranks moving on that day. The remainder, 5 officers and 95 other ranks, moved on the following day, 1 February. The journey was the same as all others with long delays and irregular meals. This time, however, there were only twenty-two to a truck and the journey lasted only fifty hours.

The total number of deaths was ninety-six, details of which have been handed in to the two Records branches.

Lieut-Col-J.Huston,
M.O.
"F" Force

Report on Tropical Ulcers at Tanbaya

Introductory

When the formation of a hospital in Burma for the treatment of all men of "F" Force who would be still unfit in two months time was first mooted, it was obvious from our experience at Shimo Sonkurai, that tropical ulcers would form a considerable proportion of the cases to be dealt with. When the hospital was ultimately started in August, we had at Shimo Sonkurai almost a hundred tropical ulcers and their treatment was a great problem. We had very little in the way of antiseptice and the routine treatment was frequent cleansing of the ulcers with hot water or saline, followed by a hypochlorite dressing made from bleaching powder. On one occasion we received a little iodoform from the Japanese, and the results we obtained with it in a limited number of patients was very promising.

Included in the first batch of patients which arrived in Burma about August 12th, were about a dozen cases of tropical ulcer, of greater severity than any I had soon at Shimo Sonkura. Ultimately of the 1900 patients who arrived, about 240 were suffering from tropical ulcers of varying degrees of severity, with or without complications. A special section of the hospital was allotted to these patients consisting of two wards capable of holding 180 and 160 patients respectively.

Over the period of existence of the hospital, approx. 420 cases of ulcer passed through our hands, of which about 185 developed in Burma.

The following clinical points were noted :

1. Etiology

The most srtiking feature in the etiology of these ulcers was that a considerable number started from very minute beginnings. A small scratch from a piece of bamboo seemed to be the commonest exciting factor, usually in a patient who was debilitated from semi-starvation and exposure, and probably suffering also from clinical or subclinical malaria, or dysentery or beri-beri.

It was the rule rather than the exception for mild skin traumata to develop into frank ulcers.

I have seen one ulcer of the arm, which ultimately proved fatal, resulting from the abrasion caused by vaccination.

Scabies which became infected were the starting point of a number of ulcers, particularly on the hands and legs, and a striking feature was their multiplicity. Others started do move, particularly in sereve cases of beri-beri, and I have seen blebs arise on an oedomatus for no apparent reason whatever, and within 36 hours these have exended into sloughing ulcers involving and tendons and muscles, with an inevitably fatal result.

Many ulcers resulted from prolonged decubitus. In patients with chronic dysentery and,or beri-beri, ulcers were very prone to develop on bony promontories particularly in view of the fact that most patients were lying on bamboo slats. Those ulcers follow same course as these in other areas of the pady. A contributory etiologies factor, as pointed out, was the extreme dobility due to recurrent malaria, dysentery, beri-beri and semi-starvation.

2. Site

Ulcers were both single and multiple, the former being the more common. Multiple ulcers adjacent to each other tended to coalosco.

The commonest site for a single-ulcer was the anterior aspect of the tibia. On other sites they tended to be multiple. The trunk was rarely affected, except in the case of pressure ulcers which involved the sacral and iliac regions. The arms, apart from the hands were relatively immune. Multiple small ulcers on the hands, particularly in the region of the dorsal aspect of the metacarpo - phalangeal and interphalangeal joints were common, usually resulting from the infected lesions of scabies. Multiple ulcers on the feet were common; these commonly followed a type of pustular eruption called tropical pemphigus.

In extremely debilitated patients, there were a few cases of multiple ulcers involving both legs, and showing very little reaction whatsoever. Most of these had a fatal termination.

The scalp was occasionally involved.

3. Pathology

As previously stated, the ulcers as a rule started from a small skin abrasion which became infected and which lead to localized death of tissue. The majority of ulcers spread with alarming rapidly, and a small infected abrasion became within 48 hours a sloughing ulcer, involving skin, subcutaneous tissue, fascia and muscle. In the later stages bone became involved with superficial necrosis. *As* a general rule there appeared to be very little associated tissue reaction, and necrosis spread rapidly. In a considerable number of cases there ultimately developed in line of demarcation, indicated by a zone of tissue reaction. In other patients, particularly those in a very debilitated state, there was no attempt at limitation, and these patients usually died very rapidly from texaemia. In others, the ulcers became limited in extent but remained in a sloughing condition with a putrid odour, and in these cases also death from texaemia usually followed.

When the anerior aspect of the tibia became exposed, the pariostoum became rapidly necrotic, and the surface of the bone developed a wormoation appearance. Sequestration of a superficial falke of bone frequently occurred. In the more severe cases, push tended to track around the entire circumference of the bone, and I have seen cases in which practically the whole of the daphysis became a huge sequestrum surrounded by pus, and completely separated from all its muscular attachments.

In favourable cases, the ulcers ceased to spread and the necrotic facial and muscular tissues separated leaving a granulating surface which continued to discharge freely. If bone had been exposed in the floor of the ulcer this slowly separated, and during this process granulation tissue grew in from the edges. Separation or removal of the sequestrum must always occur before such an ulcer can develop a floor completely covered with granulation tissues. Once grunulation had occurred opithelialization under the methods of treatment available, was extremely slow, and it was quite common to see a clean granulating ulcer of diameter less than half-acrown take nearly three months to epithelialize.

Abscesses and pus pockets frequently formed in association with ulcers. These abscesses always required incision. Such abscess formation was common with ulcers of a severe degree on the anterior aspects of the tibia where pus could be found tracking downwards and backwards, pointing on either side of the Tande Achillis. Burrowing of pus up, and down beneath the skin on the anterior aspect of the tibia was also obsorved on a number of occasions.

Outstanding in the history of these ulcers was the rapidly and extent of their spread if the patient developed malaria or dysentery.

On numerous occasions I have seen patients with a clean granulating and slowly healing ulcer, develop malaria: within 48 hour all the processes of healing had stopped, and the ulcer had rapidly increased in depth and area. The patients general condition also deteriorated rapidly and not infrequently death followed.

Despite all precautions many ulcers became flyblown, and infestation with maggots nearly always produced rapid spread of the ulcer. This was due to them absence of a surrounding wall of fibreblastic reaction to circumscribe the phagecytic activity of the maggets. The maggets burrowed deeping into the tissues and their complete eradication was extremely difficult.

In some cases there was no sign of any leucoblastic reaction what sever, and the ulcer took on a dry, greyish black appearance, with associated severe texaemia. Such ulcers were usually multiple and often fatal.

4. Complications

The majority of the patients with ulcers suffered also from malaria, from beri-beri, from amoebic or bacillary dysentery, or from a combination of these disease.

The ulcer may have proceded or followed the systemic disease. These diseases played an important part in modifying the course of the ulcers.

(a) Beri-Beri

Beri-Beri usually of the oedematous type was the most frequent accompanying disease. Ulcer usually complicated beri-beri, rather than complicated beri-beri rather than the reverse. In such cases, the ulcers were extremely indolent. Occasionally however, they spread with alarming rapidity, as the waterlogged tissues offered very little resistance to the spread of the infection. Death from texaemia was frequent.

One type of ulcer was especially associated with beri-beri. A subcutaneous bleb appeared on the dorsum of the feet. This bleb filled up with a sero-sanguineous fluid, and very rapidly increased in size. Within 36 to 40 hours, thermormis beneath the bleb had soured away; and a deep punched out ulcer had developed extending well into the subcutaneous tissue. There was always a surrounding collulitis of greater or less degree, and the patient rapidly became extremely toxic and died.

(b) Malaria

An attack of malaria in patient suffering from an ulcer was often enough to cause its rapid increase in size. The ulcer may have been healing satisfactorily for some weeks; unattack of malaria would within 48 hours undo all the improvement made in the proceeding month and would cause a rapid spread of the ulcer into healthy tissue. Death often followed.

(c) Dysentery

Dysentery was a particularly dangerous complication in a patient debilitated by ulcers. No specific therapy was available either for bacilarry or ameabic dysentery. Very few patients who suffered from a combination of dysentery and ulcer survived.

(d) Secondary Haemorrhage

This occurred only in four instances. The worst involved in each case was the posterior tibial artery behind the nodial malloolus. The cruset of the bleeding was always sudden and unexpected, and bleeding was profuse. The haemorrhage could always be controlled by direct prossuse, but one patient lost so much blood before the haemorrhage was served (it occurred at night) that he died on the following day.

5. Clinical Features

1. Pain

Pain was a universal symptom. It was severe and aching, it was felt in the area of the ulcer and it was worse at night, preventing sleep. It was frequently referred to that part of the limb immediately below the lesion.

2. Oedema

In medium and large sized ulcers of the leg there was always oedema of the foot and ankle, due to venous and lymphatic obstruction. In three ulcer patients I have seen massive oedema of the foot and leg due to thrombosis of the deep formoral veins.

3. Footer

The footing nature of the discharge particularly in rapidly spreading ulcers was very characteristic; this added greatly to the general discomfort of the patient.

4. Nutrition

The diet provided by the Japanese contained an adequacy of carbohydrates, but was grossly deficient in protein, fit, vitamins, *A*, B_1, B_2 and C. The protein lack in ulcer cases was accentuated by the continued protein loss in purulent discharges. This, associated with the lack of vitamin B, was important in the lowering of tissue resistance and the rapid progress of most ulcers. Nutrition was also grossly interfered with by intercurrent discusses such as dysentery and malaria, in which loss of appetite was a common symptom. This was particularly difficult to overcome in view of the monotony of the ration.

Treatment

The treatment of tropical ulcers at Tanbaya was fraught with difficulty. Drugs available for local application were :-

1.	Sulphanilamide	-	50 grams
2.	Water Sterilization	-	about 10 lbs Powder
3.	Sod. Chloride	-	only what could be spared from the meagre rations -4-6 ozs. daily.
4.	Flavine	-	10 grams
5.	Hydraarg Biniodide -	-	16 grams

These quantities were totally inadequate for the large number of ulcers in the camp (in all over 400). Moreover, idedoform cod liver oil or eusel, the drugs of election for the treatment of this condition, were completely lacking.

An extremely small supply of bandages, cotton wool, and gauze was available and various substitutes, chiefly mosquito nets and leaves, were used to give protection against atmosphere and against flies.

Dressing obviously had to be used over and over again and here another difficulty arose, as the water supply was at all times inadequate.

The routine local treatment was to be the ulcer with hot boiled water and then to apply the dressing soaked in hypochlorite solution which was made from W.S.P. This treatment was carried twice daily in the acute purulent stages. A thrice-daily dressing would have been desirable, but could not be carried out because of the water shortage. As to ulcer became closer and granulation tissue appeared, saline was substituted for the W.S.P. solution. These simple measures carried out diligently did produce results provided that the ulcers were not in a very advanced stage. In these cases local treatment was able to stay the rapid and usually fatal spread of gangrene.

The minute amount of sulphanilamide available was used on several cases of multiple ulcers on the hands. The results were more gratifying and I am sure that anything approaching an adequate supply had been made available by the Japanese, the deplorable death rate in these series of ulcers would have been greatly diminished.

Dietary Treatment

300 mgm. of vitamin C were administered daily for 6 days in 6 severe cases. These patients received during the same period four capsules daily each containing an unknown quantity of vitamin A.

None of these patients showed any improvement and all subsequently died.

Prior to the 16th October, the camp dietary was outstandingly deficient in Vitamin B. On this date rice polishing were first supplied. Within a few days it became possible to administer at least 3 ozs. daily throughout the camp. This dosage was continued until the 30th January when the camp broke up. It was noted that the new severe ulcers developed after the early part of November, and that from this day there was a general trend towards improvement in the majority of those patients still surviving.

Although by November most of the patients with severe ulcers had died a fact which renders comparative statistics valueless, nevertheless it is felt that this favourable trend was sufficiently outstanding to require explanation.

It is tentatively suggested that this is best provided by the great increase in the intake of vitamin B.

Surgical Treatment

Apart from palliative treatment mentioned above, the following surgical procedures came under consideration.

1. Curettage

Curettage under general anesthesia was attempted in two types of patient. Removal of hypertrophic granulation tissue gave satisfactory results. Removal of dead or dying tissue by curettage only accelerated the spread of infection into healthy surrounding tissue. The general devitalization of tissue was such that no adequate inflammatory barrier existed at the outer limit of the necrosed tissue.

2. Excision

In view of the uniformly unfavourable results of curettage of cretic tissue complete excision of ulcers was obviously impracticable, and was not stomoted.

Where the nutritional state of the patient permits of adequate natural maintenance to infection, excision is obviously a very valuable procedures in treatment of tropical ulcer. Unfortunately the resistance of our patients at Tanbaya has been reduced to a minimum by long months of hardship and privation.

3. Amputation

Comparatively small ulcers spread very rapidly. Severe texaemia developed with equal speed. In view of these facts it seen became obvious that amputation held out the only hope for the survival of a large number of patients.

The following considerations were important in deciding whether to ampute.

(a) Any patient with an ulcer more than 3" in diameter was considered a possible candidate for amputation. Such patients were watched extremely carefully, and if palliative treatment showed no sign of cracking the spread of the ulcer, amputation was performed.

(b) The tibia, apparently wormeaten, was frequently exposed in the depths of an ulcer of the leg. Amputation was always performed when such an ulcer was further complicated by the spread of suppuration lateral and pesterier to the bone.

(c) Amputation was performed in the earlier cases of acute ulcer, occurring in association with severe codomatous beri-beri. Amputation however did nothing to avert the inevitably fatal outcome in these cases, and was therefore soon abandoned.

(d) The presence of ulcers on both legs introduced a further complication. At first I did not regard a small ulcer on one leg as necessarily contra-indicating of the other leg. Experience however showed that in these patients who developed severe ulceration on one leg, the ulcer on the other leg would inevitably deteriorate also. As soon as this became obvious, bilateral ulceration became a definite contraindication to amputation.

Site of amputation was as follows :-

a. Surgical neel of the humorus — 1 case

b. Mid thigh — 25 cases

c. Upper third of leg — 14 cases

Amputation was performed as low as possible, but in a regrettable large number of cases, the "size of election" was itself included in the area of the ulceration.

Sepsis in the stump was extremely common. Tissue nutrition was so impaired that sloughing of flaps frequently occurred. The sloughing also involved vessel walls, leading to secondary haemorrhage. This was anticipated and watched for with great care. As soon as haemorrhage occurred a tourniquet was applies, the clot removed and the dressing changed. Twenty minutes later the tourniquet was removed, when it was always found that haemorrhage had ceased. In every case further haemorrhage followed at varying intervals.

Secondary haemorrhage occurred from the stump in five patients. In one case a re-amputation was necessary while in another the haemorrhage was followed by severe sepsis in the stump which caused death from texaemia. In two patients who bled from admid thing stump, the common femoral artery was tied just below Poupart's ligament. In each of these patients the wound broke down and was followed by uncontrollable haemorrhage ultimately proved fatal. One patient who bled three times from a mid thigh stump ultimately received.

Sequelac

Among the after requite special mention effects of ulcers two require special mention.

1. Joint Contractures

When any ulcer involved in skin over the flexer aspect of a joint, e.g., an ulcer in the popliteal fossil, the subsequent cicatrisation might produce a flexer contracture of the joint.

Flexer contracture of the knee joint also occurred in patients, who, to ease the pain of the ulcer, had kept the knee in a position of flexion fora long period. This phenomenon was absorbed in five patients. All the contractures responsed favourably to amputation in and to supervised active movement.

2. Sequestrum Formation

Six patients, whose ulcers exposed extensive areas of tibia, survived their taxaemia, but were left with sequestra which at a later date required removal. Each of these ulcers subsequently healed completely.

Statistics

Accurate keeping of medical records at Tanbaya was impossible. It was rendered so by the lack of paper, by the extreme shortage of technical assistance, and above all especially in the earlier days by the necessity of devoting every minute of daylight to actual treatment.

Such figures as are now presented must be regarded as approx. only : they do however give a reasonably clear picture of what happened to ulcer patients at Tanbaya.

(1) Incidence

No patients were treated in the ulcer wards at Tanbaya.

235 of these the ulcer was present on arrival at the camp.

In 185 cases, the ulcer or ulcers actually developed at Tanbaya.

(2) Mortality

Of 20 ulcer patients, 250 (60 per cent) died and 170 (40 per cent) recovered.

The mortality was much higher in these patients whose ulcer were present on arrival. Of the 235 patients in this category, 195 (83 per cent) died and 40 (17 per cent) recovery.

Of the 185 patients whose ulcers developed after arrival, 55 (30 per cent) died and 130 (70 per cent) recovered.

In approx. one third of the fatal cases, the ulcer was uncomplicated. In the reminder, one or more of the three following diseases accelerated or actually determined the fatal issue. These diseases were, in order of importance, dysentery, beri-beri and malaria.

(3) Amputation

Amputation was performed in 40 patients. No patient died during the operation. Only one patient died within 24 hours after operation. Four more patients died during the next six days. Therefore, however, the death rate steadily rise. Intercurrent disease appeared to be particularly lethal to these patients. Sepsis in the stump was a further contributory factor. Three months after the last operation, only four patients on whom- amputation had been performed were still alive.

Tropical clear at Tanbaya was a tragic affair, Mansoon writes that "Sloughing phagendena is apart to attack the half starved, malaria stricken pioneer in jungle lands, overdriven slave gangs, and soldiers campaigning in the tropics. Every ward of this description is literally applicable to the sufferers from tropical ulcer among the men of "F" Force. Grossly undernourished—deprived of adequate protein and adequate vitamin-forced to labour outrageously long hours in mud and filth constantly exposed tc trauma and infection -unable to receive adequate rest-deprived of adequate drugs and dressings, it is little wonder ulceration and gangrene spread like wildfire in these poor victims of cruelty and oppression.

Means of treatment were inadequate, water was short—food was short, drugs were short. It is possible that some part of there shortages were unavoidable. It is bad however to believe that the rice polishings and sulphur, which were supplied In October and November respectively, could not have been made available two or three months earlier. Had this been done, at least 100 lives would have been saved amongst ulcer patients alone.

In a gloomy business two things stood out in clear relief. The first was the amazing cheerfulness and fortitude of the patients in the ulcer wards. They were pathetically grateful for what was done for them and they co-operated fully in every aspect of their treatment.

The second redeeming feature was the steadfast devotion to duty of so many *of* the workers in the ulcer wards. Where so much good work was done it is difficult to single out individuals without doing apparent injustice to their fellows. The work of the following however was of outstanding merit.

Lieut L. Turner, FMSVF., who acted as my assistant for several months and look infinite trouble with the patients under his care.

Capt. E.J. Emery, RAMC, to whose skill in anesthesia was due the fact that no amputation patient, and many of these patients were appalling anesthetic risks, died during the operation.

Capt. G.W. Gwynne, 2/4 Mc. Gn. Btn. who acted as wardmaster in charge of ulcer wards and who was untiring in his efforts to maintain the fooding, washing, entertainment and morals of the patients under his care.

A/Sergeant Gerden Nichol, 2/3 M.A.O., who was in charge of nursing and was largely responsible for the relatively high standard of nursing under very difficult conditions.

Sig. N. Anderton, 8, Div. Sigs, L/C F. Deans, 2/10, Fld Amb., Cpl. Amb. A.W. Rawlings, 8 Div. Prev Coy., Pte L. Stone, 13 AGH., Pte D. Whaley 10 AGH who ware the best of an excellent collection of nursing orderlies.

QMS J.W. Franks, RASC and Cpl J. Scully, 8, Div. Signs., who were responsible for the supply of wood and water and food for the ulcer wards, and who worked long hours, day after dry, without complaint in maintaining the essential services of the ward.

Without the work of these men, the melanchely death roll, long as it is, would have undoubtedly been much longer, and I take this opportunity of recording my grateful appreciation of their work.

I would also like to express my thanks to Major B.A. Hunt, AAMC, C.O. Tanbaya Hospital, for the invaluable assistance he gave me in the preparation of this paper.

Kanburi — A. Cahill Cap, AAMC

March 1944.

Extracts From the Report of Capt. Wilson, R.A.M.C. Nutrition Expert With "F" Force

Nutrition Rations

Ready cooked food was supplied during the five day train journey from Singapore, and the three weeks or so on the march. The meals consisted of boiled rice and watery vegetable stews containing a few pieces of cucumber, pumpkin or onion-only sufficed to stave off the pangs of hunger for a few hours. The usual issue was two meals a day, plus some cold and occasionally pieces of dried fish as a haversack ration for the midnight halt. People in possession of Thai currency could buy extra food from wayside hawkers during the first week of the march, but even with this addition few men were able to maintain weight and strength during this period of exertion. At the fixed camps the I.J.A. supplied uncooked rations. Theoretically the ration was the same as at Changi, but in practical the amount handed over each day varied according to the stocks in hand, the state of communications with the outside world and the mood of the Japanese Quartermaster. Another cause of variation was the idea held by some officials and at times openly expressed by them, that sickness even though not feigned in order to avoid work, was a gross breach of discipline and an act of sabotage against the Japanese War Effort. Instructions were actually issued officially from the I.J.A. H.Q. fixing a scale of 600 gms rice daily for those working directly for the I.J.A. on the road and railway projects; 400 gms daily for those on camp duties; and only 200 gms daily for those classified as unfit or sick. As sick and convalescents always outnumbered the workers, sometimes by three or four to one, this order meant a marked reduction in the total amount of food issued to a camp. Although some adjustment and improvement of the sick mens ration was usually possible in our own cook-house, the manual workers dare not be penalised too much for the benefit of the sick. Items such as potatoes and boxed meat provided still another cause of variation. The Japanese Q.M. would issue a certain number of bags or boxes of these commodities regardless of their state of fitness for human consumption and this total number would be shown on his records. The preserved meat, a course fibred meat, probably buffalo meat without bone was partly salted of pickled and arrived packed in boxes. It usually swarmed with blow fly maggots and was often in such an advanced state of decomposition that, as a grey-green fluid it dropped through the seams of the boxes. Only one box might be salvaged of meat worth cooking from four or five issued. Sacks of potatoes suffered greatly from wet during transit and storage and many were only fit for the refuse pit. (We may add that our standard of what was fit for consumption was a local one far below anything held before leaving Changi). The rice provided was a highly milled, medium grade, Burma rice; both it and the dried beans were heavily infested with weevils. Cattle which had been driven on hoof all the way from Burma provided the fresh meat; they were just as exhausted by their walk as were the prisoners; they often died on the way and there was usually great anxiety to get our butchers to work before too many succumbed on arrival at the camps.

Supplements to the Ration

It was impossible to supplement the rations at the adequately by local purchases. Neike village was the only trading centre in the neighbourhood of the camps, and the one storekeeper with whom trading was permitted had a meagre selection of foodstuffs at high prices. Palm sugar cost 40 ticals (Thai dollars) per 15 oz tin. The men received pay at the rate of 14 tical (25 cents) when working. The sick received no pay. The camp hospitals had first claim on valuable foods such as green grams which came in later. Coconut Oil cost 35 ticals per 4 gallons, canned herrings 3 ticals per 15 oz tin. At no time were the amounts available sufficient to make any appreciable difference to the food value of the camp rations as a whole, until after the return to Kanburi at the end of November, where food was more plentiful and supplementary items cheaper. A supplement which may have made some difference to food in general was when a specimen of green leaves was shown to Maj. J.A. Reid by aBurmese at Neike. Later a large patch of these plants was found nearby and sufficient was collected daily to add to the stew for the whole camp. It was a leguminous plant, later identified as a species of Cassia (family-Leguuminosac), popularly known as wild peanut. Near Sankurai camp, a large area of ground was covered with a species of wild gourd akin to smake gourd (Family-Cucurbitaceae) the leaves of which made a palatable stew when cooked. The use of his was suggested to the officers of the camp by Maj. Reid. At Sankurai the leaves of a certain climbing plant were similarly used. This was not identified with certainty but thought to belong to the family Sterculiaciae. The leaves were large and hairy but fairly soft when boiled and produced a syrupy soup. Parties of convalescents were organised to pick these various plants daily, special quantities were given to those suffering from Beri-Beri and other deficiency conditions. The men had great faith in the value of their green stews.

Collection of eats (a) Ration figures were collected from a number of camps on the spot, others were obtained later on from the "Q" staff of the camps who had sufficient paper to keep records. One Q.M. replied to our request for information by stating that he had been in the habit of keeping his records on the shoulder blade of an ox which he had not brought back to Changi with him, (b) The figures given are the net amounts of edible food received as rations by the prisoners, and may be expected to differ considerably from the Japanese records of the foods issued for reasons already given. (c) None of the camps had weighing machines and all issues were in bulk. The amounts given in Table TV have therefore been derived from estimate weights. These estimates were made at the time by various British and Australian "Q" staff, all of whom were experienced in handling food and estimating weights in bulk and should be reasonably accurate over the period for the daily strengths were available at each camp, these have been averaged over the periods detailed in the Table.

Remarks on the Diet See Table III and III (a) Rations for June and early July were particularly poor. This was the time when some camps, notably those in Konkoita and Neike area were almost cut off from communication with the outside world. No adequate reserve stocks were laid in before the rains came, and as it was uncertain how long it would be before more supplies could get through rations were cut drastically. At Neike in the middle of June the whole camp was receiving an issue of white rice 270 gms, dried lima beans 24 gms, dried green gram 15 gms, fresh meat 50 gms including bone, per head per day. This works out at an energy value of 1200 calories, less than that required for basal metabolism. At about the same time the Konkoita camps for 8 to 10 days were on a diet of 300 gms white rice daily, and a little salt, varied occasionally by the omission of the salt. On this diet men were compelled to do heavy manual work on road and railway cuttings, (b) The later months showed an improvement in energy value except where there was a discrimination against the sick men, but only once did this food value reach a reasonable figure for the work being done. (c) Approx. 80 per cent of the total energy value was supplied by carbohydrate, and about 90 per cent of this carbohydrate was derived from highly milled rice, (d) Protein was usually small in amount and little of if was of animal origin. (e) The amount of fat was inordinately low at all camps. (f) There was a complete absence of green leaf vegetables and fruit, except later on return to Kanchanbari, consequently very low figures for vitamins A and C. (g) The Thiamin (Vitamin B1) values were well below the estimated normal requirements except at Tanbaya Hospital, Burma from the last week in Oct. onwards when rice polishings were supplied in reasonable quantities. The Thiamin-non fat calorie ration never exceeded .24 at any of the working camps (see later para). (h) The daily requirements of the different components of vitamin B2 complex is now yet known of these components, riboflavin and nicotinic acid, are approx. correct, it will be noted that the riboflavin values, while low, were not so far below the estimated daily requirements as were the values for nicotinic acid.

Further comments on the diet.

In their book, Vitamin B (Thiamin) published in 1939, Williams & Spies make several pertinent remarks on this subject :- Page 85, "The requirements for vitamin

B1 may be distinctly above the average in persons with fever, gastro- intestinal and other conditions"; page 295, "The thiamin requirement during periods of severe exertion and possibly during the course of intermittent fever such as malaria may rise considerably above the level adopted to other conditions". Fever, dysentery and other forms of enterocolitis and severe exertion were prominent features of the prisoners' life in Thailand. Page 100, (animal experiments) "The vitamin B1 requirement rises with the amount of carbohydrate consumed but falls with the increasing proportions of fat in the food". Thailand diets had an overwhelming preponderance of carbohydrates, very little fat and gravely deficient in vitamin B1. Page 102, "We shall therefore commit ourselves at the thiamin-non-fat-calorie-ratio as the best tentative index for the protection of the average individual that can be offered at present, ("While admitting the necessity for further verification of the thiamin value of foodstuffs). The thiamin-non-fat-calorie-ratio necessary to protect against beri-beri is very close to 0.3". **Note.** one obtains this ratio by subtracting the calories derived from fat from the total calories. The balance then represents the calories supplied by protein and carbohydrate, i.e., non-fat-calories. The total amount of thiamin in the diet expressed in micrograins divided by these non-fat-calories is the thiamin non-fat-calories ratio. In analysing the diets we have used Williams & Spies preferred values where available for the thiamin content of the foodstuffs except for rice. We allowed for rice 0.5 microgram thiamin per gram, a figure which more closely corresponds to local analysis of this type of rice than does the 0.3 microgram allotted to highly milled rice by Williams & Spies. This difference raises the thiamin-non-fat-calories ration of these diets well above what they would make it, but even so, the ratio never exceeded 0.24 at any working camp and was more often below 0.2, i.e., well below the protective level.

The actual figures were as follows :-

Thiamin-non-fat-calorie ratios

NF = No figures available.

	1993								*1944*
Camp	*May*	*June*	*July*	*Aug*	*Sept*	*Oct.*	*Nov.*	*Dec.*	*April*
Kankoita	.14	.16	.17	.17-,18	NF	.20	—	—	—
Neike	NF	.21	.20	NF	—	—	—	—	—
Shimosonkurai	NF	.17	.18	—	—	—	—	—	—
Sonkurai	NF	NF	.19	—	—	—	—	—	—
Kamisonkurai	NF	NF	NF	.21-.24	.20	.23	.21	—	—
Tanbaya	—	—	—	.23	.23	.31	.61	NF	—
Kanburi	—	—	—	—	—	—	—	.27	—

Given only these details one could have predicted with certainty that a severe outbreak of beri-beri must develop sooner or later. When to them we add periods of semi-starvation, the widespread occurrence of cholera, dysentery, diarrhoea and malaria, tragic results were inevitable.

III

Report by Conditions During Expedition of 3270 Prisoners of War Designated as 'H' Force as a labor organization into Thailand-Singapore during the period May-December 1943[1]

The present report is designed to bring to notice specific instances of harsh and brutal treatment accorded to the POW by the retaining power which it was not politic to include in the original report. A great deal of hardship can be directly attributed to Japanese incompetence and inefficiency as well as to a complete apathy on the part of the officers of the Imperial Japanese Army [IJA], Malaya administration. These officers seemed at all times incapable of regulating the conduct of the subordinates with the result that illiterate NCO's and soldiers entrusted with the responsibilities of supervision and administering POW were enabled to give full play to high degree of vindictiveness and sadism which seems to be an inherent part of Japanese temperament.

A general statement concerning conditions at any one camp amply illustrates the appalling conditions which applied throughout for what is true of one is equally true of all save in small variation of details, of the vicissitudes of the journey from Singapore to Thailand, little needs to be said. Suffice to reiterate that with men of one metal rice truck in torrid heat with indifferent food supplying, a practically non existing water supply and hygiene and sanitary provisions totally lacking, the standard of discomfort and suffering may well be imagined.

At the transit camp situated at intervals in the jungle beyond the railhead which were used by the marching parties travelling towards their respective destinations conditions were uniformly appalling, Food at these establishment resulted in revolting situation. Water was seldom available in quantity and often had to be purchased by the marching prisoners. Tentage was totally inadequate and often non-existant which compelled a large number of personnel sleeping in the open. As this took place in the heat of the day so that the march should take place at night, sleep for the majority of them was out of question and men were compelled to restart their march in an exhausted and dehydrated conditions, This treatment

1. F. No. 70/Historical Section.

contributed substantially to the subsequent disease epidemics which decimated personnel of the force. The camps when finally reached after long and tiresome marches during the course of which many unsavory incidents took place. The vindictiveness and brutality were the keynotes of Japanese conduct were all similar in character. Upon arrival jungle had to be cleared in order to make room for the camp .In no single instance sufficient cover was available to house personnel allotted to the area. In every case all considerations were subordinated to the demand for; abour and still more labor for carrying out the work of the railway construction undertaking and this persistant demand became operative within 24 hours of arrival in the camp of the already thouroughly exhausted and hungry troops .Every available fit man and a large portion of the sick men as well were pressed out to work leaving only thoroughly sick people to endeavor to create living conditions tolerable to Europeans. This state of affairs persisted throughout and as a result in no single instance was it found possible to even remotely approach orderliness, cleanliness and habitable conditions notwithstanding that men collapsed from illness and fatigue in this effort to clean latrines, built cooking houses bury their dead, chop wood, carry water, porter the meager ration from the close by river over rough undulating jungle paths, under the hail of cuffs and blows and abuse from all the ranks of the IJA.

No regard was paid to the location of the camps beyond their convenience to he working site concerned with the result that the camps were frequently situated heek by jowl with native coolie camps in all of which sanitary conditions were ntirely absent and throughout most of which deadly diseases were already stalking. The same lack of discrimination was displayed in the allocation of tasks of the working parties. Prisoners of war of all ranks being compelled to work side by side on cuttings mbankments, bridges etc., with coolies of every color and caste and submit to tandard ised forms of supervision and summary punishment with these people.

It was at first conceded that the officers should act as supervisors of the gangs but the incidents described hereafter will illustrate Japanese un readiness to onsider the officers as anything more than a labor unit and many of the incidents vill serve to highlight the apparent determination of the Japanese authorities to legrade in every conceivable way the officers of the various allied forces who had een unfortunate enough to fall into their hands.

Food remained at starvation level consisting for the most part of boiled rice of oor quality, a seaweed like vegetable and warm water and repeated daily. epresentations verbally and at intervals reinforced by appeals and demands in ritings failed to have any improvement. Meanwhile the persecution and abnormal bor conditions were intensified un till the whole of the force housed in all the six amps covering approximately 20 miles of jungle were in uniformly low state of ealth, emaciated, glassy eyed, bootless, practically clothe less, fever and dysentry dden but still working, working.

It was during this period that the complete incompetence or lack of desire to help or both manifested itself in all ranks of Japanese officers. For example Captain appeared not to be qualified to give orders to Lieutnent as in the case of Capt. Hachahuka who was nominally IJA, Force commander and who seemed to be unable to effect any improvement in the standards of food provided though the deliberate obstructionist tactics of Lieut. Yanakawa .

I have no hesitation in making this officer Yanakawa as a war criminal .His conduct throughout was one of complete indifference to the sufferings of prisoners indeed he seemed to take delight and derived a great delight from the spectacle of starving emaciated and oppressed whitemen. Even when clothing became available inspite of him, he succeeded in withholding in store a large quantity of footwear etc., not withstanding that thousands of men were carrying out their hard tasks barefooted and practically nude. A great many of the leg ulcers a large number resulting in amputation can be attributed in my opinion to this individual's deliberate persecution.

The next major incident of note occurred when a party consisting almost entirely of officers up to and including the rank of Liuet, Col. arrived at Tonchen under the command of Lt,.Col. W.G. Whittenburry. Prior to the departure from Changi of this party ,an assurance had been given by General Arimura that these officers would be employed on administrative and supervisory duties .This promise was contained in a letter to A, Q, Malaya Command and a copy of the same was furnished by O.C.H6 Group to the Force Commander who in turn repeatedly presented the same to the IJA Commander without results. The officer party despite their protests were made to work as coolies with native coolies. Every conceivable degradation was thrust upon them. Beating were common, hours of work were long, food was scarce and poor and in addition to working at the railway undertaking, officers of all ranks were compelled to act as porters carrying equipment and rations often over a distance of six kilometers .During the cholera epidemic an officer party from the group under Major A.M.S. Babington M.C.I.A. was compelled to carry and bury dead and dying Asiatics in a site adjacent to the British camp. protests by Major Babington resulted in his being beaten. This state of affairs continued so far as the officers party was concerned despite repeated attempts by the O.C. of the Group and the force commander at the H.Q. to have the position regulated and before the end of the expedition it was a daily sight to see officers practically nude engaged in labor tasks of the lowest and most ardous types.

Hospital accommodation in the camps consisted throughout of primitive improvisation of split bamboo, inner fabric of tents, etc, The Japanese whilst acknowledging the necessity for hospital facilities did nothing to assist in the provision of the same, and the conditions under which these soldiers suffered through the various stages of their diseases and under which many of them unfortunately died are indescrible in a report of this nature. They can be described as filthy houses and but for the untiring efforts of the medical officers and orderlies the death rate heavy as it was must have been doubled or even trebled. Japanese guards were heard to say that they hoped the sick would die and then save the Japanese rice. Medical stores were practically nil, palm leaves having to be used as bandages.

I can not recollect a single instance of the Japanese administration providing any thing except one or two kawalis in the nature of a cooking house or domestic utensils. Every bit of cooking, disinfection and food distribution, water storage was carried out by the jealously guarded and laborously prepared utensils of our own provisions or improvisation .No light was provided and even surgical operations were performed in the open by the moonlight or the light of a camp fire . The hours of work continued to be long so much so that the majority of men never saw their camp by daylight .It was the monsoon season and it rained almost incessantly. No facilities existed and no opportunities were given for the drying of the clothes clearing of bodies or resting and it is not surprising that with this combination of infamous conditions disease should be rampant .Malaria, dysentry, beri-beri and above all what the IJA resourcefully ordered to describe 'Post dysenteric Inanition' on death certificate but which was actually starvation already stalked through the camp of the force. Then without warning the cholera epidemic swept down on us. Immediate representation for the cessation of movements were spurned and a in a point of fact owing to desperation of the labor force by death movement became increasingly frequent and larger in character. The result was inevitable. The disease spread and not withstanding the noble efforts of our own medical personnel every camp throughout the Force was quickly effected. The death rate was heavy and many, stories of in-humanitarianism could be told of our captors during this period if time and space permitted in the report. It is perhaps sufficient to say at this juncture that 880 out of 3,270 people representing 27 percent lost their lives. Figures which could need no further comment and which add it the unanswerable indictment of the Japanese mal administration, in efficiency and callaouness.

The above account was compiled by Major J.F.Grossby as an appendix to the report prepared by Lieut Colonel H.R.Humpheries

IV

Conditions of Prisoners of War in Japanese Hand–An Account by Captain J. Gibson, R.A. [Extract][1]

Strange silence over the city as the 'cease fire' becomes a reality. The Japanese will not send troops into the city for 24 hours and we are allowed to keep 1000 men armed to act as police and try to preserve order in the city. I go to my gun position in Government House ground's where we have been firing for the first two days. The position has been shelled continuously and bombed but casualties are light. The guns have been rendered useless to the Japanese. Troops are rather bewildered by things in general end I talk to them and try to explain things. They have done all that was asked of them-none could say that they had let the side down. My two subalterns are in good heart, but very-very tired-we all are. We give the troops a good feed then lie down on the ground to sleep. strange stillness broods over the city–an unearthly quite after the constant roar of the guns for the last week. Soon we are all asleep and no awaking till morning. A Malya appears naked and begs for a pair of trousers. The Japanese have stripped him of his uniform and told him to go home. They are doing this to all the survivors of the Malay Regiment. Then an Indian soldier suffering from shellshock comes along. We offer him food but he is afraid to accept it and rushes away. My two subalterns and self go up to Government House to look around for something to eat and find tons of tinned frut and bottled food in the cellars. We have a Royal breakfast. After breakfast we are sitting in the hall when the first Japanese arrive–four officers. We think 'now for trouble' but the Japanese just look at us and walk out! Peculiar people. About an hour later some Japanese troops arrive and by signs tell us to clear out. I go to R.H. on a bicycle to see what is happening, passing many truck loads of Japanese on the way. They are singing and laughing and wave to me as I go past. I eventually find R.H.O on the seafront and report to the C.O. whom I have not seen for over a week. All the other troop commanders are there looking for orders. We are told to assemble at the volunteer drill Hall with all guns and vehicles so that the mechanism will be ruined during the run down to the assembly area. The guns have already been dealt with. All the guns and transport are in by midday and what a sorry sight they present. The Japanese are very cross when they see the damage and threaten reprisals-none

1. F. No. F12/Historical Section.

taken. No orders yet about where we are to be imprisoned, so a couple of us take motor bicycles and ride around the city. The Japanese are now in the town and sentries machine gun posts, etc are all over the place. They let us ride round unmolested. Back to the Drill Hall and now orders are that we proceed to Changi on foot. My CO. says 'hell to that' and we grab trucks from all over the place and set cut in parties for Changi. No one tries to stop us and finally most of the Regiment arrives - by truck. Now the trouble starts–and we are made to take the trucks right back to the far side of the city and walk back.

The Regiment has been allotted one block of barracks - rather crowded but enough room for all to lie down. We managed to get three five ton trucks (abandoned in Singapore by the Australians) full of rations into Changi so hope not to be short of food for a while. Get fairly well settled on the first day. Main trouble is water. Work on sinking a well started immediately. Ready by next day and water supply assured. The men are a bit difficult but they are good fellows and will see things more reasonably in time. They feel that they have been let down-who can say they have not-no air force, no navy, no nothing. My Regiment was the first T.A. Gunners outfit to land in Malaya on March 11, 1941. This morning an order was issued by Malay Command that all rations would be collected at a central depot and issued from there to units. This was necessary as many units had no food and it was not known when the Japanese would issue rations-if at all. Actually they started issuing rice after about three days. We had one last good meal before handing over the stuff-and then settled down-not with a very good grace-to a diet of rice and very little else. Our initial efforts at cooking this rice were amusing to say the least of it. It either turned out a sloppy mess or a solid slab. It was decided to get one of the Malay volunteers to show unit cooks how to deal with the stuff and eventually it became at least edible. It took some getting down at first but when one realized that it was to be our staple diet one held one's nose and forced it down. We had cause at this time to bless the Malay Civil Service. Some bright lad during the palmy pre-war days in the World's Playground had a bright idea, typical of the things done in this outpost of the Empire. He decided to preserve rice by adding powered lime and some other chemical. The Japanese of course found this rubbish and decided that since it was our idea of a jobs, we could eat it-while they laughed. We washed that stuff about six times before cooking it but even then it had the delicate flavour of extremely ripe eggs. It also caused quite a bit of stomach trouble and even did damage to the eating utensils. Heaven knows what our insider were like. At this stage the Japanese seemed to be keeping no check on the amount of rice issued and we were able to bury large quantity of the offending rice, and use the better, stuff again. The Japanese is in many ways a very stupid fellow and if one used a little common sense it was easy to fox him. The bad diet was now have a bad effect on the general health and malaria and dysentery were on the increase. Fortunately at this time we still had medicine available, A hospital had been started in the Selerong area and in it were all the battle casualties. It was not any too well run and despite offers from units to supply cleaning fatigues, the Medical people insisted on running the place entirely with RAMC personnel. About this time the Japanese visited the hospital and found all the medical supplies in bulk instead of being hidden. They immediately-commandeered large quantities - thus causing a serious shortage of many essential drugs, which was to be felt later.

We were allowed to go swimming in the sea at certain times and this was very useful as water was not yet available in sufficient quantities to allow baths. One morning the Japanese cleared the beach and mounted four machine guns on the foreshore. Speculation was of course rife as to what it was all about. We were soon to learn. About 11 o'clock some trucks drove up containing about 60-Chinese. These men had been members of some of our Volunteer organisations and although they had gone back into civilian clothes after the capitulation, someone had given them away to the Japanese. They were tied and forced to wade out into the sea, then the Japanese opened up with the machine guns and mowed them down in the water. The poor fellows had not a chance. The next day they turned up at the Gordon's camp. He had a dozen bullet wounds but had managed to remain afloat and had got ashore after the Japanese had gone. He was looked after by one of our Doctors and when I left Changi he was walking around quite fit again. The Japanese never discovered him. We saw very little of the Sons of Heaven at this time. They had us wired in and surrounded by the sea and seemed content to leave us to our own devices while they got their P.O.W. system organised. Only an occasional patrol on bicycles rode round the roads.

The most amazing rumours were being circulated. There had been a landing at Penang and we were advancing down Malaya. And so on ad finitum.

Three soldiers of the Coast Artillery were caught by the Japanese in civilian clothes in Singapore. They had been sentenced to death. Lieut. Col. Heath, their C.O. and the padre were allowed to be present at the execution. The whole affair was properly done and they asked not to be blind folded. They died as British soldier should - one of them asked that mother be told that he was never afraid of the Japanese. This was the first execution.

All casualty lists were now completed and handed in to the Japanese. We all hope that they will be forwarded to the proper source without delay - we know now that these lists did not get home for more than a year. There can be no possible excuse for this sort of thing. A large party of British troops including a few officers is going off to Saigon. They are mostly A/A Gunners. Lucky people - supposed the French will help them in Saigon. He did hear later on that the lads in Saigon had quite a reasonable time, mainly due to help received from the French people there.

By now Changi was beginning to look more like itself again. The roads had been repaired as far as possible by filling in the bomb craters with rubble and leveling off - roofs had been fixed up as far as possible and the place generally tidied up units. All were starting gardens and life was going on in a fairly normal fashion. There was plenty of work to be done and soon the camp at Changi was running almost normally again. About this time it was decided to start some form of education for officers and other ranks. Among Volunteer officers there were a number of professors and school teachers and we were able to offer complete course on almost any subject, candidates for these curses were selected on educational qualification and competition for enrollment was very keen. About the beginning of April the Japanese started to send large working parties into the city to be employed on building roads and shrines. Eight officers and two hundred and fifty other ranks from my unit were selected for one of these parties. We were allowed to take a certain amount of cooking utensils with us. We left Changi at 6 o'clock in the morning and marched 26 miles carrying most of our kit to Kranji going into camp at a Naval wireless station. When we arrived in this camp we found it had been rather badly knocked about during the battle and that since then the Japanese had been using the building as barracks and the whole place was in a filthy condition. We even had to remove several bodies which were of course in an advanced stage of decomposition. These were usually traced by the small. After we had been there for a few weeks we manned to get the place into some semblance of order again. Our work consisted of building a shrine on top of Bukit Timah and also cutting a road and a series of steps up the face of the hill. The first morning we were sent out to work at 6 a.m. despite the fact that, some of the men were in an extremely bad condition after the long march of the previous day, when we, had reached our destination after 8 o'clock in the evening. When we arrived on the site we found that there were already a party of Australians at work on the hill.

The Japanese guards gave us a demonstration of face slapping using the Australians as the victims; this presumably was to show us that they Intended to stand no nonsense. After the first few days things quietened down considerably and the work was not too strenuous. Rations of food at this time were extremely bad, consisting of rice, salt and one tin of M and V between48 men. At a later date the rations improved considerably and become quite reasonable. We even had for about 3 weeks a daily ration of between 4 and 6 ounces of meat and fresh pineapples, also occasionally some coconuts. The general behaviour of the Japanese during this time was on the whole quite reasonable although we were always short of medical supplies. We had one unfortunate incident on the hill when a Gordon Highlander was killed by an unexpected mortar bomb which he had picked up and was examining. Bukit Timah had been the scene of some of the heaviest fighting on the Island and we were continually finding bodies of allied soldiers in the undergrowth. These were identified as far as possible and remains were given a Christian burial, in this respect the Japanese also behaved in a reasonable manner. About the middle of June we were all returned to Changi and when we got there we were told that we were going North on another working party. 1800 of us were put in a train in cattle trucks at Singapore on June 26th bound for an unknown destination.

A Sikh-officer was in charge of us for this movement. We spent days and nights on the train in most uncomfortable conditions being fed at irregular intervals and finally reached our destination in an extremely dirty and tired condition. The destination was Bampong in Thailand. We were taken to a camp which had only partly been completed, the natives were still working on the construction of the camp when we arrived. The camp had been built in some padi fields and when it rained become a quagmire. Our work now consisted of building a road to Won Pladuk where another camp for Prisoners of War was being constructed by prisoners of war. The buildings were of bamboo and attap and we soon became experts in this form of building. There were no nails whatever in the construction; everything being tied with strips of rattan. When the building of the road was completed we proceeded to construct various smaller camps on the side of the road leading to Kanburi; these were to accommodate the Japanese engineers who were going to supervise the construction of the railway on which we were destined to work. About the beginning of October we were removed to Chunkai; here again we worked at the construction of a large camp which was to house about 4,000 British prisoners of war for the next four months and eventually became the best camp for numbers 2 and 4 groups. In November a fresh batch of British prisoners of war started to arrive from Singapore. It was now the rainy season and as the camp was not yet completed conditions were most unpleasant, many of us having to sleep in the open in torrential rain. The camp was built on the bank of a large river and after a few days several of the huts which had already been constructed were impossible to live in. Some of the troops were only in transit at this camp and moved on after few days further up the river to Wanrun. Work on the railway was now started in earnest but for the period of our stay at this camp the Japanese engineers were fairly reasonable and only on rare occasions did the men have to work excessively long hours. This section of the railway was completed by the first of February 1943 and we then moved on up the river to Wantakien; the people from Wanrun having also moved up stage then moved on to Bankaw. The food at Wantakien had been the best we had ever had from the Japanese and we were sorry to leave the camp. After another 3 weeks at Bankaw we moved back to Wantoklen and we were given a week's rest. During the timewhen we were at Banpong we had our first taste of the Korean Guards who were to be with us from then on. They arrived from Korea about the middle of July and as they marched into camp they presented most ragged and dirty appearance. Their uniforms were worn out and most of their boots were in an ' extremely bad condition. They were wearing British webbing equipment and were armed with the short Lee Enfield rifle. After they had been with us a few days they were completely re-equipped with new British uniforms. They appeared to be extremely badly trained and it used to be a source of considerable amusement to us to watch them mount guard each morning. Watching this procedure was not without its element of danger as quite frequently the odd round would go off; fortunately usually in the air. These Korean soldiers are not used in combatant units but purely for administrative work although all of them are armed. We found them to be extremely unpleasant in every respect. They were treated with the utmost contempt by the Japanese soldiers and vented their spleen on the prisoners. After they had been with us for some time by the use of judicious threats as to what would happen to them after we had won the war we were successful In subduing some of the more vicious types. They had really no Idea of the true state of the war as all the news which they received was read to them once a week by a Japanese officer in command of the camp. They were continuously making attempts to spread this news among the other ranks but without a great deal of success. During the whole time which I personally spent with the Japanese we had our own short wave radio working in at least one of the camps and the news received was spread by word of mouth throughout the camps in Thailand. This radio was constructed in a water bottle by an officer who had been an engineer with the B.B.C. and was operated by a six volt battery stolen from a Japanese truck. When the battery ran down we used to exchange it with the battery in the ration truck which called at our cook house daily. This truck was driven by a British driver accompanied by the Japanese guard who was induced to leave the truck to have a cup of tea in the cook house; while he was doing this the driver did quick change over of the battery. Despite the fact that on these occasions the vehicle had to be pushed to start it the guard never tumbled to what was going on. Later when we had moved into the jungle and car batteries were not available we used torch batteries to operate the set. These were obtained from a Thai who was of considerable assistance to us in numerous ways. He was officially pro-Japanese and was allowed into the camps to sell fruit, cigarettes, etc. This native spoke excellent English and as we proceded further up the river followed, us all the way on barges with a certain amount of food supplies. He was also able at a later date to procure for us invaluable medical supplies which must have saved many hundreds of British and Australian lives. Eventually he even cashed cheques for British, officers at very high rates of exchange. He eventually was under suspicion by the Japanese and we did not see him for some time. He managed however to persuade the Japanese somehow that he was on their side and to our relief returned to the camp again. Also during our stay at Chungkai the Japanese had a sudden blitz on the Officers. They claimed that some of the Japanese nationals had been ill-treated by the Allies in a concentration camp in America and informed us that because of this the officers would have to do manual work on the railway. We of course refused and after a long argument they finally paraded all the fit officers one morning. We were surrounded by an armed guard who were ordered to load their rifles by the Japanese officer. He then harangued us at considerable length threatening to shoot us if we did not obey his order to proceed to work. We called his bluff and still refused, eventually he lost his temper and after quite a bit of shouting and face slapping a valley was fired over our heads. We eventually had to give in as he threatened that unless we did the men would be given no rations. The type of work, allotted to us was bridge building which was the heaviest form of work on the railway and the officers were often working up to their waists in water and for extremely long hours. The men, who had by this time become extremely loyal to their officers were much upset by this treatment of us. The Japanese engineers in charge of these officers were extremely anti and the members of the party had a really grueling time. If the object of the Japanese was to break the morale of the officers they failed dismally. After our week's rest at Wantaklen we started on a ten day march right to the top section of the railway. The conditions during this march were appalling as the wet season had now started and most of the men were now without boots and had very little clothing. We had to carry our own kit and also part of the Korean guards equipment. The transit camps at which we rested at night on the way had not sufficient tents to accommodate even a small proportion of the prisoners and most nights we had to sleep in the open. We had two very poor meals each day, one before we left in the morning and the other after arrival in the evening. The coins during this march was extremely hard, many flooded streams and steep ravines having to be crossed and we were only able to make about ten kilometers each day. We finally arrived In an exhausted condition at what was to be our new camp for the next few months. This was Talanun. These camps in Thailand were normally in command of a Japanese Lieutenant with each group of camps coming under the command of a Japanese Colonel. The British side of the camp was under the command of a Lieut. Colonel usually assisted by an Adjutant, a Liaison Officer whose duty it was to arrange the daily working parties, a Sanitation Officer whose duties were most important to the health, of the camp, a Messing Officer who was in charge of all cooking arrangements and a varying number of Medical Officers according to the size of the camp. There was also an occasional Padre attached to the camp staff. The Japanese staff consisted of a number of Korean private soldiers and one or two Japanese N.C.Os.

In some of the smaller camps the highest ranking Japanese was only a first class private soldier. The Medical arrangements in all the camps were most primitive, there being a complete shortage of all medical equipment. Eventually we did set a sufficient supply of quinine to cope with Malaria cases, but other drugs were extremely scarce. At one stage we even had to use banana leaves as bondages. The health of the men was rapidly deteriorating and tropical ulcers were becoming very common. As we had very little to treat these with apart from a little Mag. Sulph. and salt and water the ulcer situation became extremely serious. Finally resulting in about 200 amputations done under the most primitive conditions. These operations were often done in the open with men standing by to chase the flies away. It is a great tribute to the Doctors that so few lives were lost during the actual operations. In May 1943 we had an outbreak of Cholera which started in a Coolie camp just north of Torsoa and rapidly spread right up the line. In some of the camps the death rate was appalling and it was all we could do to keep up with the disposal of the bodies. These were burnt in considerable numbers twice daily and the remains were buried. The Japanese had brought many natives, mainly Tamils from Malaya to work on the railway when it got behind schedule and they were dying off like flies. No medical arrangements of any sort had been made for those unfortunate people and eventually some of our Doctors were detailed to attend to them. Each morning a burial party from one of our camps was sent to the nearest native camp and their work consisted of the disposal of the natives who had died during the previous dry. At one state the Japanese were even throwing the bodies into the river as a means of disposal. Cholera eventually spread down the river because of this. In one small camp a British soldier, who was the first to go down with Cholera was ordered to be shot by the Japanese commander. Two Korean guards were detailed to execute this unfortunate man. The British officer in command of the camp pleaded with the Japanese to spare the man's life. They were adamant however and the Korean guards prepared to fire on him from about 30 yards range as they were afraid to go nearer; in order to save the man being mutilated by the inaccurate fire of the Korean guards, the British officer asked to be allowed to the man himself. He was given a rifle and one round of ammunition and went close up to the soldier who by this time was unconscious, and shot him through the head. There was an amazing squels to this incident. To fully understand this incident it is necessary to explain that the Japanese camp administration were at loggerheads with the Japanese enginees who in charge of the railway construction. The system of working was that the prisoners were leaned each day to these engineers for work on the railway and they were constantly demanding more than were available. When these people heard of the foregoing incident they reported the matter to the Japanese authorities in Bangkok. For some obscure reason this resulted in an enquiry being held finally the two British officers in the camp were charged, one with murder and the other with, being an accessary. The Japanese officer was also charged with murder. They were all taken under escort to be tried by the Japanese Military tribunal in that city. When the British officers arrived at Bangkok they were thrown into a local Military prison and very roughly treated by the guards. They were made to sit cross legged on the floor of their cell for hours at a time and were not allowed to wash or shave. One morning they were taken to the court to be tried, when they arrived at the court they found that the Japanese officer was also there and he was in a filthy condition giving the appearance of not having washed or shaved for some considerable time. The trial and after the evidence had been heard the prosecuting officer pleaded for sentences of death and 15 years solitary confinement. On the second day of the trial two Japanese Doctors appeared and screed, which when translated said that these Doctors had examined the British soldier who alleged to have been murdered and had found that he was already dead when the officer shot him of course was a complete falsehood. The court then dismissed the charges against all three prisoners. The British officers were taken back to prison and the treatment of them changed considerably. They were given a hot bath and facilities to shave and some good food. That evening one Japanese General, commanding Bangkok, came to visit the officers in their all and amidst much and bowing scraping congratulated them on the way in which they had conducted themselves in court saying that it was the way in which he expected British officers to conduct themselves. He then presented each one with a cigar and some cigarettes, also ten dollars and told them that on the day following they would be taken on a shopping tour in Bangkok. The next morning two Japanese soldiers appeared and took the officers around the town in rickshaws and allowed then to go into most of the large stores in the town. They found that most of the people in these stores were very friendly towards them. The following morning the officers were put on a train for Kanburi and from there were eventually returned to their own camps. This story was told to me by the officer who actually shot the man. The whole affair was a complete mystery to us all and we have never been able to arrive at a satisfactory explanation of the Japanese conduct.

Conditions on the railway at this time were becoming steadily worse; the Japanese were intent on getting the railway finished before a specified date regardless of the cost in lives among the prisoners. They had already made it quite plain to us that we were lucky to be alive at all and that we should consider it an honour to die building this railway for the New World Order and the Japanese Emperor. It had become abundantly clear by now that they did intend to carry out this policy. Men were dying in large numbers daily and all appeals to the Japanese were without avail. Further drafts of British and Australian prisoners had arrived from Singapore on loan to the Japanese engineers from the Japanese Malaya command. These people had been told when they left Singapore that they were going to fine camps and that any work they had to do would be of a light nature. They consisted mainly of men who had been considered unfit for heavy work and under the bad conditions prevailing in Thailand the death rate among these new arrivals was extremely heavy. They were treated even more callously than the earlier working parties as the Japanese considered that they had been ''dodging the column in" Singapore. In one of the camps where these people were the condition of the camp was so bad that even the Japanese finally had to move the location. During one of the moves between camps an ensuing incident occurred. We had several carts drawn by bullocks which were used for carrying the Japanese baggage. As there had only been rice and salt to eat for the last few weeks we had become pretty desperate for food. One night some of the Australians pinched one of the bullocks and took it into the jungle where they slaughtered it. The word went round among the lads and we adjourned into the jungle, tore the bullock apart and cooked large lumps of beef over wood fires. When the orgy of eating was over we buried all the remains. in the morning when we were ready to move again there was of course one bullock missing. The Japanese decided that it must have run away in the night; a party was organised to search the surrounding jungle. Unfortunately some portion of the beast had not been properly buried and was found by one of the Korean guards. This lead to a considerable amount of face slapping and finally a team of Australians were made to pull the cart to our destination; even then all the lads lent a hand we considered it well worth it.

In the latter part of May 1943 end early June the Japanese started to evacuate those of us who were too sick to work, to the base camps at Chunkai, Tamarkar and Kanburi. We were sent down to these camps firstly In barges and eventually as the rails were laid, by train. I personally was evacuated with chronic malaria to Tamarkan camp which was under the command of Lieut.Col, C.P. Toosey, R.A., who was the Commanding Officer of the 135 Field Regiment, R.A. This particular camp had up till then been the No. 1 group base camp and had been turned entirely into a hospital, and was one of the best run camps in Thailand. Shortly after we arrived a new Japanese commandant came to the camp and he turned out to be in the main fairly reasonable. At one time there were about 3000 British, Australian and Dutch in this camp. The buildings were in an extremely dilapidated condition at first but constant pressure by Col. Toosey resulted in extensive repairs; all of which were done by convalescent prisoners, and eventually we even achieved some complete rebuilding. It soon became evident that this was to be the show camp of Thailand and we had an official mission from the Thailand Government one afternoon who were allowed to inspect the new part of the camp. They were conducted on this tour by Japanese officials and were allowed to see the less seriously ill men. It appeared that the Thailand Government were at last beginning to show a little interest in the welfare of the prisoners held in their country by the Japanese. We thought that this was probably due to a statement made in the House of Commons by Mr. Anthony Eden when he spoke of the dreadful conditions under which the British prisoners here being forced to work. We had an extremely good system working in this camp whereby each ward was under the command of a combatant officer for cleanliness end discipline, woking in very close co-operation with the Medical staff. Regular inspections of the camp were carried out by Colonel Toosey and there was keen competition among the officers in charge of the wards to have the best turn out on inspection.

Certain facilities for sport were also presented at this camp and each evening we had basket ball, volley ball and an occasional football match. As the men became fit again they were redrafted up country on to the railway, so that we decided to cut out the games to a large extent as we did not wish the Japanese to know which men were fit. We also managed to get quite a decent canteen running and the profits from this proved invaluable in buying Medical supplies. One day the Colonel received a mysterious note asking him if he required any money to be used for food and medical supplies for the sick men. In the letter he was asked to give his time, rank and name of his bank in England and a nom de plume, also to state how much money he would require per month. After giving the matter considerable thought and discussing it with his staff, of which I was a member, it was decided to take a chance and answer the matter. We asked for 12000 dollars per month and the letter was signed "Vee". The letter was handed to the British driver of the truck which brought the rations daily and he in turn had to leave it on the counter of a certain shop in Kanburl where he had to collect the supplies daily. In a few days this same driver handed over 12000 dollars in cash to Colonel Toosey. I was in this camp for five months and during that time the money was coming in regularly. One can well Imagine what a difference this made to our supplies of medicines and extra food for the men. The amazing thing about it all was that the Japanese never once made any enquiries as to where all the money which we were spending came from. As all canteen supplies were bought by the Japanese, they obviously must have known how much money we were spending each week.

While in this camp we saw an example of the Japanese version of the Gestapo at work. Some of our men had found a Japanese tool store in a far corner of the camp and had gained access to it.

They discovered that there were large quantities of shovels and chunkels in this store and they started taking boxes of them through the wire at night and selling them to the Thais. They were getting 6 dollars per implement for them. They unfortunately were meeting with such success that they became over bold- and one night a Korean guard spotted them. This was about midnight. Immediately all Hell broke loose in the camp. The Japanese were running round shouting and screaming and finally after waking up the whole camp they rounded up 10 men. Then the trouble really began in earnest. They took the men into the Japanese office and started beating them with bamboo's and any other article they could lay their hands on; they then held one of the men down on the floor while one of the Japanese kept climbing up on to the table and jumping on to his stomach. This went on for about a couple of hours until finally Colonel Toosey managed to have it stopped. In the morning the Gestapo arrived in camp with all their Instruments of torture, which included thumb screws, hand cuffs, pieces of sharpened bamboo and whips, etc. The men, who had spent the night in the cells, were brought out and subjected to the most fiendish tortures which included sticking lighted cigarettes into their noses and ears. They also gave them what they were pleased to call the water treatment. This consisted of holding a man down on his back, placing a rice sack over his face and pouring water from a four gallon con on to his mouth. The result was that within a few minutes the man's stomach was swollen to an amazing extent with the amount of water which he had been forced to swallow. The next step was to jump on his stomach with dire results. All these were accompanied by continuous face slapping with the result that several of the men broke down and the Japanese were able to procure the information as to which Thais the tools had been sold to. That evening the Japanese accompanied two of our men to their rendezvous and we heard quite a bit of shooting. When the party returned to camp they brought with them a couple of natives and the beating began anew. A certain amount of the tools were recovered by this method. The enquiry went on for about four days and in the end we were told that six of the men had been found guilty and would be taken to Bangkok for trial by the Japanese Military tribunal. Later we learned that they had been tried and sentenced to 16 . months, solitary confinement. They were taken to Singapore to serve this sentence. A few days after this we had a visit from a high ranking Gestapo officer who spoke excellent English with a strong American accent. He had all the officers assembled and spoke to us at length on maintaining discipline among the men and finally promised us various improvements in rations and other things, all of which promises, needless to say were never carried out.

At the hospital camp at Kanburi there was a wireless set in operation and by great misfortune, combined with carelessness on the part of the operators this was discovered one day by the Japanese. By means of the usual methods the Japanese soon found out all the names of the officers implicated. They were beaten mercilessly for many days, one of them, a major, even losing his eyesight and eventually he died of injuries received. This affair had repercussions all the way up the line and many officers were brought down to Kanburi for Interrogation. There were also very strict searches made in all the caups but fortunately none of the other sets were discovered although we had to lie low for sometime. In October the Japanese decided to move all prisoners from Tamarkan to Chungkai as Tamarkan was going to be used for Australian prisoners who were to be brought from Burma. The move to Chungkai was carried out by barges and every man no matter how seriously ill he night be had to be moved by a certain date. Large numbers of the men were seriously ill and had to be carried on to the barges. There was one man not expected to live more than few hours, and we asked the Japanese to allow him to remain in Tamarkan for the few remaining hours of his life. This request was refused and the unfortunate fellow died in the barge on the way to Chungkai. As there were two more days to go before the evacuation was complete there could be no possible excuse for this treatment. When we reached Chungkai we found that the camp had grown out of all recognition and that there were now about 9000 prisoners in this camp, practically all of whom were sick. There were already over 1000 dead in the cemetary there and deaths continued at a rate of about 20 a day for the next two months. The sick were still coming down from higher reaches of the railway by barge, this necessitated a three day journey and they used to arrive in a shocking condition. Barges were crowded far above capacity and as the majority of the men were suffering from dysentery and were too weak to move, there was usually several inches of excretion in the barge, and on more than one occasion I saw a dead man in the barge when it arrived. It really was a pitiful sight to see these men in such an emaciated condition when practically all of them had to be carried out of the barges. The Japanese were completely callous about the whole affair and were yelling at us all the time to hurry with the unloading. The men had only had one meal during the journey down and very little water to drink except what they could get out of the river.

The sick were also being evacuated by rail and here the conditions were equally bad. They were crowded Into cattle trucks and there were several deaths among then during the journey. The railway was finally through in November 1943 and the general evacuation of prisoners from the top end of the line was carried out during December 1943 and January and February 1944. Once the work on the railway ceased the general condition improved considerably. Rations became much better and general treatment of prisoners by the Japanese showed a marked improvement. The only work done in Chunakai camp consisted of camp fatigues and we started quite a large garden under Japanese supervision. When this garden began to produce vegetables, most of the produce went to the Japanese and if there was any over this was given to the sick, one dry a had of extremely lean cattle arrived and from then on we had a small ration of meat daily, excepting Wednesdays when we had one small fresh fish per man. During this time we managed to contact the Australians and learned from them that conditions in Burma had been very similar to those prevailing in Thailand. They seemed to be in a better position than we were for clothing and we were able to buy a few articles from them, A party of 200 men from Chungkai under three officers was detailed to build a memorial to prisoners of war and Japanese soldiers who had died on the construction of the railway; this took the typical Japanese form and was sited on the river bank near the large steel bridge which crosses the river west of Kanburi. When the memorial was completed it was unveiled by a high ranking Japanese officer with the usual oriental ceremonial, a detachment of prisoners of war being present. The camp at Chungkai was commanded by Major Outram who had been second in command of the 137 Field Regiment, R.A. Although there were British officers in the camp senior to Major Outram and he offered to relinquish command to them, none of them would accept the responsibility. The camp was extremely well run a credit to the British commander. Life at Chunkai was not without its little Incidents and the occasional beating up still occurred. Three British officers were beaten for small offences and two of them suffered from broken jaws and one from a broken arm. On January 1,1944 a party of Scottish officers which included myself, decided to celebrate new year by absorbing some extremely raw alcohol which we had previously produced from fruit skins, rice, sugar and various other ingredients. We having quite a party at the end of one of the huts when a Korean guard appeared on the scene removed one rather roudy member of the party to the guard room. The Commander very wisely decided that as this gentleman was in an extremely ripe condition it was unlikely that he had achieved without the assistance of friends, so in a few minutes some guards arrived and collected remainder of the party. We were all taken to the guard room and lined up at attention. The guard commander apparently had an unusual sense of humour for a Korean, because he pushed the end man just the rest of us with the result that we all fell down. He then walked along the line saying one of us "Scot soldier?" If we replied in the affirmative he passed on. There was one unfortunate Sassenach in the party who said "No English" he immediately received a belt on the ear because apparently the guard considered that an English man should not be celebrating New Year. A few minutes afterwards we were all dismissed and what might have been an ugly incident finished happily. Next day a miserable time was had by all the revellers as this type of alcoholic refreshment was not the best thing for the system.

During January a party of about 100 fit men and an officer were sent off to construction of a new hospital camp for the sick men who were suffering from chronic malana and any other ailment which made them of no further use as labour. This camp was well laid out and the huts were of weather boarding with wooden floors; reasonable sanitary arrangements were to be provided and it was understood that the camp would be under the supervision of the Red Cross authorities. The work was completed by the end of May and we started evacuating the sick of No. 2 and No, 4 groups in parties of 500. Also at this time the Japanese authorities held a complete medical inspection of all prisoners of war and about 2000 British prisoners were selected for transfer to Japan. In this party no officer above the rank of Captain was included; the ratio being one officer to each 150 men, I was in command of this party. We were segregated from the rest of the troops in the camp and were fitted out with one shirt, one pair of shorts, one pair of boots (rubber), one singlet, one pair of under pants. Eventually after a long wait we were entrained for Singapore on the morning of June 7, 1944. It was the original intention to embark at Bangkok but apparently this was found to be owing to allied bombling activities. Before we left we received the news of or D Day and as can be well imagined this gave us a tremendous uplift. Before we left we used to have frequent air raid alarms both day and night and on several occasions we were able to see allied bombers passing over the camp. This always heartened us considerably. The day before we left a Japanese newspaper man came to the camp and I was sent for to be interviewed by him. He asked me lots of stupid questions, one of which was "Are you afraid of being sunk by American Submarines?" He gave me to understand that the Americans made a habit of lying in wait for ships carrying British prisoners of war and sinking them, but assured me that as the Japanese ruled the ocean, and as we would be heavily escorted, we need have no fear. All of which was extremely amusing. I am afraid the gentleman was under the impression that the best place for me was a lunatic asylum owing to some of the frivolous answers which I gave to his questions. We arrived in Singapore after a most uncomfortable four days and we were accommodated at River Valley Road camp. This camp was in an advanced state of dilapidation and as the supply of fire wood during our stay there was quite inadequate, I am afraid that the whole place must have fallen down shortly after we left as we supplemented our supplies considerably from the buildings. In the next camp there were about 3000 Indian troops who had been captured when Singapore fell and who had been working on the island ever since. Although we were strictly forbidden to have any contact with these people we managed to speak to them quite a lot and it, was really a pathetic sight to witness their delight at seeing British officers again. There could not be the slightest-doubt as to the loyalty of these men, as the Japanese had used every form of persuasion to turn them against us, without success. They had been beaten and on occasions starved in an attempt to make them go over to the Japanese, but still remained loyal.

We had an officer of the Gurka Regiment with us and he was able to hold quite a few conversations with the Sepoys who described to him the methods used by the Japanese in attempting to force then to join the Free Indian Army. During the earlier days of our captivity while we were still in Changi, Sikh guards had been placed over us and British officers had been made to salute them. We later found out that these men had been enlisted mainly from the Naval Base, and other police forces. While we were in transit in the camp at Singapore the rations consisted of rice, tapioca root, which was almost inedible, and a small quantity of extremely odorous dried fish, and in quantity were quite inadequate. The health of the men who were all fit when we arrived In Singapore began to decline rapidly. We were finally marched down to the docks for embarkation on June 26th. We were divided into two parties, one of 1250 under my command and the other consisting of 750 under command of Captain R. Hall of 118 Field Regiment, R.A. The ship on which ray party embarked was the Hofoku Maru, a vessel of about 5000 tons built on the Clyde in 1902. She was In a very bad state indeed, the plating on the decks being eaten through by rust in several places, and she did not look as though she had seen any paint since the war began. We were to be accommodated in two holds, one forward and one aft, which meant putting 625 men in each hold. As we were carrying a cargo of bauxite in the lower parts of the holds only the top section of each hold was available to us. I immediately protested to the Japanese officer in charge about the conditions but despite a lengthy argument we were finally forced to embark. The crowding in the hold was such that no man could lie down and all had to sit up In a cramped position. He had however promised that once we left the port we would be allowed to sleep a certain number of men on the deck. This helped to ease the congestion a little. We finally got under way in a convoy of eleven ships with an escort of four small destroyers. We sailed within sight of land all the way to In British North Borneo when we stopped for refuelling. This port which is an important oil centre was crowded with shipping and there were a large number of tankers being loaded with crude oil. Something went wrong with our engines while we were here and the rest of the convoy Including the ship with the 750 British prisoners sailed without us. Eventually after ten days we put to sea again in a convoy of eleven ships with an escort of four destroyers and sailed close to land all the time until we finally reached Manila on 23rd July. We arrived in the bay about mid afternoon and next morning went along side. Here we unloaded about a hundred hen coops on to the decks and then pulled out into the bay again and dropped anchor about three miles off shore. At this time Manila bay was crowded with Japanese shipping of all sorts and transports loaded with Japanese troops were continuously passing through. As far as we could observe they did not seem to land many of these troops in Manila. The ship containing the 750 British prisoners was in the bay when we sailed a few days later. By now the health of the troops was causing us serious concern and I used to spend quite a bit of time on the bridge in appealing to the Japanese for more reasonable treatment. Although we had four

Doctors with us we had practically no medical supplies except a small quantity of quinine. Very soon we had our first death which was rapidly followed by others. Our Doctors despite the fact that they did everything humanly possible. In attempt to save lives, were unable to cope with the situation. Finally the Japanese agreed to make some attempt to procure some medical supplies for us and in a few days two boxes containing these were brought aboard. Out of these supplies we were given a small quantity of vitamin injections and some vitamin pills. The bulk, which was all American Red Cross, was kept by the Japanese for the use of themselves. We also did everything possible to procure better rations for the men but here again not with little success. Daily rat:ons consisted of six boxes of rice, one large basket of vegetables, and half a bucket of fish, also salt and a spoonful once every five days. All this between 1250 men. Sickness was steadily increasing and the death rate became higher. The majority of the men were by now in a very weak state and were suffering so badly from beri beri that many of them could not retain even the small amount of food which they got. To make matters worse it was now the rainy season and we had about six weeks continuous downpour. As it was quite impossible to cover the 'holds without suffocating the men we lived in a state of continuous wetness. There apparently was something seriously wrong with our engines and they were working continuously on them. The local Philippines used to come aboard when they were coaling end from them we gleaned quite a bit of news. They used to bring us the local newspaper called the Manila Tribune. This was printed in English and although it was full of Japanese propaganda we were able to form some idea from it of the local conditions. Most of the natives spoke quite a bit of English and we were extremely friendly with them. Eventually the Japanese when they saw that we were fraternising with those people increased the guards and to shoot any of us seen talking to the natives. After we had been lying in the bay for few weeks they proceeded to off-load our cargo on to another ship. Three ships came alone side at different times and sings of Formosans who were dressed in Japanese uniforms unloaded our cargo of bauxite end quite a quantity of into them.

These Formosans appeared to be in pretty bad physical condition and were also Inclined to be friendly towards us. Our men by now were dally and finally we had reached the rate of five or six deaths per day. The first man who died had been burled ashore in a large ceraotary or the outskirts of the town but now all the- men who dice; were thrown overboard wrapped in rice sacks with c box of bauxite tied on to feet. We had padre with us and we were able to give all the men a Christian burial although the Japanese adopted most callous attitude towards this and insisted on the bodies coin overboard a few minutes after death. By now about hall the pen were quite unable to move at all and most of those who could walk about were so weak that the few who were strong enough to do any work with the sick were rapidly losing strength though lack of sleep. The hole's were in a filthy conditions we had no feetilities for cleaning them and the Japanese made no attempt to help us in any way. The majority of the men were unable to climb out of the holds to use the latrines and the stench in the hold became unbearable. We appealed to the Japanese to allow us to put at least some of the men ashore and finally we were allowed to evacuate only 50 of the worst cases. These men were taken to a hospital in one of the American camps in Manila and we understood that they were being well cared for. By the time we finally sailed from Manila Bay on September 20, over one hundred men had died including one of our Medical Officers, Capt. M.G. Braham.

During the last few weeks of our stay in Manila Bay there had been quite a number of air raid alarms and we had-moved to dispersal areas on quite a few occasions but so far had seen no sign of any allied aircraft. We had also heard that the American fleet were somewhere in the vicinity. By this time the men were in such bad shape that they really did not seen to care whatrain happened and one men jumped overboard in an attempt to end it all. We managed to rescue him, one of his friends jumping overboard and holding up until a rope was thrown in, but when we got him on board he lay down and refused to eat and died within few days. Many of the other men also adopted this attitude. We left in a convoy of seven ships of midday on September 21 and we were escorted by two small destroyers and two very small escort vessels. At 6 o'clock that night just as it was getting dark we sailed into a little bay on the Luzon coast anchored for the night. We sailed again at 6 o'clock next morning. The Japanese were extremely nervous and the guards had been issued with hand grenades to be thrown into the holds in event of any trouble. The majority of our men had been supplied with lifebelts. At nine o'clock on the morning of September 21st I was down in one of the holds talking to the men when suddenly there was terrific rear of a burst of machine gun fire. The bullets came rattling alone the deck but few of them penetrated into the hold. I ordered the men to keep under cover and ran up on to the dock to find out what was happening. I saw that the convoy was being attacked by about 60 American dive bombers and two of the ships were already sinking. They now seemed to be concentrating on our ship and several more planes machine gunned us completely wrecking the few lifeboats which we had and killing several people. The only means of defence which we had was an ancient field gun mounted on a platform astern and after firing one round the gun crew went overboard. The first hit on our ship was an aerial torpedo which hit us a midships and lifted us well out of the water. I ran round to the side of the ship which had been hit to see what the damage was. I thought that although we appeared to be listing slightly, as the decks were still being machine gunned it would not be advisable to bring the men out from the holds just yet. I ordered then to stand fast and put on their lifebelts. Just then two live bombers appeared, they headed straight for us and I could see the bombs-being released; on of the bombs fell into the forward hold and exploded causing frightful casualties among the men. The second bomb fell into the aft hold and blew a large hole in the bottom of the ship. Almost simultaneously another two bombs hit us a midships. As we now seemed doomed I ordered the men to abandon ship getting as many of the sick as possible out of the holds first. I was still shouting this order when she broke in the middle and plunged under in a matter of seconds. I found myself in the water surrounded by wreckage of oil sorts. The Korean guards had gone overboard as soon as we were hit by the first bomb and no attempt was made to interfere with the prisoners in any way. It had been quite Impossible to move any except the few sick men from the holds and hundreds of them were drowned like rats In a trap. It was dreadful to hear the men crying for help which they never received. When we were in the water, planes dived down and started machine running is causing quite a number of casualties. After a few minutes they must have seen that we were white men and the machine gunning stopped, .As far as I could see most of the convoy seemed to have been sunk excepting one large tanker which had managed to run a ground on the beach which was about four miles distant. None of the escort vessels was hit although there were many near misses on them. Soon lifeboats were lowered from these vessels but they refused to pick up anyone but Japanese survivors. It had been our intention to kill the Japanese officer in charge of us in the event of anything like this happening but it was all over so quickly we never had a chance to get to them. We had however succeeded in killing one particularly nasty member of the crew, As soon as I got to the water I decided to try to reach the beach and escape Into the hills. I spoke to several of the men who were near so in the water and told them to make for the beach and get Into the jungle when I would try to find them later. After being in the water for six hours I at last approached the beach only to find the Japanese from a nearby garrison there waiting our arrival. Fortunately there were large breakers running near the beach and I was able to swim a few yards north of these Japanese and escape into the undergrowth which was only a few yards from the water's edge. I was so exhausted that I am afraid I passed out for a few hours but fortunately the Japanese did not discover my hiding place. I started to make my way inland and ran into a bunch of Philippines, some of who were the local constabulary and were armed with rifles. They asked me who I was and I told then that I was a British officer and was trying to escape from the Japanese. At this time I was dressed only in a pair of underpants. They agreed to help me although the constabulary were supposedly pro Japanese. They took no to one of their hiding places in a sugar came field near the town and promised to bring a Philippine who had served in the American Amy during the battle of Dataan after dark. This man duly arrived accompanied by some friends. I found that they were all pro-American and had been officers in the Philippine Amy. They took be to one of their houses and gave no some clothing and a good meal, the first one I had had for three years. Much to my disappointment I found that I was unable to do it justice. Later that night I was moved to another house on the outskirts of the town where I stayed for the next few days. While I was there quite a number of Philippines who could be trusted came to visit me bringing food and cigarettes. They asked me if I would form a guerilla band in the district as there was no active organisation in that particular place at the tine; although the guerillas were active in many other localities. The name of this town was San Narciso in the province of Zambales, T agreed to orcanise a company of guerlllcs end eventually we enlisted four officers and eighty men. The names of the officers were Fred Posadas, who was to be second in command, R.E. Aguirre, Tony Pasadas and Attorney Evangelista. Out of the eighty men we had a strong armed squad of four whose duty it was to procure arms. A number of natives had collected side arms and rifles during the American retreat and had kept these hidden from the Japanese. My men knew where quite a number of these were to be found and used to go off at night and threaten the owners until they handed over the arms to us. There were Japanese garrisons in quite a number of the towns around us so we had to be extremely careful. I personally only moved about during the hours of darkness. In the meantime I had learned front the chief of the constabulary that eight British soldiers had succeeded in escaping. I arranged for him to send these men about thirty miles inland to the foot of the hills where there were no Japanese. This was done to aid the men hidden away in a small hut in a safe place. The question of feeding the men was rather difficult at first but eventually we arranged to find a men called Rodriguez who agreed to 'see to the food supply. After I had been living near the town for about six weeks a Philippine spy gave me away to the Japanese. This caused a quick evacuation to a rice for a about three miles out of the town. A few nights later some of my men collected this spy who had previously been responsible for the arrest and execution of several Philippine patriots, and he was suitably dealt with. Shortly after this I set off one night mounted on a small pony and escorted by eight armed Philippines to visit the British soldiers who had escaped with fie. As it was about 30 miles to the place where they were living we did not arrive there until the middle of the next morning after having been on the move continuously. As I had not done any riding since leaving England in 1940 you can imagine that I had to eat standing for the next week. The saddles on the horses had been made for a very much smaller posterior than mine and by the time I arrived I was in an acute state of discomfort. I found the men living in a hut among some trees by the side of the river and they were as comfortable as could be expected under the circumstances. They had been provided with a certain amount of clothing but were unable to find any footwear enough for them. Food was still proving a bit of a problem and I had brought a bullcart of vegetables and rice and sugar which I hoped would last them for at least two weeks. Four sacks of rice which I had brought in San Narciso had been way laid by another guerilla outfit and consumed. Although I had words with the Captain of this band I was not in a position to do much about it. In this part of the country where the men were living there were no Japanese within 15 miles and owning to the nature of the country it could only be approached by one trial which could be kept under observation. The men were able to move about freely in the daytime. All the Philippines in this part of the country were pro American and were most helpful to us, also the Negritos who lived in the mountains used to come to feed the men bringing then small gifts of food and tobacco. After being with them for a week I returned to San Narciso. The chief purpose of Guerilla Company was to procure information regarding the disposition of Japanese garrions and troop movement in

Zambeles province. Also to observe shipping movement on coast. By now aircraft from America naval forces were flying over the territory almost and one day in particular we had the thrill of seeing nine American fighters shoot down 11 Japanese twin bombers which were coming in to land at Son Marceline aerodrome. One of these planes came down in a pedi field quite near where I was living. There were 11 Japanese in, all of them officers. Eight of them were killed and the remaining three slightly injured, From information collected it was ascertained that all of the machines had been carrying passengers and had no bomb load. In the afternoon some of ray men removed 2 twin barrel 30 calibre machine guns from the plane, also quite a quantity, of cmunition and an excellent map which included the south island of Japan proper, Formosa and the whole of Luzon. From this map we gathered that the planes had cone from aerodrones in the south of Fornosa. and were makins for Manila. Unfortunately shortly after we had removed the machine guns from the plane about a dozen Japanese soldiers appeared they found that the guns were missing they threatened, to bum the nearest barrio unless the guns were returned immediately. This of course had to be done. We had better luck however with a machine which had come down a bit further away and we were able to secure one twin barrel machine gun from this. Soon afterwards I had a message from an American Colonel who was living with the Negritos in the Zambeles mountains. I had heard of his presence previously but as I had been told by the Philippines that he was not taking any active part in the guerilla organisation I had not bothered to get into touch with him. About this time mother Japanese spy had given information as to my whereabouts and the Japanese were offering of rice for my capture. Fortunately for me one of my men found out about this and I managed to get away about an hour before the Japanese party arrived to collect me. Unfortunately however they did manage to arrest the there Philippine officers, Posadas Aguirre and Evangalista. By this time, I was well on my way towards the mountains, once again on horse back and accompanied by my armed guard of Philippines. The Japanese tied the three Philippines with their hands behind their backs and started to work on, then in their usual way in an attempt to make then give away my whereabouts. Unfortunately Evangelista broke down after he had been immersed in a Msh pond several times and almost drowned and gave the Japanese all the inform nation they wanted. He gave this in the form of a written statement to the Japanese officer and told him all about our company of guerillas, also the fact that I had gone off to see the American Colonel in the hills and was expected back in a few days. After he had given this statement he was apparently overcome with remorse and when his hands were untied to allow him to sign the statement he snatched up the Japanese officer's revolver and shot him twice through the head killing him instantly. He then turned the gun and shot himself through the head. During this interlude the Japanese soldiers who had been standing on Guard ran out of the house and the local Mayor who had boon forced to accompany the Japanese was able to snatch the statement from the table and conceal it on this person. The most amazing thing, about it all was that the statement apparently had been completely written by the Japanese soldiers and they never asked for it again. It was really the greatest stroke of good luck that this particular officer had been killed as apparently he had a very considerable amount of information about the whole of the guerilla movement in Zambeles and was about to send out punitive expeditions. In the usual Japanese fashion he had been keeping this information to himself probably so that he got all the glory for cleaning up the guerillas and of course it all died with him. The next day the Japanese arrested the families including the children of all the Philippinos concerned and threw them into prison. For some reason best known to themselves they made the wife of Evangelista sign a statement to the effect that her husband had been killed by the Japanese guards while attesting to escape. In the meantime the other two officers were being tortured in an attempt to note then talk. They told the Japanese that they knew and that I had come to them for help sometime before in a very creak condition; they said that they had given some food and sent railway as they felt sorry for no but were afraid to give no shelter. Despite everything they did and finally after two weeks imprisonment they were, all set free, but were told that they must live in future in the provincial capital, a town called iva and must report to the Japanese garrison there daily. During all this time I had been living in the hills with the American Colonel. When I first met him. I was escorted to his hideout by a band of Negritos some of whom were armed with rifles and some with bows and arrows. Before we proceeded to the hideout which was about 2000 feet up the steep mountain covered in jungle and only approachable by one narrow trail, they disarmed no. By the time we readied the top of the hill we were winging wet with perspiration. The Neg ritos cool as they were when they started off. I found the Colonel very comfortably housed in a small hut well hidden away some banana trees and impossible to find without the aid of a guide. The Japanese had already on one occasion tried who find the hide out without success. His cooking done for him by a Philippines soldier who had been his constant companion for two years. I found the gentlemen to be in not too good a state either mentally or physically. He started our conversation by telling me that as I was a British officer he would prefer to discontinue by command of the guerilla company in San Karclso and that it should be handed over to one of the Philippines officers. He had apparently decided to take an active part in gurillo activities and had made himself commander of all Luzon. He had formed a staff consisting of many American officers who were running loose around the Island one used to send out orders employing Negrito runners. Just before I arrived he had been able to secure a short wave receiving set and it had become any job while I remained with hin to listen in to the news usually from San Francisco and take it down for distribution. After I had been *there* for a couple of weeks one of his officers arrived from Panpanga and we finally persuaded him that it was now safe to leave the mountains and go down into the foot of the hills where he would be better able to establish a headquarters with more control. Eventually we moved out to new site near the barrio of Mynamar and within a few hundred yards of where my men were living. We lived in a small house which belonged to Tentient Vernon De La Creuz. From here I was in a position to see my men each day. The only trouble about this area was that, there was a lot of Malaria and as my men and myself had already had n considerable amount of malaria whilst in Thailand we found it very trying. The men in particular were continuously getting the fever and as we were not able to attain the necessary medicines the health was causing quite a lot of concern, One of them who had been badly beaten about the head by the Japanese in Thailand became very ill and eventually died after having been in a coma for eight days. This was on November 21st. I gave Christian burial as well as I could and some of the guerillas fired a volley over the grave. The health of the remainder of the men was getting worse and after trying to got a Doctor to visit then; from one of the towns in Zambeles one of the American officers told me that he knows a doctor over in Pampanga who was a member of the guerilla force and cave me a letter to him ordering him to come over and see the men, I was supplied with a guide and set off for Pampanga early one morning. This involved two day journey over three ranges of mountains and was extremely hard going. I was met on the other by a fresh lot of guides who took me to where another American officer was living in the barrio of Natividad near the town of Gua gua. He was able to help me to procure a large supply of drugs which the Doctor considered would be necessary and eventually after about a week we set out on the return journey. In Panpanga the guerillas were extremely well organised and it was possible to move about more freely at night although there were many Japanese garrisons in this district. We used to have men in each barrio who would contact us and let us know if the district was clear of Japanese and safe to move about in.

In one town, San Fernando, there was a Japanese garrison of about 1000 and we used frequently to pass very close to one of their guard posts without ever been suspected by the Japanese sentries. One evening an American officer who had gone to the town to meet one of the guerilla leaders, stepped out of a bull cart and found himself face to face with a Japanese soldier. They stared at one another for a split second then the Japanese ran one way and the American the other. The reason for this sudden disappearance of the Japanese was that he was unarmed and the American had a 45 hanging from his waist. We never moved about any time without our side arms. During the time I spent in Pamponga I lived In a house on the outskirts of the barrio. This house belonged to three extremely plump sisters who had been harboring Americans all the time since the fall of Manila. They were completely unafraid of the Japanese and although their house has been searched on several occasions they had so far managed to keep clear of trouble. Also living in this district was the ex-Governor of the province of Masbate, Dr. Pecson. The Doctor was one of the few Governors who had persistently refused to co-operate with the Japanese and he had spent some considerable time in prison. When he was finally released he was forbidden to go back to his province on pain of death. He was doing extremely good work among the natives in the district although he had to be constantly on his guard and had to go into hiding whenever any Japanese appeared in the district. The Americans had by now practically cleared Leyte and were making daily raids on the aerodrome in Luzon. In the district where I was we were within twelve miles of Clark Field which is the largest aerodrome in Luzon and there, was also a string of smaller airstrips all within a ten mile radius, Clark Field was bombed almost daily by heavy bombers and the smaller airstrips were straffed almost continuously. A lot of this straffing was anything but accurate and; it paid to take cover whenever allied aircraft were sighted. The Japanese in the district must have got wind of our presence as they started to raid the nearby barrios forcing us to get out of the house and hide in the padi fields during daylight hours. On one occasion they actually got within a hundred yards of our hiding place but fortunately they turned away in another direction.

In the meantime I had sent the Philippine Doctor with an American pilot over to Zambeles with the Medical supplies and orders to proceed direct to my men and give them treatment immediately. I was delayed with an abscess on my leg and an attack of Malaria which made it quite impossible for not to travel. We had been sending out patrols to collect American pilots who had been shot down during the raids on the air fields and in all we were able to luring in 12 officers and men whom we supplied with guides and sent, to; the American Colonel's headquarters in Zambeles, any American pilot to be caught by the Japanese was immediately bayoneted. By the first week in January the Americans gained complete air superiority and for some time now there had been no opposition from the Japanese. Japanese troop movements were now going on a fairly large scale. Considerable nmbers of troops were moved both by hut and on foot going North; presumably In anticipation of an American landing in the gulf of Lingayen. Quite a number of tanks and heavy guns were included In this move. There appeared to be a shortage of food and each town that we stopped at they were in a habit of confiscating all the rice, chickens and pigs which they could find. They were also commandeering bullcarts to transport these supplies. The Philippines did their best to hide the rice and live stock. The fact that the Japanese had begun to make house to house searches forced us to move out of the district. They were taking reprisals against the Natives and every time Japanese soldiers appreciated barrio the natives used to run into the padi fields and hide. This annoyed the Japanese and they began Co use machine guns. Many natives were killed in this way. The Americans were now dropping pamphlets warning, the natives to keep away from the main roads as they were bombing bridges and straffing any transport, seen moving on the roads. When I was fit again I moved off accompanied by an American officer and some native guides across the mountains to Zambeles.

V

Statement made by Major F.J. H. Nelson R.A. B.M.R.A. 9th Indian Div. on Conditions in the P.O.W. Camp Under Japanese Control[1]

Prisoner from February to November 1942 – Changi

Prisoner from November 1942 to March 1943 - Thailand

(Personally administrating Battalion, On Railway Work)

Prisoner – March, 1943 to September 1944 - BASS CAMP CHUNGKAI.

(Was employed in Hospital on Ward Welfare Work) Prisoner September 1944 to January 1945-In command of a Jungle Camp of 500 men working on wood, cutting) Prisoner January 1943 to August 1945 - Officers Camp KANPURI.

Medical

Generally speaking supplies were, very short. Quinine in the Camp with which I personally was concerned was given out originally in half of the correct dose, reduced to a quarter and finally after a few weeks small doses only given to fever cases of 101° and over, Bandages very, very short and here is a personal example: a medical orderly in charge of ulcer cases, the worst of which was knee to ankle and meeting at the back of the leg (bones, and sinews exposed), and the average was 4 or 5 deep ulcers on the leg, was given a piece of gauze about a yard long and three inches wide to treat his patients. Sometimes salt was the only drug available. The smell in the ulcer ward defies description.

Hospitals

Were composed of huts the same as the ordinary living quarters. The huts were dark and adequately roofed. Beds consisted of Bamboo slats about 7 feet long and each man had rather less than a metre apace. The men were lousy and in places too ill to be deloused. In one hospital ward which I commanded while standing at the and of the bed I could easily see the lice crawling over the patient, lie was too ill to be isoved and in a couple of days died Bamboo slats were riddled with bugs and despite weekly cleaning they were never really cleared. Only very sick men were admitted to the hospital on account of lack of space. S.A.M.C. personnel inadequate and a large proportion of the nursing orderlies were amateurs, operations carried out on the primitive conditions, no dust proofing possible, no proper clothing for

1. F. No. F12/Historical Section.

doctors, usually adequate antiseptics. Bed pans, bottles etc. had to be locally manufactured and they were never enough. Most troops had about one blanket, frequently threadbare, some Red Cross blankets were received, one example was — 19 issued to 500 men and these were kept in the hospital, Improvised blankets were made of rice sacks.

Food

No distinction made between hospital patients and fit men with regard to issue of rations except that a lower scale was issued for sick men. British authorities used to take out from the Camp ration a proportion of the more nutritious food for the hospitals i.e. offal.

General

Clothing

The average man lived in a "G" string, i.e. to say a loin cloth. Most of them. had one or two pairs of shorts mostly in tatters and usually some sort of shirt. These were usually kept for evening wear.

Food

Cooking was difficult owing to shortage of containers (Cooking pots) and in some cases to shortage of wood. Three meals were served each day. The daily rice ration varied between 12 Dozs and later up to 24 ozs in working camps per day. This last was adequate. The following is an average menu for a day.

Breakfast

Paprice or Ground Rice—pint or pint and a half per man, and in later days two or three thick slices of bread instead *of* rice, sometimes locally made Jam or spread.

Lunch

Adequate rice. Usually some form of dried fish, possibly a weak vegetable stew.

Dinner

Rice. Rather better stew containing meat when available, and usually a fried or baked rice ball, flavoured.

One or two pints of drinking water every day and weak tea with every meal. Meat or fish when available was issued in quantities of about two ozs per man. In general the Japanese were never short of Rations, in particular they had quantities of eggs and protein bearing food, for example in a camp of 500 men at one period six hundred per day came into the camp and all were eaten by 23 Japanese soldiers (who complained about too many eggs). In the same camp the Japanese (23) took roughly one half of the meat available for the whole camp - Allied strength 500.

Fruit was available through local purchase, rarely issued in rations. In the early days money went *very* much further than in later days, for example at the end of 1942 eggs were 5 each or sometimes less, at the and, they were 20 each. Tobacco started at 50 and rose to 70 per two lbs. At the beginning local purchase was opened to all ranks but in later days somewhat restricted through British run canteen under Japanese supervision.

Red Cross Food

One consignment of parcels arrived (one man parcel) and (3 *man* parcel American. This was excellent stuff issued at Chunkai Camp at one parcel to six men. Occasionally issues of local purchase commodities food, tobacco, beans, peas, salt fork fat, sugar, tea; coffee and butter and milk. These purchase were made from money given from Red Cross sources to the Swiss consul at Bangkok, who at Bangkok told us that he was buying on the assumption that we only got a percentage of what he sent us. At Liason Camp, September 1944 to January 1945 a consignment valued at about 6000 lecal prico was received, 33 4 galloos tins of pork, peas, beans, etc. were received in November. The Japanese immediately reduced the rations. These stores wero kept in a store to which the Japanese had daily access, by the ruse of issuing for every tin or sack sent to the cook house and putting a second one in a hiding place under the beds, the Japanese got the impression that we had none left and ration improved. We issued the remaining stuff under cover of darkness to the kitchen.

Treatment

Individual treatment of men by Japanese was on occasions extremely brutal. Japanese discipline is maintained by face slapping, standing outside guard rooms for periods up to four days without food or drink or shelter, benting with bamboos usually until the man insensible (after which ho was not allowed medical treatment) confining in very restricted quarters with no facilities fur latrine and very low diet, consisting of a ball of rice kneaded between the hands, was and sometimes a little salt for a period of three days, followed by one day food and then a further three days on rice and so on. The period of the detention varied from a few days to - months and in one case of an Officer three months. Collective punishment was the order. The whole camp would be punished for the misdoings of one man (strictly against international law). Punishment were taken in the form of a restriction in diet, liberty, smoking or the whole camp kept standing about on parade for hours on end.

Working Conditions

During the rush period at the end of 1943 working conditions were extremely bad. Sick men were carried out on stretchers and were made to work, malaria was not recognized as a disease any suffering from ulcers had to have in many cases amputation and often died. Food was so bad that deficiency diseases were prevalent causing a large number of deaths. Dysentery, Cholera and Diptheria broke out owing to poor sanitation. Every available man and officer was made to work on the Railway with the bare minimum allowed for Camp duties. At this period accommodation was in leaking tents on the wet ground; the men were never dry for periods of 3 weeks at a time, working hours here sometimes from before daylight in the morning to after dark at night, in some cases out all night without rest. One party from Singapore (F & H parties) arrived in Thailand early '43 at the end of the year with about '45 per cent of their original strength.

Mail

Arrived about a year late and then not complete. Received intermittently at periods of three to five months. Personally my last mail outwards is up to November 1944 only one post card reached home and one reached India.

Books

Books were allowed through out but never in sufficient quantity to admit of more than a very small proportion getting to the other ranks. The natural destructiveness of the O.Rs. precluded making the Officers books available to them.

Anti Malaria

In my camp of 500 men there were only about; ten who in the period of 5 months did not get malaria I personally had 17 bouts in ten months. Anti-malaria measures very lax. Mosquito nets were provided but seldom to full scale and grass matting to cover the Bamboo slats was not always provided and mosquitoes could get up through the slats. In some camp oil was provided. Men had little or no protection in way of clothing and at Linson smoky fires were kept in the huts night in an attempt to keep mosquitoes down frequently men had to wash at dusk when the mosquitoes were at their worst.

Wireless

Receiving sets were maintained though at great risk to the operators. In one case the aerials were disguised as clothes line.

Sanitation

Latrines were usually too close to the hut and the cook houses, and very difficult to fly-proof, usually on account of lack of labour. No seating accommodation for hygienic reasons, though there were one or two seats for amputation cases. No privacy. Latrines were seldom roofed.

Miscellaneous

Some times there were extra rations for Christmas but not at Linson last Christmis. On the Emperor's birthday we received we cubes of our own pine apple each. In 1944 Japanese were sent straight from Japan to take charge of the camps. Politeness in them was in evidence and there was great courtesy between the Officers and the Commanders, in personal dealing. One Japanese N.C.O. even went so far as to ask his prisoner for time off.

N.B. In most cases full cemetery records have been maintained. Buried under grounds and will be recovered.

VI

Report by Capt. J.W. Chapmen Ist Gurkha Rifles Regarding the Organisation etc. of Prisoners in the Taka-nun Camp, Thailand [Extract][1]

In February 1944 the Japanese Authorities organised all available fit men in the Taka-Nun Camp, Thailand, into Groups of 150 men under the command of a British officer. Japanese Groups were numbered off in Battalions and I (Captain J.W. Chapman of the Battalion 1st Gurkha Rifles) was placed in command of the first group formed i.e., No. 25 Battalion. The object of the Japanese in forming these groups was to facilitate the-transport of all fit men from Thailand to Japan for further duties of an industrial nature, the railway construction task from Bampong to Moulmein having been completed.

I was appointed O/C of this party as I possessed a good working knowledge of the Japanese language. The number of groups or battalions formed from the available men at Takanun was five i.e., Nos. 23, 26, 28, and 29 Battalions.

No. 5 Battalion left Takanun on the first stage in the long journey to Japan on both February 1944 at 14.00 hours. A halt would be made at Cungkai–No. 2 Group Headquarters -where the overseas party would be equipped with warm clothing and other necessities before embarkation. The sartorial appearance of the battalion suggested that an immediate issue of tropical clothing should have been made first of all. Nearly every man was in, rags and quite a number were improvised hats fashioned from bits of wire and old clothes, kit tags, etc., some were without footwear of any description, and had been in this sorry condition for some months past. The Japanese had issued a few days previously some old rice sacks to those of the party who were without blankets. These sacks were not issued as a temporary expedient, but were for use on the voyage and a roster of names was kept of those to whom they were given in order to keep a check on these valuable items of warm equipment!

The train conveying the battalion to Chungkai (Base Camp in Thailand) consisted of a number of cattle trucks and thirty two men were allotted to each of these wagons. The floors of these trucks were covered with cattle droppings and mud, and when the allotted number of men had crammed themselves inside the carriage there was little possibility for each man to avoid sitting in the filthy or

1. F. No. F32/Historical Section.

depositing his kit on it. However, the men were grateful that the accommodation provided, did, at least, allow some fresh air to penetrate inside, and the open nature of these trucks enabled them to view the passing countryside.

The haversack rations which were intended to last for twenty-four hours consisted of two rice rissoles, one of meat and the other of dried fish. These rations were far from adequate; but as most of us had many past experiences of the indifference of the Imperial Japanese Army to the welfare and comfort of their prisoners, especially if attention to such matters involved the in the last bit of trouble, we' were therefore not surprised at this state of affairs.

The majority of the battalion looked forward to the trip to Chungkai as they would soon be seeing some of their old friends again who had previously been evacuated there on account of ill health. Above all, most of them were glad to get away at long last from the up-country districts of Thailand in which they had suffered untold misery and privation; especially during the wet weather period which also coincided with the cholera epidemic with its appalling death rate.

The train was in charge of a Japanese Serjeant who had under him a number of Korean guards. I recieved my orders from this serjeant through these guards and It was my duty to maintain discipline and see that all instructions were obeyed by the men. This task was rendered more difficult by the presence of the above-mentioned guards who did their best to interfere in small matters of discipline which could easily have been settled by myself and my N.C.Os.

The journey was uneventful except for a somewhat severe thunderstorm which occurred during the night and gave us all a severe soaking, and some of the carriages received considerable battering from dislodged rocks when passing quarries through which the railway had been blasted.

Chungkai was reached at 5 a.m. on the 29th and after unloading the train the battalion was marched off to the Camp and allowed to snatch a few hours sleep before being summoned to breakfast. This meal which took place at 5 a.m. consisted of a plate of boiled rice and a spoonful of sugar. This was the ration issued by the Japanese; but owing to the good graces of the P.R.I. each man was given a hard boiled egg in addition. After this, the men spent the rest of the day in carrying out camp fatigues, which consisted for the most part in unloading trains from up-country. The battalion was also liable to be called out at any time during the day or night to deal with these trains and was responsible for this work for the ten days that they spent at the Camp, as well as catering for their own feeding arrangements, which proved very difficult with the minimum of utensils in our possession together with those which could be procured.

The daily rations were at all times very poor, consisting of boiled rice, or "Pap" rice and sugar in the morning, and boiled rice with a thin stew of meat and vegetables at midday and evening. Fortunately it was possible to supplement these meagre rations. providing one had the money by purchases at the canteen where one could obtain all manner of delicacies ranging from passable gingerbread to curried stews and omelettes. There were also hot and cold drinks of all kinds which were hawked around for sale at all hours of the day. It was also possible to buy bananas from good natured Thai people who risked the wrath of the Japanese by bringing their small canoes into the river bank adjacent to the camp. The only drawback to these amenities was the lack of money, and as the great majority of the P.O.Ws in this camp were sick, or semi-sick men who received no pay, only the minority of the O.Rs could afford to indulge in these facilities.

Chungkai was in reality an overgrowing version of the typical type of jungle camp which the Japanese provided for the accommodation of P.O.W. in Thailand. It was more elaborately planned out, and being the base camp, food supplies were more plentiful, and consequently the P.R.I, facilities were better than those that could be obtained in the more advanced camps. In other respects Chungkai had little more to offer. Accommodation was of the usual structure consisting of bamboo slats for beds, bamboo slats for walls and an at tap roof. These buildings together with those, in the hospital area were built for living and sleeping in and there were no buildings in the whole camp for the serving of food, or where one could sit down, read, and have one's meals. In fact, the food was served in the open and in fine weather it was a common sight to see hundreds of men squatting on the-bare ground outside their huts and eating their rice to the buzzing accompaniment of swarms of flies. The only food containers for carriage of food from cookhouses to food queues were 4 gallon Ghee-tins with improvised handles, the existing remnants of British cookhouse utensils being far too valuable for such rough usage outside the cookhouses (kitchens).

All bathing took place in the river adjoining the Camp and at certain specified times of the day. Hundreds of men could be seen washing themselves and their clothes, and splashing about in the water like a scene from the river Ganga. The indiscriminate mixing of men suffering from various skin ailments and other diseases was possibly the reason why such afflictions were rampant everywhere.

A distressing feature of Chungkai was the sight of legless and armless men to be seen wandering round the camp. In the majority of cases a small ulcer which had received little or no medical treatment in its early stages, contracted during the course of the work up country on the railway, was the primary cause of their misfortune. Some shocking cases of erstwhile robust men, now reduced to living skeletons, could be seen at any time in the hospital area.

The resources of the P.R.I, were most useful item in the life of the prisoner of war in Thailand. The basic rations as issued by the Japanese seldom consisted of more thai three meals of rice a day with just sufficient scraps of meat and vegetables to go with two of these meals. Tea without milk or sugar was also provided.

The P.R.I. enabled the men to supplement these inadequate rations by the purchase of eggs, fruit, dried fish, curry powder, salt and pepper, etc., and undoubtedly helped to decrease the number of cases of acute mal-nutrition to be seen in every camp along the line. The sick cases were in particular especially catered for and many lives were saved by its agency.

Within a few days of the arrival of No. y5 Battalion, all the other groups, Nos. 26, 27, 28 and 29 had also turned up at Chungkai and an issue of captured British clothing was handed out to the men at a formal parade at which the Japanese Colonel in charge of No. 2 Group. Yanagida was present. The kit issued consisted of an odd assortment of clothing such as Khaki Drill tunics, woollen shirts Woollen long pants hospital blues, and navy long woollen trousers. There were R.A.F. thick tunics, thick woollen tartan trousers, and a few suits of battle dress. These articles were handed out to the men irrespective of size and fitting with the result that the appearance of the me provoked some laugnter from an amused audience of camp loafers who were watching the proceedings especially when the whole parade were made to strip absolutely naked and dump the existing wardrobe of rags and tatters which were eagerly gleaned up by the Japanese quartermaster.

Each man received a pair of long woollen under pants. Those who got a K.D. tunic received in addition a blue woollen shirt and a pair of K.D. Shorts. Those who were given a battle-dress or R.A.F. serge tunic received a cotton singlet and a pair of navy blue woollen or tartan trousers. All men received a pair of thin rubber shoes to-go with their outfit and this completed what the Japanese considered to be a suitable kit for a voyage overseas.

While at Chungkai, as at other Camps, we of course received the current news from secreted wireless sets set up in such articles as water-bottles, ghee-tins, bamboo poles, etc., and sent round in News letters and I was able to cheer up the men with the same. A Thai merchant who carried out considerable business on the river was a great news vendor, and supplied a considerable amount of useful and heartening heartening information and news. This Thai's name was, I believe, Pong.

The Five Takanun battalions left Chungkai on the second stage of the Journey on the 10th March,1944, for Non Pladuc. This camp was some sixty miles from Bangkok and it was at first thought the battalions would remain there for a couple of days until they proceeded further to either Bangkok or Singapore for embarkation. The original arrangements evidently went astray as the battalions remained in this camp for nearly three months before finally leaving for Singapore. The overseas party i.e. Nos. 25, 26, 27, 82 and 29 battalions left Chungkai at 1400 hours and arrived at Non Pladuc at about 20.00 hours. There the seven hundred odd men of the comprising battalions together with five Officers and the Medical Officers were billeted in a small corner of this Camp in the usual bamboo huts. The men were warned that they were in quarantine and were not allowed to stray outside this area or get in contact with the other Dutch and British P.O.W. in this camp.

The area allotted to the party was roughly an acre and a half in extent and within this small space all forms of activity such as P.T. and games had to be confined. Two large latrines also occupied a spac in this area and, owing to their close proximity, the number of flies increased to such an extent that regular fatigues for fly-killing had facing to be instituted and were rigorously carried out. The Korean guards were also accommodated in the same sector of the camp and were to all intents and purposes as much restricted in their movements as were their prisoners, except that they had their evenings in afternoons out which to them appeared rare treats.

Our food was cooked in the main Camp Kitchens and food orderlies were allowed access to them for the purpose of fetching which were prepared cooked by the Dutch, who were in control of the whole camp. The quality of food served was fairly good and considering the fact that the men did little work was adequate to keep soul and body together. Later on, the Takanun party was able to have its own Canteen and such food as cooked Soya Beans, bananas, pea Nuts, Fried eggs, etc., could be obtained cheaply and were greatly appreciated. The purchase of these commodities was undertaken through the medium of the Serjeant in charge of the Korean Guards, who, no doubt, exacted a handsome commission from us for his good graces.

Washing and bathing facilities were afforded by two wells dug lose to the latrines from which some dirty muddy water could be used provided they were not stirred up too much. On two occasions heavy rainfall entirely filled up these wells with water so that it was not possible to trace their site and, as the latrines were, adjacent, all the effluent from them tended to spread/all over the ground in their Immediate vicinity and rendered them unfit for bathing purposes. The lack of pails and buckets tended to make matters even more difficult.

The health of the men gradually deteriorated under these conditions, and the camp provided bad place for both Malaria and mosquitoes. There were many cases of Dysentery and Beri-beri and we deaths occurred during the three months stay. Fortunately, the lental condition of the men was kept in a healthy condition by the valiant efforts of both Officers and men in organising bridge and tournaments and battalion concert parties.

The Japanese major in charge of the Non Pladuc Camp finally gave permission for the visit of the Camp Concert Party, comprising a first rate Dutch Orchestra, once a week to our sector. One or two games of football were played between Takanun and the Dutch POWs, and the .party was allowed to proceed to the main camp to fitness these contests.

To allow the men the opportunity of stretching their legs and to help pass away the time permission was sought by the officers and eventually obtained to undertake small fatigues. This took the form of transporting firewood from the local station to the main camp and was considered a privilege by all ranks. On the way to the station the party had to pass a camp consisting of Free Indians who were in charge of a number of anti-aircraft guns under the Nipponese supervision. This camp flew the tri-colour flag of the Azad Hind party. On a number of occasions these renegade gunners opened up fire on passing British and American aircraft. They were also armed with the Lee-Enfield rifle and were equipped with an odd assortment of British and Dutch , tunics and trousers. Their officers had the colours of the Independence flag displayed on their epaulettes.

The health of the five battalions gradually deteriorated under these trying conditions and many new. cases of malaria cropped up together with a number of recurrent ones. A hospital for the treatment of the more serious cases was made by partitioning off one of the hiits. This enabled the two Medical Officers Drs. G.C. Petrovsky and D.J. Longbottom -with the aid of their staff., to keep a personal eye on their patients. Medical supplies were obtained from the main Camp hospital as, until the timely arrival of Red Cross supplies, medical equipment and drugs possessed by the two above-mentioned Os were extremely limited.

An outstanding event took place on June 19th when tnere arrived a number of American Red Cross boxes and medical supplies. Each box contained four individual invalid parcels containing tinned milk, chdcolate, coffee, soup powder, cigarettes, etc., but the number was insufficient to provide one for each man and the fin-El distribution was at the rate of eleven men per parcel. Although this greatly diminished the beneficial value of these comforts the la en were delighted and grateful enough for even this small measure; as these parcels were the first that many of them had ever received since their capture.

Number 25 Group finally left Non Pladuc on the night of 8th June for Singapore,the other groups-followed us the next day. This time the accommodation was even more restricted and some thirty ‘two men were piled into each truck, or gooas wagon, with- a Korean sentry to each carriage which was already half full of packing cases containing various forms of dried greens, etc. The journey to Singapore was a nightmare. It was almost impossible to stand upright, or to stretch one's legs. It was considered necessary by the guard to occupy the space of two men close to the sliding doors of the wagon to uphold the dignity of his position. Furthermore, during the night, he insisted on one of these two doors being closed, which aggravated'the intolerable state of affairs still further. During the journey there was a constant struggle to obtain positions where cooler conditions prevailed, and it was eventually found necessary to allov, each man to sit by the doors in turn.

Three meals a day were provided by the railway authorities and were partaken at the various stations on the. way down. These consisted of boiled rice and dried fish with a few scraps of stewed vegetables throv.n in. The food -was usually eaten in the trucks and on one occasion at one of the larger stations the men were compelled to eat their rations inside the wagons with all the doors closed. They were informed by the guards that the reason for this was that an important Japanese Official was at the station and possibly the sight of semi-starving Ps.O.W. devouring their rations might prove offensive to him.

A noticeable feature of the journey down the Malayan Peninsular was the number of Chinese and Tamil children who surrounded the train at the country stations begging for food. Two years previously such a sight was not to be seen as Malaya was then a land of plenty. Another feature was the gloomy and silent atmosphere of such busy towns as Ipoh and Kuala Lumpur. From what one knew of Malaya under British administration it was very evident that the former atmosphere of prosperity no longer pervaded the country and this state of affairs was further reflected in the very faces of the inhabitants themselves.

After a journey occupying four nights and three days Singapore was finally reached in the early hours of 15th June 1944. The party was marched from the train to the Havelock Road P.O.W. Camp which had been revived by the Japanese for the reception of overseas parties from Thailand. There were already a number of battalions from other Groups awaiting embarkation in the camp and during the five days sojourn in Singapore a constant stream of men arrived daily from Thailand for the same-purpose including of course, the remaining four battalions comprising the Taka Nun party.

The rations were again very poor and consisted of a mixture of boiled rice and tapioca root three times day and on these meals the men had to be content as it was hot found possible to buy food from outside the Camp to supplement this meager daily allowance. The Chinese very kindly presented the P.O.W.s, with a large shark, which was greatly appreciated, and this was the only meat ration that they had during the stay at Singapore.

Adjoining the Camp and separated by a narrow creek was an Indian P.O.W. Camp. As it was necessary to fetch daily rations from the stores of this Camp, it was found possible for the fatigue parties detailed for this task to contact with their Indian compatriots. In this way news of the invasion of France by Britain and America filtered through the Camp and greatly enheartened the men on the eve of their departure overseas.

I managed to be in charge of several of these fatigues and was able to get into touch with a number of Gurkhas of my own regiment the 1st Gurkha Rifles. They were delighted to see me and were able to give me a newspaper, obtained from a Chinese, in which the news of the landing in France by our forces was contained, and I was thus enabled to give out this item of news as if from an official source. In return, thanks to donations from members of the Takanun battalions, I was able to present them with a sum of 150/- to be divided amongst them.

The attitude of our fellow Indian Ps.O.W. towards us was one of intense friendliness. Everywhere we went they gave us the thumbs up sign, and made uncomplimentary gestures behind the backs of their Japanese guards. They were very punctilious in saluting their own officers and, altogether, their morale can be said to be of the highest and was a source of encouragement to all of us who had been under the impression that all Indian Ps.O.W. had finally gone over to the Japanese, and to the Indian Independence Party. All kinds and classes of Indians were represented in this Camp and all appeared to get on very well together. The only possible element of doubt being a number of Sikh.

Prisoners who were regarded with some suspicion by their fellows owing to the early disloyalty of a large number of this race of warriors.

I was unfortunate enough to be caught talking to one of my Gurkhas by a Japanese sentry and was taken to the Guardhouse. Here I was interrogated by the Nipponese who asked me whether I was in the Indian Army. I denied this, although I was wearing a Gurkha type hat and badge at the time. This incident resulted in the severe knocking about and bruising of my face several times, together with a warning of further dire consequences to follow should a repetition occur in the near future. However, it was worth its.

On the eve of our departure the whole camp was summoned to a parade at which a message from Col. Nakamura O.C. i/c of all P.O.W. in Thailand was read out to us as follows:

"You are to be transferred from the jurisdiction of the P.O.W. Camp Thailand to that of Japan, where you are to assume labour duty. Since the opening of the Thailand Camp you were diligently carrying out imposed labour duty for more than twenty months; especially you were employed on railway construction in which your discharge of duty attained the aimed objective, as scheduled, which we warmly appreciate. On completion of the above mentioned, task you are, to be transferred to the Holy Land of the Rising Sun, where the scenery is simply superb. The Empire of Great Japan the proper appellant of which is BEO-Y-YASIMA-DAI NIPPON TEIKOKO is populated with nationals of up righteousness, morality, brave yet courteous, humane, yet strictly severe on vices. The proverb most common in use. Even the hunter himself will not slay a stray bird seeking refuge on his lap will probably explain the attitude and habitude of Japanese sentiments. The land has four distinct seasons spring with an abundance of various .blossoms where birds chirp peacefully everywhere; evergreen summer with cool breezes easing the universe;, transparent autumn skies with clement moon, and with winter in which the snow white washes the whole country; purifying the inhabitants. These are nothing but the image of His August Majesty's greatest virtue to which all nationals are bidden to follow in loyalty towards the imperial creation of benevolency,etc., etc. Therefore I tell you Officers and men, go to Japan with ease of mind find do your imposed labour duty to perfection. Then I verily tell you that our billion nationals will be welcoming you to share the Imperial favour you. On the other hand, should any one of you still retain conscience of any inimical projects or things detrimental to the interests of Japan, the consequential result must be borne on his own shoulders, however severe ozs regrettable to all concerned. I reiterate believe in Japanese chivalry and go forward in the right way, not astraying, on proper and mature consideration.

In conclusion I should like to call your attention to take good care of your health for the sudden change of climatically conditions, and wish you the happy future with my blessings for your bon voyage.

Finally on 18th June at early dawn Number 25 Battalion, followed in turn by the other four battalions, was marched out out of Havelock Road to the Pagar Docks for embarkation. On arrival at the whare side the party had to sit down for several hours before finally proceeding aboard ship. Opportunity was taken during this interval of filling all, available water containers with fresh water on the advice of the Japanese who predicted a water shortage should the ship have to remain at anchor for any length of time owing to unforeseen circumstances.

The moment of embarkation having arrived the party filed off led by No. 05 battalion, and boarded the Asaka Maru each man being handed a parcel of rubber containing a handle which was to serve as a life buoy.

The Asaka Maru was a cargo .boat of the tramp variety, of some 4,000 tons yet in size. The accommodation provided for some seven-hundred men with their kit was contained within the space of one hold placed between the stern and midships Platforms had been arranged around the walls of the hold three tiers high. When only half the party had embarked the hold had been filled up to the extent that it was impossible for the men to stretch themselves out full length. The middle of the hold was filled up by men seated on their kit, amidst a heap of extremely musty and evil smelling lifebelts and it was literally impossible to force any more men down the hold. The Korean Guards grew very excited and a number of men were assaulted for not climbing down in the already well filled inferno, and it looked at one time as though an ugly incident was about to develop, as the ugly temper of the Ps.O.W. themselves was revealing itself by the number of uncomplimentary remarks shouted to those to whom they attributed their, present miserable plight.

After some twenty odd men had fainted away owing to the intense heat and when the officers had appealed to the Japanese to supply further accommodation, the strain was temporarily lessened by the ship's Captain who agreed to allow some-of the party to accommodate themselves in the fore, well deck and a-small number on the lifeboat deck .admidships. The balance of the battalions as to remain in the original hold. Although this greatly eased the accommodation in the hold the, position was still intolerable and much resembled one of the unsavoury holds of an Arab slave dhbw. After some deliberation, the party was finally distributed over the ship as follows 400 men in thre aft well flick 800 men in the fore well deck, and 100 men on the lifeboat deck amidships. The above figures are approximate. The Korean guards installed themselves amidships below the deck occupied by the Ps.O.W. and posted sentries which paced the areas occupied by the two decks amidships, or what -would be the promenade decks on a passenger steamer. This arrangement enabled the guards to keep the three parties separated and it was necessary, to pass the improvised guard-house every time one wished to go to. the aft well deck where salt-water .bathing facilities were available at certain times of the day. There was constant friction between the men and the guards, owing to the arbitrary manner in which each individual Korean sentry imposed his own rules and regulations as to when passage from one area to another .was permissible. Some of the guards were worse than others in this respect and appeared to be out for trouble at all times. However, as the weeks lengthened out and weather conditions became more and were intolerable, the guards became too absorbed in their own misery to worry over such trifles and discipline lagged accordingly.